◆ **T**he resistant virtues of the structures that we seek depend on their form; it is through their form that they are stable, not because of an awkward accumulation of material. There is nothing more noble and elegant from an intellectual viewpoint than this: to resist through form.

• Eladio Dieste,
La Estructura Ceramica
(Bogotá: Escala, 1987)

SHAPING STRUCTURES
STATICS

Wacław Zalewski and Edward Allen

Drawings *by* Joseph Iano

John Wiley & Sons, Inc.
New York Chichester Weinheim Brisbane Singapore Toronto

This text is printed on acid-free paper.

Copyright © 1998 by John Wiley & Sons, Inc.

All rights reserved. Published simultaneously in Canada.

Reproduction or translation of any part of this work beyond
that permitted by Section 107 or 108 of the 1976 United
States Copyright Act without the permission of the copyright
owner is unlawful. Requests for permission or further
information should be addressed to the Permissions Department,
John Wiley & Sons, Inc., 605 Third Avenue, New York, NY
10158-0012.

This publication is designed to provide accurate and
authoritative information in regard to the subject
matter covered. It is sold with the understanding that
the publisher is not engaged in rendering legal, accounting,
or other professional services. If legal advice or other
expert assistance is required, the services of a competent
professional person should be sought.

Library of Congress Cataloging in Publication Data:
Zalewski, Wacław.
    Shaping structures: statics / Wacław Zalewski, Edward Allen.
      p.   cm.
    Includes index.
    ISBN 0-471-16968-4 (cloth : alk. paper)
    1. Structural analysis (Engineering) 2. Statics. I. Allen,
  Edward, 1938- . II. Title.
  TA648.Z35   1997
  624.1'71—dc21   96-37609

Printed in the United States of America

10 9 8 7 6 5 4 3 2 1

CONTENTS

PREFACE

The essence of structural design is to shape each structure to respond effectively to the forces that it must withstand and the human activities that it nurtures. Thus students of architecture and structural engineering should be involved in the process of creating suitable structural form throughout their years of schooling, from their first fundamental lessons to the extended design projects of their advanced courses.

This is the first of a projected series of volumes on the creation of structural form. These fourteen chapters comprise both a treatise on the rudiments of statics and an introduction to the art of shaping structures. The two topics are natural, comfortable companions. A knowledge of statics, which is the study of the effects and distribution of forces on bodies that remain at rest,

is a sufficient basis for finding good forms for hanging structures, arches, and trusses. And because all structural wisdom grows from an understanding of these simple, elegant devices, the student who emerges from a course in statics with a confident command of them is well prepared to undertake the study of the internal flows of forces in beams, slabs, plates, columns, frames, connections, and foundations.

These chapters are rich in examples that show how to find form and forces for a spectrum of graceful, efficient structures for buildings and bridges. Most examples feature parallel presentations of numerical and graphical design techniques. Solutions are pursued alternately in conventional and SI metric units of measurement. Because more material is presented than can be covered in a single academic term, the

teacher and student should select freely from what is offered, choosing the demonstrations that interest them most and following the solution paths that seem most natural. It would be a mistake, however, to ignore consistently either the graphical or numerical techniques, because both have much to offer. For more than a century, the greatest structural designers, those whose work graces these pages, have conceived and developed their masterpieces through a combination of numerical and graphical methods, the latter being especially valuable during the early, conceptual stages of design.

The computer-literate reader will soon realize that all the techniques presented in this book, both numerical and graphical, are readily susceptible to computerization. To give these tasks over entirely to the computer, however, would be to place them in a "black box" that would obscure their inner workings. This would deprive the designer of valuable insights into the behavior of the structure that is being designed and invaluable clues as to how to improve its form.

Finite element analysis, readily available through the growing power of small, inexpensive computers, is a useful adjunct to these methods because it facilitates a detailed examination of stresses and deformations. But it does not replace a sound, fundamental knowledge of the laws of statics and, being merely an analytical technique with no powers of discernment, it is as happy to find the forces in a badly shaped structure as in one that is perfectly suited to its task. The finding of a suitable form for each structure is still the worthiest goal of the engineer and architect, as it has been since the beginning of time.

Wacław Zalewski • *Edward Allen*
Belmont, Massachusetts
South Natick, Massachusetts
August 1997

ACKNOWLEDGMENTS

The authors wish to express their sincere thanks to the many people whose assistance was indispensable during the preparation of this book. Wacław Zalewski wishes to acknowledge particularly the encouragement and suggestions of his distinguished colleagues, Professors Jerzy Sołtan and Eduardo Catalano. Edward Allen acknowledges the intellectual contributions of Professor Arnold Rosner, whose ingenious work with hanging string models will appear in a future volume of this series. The present volume evolved from notes prepared for various seminars, classroom courses, and design studios that the authors have taught at both undergraduate and graduate levels over a period of several decades at the Massachusetts Institute of Technology, the Politechnika Warszawska, the Universidad Central de Venezuela, Yale University, the University of Washington, Montana State University, the University of California, San Diego, and the University of Oregon. Among our students, we thank especially John Ripley Freeman, Donna Harris, and Don Livingstone. The authors thank the staff of John Wiley & Sons, Inc. Senior Editor Amanda Miller guided the project with energy, imagination, and a sure hand, assisted by MaryAlice Yates and Mary Masi. Eloise Donnelly, Mary Masi, and Rose Leo Kish worked long and tirelessly to locate and acquire the photographs. Donna Conte oversaw production of the book with impressive ease and expertise. Karin Kincheloe directed her limitless talent to the design of the book.

The gifted Joseph Iano, friend and coauthor, gave much more than was asked of him to the preparation of the drawings. The human figures in the CAD drawings were created with the Posed Human Figure Library of the CAD Technology Group. Friends and colleagues Jerry Bancroft, Susan Ubbelohde, Tim Becker, Robert Dermody, Doug Kelbaugh, Chris Luebkeman, Maynard and Lu Lyndon, and Lisa Ronchi gave special assistance at crucial times. We thank especially our wives, Irena Zalewski and Mary M. Allen, for their assistance and support during the preparation of the manuscript.

CHAPTER ONE

A VERTICAL TENSILE STRUCTURE

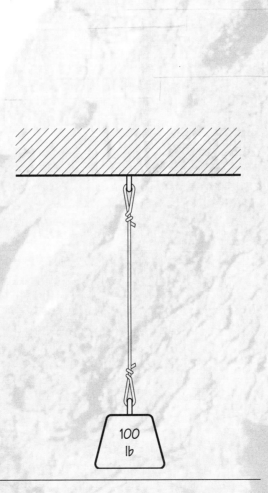

◀ **A rock climber's life hangs by a vertical tensile structure: a climbing rope. (Photo: Tony Stone Images.)**

▲ *Figure 1.1*
A vertical tensile structure.

The most important concepts of structural design are embodied in even the simplest of structures, a wire hanging vertically with a weight attached to its lower end. In the accompanying diagram (Fig. 1.1), the weight is a 100-lb block of iron. The wire is 1/8 in. in diameter. The wire weighs very little as compared with the load that it supports, so for our present purposes we will ignore the weight of the wire itself and concentrate on what happens to the structure as a result of the 100-lb load.

To analyze any structure successfully, we must be able to represent clearly and unambiguously the *forces* that act on each of its *members*. In this example the structure has only one member, a vertical wire.

CONSTRUCTING A FREE-BODY DIAGRAM

We begin our analysis by drawing a picture of the wire only, free of its connections to the weight below or to the ceiling above (Fig. 1.2). This is the first step in drawing a *free-body diagram*, which is a representation of a structural member or a portion of a member, together with all the forces that act on it, as a body that is free

▲ *Figure 1.2*
To begin construction of the free-body diagram, we show only the wire, free of the ring above or the iron weight below. An arrow indicates the direction and magnitude of the force exerted by the iron weight on the bottom end of the wire.

of all the other parts of the structure. The iron block is a *load* that exerts a downward force of 100 lb on the lower end of the wire. We represent this force with a downward-pointing arrow at the lower end of the wire accompanied by the notation "$P = 100$ lb." The arrow represents the *direction* of the load, and the figure of 100 lb represents its *magnitude*. The letter P is conventionally used to represent a force that acts on a body at a single point. We can think of P as an abbreviation for "pull" or "push"; in this case it represents a pull on the wire.

We have drawn the wire and the force that pulls on it from below. As we look at this diagram, however, we recognize that it is not complete. If the only force that acts on the wire is the 100-lb downward pull, the wire will not stay where it is. It will move in the direction of the pull. But we know that the wire remains where it is, firmly attached to a ring in the ceiling.

In order for the wire to remain where it is, there must be another force acting on it that balances exactly the 100-lb pull at the bottom. To create this exact balance, the other force must also be 100 lb in magnitude, and it must act directly upward, opposite to the direction of the pull of the weight. This force is exerted by the ring in the ceiling, which reacts to the downward pull by pulling in an upward direction on the wire with a magnitude of 100 lb. Because this upward pull is exerted in reaction to the downward pull at the bottom of the wire, we call it, naturally enough, a *reaction*, abbreviated into the letter R. We represent this force on the free-body diagram with an upward-pointing arrow at the top of the wire, accompanied by the notation "$R = 100$ lb" (Fig. 1.3). We have completed the free-body diagram of the wire.

▲ *Figure 1.3*
The complete free-body diagram shows also the upward force exerted on the top end of the wire by the ring in the ceiling.

STATIC EQUILIBRIUM

If the wire is pulled by a force of exactly 100 lb at each end, it will not move, just as the rope in a tug-of-war will not move when it is pulled by evenly matched teams of people. In the language of structural design, the wire is in *static equilibrium*, which means that the forces that act on it balance each other in such a way that the wire will not move.

We can express numerically the condition of static equilibrium for the wire. To do this, we assign positive numbers to downward forces and negative numbers to upward forces. (This is an arbitrary convention often used in the representation of forces in structures.) We add all the forces that act on the wire and set the sum equal to zero. A zero sum indicates that the forces balance one another exactly. For the wire in our example, the numerical expression of equilibrium looks like this:

$$100 \text{ lb} + (-100 \text{ lb}) = 0$$

Putting this expression in general terms:

$$\sum F_v = 0 \qquad [1\text{-}1]$$

The Greek letter sigma, Σ, stands for "sum." F_v means "forces in the vertical direction." We read this expression as "The sum of the forces in the vertical direction equals zero." It means that there must be as much upward force on a structural body as there is downward force. This elementary relationship is used in the design of every structure, from the simplest to the most complex. It represents one of three fundamental conditions of static equilibrium that apply to all structural members subjected to forces acting in a single plane. We will develop expressions for the other two conditions a bit later, as we address structures that are acted upon by forces in directions other than vertical.

TENSION

Examining the free-body diagram that we have just completed, we see that the wire is pulled by

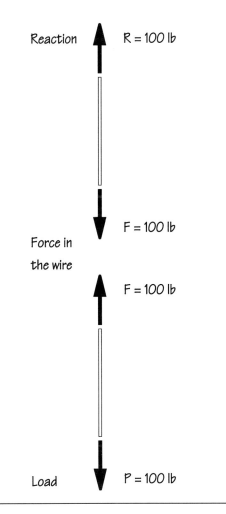

▲ *Figure 1.4*

A cut through any horizontal plane along the length of the wire produces two free-body diagrams that show an internal force of 100 lb in each of the two portions of the wire.

a force of 100 lb at each end. These forces tend to stretch the wire, to pull it apart. When a structural member is being pulled or stretched, we say that it is in *tension*, or that it is subjected to a *tensile force*. The tensile force within the wire in this example is 100 lb. This is also an *axial force*, a force that acts along the imaginary longitudinal centerline, or axis, of the wire.

Some people might look at the free-body diagram with a force of 100 lb at each end and conclude, with apparent logic, that the tensile force in the wire is 200 lb. Do not be fooled: Whenever a load pulls on the lower end of this wire, the ring in the ceiling automatically pulls back with a force that is exactly equal to the load. The pull of the ring does not add to the force in the wire, it merely keeps the wire from moving. We can make an imaginary cut through the wire at any point and draw a free-body diagram of only that portion of the wire that lies above or below the cut (Fig. 1.4). No matter how we slice it, the force inside the wire is always 100 pounds.

STRESS

If the wire were very small in diameter, like a human hair, the 100-lb tensile force would break it. If the wire were very large in diameter, like a thick steel rod, the 100-lb tensile force would not even come close to breaking it. In designing structures, we need a way to decide how big each member of the structure has to be. A member that is too small may break. A member that is too large will cost too much and will look clumsy. In our example, it would be useful to know whether the 100-lb load is likely to break the 1/8-in. diameter wire. For this purpose, the concept of *stress* has been developed. Stress is a measure of

WHAT IS A FORCE?

Force is a physical phenomenon that we recognize instinctively when we push or pull on a heavy object and feel the stretching in our muscles and tendons. A force can be described by means of the two basic consequences of its action, **external effects** and **internal effects.**

The **external effect** of a force that acts on a body can be either to change its velocity or to give rise to opposing, reactive forces that prevent the movement of the body. These reactive forces are of particular interest to us as we design structures, because they establish a state of static equilibrium. The combined external effect of the forces that act and react on a body in equilibrium is the same as if no force were acting on it; this is why a body in equilibrium does not move.

The **internal effect** of a force on a body in equilibrium is that it produces along its path deformations and stresses in the material of which the body is made. The intensity of these internal exertions depends on the magnitude of the external force and on the dimensions and shape of the body. The ability of a structural body to resist external forces depends on the degree to which it is stressed.

When designing a structure, our usual goal is to give it a shape that uses the least material while transmitting its internal forces without overstressing it. The influence of shape on the internal response of a structural body to an external force is illustrated in Figure A: A force that might easily break a curved bar, (b), will do no harm whatsoever to a straight bar of the same dimensions, (a). This is but one example of the many that we will study in these chapters. ■

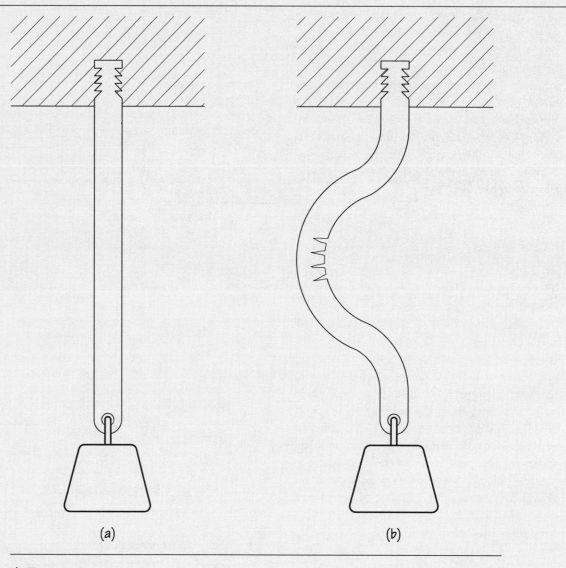

(a)   (b)

▲ *Figure A*

the intensity of the action of a force on a material.

The stress in a wire under axial tension is equal to the force in the wire divided by the area of the cross section of the wire. Expressed algebraically,

$$f = \frac{P}{A} \qquad [1\text{-}2]$$

Here, f represents stress. Because the wire is in tension, the f is *tensile* in this case. P is the force in the wire. A is the area of a cross section of the wire.

In our example of the weight hanging on a wire, f, the tensile stress, is the unknown quantity that we are trying to determine. P, the force, is 100 lb. A, the cross-sectional area of the wire, we will have to calculate. The area of a circular section of a solid is found by using the formula

$$A = \frac{\pi d^2}{4}$$

in which d represents the diameter of the wire. The wire is 1/8 in. in diameter, which is easier to work with if we express it as 0.125 in. Substituting this in the formula and solving, we find that the cross-sectional area of the wire is 0.0123 square inches (usually abbreviated as $in.^2$). Now we can complete the computation of the stress in the wire:

$$f = \frac{P}{A} = \frac{100 \text{ lb}}{0.0123 \text{ in.}^2} = 8130 \text{ lb/in.}^2$$

Stress is always expressed in units of force per unit of area. In this example, the units are pounds per square inch, shown here as *lb/in.*² They may also be abbreviated as *lb/sq in.*, or, most commonly, as *psi*.

ACTUAL STRESS AND ALLOWABLE STRESS

8130 psi is the *actual stress* caused in the 1/8-in.-diameter wire by the load of 100 lb. Actual stress becomes meaningful when we can compare it with the maximum stress the wire can be expected to resist safely. This maximum safe stress is called the *allowable stress* (f_{allow}) or, sometimes, *working stress*. If we look in an engineering handbook and find that the recommended allowable tensile stress in so-called mild steel, the most commonly used structural steel, is 22,000 psi, we see that the actual stress in our example is only about a third as large as this allowable stress. This means that the 1/8-in. wire could hold safely nearly three times as much load as we have put on it. If we are designing this simple structure to support a load that will never be larger than 100 lb, we could save money by using a smaller wire, one just large enough to carry the load safely. But how small a wire could we use?

We answer this question by substituting an f_{allow} of 22,000 psi and the 100 lb force into the general formula for stress, keeping the cross-sectional area of the wire as an unknown for which we solve:

$$f_{\text{allow}} = \frac{P}{A}$$

$$A = \frac{P}{f_{\text{allow}}} = \frac{100 \text{ lb}}{22,000 \text{ psi}}$$

$$A = 0.00455 \text{ in.}^2$$

We need a wire whose cross-sectional area is 0.00455 in.² To find how large a diameter, d, this wire must have, we substitute into the formula for the area of a circle:

$$A = \frac{\pi d^2}{4}$$

$$d = \sqrt{\frac{4A}{\pi}} = \sqrt{\frac{4(0.00455 \text{ in.}^2)}{\pi}}$$

$$d = 0.0761 \text{ in.}$$

A wire 0.0761 in. (about one-thirteenth of an inch) in diameter is the smallest and most economical tensile member that we can use safely in this structure. In practice, we would consult an engineering reference book and select wire of the smallest standard diameter that equals or exceeds the diameter we have calculated. We find in the American Institute of Steel Construction's *Steel Construction Manual* that a 15-gauge wire has a diameter of 0.072 in., which is just a bit too small. A 14-gauge wire, the next larger size, has a diameter of 0.080 in. We choose the 14-gauge wire.

SIZING STEEL HANGER STRAPS FOR A TALL BUILDING

Suppose we are designing an office building with 10 floors, to be built in Singapore. The entire weight of the building is brought to earth by the steel wide-flange columns of a central core structure, rectangular in plan, that contains elevator shafts, stairways, and shafts for the vertical pas-

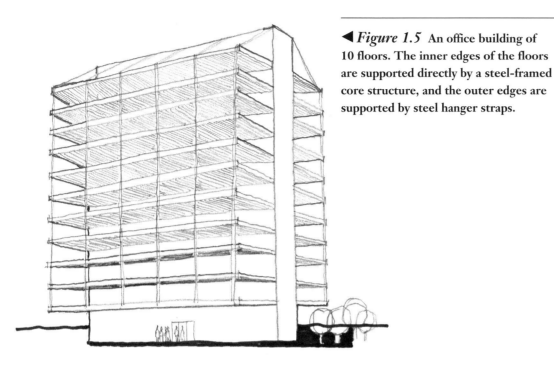

◄ *Figure 1.5* **An office building of 10 floors. The inner edges of the floors are supported directly by a steel-framed core structure, and the outer edges are supported by steel hanger straps.**

SI UNITS OF MEASUREMENT

The United States is the only industrialized country in the world that still uses the ancient and inconsistent units of measurement that are part of our English heritage. Elsewhere, SI units, a streamlined version of the metric system of measurement, are used. To hasten the conversion of the U.S. building industry to SI units, the U.S. government requires their use on all federal building projects. The basic units of the SI system are the meter (m) for length, the kilogram (kg) for mass, and the second (s) for time. The millimeter (¹⁄₁₀₀₀ of a meter, abbreviated mm) is the preferred subdivision of the meter. To avoid confusion, the centimeter (¹⁄₁₀₀ of a meter) is not used in SI. Area is measured in square meters (m²) or square millimeters (mm²), and acceleration in meters per second per second (m/s²). The SI unit of force, kg·m/s², is called a newton, abbreviated N. (Notice that in SI notation, units that are multiplied by each other are separated by a dot, as in kg·m.)

Three standard prefixes are commonly applied to units used in SI structural calculations: milli-, kilo-, and mega-. "Milli-" always means one one-thousandth. "Kilo-" means one thousand, and "mega-" means one million. Most forces in building structures are many newtons in magnitude, so they are usually expressed as kilonewtons (kN) or meganewtons (MN). A kilonewton is 1000 newtons, and a meganewton, 1,000,000 newtons. Preferred practice in SI computations is to eliminate the commas that we use to divide large numbers into groups of three digits, and to replace the commas with spaces. Thus a meganewton can be properly represented as 1 000 000 newtons. Most countries customarily use a comma as a

sage of pipes, wires, and ducts (Fig. 1.5). The inner edges of each floor slab are supported directly on this core. The outer edges are supported at 12 points by steel straps (*hangers*) that are suspended from the top of the central core. Each hanger must support a mass of 24 500 kilograms (kg) at each floor. If the allowable tensile stress in the steel used for the hangers is 150 megapascals (MPa), how large must each strap be at a point just above the lowest floor, and how large must each be at a point just above the highest floor?

This problem is not very different from finding the required size of wire for the 100-lb weight, but the units of measurement in which the problem is presented may be unfamiliar to you. So far we have been working in *conventional units* of measurement, inches and pounds. Here the units are *SI*, which stands for *Systéme Internationale d'Unités.* It is important for you to develop an intuitive grasp of SI units so that they become as natural to use and easy to conceptualize as conventional units. This will take time, but the accompanying sidebar spells out the system and gives some easy-to-remember approximations that will speed the learning process a bit.

decimal point instead of a period. In this book we will work interchangeably in both conventional and SI units, so to avoid confusion we will use a period as a decimal point in both systems of measurement.

The unit of stress in the SI system is the pascal, abbreviated Pa. One pascal is equal to one newton of force per square meter. As with newtons, structural calculations are usually carried out in kilopascals (kPa) or megapascals (MPa).

In calculating with conventional units, we customarily use units of pounds to represent both force and mass. This practice is ambiguous. Strictly speaking, force equals the mass of a body times acceleration. The SI system is unambiguous in this regard: The force that gravity exerts on a mass is its weight, which is equal to the mass in kilograms times the acceleration of gravity (g). In physics this relationship is expressed by the equation $P = Ma$, where P represents force (push or pull), M, mass, and a, acceleration. The acceleration of gravity, g, at the surface of the earth in SI units is approximately 9.8 meters per second per second (m/s²).

If you are not accustomed to thinking in SI units, the following approximations may be helpful:

Length

The handiest figure to keep in mind, and a very close approximation, is that **100 millimeters equals about 4 inches.** This is especially useful because both 4 in. and 100 mm are preferred dimensional modules for construction. One foot is three modules long, or approximately 300

mm. A standard sheet of plywood is 4 by 8 ft, which is 12 modules by 24, approximately 1200 by 2400 mm. One meter is approximately 40 in., or 3 ft 4 in. A millimeter is so small, about the thickness of a dime, that except when working with detailed dimensions of precision-crafted components, it is good practice in designing and constructing buildings to work to the nearest 50 mm dimension, which is about 2 in. Remember that in SI, centimeters are not used, only millimeters and meters. Dimensions on construction drawings are generally given in millimeters only. A dimension of 44 500 may be read either as 44,500 mm or 44.5 m.

Area

One square meter is equal to about 10.76 square feet. For really quick mental calculations, you can think of this as 10 square feet per square meter; this results in an inaccuracy of about 8%. If you use 11 square feet per square meter in your computations, your error will be only about 2%.

Mass

A kilogram of mass is equal to about 2.2 pounds. To convert kilograms to pounds in your head, multiply the number of kilograms by 2, then add another 10%. Thus, to convert 1450 kilograms to pounds, first multiply by 2 to get 2900 pounds, then increase this number by 10%, which is 290 pounds, for a total of 3190 pounds. To convert pounds to kilograms, multiply the number of pounds by 0.45, or divide by 2 and subtract 10%.

Force, Weight, Load

One newton is the weight of a small apple, a fact that is easy to remember because we associate Sir Isaac Newton's theory of gravitation with a falling apple. **One pound of force is equal to about 4.5 newtons** (there are four or five small apples in a pound). Later in this book we will be calculating loads and forces in kips (short for kilopounds), which are units of 1000 pounds. A kip is equal to approximately 4.5 kilonewtons.

Stress, Pressure

One pascal (Pa) can be visualized as the weight of one small apple distributed over one square meter of surface area. This is a very small pressure indeed: the apple weighs less than a quarter of a pound, and a square meter is nearly 11 square feet. In fact, **a single sheet of paper exerts a pressure of a little less than 1 Pa on a desktop.** A book with 300 pages puts a pressure of about 200 Pa on a table if it is lying flat. Structural analysis is generally done in kilopascals or megapascals. A kilopascal (kPa) is the pressure exerted on a tabletop by a stack of five average hardcover novels, about 0.145 pounds per square inch (psi). A megapascal (MPa) is a thousand times larger, approximately 145 psi. A handy fact to remember is that 1 MPa = 1 N/mm². A very close approximation of atmospheric pressure at sea level is 100 kPa. ∎

NUMERICAL ACCURACY IN CALCULATIONS

It is the mark of an instructed mind to rest satisfied with the degree of precision which the nature of the subject permits and not seek an exactness where only an approximation of the truth is possible.

ARISTOTLE

How accurate does a structural calculation have to be? Using a hand-held electronic calculator, we can carry almost as many digits through a calculation as we wish. But the final result cannot be more precise than the least accurate figure used in the calculation. In most structural work, the values we use for the loads on a building are taken from tables in building codes. These values often differ from the actual maximum loads on a building by very large amounts. Typically, an American building code specifies a residential floor loading as 40 pounds per square foot (psf), which is about the same as filling every room with adult men standing two feet apart in each direction, or covering the floors with a solid layer of books a foot deep.

Few residential floors are loaded so heavily. More significant, we have no way of knowing with any certainty whether a given floor of a building will be loaded to 5 psf, 40 psf, something in between these figures, or perhaps even something more. There are other uncertainties that lie behind every structural calculation. These include uncontrollable actions of nature such as high winds, heavy snows, and seismic activity; dimensional inaccuracies that occur during construction; variabilities in the physical properties of structural materials; and the many small mistakes that occur inevitably as a building is designed and built. Clearly, an error of 1 or 2% in calculating the sizes of the structural members that make up a building is of no significance in relationship to the potential magnitudes of these uncertainties. It is useless to attempt to achieve an accuracy greater than plus or minus 1% in structural calculations.

There is no advantage in carrying more than three significant figures through any structural calculation. In fact, much rougher calculations often suffice. If the number 10.09 is simply truncated to 10.0, the loss of accuracy is less than 1%. In SI units, the acceleration of gravity at sea level at a latitude of 45°, carried to six significant figures, is 9.80665 m/s^2. We can truncate this to two significant figures, 9.8 m/s^2, with an inaccuracy of less than 1/10 of 1%.

If you follow a general rule of retaining three significant figures in your calculations, you will often be able to streamline your work by dropping digits from the answers that your calculator displays. A displayed answer of 24,557.25, for example, can be rounded safely to 24,600, keeping only three significant figures. On the other hand, if a displayed answer is 0.01, it is wise to display and record two more decimal places in order to retain 1% accuracy, because the calculator could be using this displayed value to represent an answer of 0.005 or 0.0149, exposing you to a potential error of as much as 50%. ■

We begin the solution process by drawing free-body diagrams of the hanger straps at the two locations that we wish to study (Fig. 1.6). At the lowest floor, the strap must support a mass of 24 500 kg. How great a force does this exert on the strap?

$$P = Ma$$

$$P = (24\ 500\ kg)(9.8\ m/s^2) = 240\ 000\ N = 240\ kN$$

For simplicity in making connections, we would like to keep the width of the strap constant at 150 millimeters (mm), and vary the thickness as required. As compared with the mass that it supports, the mass of the hanger strap itself will be so small that we will not con-

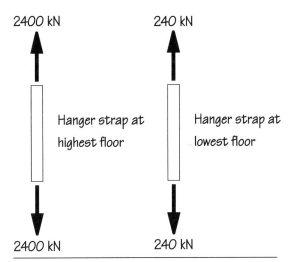

▲ *Figure 1.6*
Free-body diagrams of hanger straps above the highest and lowest floors.

sider it in our calculations. We are ready to find A_{req}, the required cross-sectional area of the hanger strap at the lowest floor:

$$f_{allow} = \frac{P}{A}$$

$$A_{req} = \frac{P}{f_{allow}}$$

We can save a step in the solution by substituting for A_{req} an expression for the area of the strap in terms of its thickness and its width:

$$t_1(0.150\ m) = \frac{240\ kN}{150\ MPa}$$

The allowable stress (f_{allow}) in the steel of the strap is 150 MPa. The desired width of the strap is 0.150 m, which is the same as 150 mm; it is expressed in meters so as to maintain consistency of units in the computation. We have used the term t_1 to represent the unknown quantity, the thickness of the strap just above the first or lowest floor of the 10-story building (we will use t_{10} to represent the thickness of the strap at the highest floor, the tenth). We rearrange the equation in terms of t_1 and change all the units to meters, newtons, and pascals so that the answer will be in meters:

$$t_1 = \frac{240\ 000\ N}{(0.150\ m)(150\ 000\ 000\ Pa)}$$

$$t_1 = 0.0107\ m = 10.7\ mm$$

Assuming that steel plate material comes in standard thicknesses that are integral numbers of millimeters, we will use a strap 11 mm thick and 150 mm wide to support the lowest floor of the

building (Fig. 1.7). You can convert this answer to inches for purposes of visualization by using an approximate conversion factor of 25 mm per in.: The strap is about 6 in. wide and less than 1/2 in. thick. This is a remarkably small member to support a substantial portion of the floor of a building. In general, tensile members can be much more slender than *compressive members*, members that are squeezed rather than stretched, for reasons that we will discover in the next chapter.

At the tenth floor, the free-body diagram shows that the hanger strap must support not

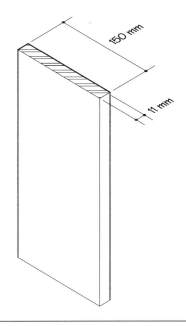

▲ *Figure 1.7*
A section of the hanger strap for the lowest floor.

only the mass of that floor, but also the masses of the nine floors below. The force in the strap at this point is therefore 10 times as great as it is at the lowest floor, and the strap must be 10 times as large in cross-sectional area. Holding the width of the strap constant at the specified 150 mm, we find that the strap must be 107 mm thick. You may wish to convert this mentally to conventional units to get an idea of how large it is, or to draw it full-size using an SI ruler or scale.

If we were doing a full design of this structure, we would repeat this procedure for each floor of the building. The strap will be twice as thick above the second floor as it was at the first, three times as thick above the third floor, and so on. The floor-by-floor change in the dimension of the hanger strap is expressive of the way that loads accumulate in this structure and can become a meaningful part of the architecture of the building if we wish. We decide to do this by making up the strap from 11-mm layers. One layer will extend all the way from the roof to the lowest floor. One will extend from the roof to the next-lowest floor, and so on. The straps will be fastened into a tight bundle at each level by wrapping small steel straps around them at intervals.

There are three major problems that have to be solved in detailing the hanger strap. One is how to connect it to the steel girder at each floor. Another is how to prevent corrosion of the straps. A third is how to protect the straps from losing strength if the building should catch fire and the steel should soften in the heat. These are complex questions that go beyond the scope of this chapter. The preliminary design sketch of a detail shown here (Fig. 1.8) uses high-strength

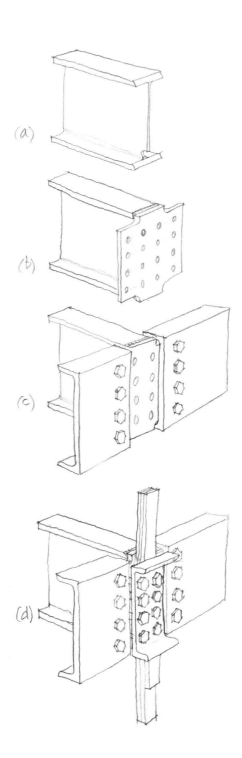

(a)

(b)

(c)

(d)

◀ *Figure 1.8*
Preliminary design sketches for the detail of a typical connection between a hanger strap and a wide-flange steel floor girder. (a) In the steel fabricator's shop, the end of each roof beam is prepared by beveling the flanges to facilitate the deposition of weld metal to the full depth of each flange. The lower flange is beveled in the same direction as the upper one, and a clearance hole is provided in the web so that this flange can also be welded with the beam sitting upright. This saves the time and expense of having to turn the heavy beam over between welds. (b) A thick steel connector plate with four rows of bolt holes drilled into it is welded to the end of the beam in the shop. (c) For a smooth, flush exterior appearance, steel channels are used for the perimeter beams. As the steel frame is erected on the construction site, these are bolted to the outer lines of holes on the connector plate. (d) A short piece of steel channel is used to clamp the steel hanger straps to the connector plate, using the inner lines of holes. The flanges on the channel help to stiffen it against the tendency to bend under the intense pressure of the bolts. Steps (c) and (d) may be reversed if it facilitates the erection process.

steel bolts to clamp the bundle of hanger straps tightly between a short piece of steel *channel* and a steel plate that is welded to the end of the floor girder. This transmits the force from the girder to the strap by friction and avoids piercing the strap with bolt holes that would weaken it. Such connecting of members by friction, using high-strength bolts to apply the clamping force, is very common in steel construction. A table in the *Steel Construction Manual* tells us that a 19-mm diameter bolt can safely transmit 34.4 kN in this manner. The required number of bolts is found by dividing the force to be transmitted by the force that each bolt can transmit:

$$n_{\text{req}} = \frac{P}{P_{\text{allow}}}$$

$$n_{\text{req}} = \frac{240 \text{ kN}}{34.4 \text{ kN/bolt}} = 6.98 \text{ bolts}$$

Seven bolts are needed, but for symmetry we show eight bolts in the detail.

The problem of fire resistance can probably be solved, at least in part, by keeping the strap in the open air, well away from the exterior wall. Further fire resistance can be imparted by covering the strap with an *intumescent coating* that swells when subjected to heat and forms a stable insulating layer over the steel. A properly selected coating system will also protect the steel from corrosion.

In addition to the bundled strap idea that we have developed, we might wish to consider other ways of expressing visually the accumulation of loads in the hanger straps of this structure, several of which are shown in Figure 1.9.

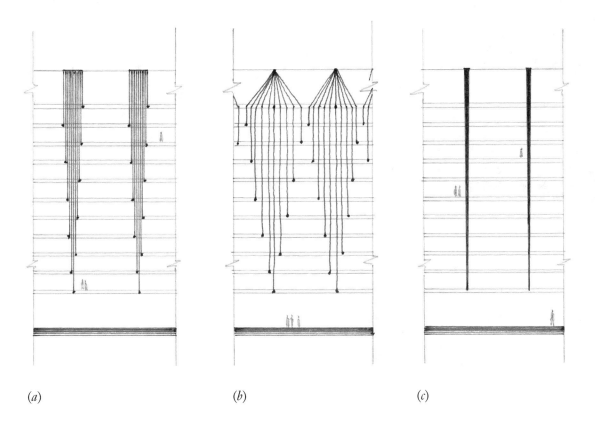

(a) *(b)* *(c)*

◄ *Figure 1.9*
Other ways of expressing visually the accumulation of floor loads in the hanger straps. (a) Each individual strap is kept separate from all the others, but the straps are clustered to create an inverted tree at each girder line. This scheme has the practical difficulty that most of the hangers do not align with the girders they support unless the girders change location to match the hangers, a difficult and costly expedient. This could be overcome by installing a stiff perimeter girder to transfer forces from the straps to the main girders. (b) The individual straps are uniformly spaced around the perimeter of the building. This scheme shares the problem of scheme a. (c) The straps are consolidated into steel bars that are tapered so that the taper is visible when viewing the building straight on.

In Figure 1.10 we see a construction photograph of the Westcoast Transmission Company Building, built in 1969 in Vancouver, British Columbia, to the design of architects Rhone and Iredale and structural engineer B. Babicki. It is very similar to the building that we have just analyzed, but its designers chose to use pairs of high-strength steel cables for the hangers rather than mild steel straps. Because of the high strength of the steel, the cables are even

---

◀ *Figure 1.10*
The Westcoast Transmission Company Tower under construction. (Rhone & Iredale Architects, Vancouver, B.C. Partner in charge: William K. Rhone. Structural Engineer: Bogue Babicki.)

smaller than the straps that we have designed, and the designers have chosen to make them constant in dimension throughout the height of the building. Although these cable pairs may not be as expressive visually as the tapering bundles of steel straps that we have designed, there were good reasons for their adoption. The cables were less expensive than straps because they could be simply pulled off a reel and installed full-length, without requiring the cutting and assembly of multiple steel straps of varying lengths for each hanger. The connections to all the floors are identical and use standard cable hardware that attaches with very little labor; this also saved money. The cables were subsequently coated with a thick insulating layer of fireproofing material and enclosed within the outer skin of the building; thus they were protected from the weather and problems of fire and corrosion were avoided. Design decisions such as the choice between layered straps and pairs of high-strength cables usually must take into consideration a number of nonstructural factors like material cost, labor cost, weather protection, fire protection, and ease of detailing. These non-structural factors often become the critical ones in making a decision.

▲ *Figure 1.11*
Two mezzanine levels of the Arrow International Building in Reading, Pennsylvania, are supported by steel channel hangers, leaving the main floor free of columns. (Architect: Kallman, McKinnell & Wood. Photo by Steve Rosenthal.)

▲ *Figure 1.12*
Vertical hangers transmit the loads of the roadway and vehicles to the twin steel arches of the Roosevelt Lake Bridge in Arizona. (Engineer: HNTB Corporation.)

Key Terms and Concepts

force	$\Sigma F_v = 0$	actual stress	newton
member	tension	allowable stress	pascal
free-body diagram	tensile force	working stress	milli-
load	axial force	hanger	kilo-
direction of load or force	stress	SI units	mega-
magnitude of load or force	$f = \dfrac{P}{A}$	Systéme Internationale d'Unités	compressive member
reaction		meter	channel
static equilibrium	tensile stress	kilogram	intumescent coating

Exercises

1. Two 16-year-olds have challenged three 12-year-olds to a tug-of-war (Fig. 1.13). They discover that the two teams are very evenly matched, and the rope tends not to move in either direction. If each of the older contestants exerts a force of 300 N on the rope, how much force is exerted by each of the younger contestants, if they share the force equally? What are the forces in segments *a*, *b*, *c*, and *d* of the rope? (*Hint:* Draw free-body diagrams to represent each of the segments.)

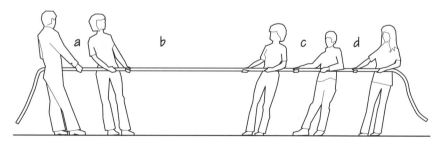

▲ *Figure 1.13* **A tug-of-war.**

2. The balcony of a theater will be supported by steel tension rods that are hung from the roof structure above (Fig. 1.14). Each rod will be attached to a balcony floor beam at its lower end and must support a mass of 14 000 kg. The allowable tensile stress in the rod is 150 MPa. How large in diameter must the rod be? Round up the answer to the nearest whole millimeter.

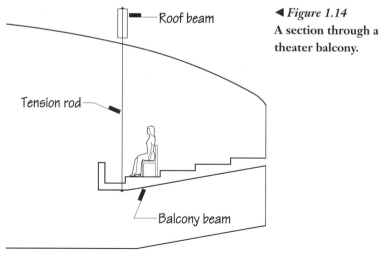

◀ *Figure 1.14*
A section through a theater balcony.

3. Find the **actual** stress in the 14-gauge wire that we selected to support the 100-lb iron weight.

4. You are designing a wooden bridge that will be supported by tensile members on either side (Fig. 1.15). You have found that the maximum axial force in each tensile member is 6000 lb. The allowable tensile stress in the wood is 750 psi. What is the smallest standard piece of wood you can use for this purpose? Is it a 2 × 4 ("two-by-four"), which is actually 1.5 by 3.5 in. in cross section; a 2 × 6, which is 1.5 by 5.5 in.; or a 2 × 8, which is 1.5 by 7.25 in.? What is the **actual** stress in the wood member you have selected?

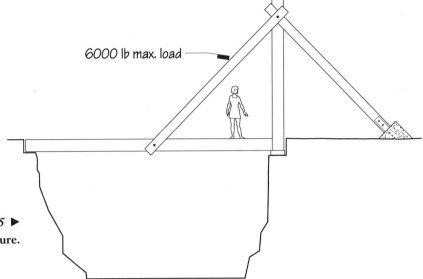

6000 lb max. load

Figure 1.15 ▶
A wooden bridge structure.

A VERTICAL COMPRESSIVE STRUCTURE

◀ The roof of this Greek temple from the sixth century B.C. is supported on stacks of stone blocks that are carved into the characteristic shapes of Doric columns. (Photo courtesy of Photo Researchers.)

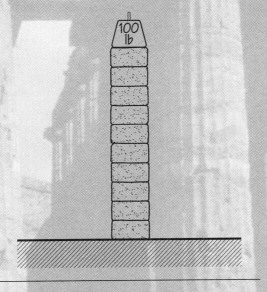

▲ *Figure 2.1*
A vertical compressive structure.

In the preceding chapter we examined the behavior of a simple tensile structure, a vertical wire supporting a 100-lb block of iron. In this chapter, we begin by supporting the same block of iron on a different kind of vertical structure, a stack of 10 stone blocks, each of which weighs 20 lb and is 8 inches square and 4 in. high (Fig. 2.1).

CONSTRUCTING A FREE-BODY DIAGRAM OF THE COLUMN

The first step in analyzing this structure, as with any structure, is to construct a free-body diagram of it. We draw the stack of blocks as if it were floating in space, without showing the ground below or the iron block above. We begin adding the forces that act on the stone blocks by showing at the top a downward-pointing arrow accompanied by a figure of 100 lb to represent the weight of the iron block (Fig. 2.2).

The iron block is a *live load*. Every structure is designed to support a live load, which is made up of forces that are sometimes present and sometimes not, and that vary in intensity—things like people, furniture, machinery, automobiles, boxes of merchandise in a warehouse, or snow on a roof. Also included in the general category of live loads are wind pressures on walls and roofs, and forces caused by seismic motion.

In addition to live loads, every structure must support a permanent *dead load*. The dead load includes the self-weight of the structure, such as the weight of a concrete block column or wall, a wooden beam, a steel truss, or a reinforced concrete floor slab. The dead load of a building also includes the weight of fixed but nonstructural features such as partitions, ceilings, exterior walls, and mechanical equipment. In the instance of the wire hanger considered in the first chapter, we decided that the dead load of the wire was so small, a miniscule fraction of the weight of the iron block, that we did not have to consider it in our calculations. This was an exceptional case; in nearly every structure, we must take into account the weight of the building itself and include it in our analysis as a dead load that has to be supported in addition to the live load. The weight of the stone blocks in the simple compressive structure that we are examining is a dead load that must be taken into account.

Gravity acts on all parts of the stack of stone blocks. Theoretically, we should represent the dead load of the blocks on our free-body diagram as a very large number of tiny, downward-pointing arrows distributed evenly throughout the volume of the stack. For most purposes, however, we can simplify the representation of the dead load by assuming that it consists of a few forces, one per block, that act at the centers of the masses that they represent. In the free-body diagram, we represent the dead load as a series of ten 20-lb arrows, each acting in a downward direction at the center of one of the 10 blocks (Fig. 2.3).

STATIC EQUILIBRIUM

We know that our free-body diagram is incomplete, because so far it includes only forces that act downward. These forces would move the stack of blocks in a downward direction if they were not balanced by an equal force or forces acting in the opposite direction. Consider the expression for static equilibrium that we developed in the first chapter:

$$\sum F_v = 0 \qquad [1\text{-}1]$$

The sum of the forces in the vertical direction must be zero if the stack of blocks is to remain stationary. In order for this to be true, there must be a force or forces acting in the upward direction that we have not yet added to our free-body

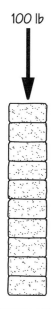

▲ *Figure 2.2*
Starting construction of the free-body diagram.

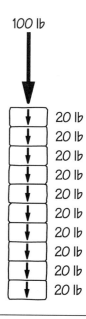

▲ *Figure 2.3*
Continuing construction of the free-body diagram.

diagram. The only other body acting on the stack of blocks is the ground on which they sit. The ground must exert an upward force to balance the dead load of the stone blocks and the live load of the iron block. Using eq. [1-1], we can find out how large this force is. We are careful to follow the convention of using positive numbers for downward forces and negative numbers for upward forces. We represent the force exerted by the ground as R (remember that R stands for *reaction*). Our computations look like this:

$$\sum F_v = 0$$

$$100 \text{ lb} + 10(20 \text{ lb}) + R = 0$$

$$R = -300 \text{ lb}$$

The reaction is 300 lb. The minus sign tells us that it acts in an upward direction. We complete the free-body diagram by adding an upward-pointing arrow at the bottom with a magnitude of 300 lb (Fig. 2.4).

COMPRESSION

Examining the completed free-body diagram, we see that the stack of blocks is acted on by forces that tend to squeeze it together. When a structural member is squeezed, we say that it is in *compression*, or that it is subjected to a *compressive force*. A linear vertical structural member (such as this stack of blocks) that is acted on by vertical forces that cause compression is called a *column*. A planar vertical structure (such as a wall of stone blocks) that is acted on by vertical forces is called a *loadbearing wall*, or more commonly, a *bearing wall*.

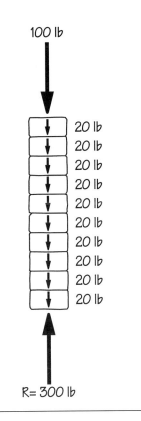

▲ *Figure 2.4*
The completed free-body diagram.

FINDING THE FORCE AT ANY POINT IN THE COLUMN

How large is the compressive force in the column? In the earlier example, the wire weighed so little, just a fraction of a pound, that we could achieve a very close approximation of the tensile force at any point in the wire by assuming that the total force at that point was 100 lb. In this example, the total dead load of the column is twice as much as the live load that it supports. Examining the free-body diagram in Figure 2.4, we can say that the compressive force at the very bottom of the column is 300 lb, the same as the reaction. But how large is the force at some location in the middle of the column, between the fifth and sixth blocks, for example? To determine this, we must construct another free-body diagram that includes only the portion of the column above this plane.

We make an imaginary cut through the column between the fifth and sixth blocks and draw free-body diagrams of both portions of the column (Fig. 2.5). We add the live load arrow at the top of the upper portion, and five arrows to depict the dead loads of the blocks. All these arrows act in a downward direction; what force acts in the upward direction to balance them? It must be a force exerted on the top half of the column by the bottom half. We represent this force as an upward-acting arrow on the bottom end of the upper portion. We label this force $P_{5\text{-}6}$, indicating that it is the force between blocks 5 and 6. (Remember that P stands for "pull" or, in this case, "push.") What is the magnitude of $P_{5\text{-}6}$? Once again we use the expression for static equilibrium, eq. [1-1], to find the answer, giving positive values to downward-acting forces:

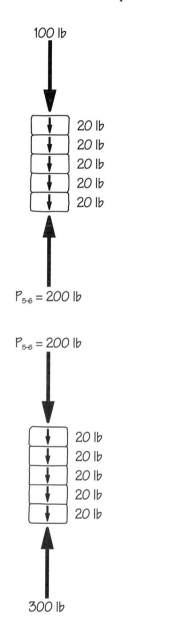

▲ *Figure 2.5*
Free-body diagrams of two portions of the stack of stone blocks.

$$\sum F_v = 0$$

$$100 \text{ lb} + 5(20 \text{ lb}) + P_{5\text{-}6} = 0$$

$$P_{5\text{-}6} = -200 \text{ lb}$$

The force at the midheight of the column is 200 lb. The negative value tells us that it acts upward on the top half of the column. We add an arrow to represent this force to the free-body diagram.

The free-body diagram of the upper portion of the stone column is now complete. To complete the diagram of the lower portion, we add a downward-pointing arrow at the top with a value of 200 lb; this is force $P_{5\text{-}6}$. Together with the five 20-lb forces in the blocks, it balances the 300-lb reaction at the bottom.

In similar fashion, we may find the force at any point we wish to study in the column. We simply make an imaginary cut through the structure at that point and construct a new free-body diagram of the portion of the structure above or below the cut (usually there is no need to diagram both portions). Then we sum up the forces in the vertical direction to find the magnitude of the force. This technique of making imaginary cuts and free-body diagrams of portions of a structure is very valuable to the designer and is used constantly in examining the forces in every type of structure, as we shall do again and again throughout this book.

FINDING FORCES GRAPHICALLY

We have just found the force at a selected point in the column by using a *numerical solution* based on the manipulation of numbers and symbols. There is another method of arriving at the same

result. It is called a *graphical solution*. Graphical solutions are based on the construction and evaluation of scaled drawings.

As a way of understanding the fundamental principle of graphical solutions, let us construct a bar graph that represents all the forces that act on the stone column. Because all the forces act in a vertical direction, we make the bar vertical. Because the loads of the iron block and the stone blocks all act in a downward direction, the bar will be measured **downward** from a horizontal zero axis. We choose a convenient scale to which to construct the graph, in this case 1 in. equals 100 lb. We keep the free-body diagram of Figure 2.4 nearby to guide us.

We begin at the top of the structure and construct the bar graph systematically (Fig. 2.6). The first segment of the bar descends 1 in. below the zero axis to represent the downward push of the 100-lb iron weight. We add below this a bar segment 0.2 in. tall. This represents the 20-lb weight of the topmost stone block. In similar fashion, we add nine more connected bar segments, each 0.2 in. high, each extending downward to match the direction of the force. We label each bar segment with the number of the stone block whose weight it represents.

The bar graph now shows all the downward-acting forces connected end-to-end in a downward-extending bar. In checking the free-body diagram, we see that there is also an upward-acting force that we have not yet represented. This is the reaction at the bottom of the column, an upward push of 300 lb. For this we must construct a bar segment that starts from the bottom of the bar that we have drawn and proceeds **upward** for a distance of 3 in. In laying out this segment accurately on the graph, we find that it reaches back exactly to the horizontal zero

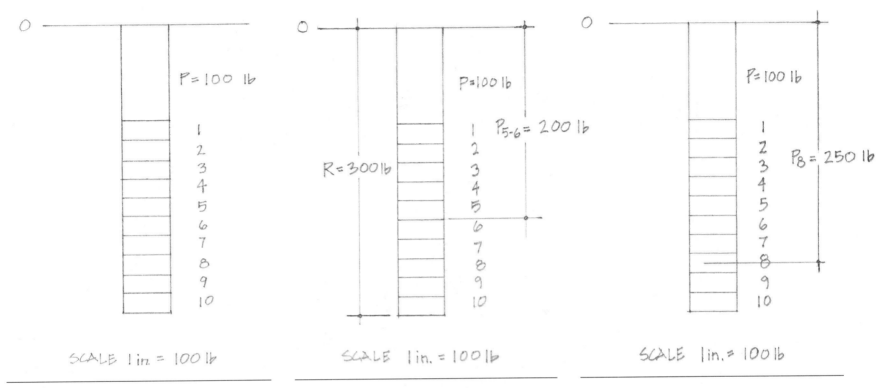

▲ Figure 2.6
A bar graph representing the loads on the stack of stone blocks.

▲ Figure 2.7
The reaction is added to the bar graph; scaling the graph to find the force between the fifth and sixth blocks.

▲ Figure 2.8
Scaling the bar graph to find the force at the middle of the third block.

axis of the graph. The bar has folded back on itself and has ended up at the same point at which it began (Fig. 2.7). This construction, like every graphical construction that we will do throughout this book, is self-checking in this respect: The graphical representation of all the forces that act on a free-body must begin and end at the same place. If it does not, there has been an error either in computing the reaction or in constructing the graph.

The bar graph has closed accurately on itself, and we are now ready to use it to find the

force at any point in the column of stone blocks. To find the force between blocks 5 and 6 using Figure 2.7, we merely measure the height of the bar from the horizontal zero axis to the line that separates segments 5 and 6 of the graph. The measurement is 2 in., which represents 200 lb. This agrees with the solution that we found numerically a few paragraphs earlier.

One of the advantages of a graphical solution is that, once the graph has been drawn, we can use it easily and rapidly to find answers to as many other questions as we care to ask about

forces in the structure. We can find the force between blocks 8 and 9, or blocks 1 and 2, just by taking another measurement on the same graph. We can also find the force at **any** point in **any** block just as easily. The force at the midheight of block 8, for example, can be measured in a matter of seconds as 250 lb (Fig. 2.8).

In solving structural problems graphically, we do not usually go to the trouble of constructing bar graphs. Instead, we use a single-line representation of the forces to save time. In the case of the stone column, the bar is replaced by a sin-

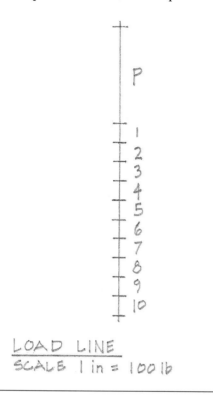

P

| 1
| 2
| 3
| 4
| 5
| 6
| 7
| 8
| 9
| 10

LOAD LINE
SCALE 1 in = 100 lb

▲ *Figure 2.9*
A simplified graphical representation of the loads on the stack of stone blocks: the load line.

gle vertical line, the *load line* (Fig. 2.9). We will see in subsequent chapters that every graphical solution, no matter how complex the structure under investigation, begins with the simple act of constructing a load line. If all the forces that act on the structure result from the action of gravity, as they do in this example, the load line is vertical. Horizontal ticks divide the load line into segments that represent the magnitudes of the various vertical forces. The load line is always accompanied by a notation of the scale to which it is constructed. Graphical solutions are gener-

ally done at a drafting board using drafting tools and a sharp pencil, working carefully to attain a high level of accuracy.

COMPRESSIVE STRESS

In the first chapter, the concept of stress was presented. The formula for stress is

$$f = \frac{P}{A} \qquad [1\text{-}2]$$

where f is the stress, P is the internal force, and A is the cross-sectional area on which P acts. The stress in the wire in the previous example was a tensile stress, which may be represented as f_t. We read f_t as "stress in tension" or "tensile stress."

The stack of stone blocks is under a compressive force; therefore its stresses are compressive. To make this clear we represent its stresses as f_c, which we read as "compressive stress" or "stress in compression."

To find the compressive stress between the fifth and sixth blocks of the column, we use the general formula for stress, substituting the reaction of 200 lb for P, and the dimensions of the bottom face of the stone block, 8 in. by 8 in., for A:

$$f_c = \frac{P}{A}$$

$$f_c = \frac{200 \text{ lb}}{(8 \text{ in.})(8 \text{ in.})} = 3.13 \text{ psi}$$

The stress in the middle of the column is 3.13 lb per sq in. (psi). We can follow a similar procedure to determine that the maximum stress in the column, which occurs at the bottom, is 4.69 psi.

It is a good practice to carry all the units of measurement through a calculation, as we have

done here in keeping the "lb" abbreviation after the 200 in the numerator, and the "in." abbreviation after each of the eights in the denominator. This allows us to check to be sure that we have substituted values correctly into the equation and that we have been consistent in our use of units. We do this by solving the equation for units only, leaving out the numerical values:

$$\text{psi} = \frac{\text{lb}}{(\text{in.})(\text{in.})} = \frac{\text{lb}}{\text{in.}^2} = \text{psi O.K.}$$

The units check. This does not guarantee that we have not made an arithmetical or clerical mistake, but it does mean that we have probably set up the equation correctly.

ALLOWABLE STRESS

The actual maximum stress that we have found in the column, 4.69 psi, is very low. A typical building stone might have an allowable compressive stress (f_{allow}) of 1000 psi. Can we make the blocks smaller in cross section, so that they are stressed to the 1000 psi maximum? We can find the minimum cross-sectional area for the blocks by substituting the allowable stress in the general formula for stress, using the maximum force in the structure, which occurs at the bottom of the column. Earlier we computed this force to be 300 lb, but we cannot use this figure, because it is based on the dead load of a stack of blocks that are 8 in. square. We expect the blocks in the fully stressed column to be much smaller than this. In our original structure, the stress in the blocks is approximately 5 psi, and in the structure that is stressed to its maximum safe load-supporting capacity, it will be 1000 psi. This means that the blocks could be only about 5/1000 as large in the fully stressed structure. We estimate the new dead load by applying this ratio to the old dead load:

$$Dead\ load \cong \frac{5}{1000}(200\ lb) \cong 1\ lb$$

If the dead load for the fully stressed column is only about one pound, then the total of the live and dead loads at the point of maximum stress, the base of the column, is the sum of the 100-lb live load and the 1-lb dead load, or 101 lb. Using this value, we compute the required size of the column. We use the symbol A_{req} to represent the required cross-sectional area of the column:

$$f_{allow} = \frac{P}{A_{req}}$$

$$A_{req} = \frac{P}{f_{allow}}$$

$$A_{req} = \frac{101\ lb}{1000\ lb/in.^2} = 0.1\ in.^2$$

This tells us that we need stone blocks that are only one-tenth of a square inch in cross section. If the blocks are square, this works out to a dimension of 0.32 in. on each side.

What would happen if we adopted this size for the column? For one thing, the blocks would be difficult to make, because 0.32 in., about one-third of an inch, is far too small a dimension for a block made of stone, which is a coarse-grained, brittle material that breaks easily when cut to very small dimensions. (A 0.32-in.-square bar of steel, on the other hand, is easily manufactured and is perfectly reasonable to use in a structure, because steel is fine-grained and not brittle.)

More important, however, a stack of 10 blocks that are only 0.32 in. square will be very

unstable. It will tend to *buckle*, because the compressive action of the load in the column will magnify the effect of any tiny imperfections in the way the blocks are made or joined, causing the stack of blocks to tip over or to push out sideways (Fig. 2.10). A column of this dimension would be sure to fail by buckling, because it is much too *slender*.

A potential for buckling is present in any structural element that is compressed. Buckling is a difficult phenomenon to quantify accurately, and we will not go very deeply into it at this time. Expressions for predicting buckling behavior are based on the *slenderness* of the column, which in most structural materials is represented by a *slenderness ratio*, which is its length divided by its

smallest transverse dimension (its dimension at right angles to the longitudinal axis of the column). The more slender the column, the less load it can carry without buckling. The original column of stone blocks had a slenderness ratio that can be computed as follows:

$$Slenderness\ ratio = \frac{height}{transverse\ dimension}$$

$$= \frac{40\ in.}{8\ in.} = 5$$

Looking at a scaled drawing of this column, most of us would judge that a stone column with a slenderness ratio of 5 is probably highly resistant to buckling (Fig. 2.11). The slenderness ratio of

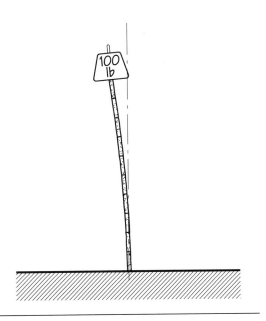

▲ *Figure 2.10*
A column that is too slender will buckle.

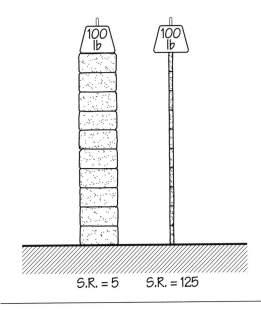

▲ *Figure 2.11*
Slenderness ratios.

OF MOSQUITOES AND MASTODONS

Why are a mosquito's legs so slender relative to the size of its body, whereas an elephant's legs are so thick and clumsy? We can gain insight into this phenomenon of nature by considering an animal's legs as structural columns. In doing so we will make some gross simplifications: we will ignore the dynamic loads of running and jumping to which animals subject their legs, and take into account only static gravitational loads. Animal bodies and legs are very complex geometrically, but we will represent them as simple rectangular solids. We will further assume that the average allowable compressive stress in muscle and bone is more or less the same for an elephant as for an insect; we will assign to it a value of 100 kPa. For the density of animal flesh we will adopt the density of water, 1000 kg/m^3.

A mosquito is a bit small to deal with conveniently, so we will examine instead the leg structure of a large grasshopper, whose body we represent as a cube 10 mm on a side (about four-tenths of an inch). First we calculate the volume of the body:

$$Volume = (0.01 \text{ m})^3 = 1.0 \times 10^{-6} \text{ m}^3$$

Next we figure its mass and weight:

$$Mass = (1.0 \times 10^{-6} \text{ m}^3) \times (10^3 \text{ kg/m}^3) = 10^{-3} \text{ kg}$$
$$\text{or } 0.001 \text{ kg}$$

$$Weight = (10^{-3} \text{ kg}) \times (9.8 \text{ m/s}^2) = 9.8 \times 10^{-3} \text{ N}$$
$$\text{or } 0.01 \text{ N}$$

Now we can determine the total required cross-sectional area of its legs:

$$A_{req} = \frac{9.8 \times 10^{-3} \text{ N}}{100 \text{ kPa}} = 9.8 \times 10^{-8} \text{ m}^2$$

To level the playing field between the grasshopper, which has six legs, and the elephant, which has only four, we calculate the required size of the legs as if each animal had but a single, square leg. For the grasshopper:

$$\text{Dimension of a single square leg}$$
$$= \sqrt{9.8 \times 10^{-8} \text{ m}^2} = 0.0003 \text{ m}$$

This leg dimension is equal to about 3% of the grasshopper's linear body dimension. Now we repeat these calculations for a baby elephant, which we approximate as a cube of flesh one meter on a side:

$$\text{Volume} = 1 \text{ m}^3$$

$$\text{Mass} = (1 \text{ m}^3) \times (1000 \text{ kg/m}^3) = 1000 \text{ kg}$$

$$\text{Weight} = (1000 \text{ kg}) \times (9.8 \text{ m/s}^2) = 9.8 \text{ kN}$$

$$\text{Total required area of legs} = \frac{9.8 \text{ kN}}{100 \text{ kPa}}$$

$$= 0.098 \text{ m}^2$$

$$\text{Dimension of a single square leg} = \sqrt{0.098 \text{ m}^2}$$

$$= 0.3 \text{ m}$$

The leg dimension of the baby elephant is equal to 30% of its linear body dimension, compared with 3% for the grasshopper. The elephant has very pudgy legs, and the grasshopper, very skinny ones.

Why is this so? It is a simple matter of geometry. The body of any animal is a solid whose weight varies as the cube of its linear dimension. The cross section of a leg is a planar area that varies only as the square of its dimension. As a body grows larger in linear dimension, its legs must thicken at a much faster rate than the body in order to keep the stresses in the bone and muscle to safe levels. Thus, a grasshopper's legs are proportionally thicker than those of a mosquito, and a mouse's thicker than those of a grasshopper, and so the pattern continues through cats, dogs, humans, draft horses, hippos, and mastodons.

We can conjecture that if there were another planet that had living creatures made of organic tissue similar to that of animals on earth, and this planet had a gravitational pull only half as strong as ours, its animals would be proportioned very differently. Insects the size of our grasshoppers would have shapes similar to our mosquitoes, and animals as tall as our elephants would have the bodies of antelopes. ∎

the new column is much greater than 5, however:

$$Slenderness\ ratio = \frac{height}{transverse\ dimension}$$

$$= \frac{40\ in.}{0.32\ in.} = 125$$

Most of us would conclude intuitively from looking at Figure 2.11 that a stone column should not have a slenderness ratio as high as 125, because it will surely buckle. We would like to find a slenderness ratio that is somewhat larger than 5 and a lot less than 125 that would be appropriate for the design of a stone column that is safe from buckling. At this point in our learning, we have not developed analytical tools to help us resolve this dilemma; we will have to take up this discussion in a future volume.

INVERTIBILITY

In this chapter and in the preceding one, we have studied two simple vertical structures for supporting a 100-lb weight. One is a hanger with the weight attached to its lower end. The other is a column of stone blocks with the weight sitting on its top. The wire is stressed in tension, the column is stressed in compression. Each is a physical inversion of the other. In other words, if we turn the wire upside down, together with its support and its load, while preserving the downward direction of the external load, it acts (or at least tries to act) as a column (Fig. 2.12). The *character* of the force in the structure reverses when this is done: tension becomes compression. Similarly, if we turn the column upside down, together with its support and its load, compression becomes tension. As we shall see again and

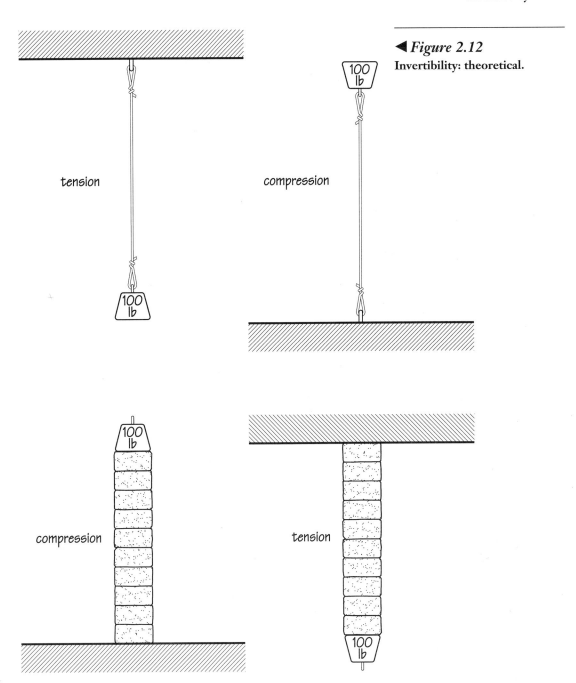

◀ *Figure 2.12*
Invertibility: theoretical.

again in examples to come, if any structure is inverted while the external loads that act on it remain the same in magnitude and direction, all the forces within it change character. Their absolute values do not change: 100 pounds of tension become 100 pounds of compression, and vice versa.

As we have seen, however, there is an important difference between a structural element in tension and one in compression: a tensile element corrects its own shape if it is not exactly straight and becomes more stable under load, whereas a compressive element tends to magnify its own imperfections of shape and to become unstable by buckling. The wire in the first example might have some kinks in it before it is loaded, but these would start to straighten as soon as any load is applied. A large tensile force would pull the wire into a perfectly straight line. The column of stone blocks in the second example, if it were made too slender, would tend to magnify the ever-present inconsistencies within the blocks as well as any slight misalignment between the blocks and, thereby, to buckle. Thus, structural elements acting in compression must be fatter than elements acting in tension (Fig. 2.13).

There is another difference between compressive and tensile members. Compressive members may be discontinuous, held together only by the pressure of one element upon another, as is the case in the column built of discrete blocks of stone. Tensile members must be continuous, so that the tension cannot pull the elements apart. Thus, we cannot actually invert the stone column, because it would fall apart at the joints. We cannot actually invert the wire, either, because it is so slender that it would buckle under its load. A compressive element

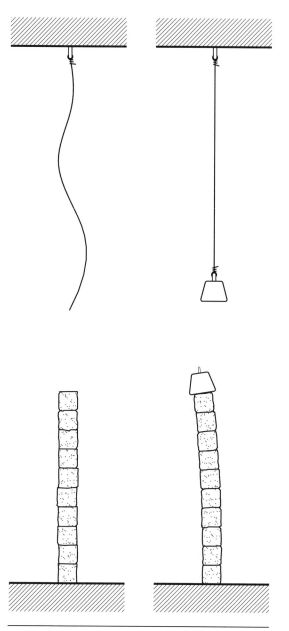

▲ *Figure 2.13*
Invertibility: practical.

must be stiff as well as sufficient in cross-sectional area. Nevertheless, we will find in later chapters that this principle of invertibility is valuable in helping us to understand easily many structural ideas that would otherwise be difficult to grasp.

SIZING CONCRETE COLUMNS FOR A TALL BUILDING

The detailed design of reinforced concrete columns for a building is a fairly involved process. However, it is often useful in early stages of design to determine approximate required sizes for the columns of a building by means of simple computations that are based on an average stress for the composite action of the concrete and the vertical steel reinforcing bars that make up the column. Let us apply such computations to a 10-story building with floor-to-floor heights of 3.5 m (Fig. 2.14). Each column must support a mass of 16 000 kg from the roof structure and 24 000 kg from each floor structure. These figures include both dead loads and live loads for the roofs and floors, but they do not include the dead load of the column itself. We will assume an allowable average compressive stress in the columns of 15 MPa. The density of reinforced concrete is approximately 2 400 kg/m³. The building is designed so that all the *lateral forces*—wind and earthquake—are resisted by a rigid shaft at the center of each floor that houses the elevators and stairways. This means that the columns resist only vertical *gravity loads*, which include the dead and live loads of the building and its contents. We assume that all the columns are square in cross section, and that they are stocky enough that buckling is not a consideration in their design.

A bit of preliminary thinking about this problem reveals that the column bearing the smallest load is at the top of the building, where it supports only the roof. The column that bears the next smallest load is the one just below it that supports the roof plus the top floor, and so on down to the foundations. Loads on a stack of columns accumulate from top to bottom. Accordingly, the columns at the top of the building are likely to be smaller in cross section than those at the bottom. It is also apparent that the mass of the concrete columns themselves could become a significant portion of the total mass that the columns must support. Both these facts suggest that it is wise to start calculating column sizes at the top of the building and work our way to the bottom floor by floor. In this way, we can include the weights of the columns themselves in the calculations as we go along.

We begin by drawing a free-body diagram of the column at the top of the building (Fig. 2.15). The maximum force in this column will occur just above the top floor, where the weight of the roof, which has a mass of 16 000 kg, plus the entire self-weight of this portion of the column, must be supported. We have not yet calculated how big this column must be, so we do not know how large its mass is. This is a typical situation that we encounter in designing any structural element. Every element must support its own mass as well as the mass it is designed to support. We do not know what its mass is until we design it, but we cannot design it until we

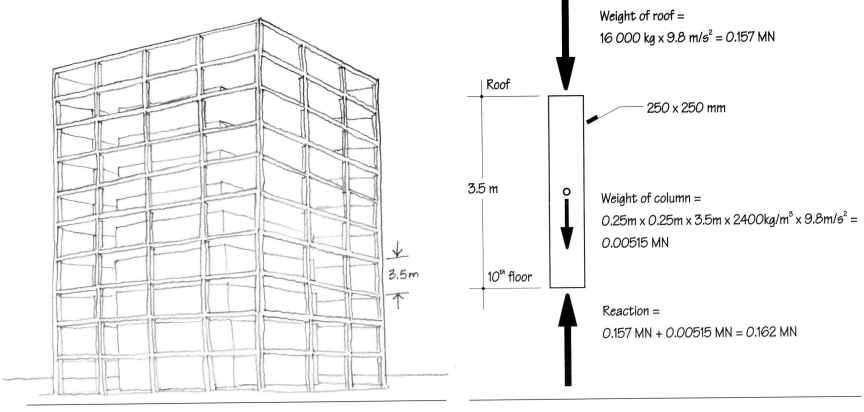

Weight of roof =
16 000 kg x 9.8 m/s^2 = 0.157 MN

250 x 250 mm

Weight of column =
0.25m x 0.25m x 3.5m x 2400kg/m^3 x 9.8m/s^2 = 0.00515 MN

Reaction =
0.157 MN + 0.00515 MN = 0.162 MN

▲ *Figure 2.14*
A 10-story building with reinforced concrete columns.

▲ *Figure 2.15*
Free-body diagram of the tenth-floor column.

know what its mass is. To escape this dilemma, we must estimate what the mass is likely to be, determine the size of the element on this basis, and check to see whether our estimate of size was close enough to the actual size that our result is valid. If the estimate is too far off, we must reestimate and do the calculations again.

In this concrete building, we have some guidance in approximating the size of the top-most column. The applicable building code specifies that a column may not be smaller than 200 mm in any dimension; this assures that the column is not too slender and that there is sufficient concrete in the column to protect the steel reinforcing bars from fire. Moreover, experience has shown that concrete columns are unlikely to buckle if their slenderness ratio is fifteen or larger. This relationship suggests a minimum column dimension of 233 mm for the 3.5-m-long columns in the building we are considering. For convenience in construction, we round this up to the next multiple of 50 mm, which is 250 mm. The topmost column does not support very much load, only the roof, so a good guess is that this column will not have to be larger than 250 mm square. From this assessment, we can make a preliminary estimate of the mass of the column:

$$Mass\ of\ column = volume \times density$$
$$Mass\ of\ column = (0.25\ m)(0.25\ m)(3.5\ m)$$
$$\times (2\ 400\ kg/m^3) = 525\ kg$$

We follow the units through the equation to check whether we have set up the equation properly:

$$(m)(m)(m)(kg/m^3) = kg\ O.K.$$

The maximum force in the top-floor column can now be calculated. We work in meganewtons (MN) to match the allowable stress in megapascals:

$$P = (16\ 000\ kg + 525\ kg)(9.8\ m/s^2) = 0.162\ MN$$

Next we find the required size of this column:

$$f_{allow} = \frac{P}{A_{req}}$$

$$A_{req} = \frac{P}{f_{allow}}$$

$$A_{req} = \frac{0.162\ MN}{15\ MPa} = 0.0108\ m^2$$

To find the side of a square column with this area, we take the square root of 0.108 m², which is 0.104 m, or 104 mm. This is less than the 250-mm minimum column required by code, so we adopt a column size of 250 by 250 mm for this floor. Our estimate of the size of the column was

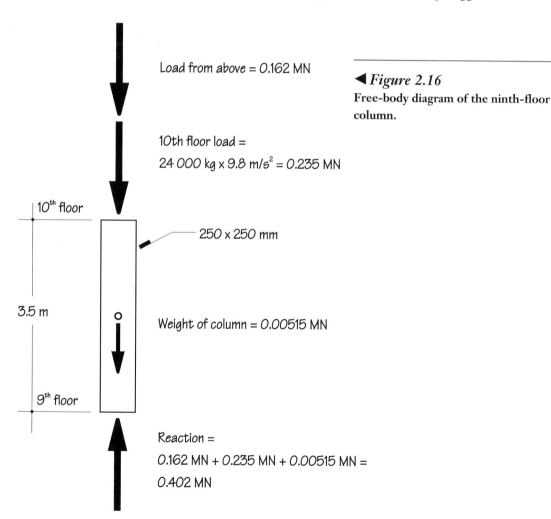

Load from above = 0.162 MN

10th floor load =
24 000 kg x 9.8 m/s² = 0.235 MN

10th floor

250 x 250 mm

3.5 m

Weight of column = 0.00515 MN

9th floor

Reaction =
0.162 MN + 0.235 MN + 0.00515 MN =
0.402 MN

◄ *Figure 2.16*
Free-body diagram of the ninth-floor column.

correct, and we can go on to the next stage of our computations.

Moving down to the next floor, the ninth, we can guess with confidence, based on the huge surplus of area in the tenth floor column, that the minimum-size column will again suffice. We draw another free-body diagram (Fig. 2.16) and repeat the computational process. The mass that this column must support comes from the roof,

one floor, and two stories of column. This process is repeated for each floor until we reach the ground.

The key figures derived from these calculations are summarized in tabular form in Figure 2.17. (Constructing a table such as this is a good way to organize repetitive calculations.) The table shows that a 250-mm-square column suffices for the seventh through tenth floors. By

keeping track, as we went along, of how quickly the calculated column dimensions in column 6 of the table were approaching the rounded column dimensions in column 7, we were able to anticipate the points at which the column size had to be increased. In reviewing as a group the calculated sizes for the columns, which we have rounded to the nearest 50 mm, it is apparent that we could round their sizes still further to allow a

	COL. 1	COL. 2	COL. 3	COL. 4	COL. 5	COL. 6	COL. 7	COL. 8	COL. 9
COLUMN JUST ABOVE FLOOR No.	TOTAL MASS SUPPORTED FROM ABOVE, kg	ESTIMATED MASS OF COLUMN ON THIS FLOOR, kg	TOTAL MASS SUPPORTED, kg, COL.1 + COL.2	TOTAL FORCE, MN COL.3 × 9.81 m/s²	REQUIRED COLUMN AREA, m² COL.4 ÷ 15 MPa	CALCULATED COLUMN DIM. REQUIRED, mm² $\sqrt{COL.5}$	COLUMN DIMENSION ROUNDED TO 50 mm	ACTUAL MASS OF COLUMN ON THIS FLOOR, kg	TOTAL MASS TRANSMITTED TO FLOOR BELOW, kg COL.1 + COL.8
10	16 000	525	16 525	0.162	0.0108	104	250	525	16 525
9	40 525	525	41 050	0.402	0.0268	164	250	525	41 050
8	65 050	525	65 575	0.643	0.0428	207	250	525	65 575
7	89 575	525	90 100	0.883	0.0589	243	250	525	90 100
6	114 100	760	114 860	1.126	0.0750	274	300	760	114 860
5	138 860	760	139 620	1.369	0.0913	302	300	760	139 620
4	163 620	1 030	164 650	1.614	0.108	329	350	1 030	164 650
3	188 650	1 030	189 680	1.860	0.124	352	350	1 030	189 680
2	213 680	1 345	215 025	2.107	0.141	375	400	1 345	215 025
1	239 025	1 345	240 370	2.356	0.157	396	400	1 345	240 370 TO FOUNDATION

GIVEN: ROOF L.L. + D.L. = 16 000 kg/column
FLOOR L.L. + D.L. = 24 000 kg/column
f_{allow} = 15 MPa
DENSITY OF CONCRETE = 2 400 kg/m³
MIN. COLUMN SIZE = 250 × 250 mm

▲ *Figure 2.17*
Calculating the sizes of the columns for all 10 floors.

How Tall Can We Build?

Imagine a vertical bar of constant cross section, hanging freely without any external load (Fig. A). How long can the bar become before it breaks under its own weight? The tension in the bar varies from zero at the bottom to a maximum value at the top. The stress at the top is equal to the total weight of the bar divided by the cross-sectional area of the bar. When the bar is lengthened to the point that this stress reaches the ultimate strength of the material in the bar, the bar breaks. The total weight of the bar at its maximum length is equal to its density, ρ, times its cross-sectional area, A, times its breaking length, L_{br}. (In SI units, ρ in this expression must be multiplied by g, the acceleration of gravity, 9.8 m/s^2, to convert it from mass per unit of volume to weight per unit of volume.) The force in the bar at its breaking point is equal to its ultimate strength, f_{ult}, times its cross-sectional area. Thus, we can set weight equal to breaking force to formulate an expression for the length at which the hanging bar will break. In conventional units:

$$\rho A L_{br} = A f_{ult}$$

In SI units:

$$\rho g A L_{br} = A f_{ult}$$

In both versions of this expression, the term A appears on both sides of the expression and can be cancelled; hence, in conventional units:

$$L_{br} = \frac{f_{ult}}{\rho}$$

In SI units:

$$L_{br} = \frac{f_{ult}}{\rho g}$$

Breaking length, also called *specific strength*, is the ratio of ultimate strength to density. It is a

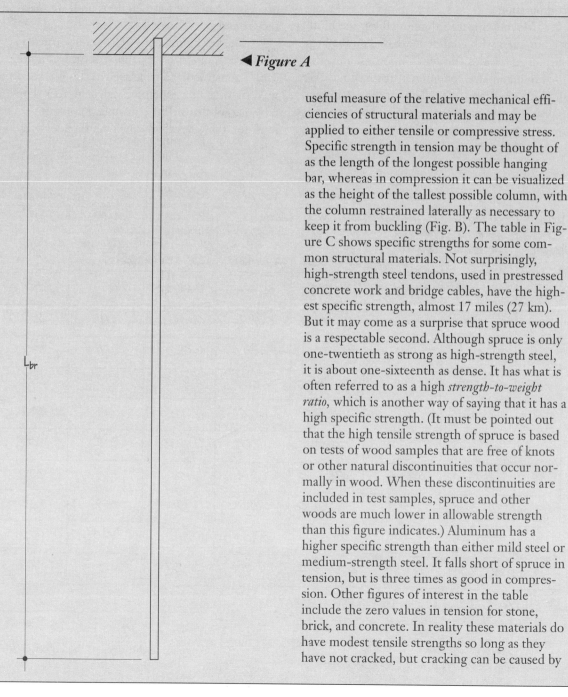

◀ *Figure A*

useful measure of the relative mechanical efficiencies of structural materials and may be applied to either tensile or compressive stress. Specific strength in tension may be thought of as the length of the longest possible hanging bar, whereas in compression it can be visualized as the height of the tallest possible column, with the column restrained laterally as necessary to keep it from buckling (Fig. B). The table in Figure C shows specific strengths for some common structural materials. Not surprisingly, high-strength steel tendons, used in prestressed concrete work and bridge cables, have the highest specific strength, almost 17 miles (27 km). But it may come as a surprise that spruce wood is a respectable second. Although spruce is only one-twentieth as strong as high-strength steel, it is about one-sixteenth as dense. It has what is often referred to as a high *strength-to-weight ratio*, which is another way of saying that it has a high specific strength. (It must be pointed out that the high tensile strength of spruce is based on tests of wood samples that are free of knots or other natural discontinuities that occur normally in wood. When these discontinuities are included in test samples, spruce and other woods are much lower in allowable strength than this figure indicates.) Aluminum has a higher specific strength than either mild steel or medium-strength steel. It falls short of spruce in tension, but is three times as good in compression. Other figures of interest in the table include the zero values in tension for stone, brick, and concrete. In reality these materials do have modest tensile strengths so long as they have not cracked, but cracking can be caused by

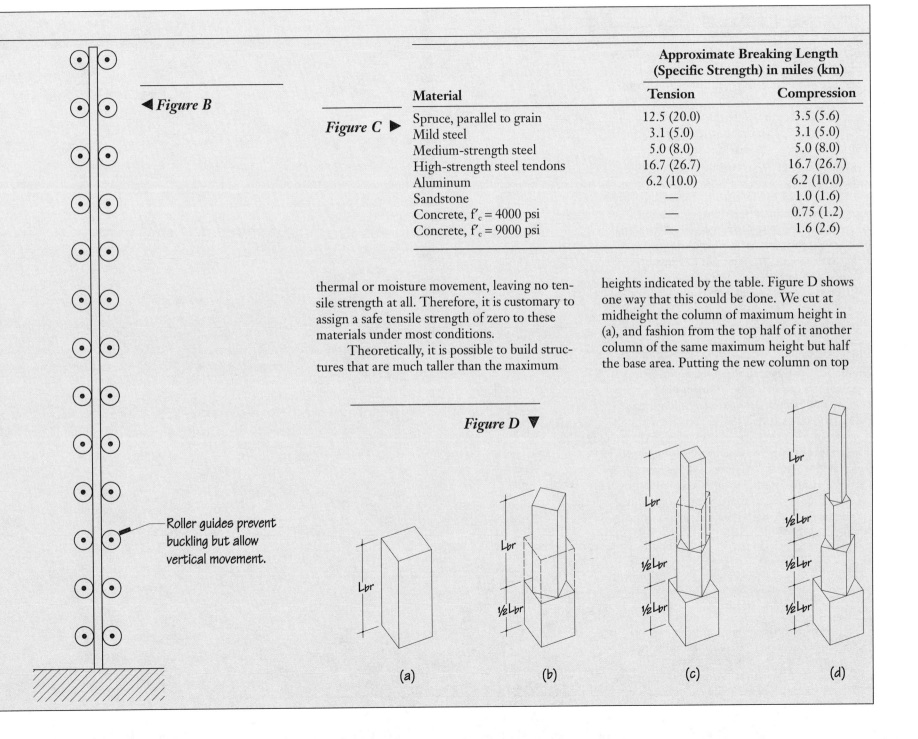

◀ *Figure B*

Roller guides prevent buckling but allow vertical movement.

Figure C ▶

Material	Approximate Breaking Length (Specific Strength) in miles (km)	
	Tension	Compression
Spruce, parallel to grain	12.5 (20.0)	3.5 (5.6)
Mild steel	3.1 (5.0)	3.1 (5.0)
Medium-strength steel	5.0 (8.0)	5.0 (8.0)
High-strength steel tendons	16.7 (26.7)	16.7 (26.7)
Aluminum	6.2 (10.0)	6.2 (10.0)
Sandstone	—	1.0 (1.6)
Concrete, $f'_c = 4000$ psi	—	0.75 (1.2)
Concrete, $f'_c = 9000$ psi	—	1.6 (2.6)

thermal or moisture movement, leaving no tensile strength at all. Therefore, it is customary to assign a safe tensile strength of zero to these materials under most conditions.

Theoretically, it is possible to build structures that are much taller than the maximum heights indicated by the table. Figure D shows one way that this could be done. We cut at midheight the column of maximum height in (a), and fashion from the top half of it another column of the same maximum height but half the base area. Putting the new column on top

Figure D ▼

(a)   (b)   (c)   (d)

HOW TALL CAN WE BUILD? (*continued*)

of the remaining half of the original one (b), we build a column that is half again higher. In (c) we repeat the exercise, cutting the top portion of structure (b) in half and creating another column of maximum height, to arrive at an overall height that is twice that of the original column. Hypothetically, we could repeat this process again and again to make the column as high as we want.

Comparing the three tower configurations shown in scaled-down heights in Figure E, the maximum height for any material of the parallel-sided tower, (a), is equal to the Specific Strength in Compression value in the table shown in Figure C. A tower of uniform taper with the same base area, (b), could be three times as tall. Tower (c), again with the same base area, is tapered logarithmically so that its material is fully stressed at every point along its height. In theory, tower (c) could be infinitely high. Surprisingly, all three towers contain exactly the same volume of material.

To this point, we have considered structures that are stressed to the breaking point. It is obvious that they are unsafe; in theory, even a butterfly alighting on one of them would precipitate its failure. We can get around this problem by assigning a factor of safety, *S*. We might decide that it is safe to stress the material in a structure to only half of its ultimate strength, in which case $S = 2$. The *allowable length*, L_{allow}, of that material can then be determined using this expression:

$$L_{allow} = \frac{L_{br}}{S}$$

If an arch or suspension cable has a rise or sag that is equal to 15% of its span, the maxi-

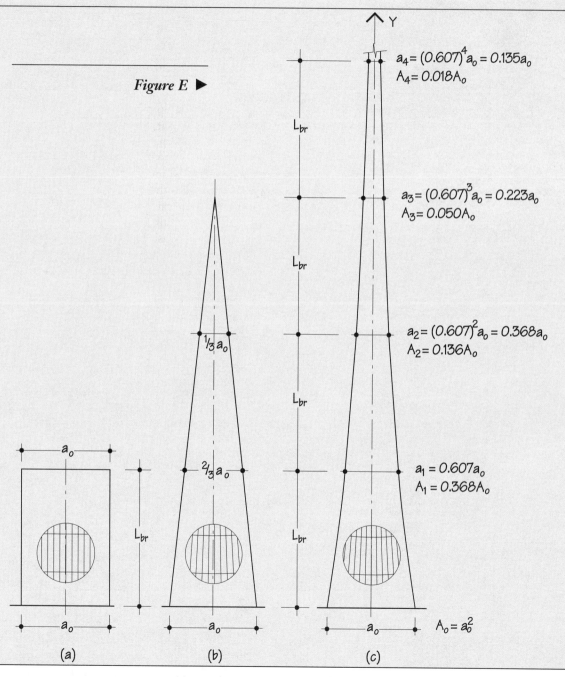

Figure E ▶

$a_4 = (0.607)^4 a_0 = 0.135 a_0$
$A_4 = 0.018 A_0$

$a_3 = (0.607)^3 a_0 = 0.223 a_0$
$A_3 = 0.050 A_0$

$a_2 = (0.607)^2 a_0 = 0.368 a_0$
$A_2 = 0.136 A_0$

$a_1 = 0.607 a_0$
$A_1 = 0.368 A_0$

$A_0 = a_0^2$

$\frac{1}{3} a_0$

$\frac{2}{3} a_0$

a_0

L_{br}

(a)   (b)   (c)

mum force in the arch or cable is approximately equal to its self-weight (Fig. F). Therefore, the theoretical maximum span for such structures is the same as the breaking length of its material. Applying a factor of safety of 2, the maximum allowable span for a medium-strength steel arch with a rise of 0.15 times its span can be figured as follows:

$$L_{\text{allow}} \approx \frac{L_{\text{br}}}{S} \approx \frac{5.0 \text{ miles}}{2} \approx 2.5 \text{ miles}$$

This is about 4 km. In designing a similarly proportioned arch in 9000 psi concrete, a less consistent material than steel, we might be wise

to apply a factor of safety of 3. This arch could span under its own weight only:

$$L_{\text{allow}} \approx \frac{L_{\text{br}}}{S} \approx \frac{1.6 \text{ miles}}{3} \approx 0.53 \text{ miles}$$

If the arch had to support a superimposed load equal to its self-weight, its allowable span would be only half this much, or about 0.265 miles, which is roughly 1400 ft or 425 m. By judicious tapering of these arches to create uniform stresses throughout, their maximum spans could be extended somewhat, although not indefinitely, as is theoretically possible with a tower.

Taking into consideration such problems

as buckling and foundation stability, no real arch could be built to these spans. No actual tower could be built to a height even remotely approaching any of the extreme limits we have contemplated here, even with a safety factor of 2 or 3. No hanging bar could be constructed to these lengths, if for no other reason than the impossibility of building a tower of equal height to support it. But these theoretical investigations reveal an intriguing glimpse of future possibilities for structures that are very tall or that span very long distances, and the resulting forms offer lessons that can be applied to structures of any size. ■

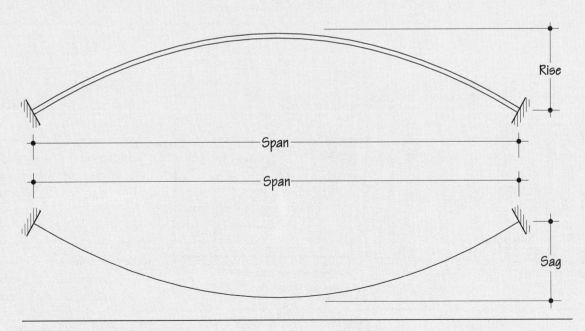

▲ *Figure F*

maximum reuse of concrete column formwork on the job site for increased economy of construction. A 250-mm column could be used for the top four stories, then a 350-mm column for the next four, and a 400-mm column for the remainder. In many buildings that are not too tall, it even proves economical to simplify formwork and detailing by using a single column size throughout all the floors. In this building, it might make sense to adopt a single column size of 400 mm square for all the floors. There is not much cost saving in standardizing the reinforcing steel in the columns, so we could save money by varying the amount of steel reinforcing bars in proportion to the loads in each segment.

The safety of a building is especially dependent on the safety of its columns. If a floor slab or beam fails, the damage is usually limited to one

or two floors in the immediate vicinity of the collapse. If a column fails at the bottom of a multi-story building, all the floor areas that it supports will collapse. This is why building codes mandate more fire protection for columns than for any other structural elements, and it is why we always take special care in designing columns.

Assuming that we retain the variations in column size as originally tabulated, and summing the masses of the columns for all the floors, we find that the self-weight of the columns is less than 4% of the total load that each ground-floor column supports. Even a 50% error in figuring the weights of the columns for this particular building would result in only a 2% error in the estimated total load on the column, which is not likely to be significant. It is apparent that we are using materials of fairly high strength to achieve

so low a percentage of dead load in the columns. The percentage of self-weight of columns would be even lower for the columns of a steel building frame, because steel has a higher ratio of strength to weight than does reinforced concrete. For very tall concrete buildings, it has become standard practice to reduce the self-weight of the columns by making them of concrete with ultimate strengths as high as 125 MPa (18,000 psi).

In the preceding chapter, we designed steel hanger straps for a building with the same height and loads as this building. The straps, being tensile members and therefore not subject to buckling, and being made of steel, were very small in cross section as compared with the reinforced concrete columns that we have just designed. The largest of the straps was only 110 by 150 mm in size, about one-tenth of the area of the largest concrete column.

In assigning sizes to the hanger straps, we worked from the bottom of the building to the top, whereas in sizing the columns we worked from the top to the bottom. This is consistent: in every building, we begin by sizing the portion of the structure that is most remote from the foundation as measured along the path that the loads must follow. In most buildings, this means working from top to bottom, analyzing how the loads accumulate in the columns floor by floor. In a suspended structure, however, the loads accumulate from the bottoms of hangers to the tops. Thus, hangers are largest at the top of a building, whereas columns are largest at the bottom.

As with the suspension hangers, we may wish to consider how to express visually the variation in the load carried by the columns from one floor of the building to another (Fig. 2.18). In this building, we could choose to ignore this

(a) COLUMNS UNIFORM   (b) COLUMNS TAPERED   (c) NONUNIFORM COLUMNS INSIDE WALL

▲ *Figure 2.18*
Some options for visual expression of the variation in the required sizes of concrete columns.

variation by making all the columns 400 mm square. With an additional expenditure of money, we could express the variation as a uniform taper in columns that project out through the face of the building. This might involve fixing the width of all columns at the practical minimum dimension of 250 mm and letting the depth vary from 250 mm at the top to 650 mm at the bottom, which gives the column at each floor about the same cross-sectional area as we had

calculated originally (columns do not have to be square in cross section). The increased cost of this option would result from having to fabricate special column forms for each floor of the building rather than reusing forms as much as possible, and from the additional labor required to fabricate and install tapered assemblies of reinforcing bars. In everyday practice, the most common way of handling column size variation is to let the columns change in dimension in the most

economical way, and to set the outside faces of the columns back a few inches from the face of the building so that they lie completely inside the exterior wall. This avoids thermal expansion and contraction in the columns and eliminates any potential problems of sealing against the penetration of air and water around the columns. It also simplifies greatly the task of installing the exterior walls.

▲ *Figure 2.19*
The tower of the cathedral in Siena, Italy, completed in about A.D. 1360, expresses the variation in forces in its stone bearing walls by varying the amount of window opening at each level. (Photo courtesy of Photo Researchers.)

▲ *Figure 2.20*
Chicago's Monadnock office building, built in 1891 by architects Burnham and Root, is supported by unreinforced brick masonry loadbearing walls. The wall thickness varies from 18 in. (460 mm) at the top story to 72 in. (1830 mm) at ground level. (Photo by William T. Barnum. Courtesy of Chicago Historical Society, IChi-18292.)

Key Terms and Concepts

compressive structure
live load
dead load
reaction
compression
compressive force
column

loadbearing wall, bearing wall
numerical solution
graphical solution
load line
f_t
f_c
f_{allow}

A_{req}
buckling
slenderness
slenderness ratio
lateral bracing
invertibility
character of forces

lateral forces
gravity loads
breaking length
specific strength
strength-to-weight ratio

Exercises

1. A diagonal member in an upper chord of a steel roof truss must carry an axial compressive force of 97,500 lb (Fig. 2.21). If the allowable stress in the steel is 22,000 psi, how many square inches of steel must there be in the cross section of the member, assuming that buckling is not a problem?

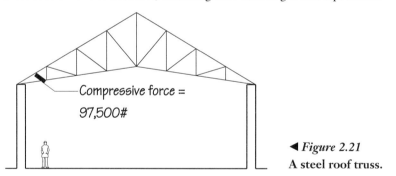

Compressive force = 97,500#

◀ *Figure 2.21*
A steel roof truss.

2. You have been hired as a consultant to investigate whether additional floors can be constructed on top of an existing hotel with loadbearing reinforced masonry walls (Fig. 2.22). The walls are 250 mm thick. On the basis of laboratory load tests on samples of material taken from the existing walls, the allowable compressive stress in the masonry has been established to be only 1.90 MPa. A 1-m-wide vertical strip of wall presently supports both a roof mass of 600 kg and 12 floor masses of 950 kg each. Each story is 3.00 m tall from floor to floor. The density of the masonry wall is 2 250 kg/m³.

How many additional floors can these walls support, assuming that the foundations have sufficient excess capacity, the new floors are loaded the same as the existing ones, and the thickness of the wall remains constant in the new construction? (*Hint:* Consider a 1-m-wide vertical strip of wall as if it were a column 1 m wide and 250 mm deep.)

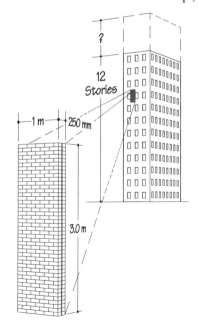

?

12 Stories

1 m — 250 mm

3.0 m

◀ *Figure 2.22* **A hotel supported by reinforced brick masonry walls.**

3. A laminated wood arch carries an axial compression force that reaches a maximum of 170,000 lb near the points of support on either end (Fig. 2.23). It is prevented from lateral buckling by the bracing action of the roof enclosure. If the arch is 5.125 in. thick in cross section, how deep must it be to limit the compressive stress to 2000 psi? Laminated wood members are manufactured in depths that are multiples of 1.5 in.; round your answer up to the nearest standard depth. What is the actual stress in the member you have chosen?

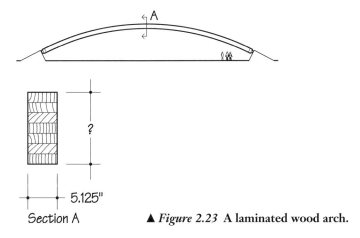

▲ *Figure 2.23* **A laminated wood arch.**

CHAPTER THREE

FORCES IN MANY DIRECTIONS

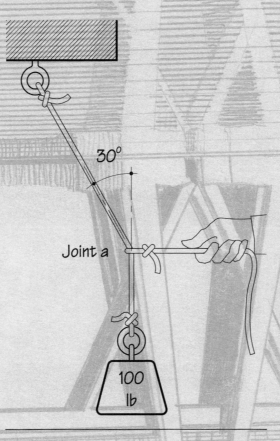

◀ The Lake Maracaibo Bridge in Venezuela, completed in 1962, was designed by Italian engineer Riccardo Morandi. Inclined cable stays support the ends of concrete beams that cantilever 80 m from each side of each tower. A concrete beam spanning 46 m is supported on the ends of the cantilevers. (Drawing by Edward Allen.)

▲ *Figure 3.1*
A simple suspended structure.

We attach a 100-lb weight to the lower end of a rope that hangs from the ceiling, tie a second rope to the middle of the first rope, and pull horizontally until the first rope is inclined at an angle of 30° from the vertical (Fig. 3.1). How hard must we pull on the horizontal rope to sustain the weight in this position? And what is the magnitude of the tension in the inclined portion of the rope? These two questions present us with two unknown forces that we must find.

CONSTRUCTING THE FREE-BODY DIAGRAM

To answer these questions, we begin, as we do in finding the forces in any structure, by drawing a

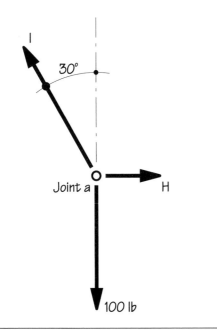

▲ *Figure 3.2*
Free-body diagram of the structure in Figure 3.1.

know its magnitude. We name it *I*, to remind us that it is the inclined force. All three forces that act on this joint are *concurrent*, which means that they all pass through the same point, *a*.

We examine the completed free-body diagram of joint *a*. There is one given force, the weight of 100 lb. There are two unknown quantities, the magnitudes of forces *H* and *I*. Because joint *a* does not move, it is in static equilibrium, meaning that the three forces must balance one another.

Solving for the Unknown Forces

For the vertical structures that we analyzed in Chapters One and Two, we developed an expression of static equilibrium:

$$\sum F_v = 0 \qquad [1\text{-}1]$$

We arrived at this expression by reasoning that if a free body is acted upon by any unbalanced force in the vertical direction, it will move up or down. If we do not want the body to move verti-

cally, all the forces in the vertical direction must balance out to zero: there must be as much force pulling up on the body as there is pulling down on it. In our free-body diagram of joint *a*, however, two of the three forces are not vertical. One is horizontal, the other is inclined. A single equation of static equilibrium will not suffice. We must find at least one other mathematical expression to give us the two equations we need to be able to solve for the two unknowns, *H* and *I*, that are presented by this problem.

Characteristics of a Force

A force has three characteristics (Fig. 3.3):

1. Its magnitude
2. The position of its *line of action*
3. The direction in which it acts along its line of action

The **external** effect of a force on a body is independent of its *point of application* on the line of

free-body diagram (Fig. 3.2). We take as a free body the joint *a* where the two ropes meet, because both of the unknown forces act on it. We sketch first an arrow and a number representing the downward force of the 100-lb weight. Next, we add an arrow representing the pull of the horizontal rope. We know the direction of this arrow (horizontal, pulling to the right), but we do not know its magnitude. We name this force *H*, which will help us remember that it is horizontal. To complete the free-body diagram, we add the arrow representing the pull up and to the left by the rope that is 30° from the vertical. Again, we know its direction, but we do not

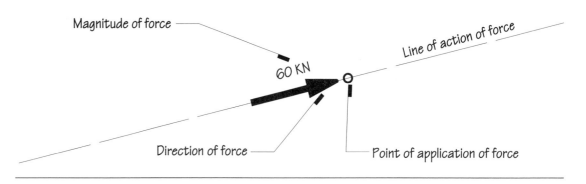

▲ *Figure 3.3*
The characteristics of a force.

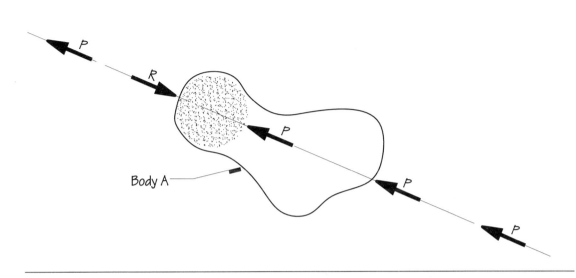

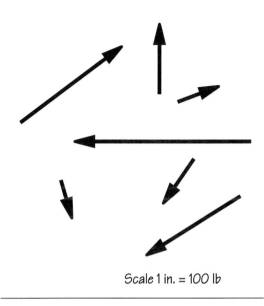

Scale 1 in. = 100 lb

▲ *Figure 3.4*
External and internal effects of a force.

▲ *Figure 3.5*
Using arrows to represent vectors.

action: in Figure 3.4, force *P* tends to move body *A* in exactly the same manner, regardless of where *P* is applied along its line of action. The **internal** effect of a force on a body, however, is very much dependent on its point of application: if *P* is applied at the lower right end of *A*, the entire body is compressed between *P* and reaction *R*. If *P* is applied inside body *A*, only the material in the shaded area between *P* and *R* is compressed. For the present, we are concerned only with the external effects of forces.

SCALAR AND VECTOR QUANTITIES

In earlier chapters, we dealt only with *collinear* forces, those that all shared the same line of action. In the first example (Chapter One), that

line of action was the axis of a steel wire. In the example in Chapter Two, it was the axis of a stack of stone blocks. This collinearity allowed us to treat the forces as if they were *scalar* quantities, different in magnitude but having the same line of action. All we had to do to sum collinear forces was to assign a plus or minus sign to each to designate its directional sense, then add the signed numbers.

The forces that are represented on the free-body diagram that we are currently considering in Figure 3.2 are not collinear; they have three different lines of action. They are, however, *concurrent*, which means that their lines of action all pass through a single point, *a*. To add concurrent forces that are not collinear, we must use *vector addition*.

A *vector* is a quantity that has both magnitude and direction. It is convenient to represent a force vector with an arrow. The shaft of the arrow lies on the line of action of the force. The head of the arrow indicates the direction in which the force acts. The length of the shaft and point, measured to any convenient scale, represents the magnitude of the force (Fig. 3.5). Using this representation, we are prepared to visualize a simple way of adding forces that act at various angles.

Imagine that we knot three pieces of cord together at a single point. We tie three unequal weights to their ends, then run two of the cords whose weights total more than the third weight over frictionless pulleys mounted on a wall. We allow the system of cords and weights to reach

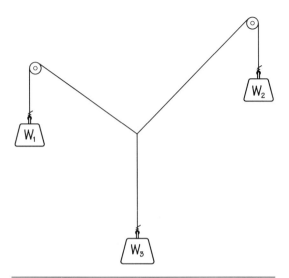

▲ Figure 3.6
A system of weights, cords, and pulleys in equilibrium.

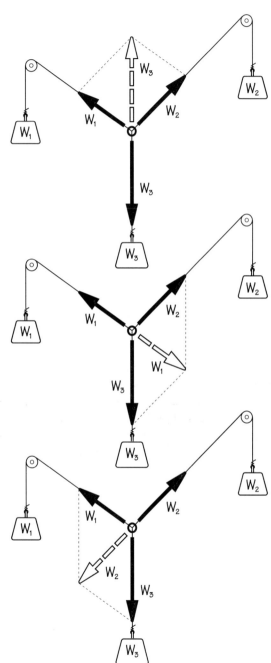

equilibrium (Fig. 3.6). The magnitude of the tension in each cord is equal to the weight fastened to its end. The line of action of each of the three forces can be traced from its cord onto a sheet of paper mounted behind the cords on the wall.

When we construct on this sheet the vectors of these three concurrent forces over their lines of action, we discover that **the vector of any force is the same in magnitude and direction as a vector constructed on the diagonal of a parallelogram formed on the vectors of the other two forces** (Fig. 3.7). This is the *parallelogram law*, a fundamental axiom of structural mechanics.

The vector constructed on the diagonal of the parallelogram with its tail on the same point

as the tails of the two original vectors represents the *resultant* of the two forces. A resultant is a single force whose magnitude and direction are such that it has the same external physical effect as two or more forces acting together.

As an example of the use of the parallelogram law, consider the two vectors *J* and *K* (Fig. 3.8). We can find the magnitude and direction of their resultant (their vector sum) by constructing a parallelogram in which *J* and *K* form two adjacent sides. The sum of vectors *J* and *K* is the diagonal *L*. *L* is the resultant of *J* and *K*, a single force whose external effect on a body is identical to that of the two forces acting together. If we reverse the direction of *L*, it will exactly balance *J* and *K* in an arrangement of weights, cords, and pulleys. A reversed resultant, representing a single force that will exactly balance two or more forces, is called an *antiresultant* or *equilibrant*.

If we wish to find not only the magnitude and direction of the resultant of two concurrent forces, but also the position of its line of action, we must follow the procedure illustrated in Figure 3.9. Vectors *M* and *N* are moved along their respective lines of action until their tails coincide. At this location, *a*, the parallelogram is constructed, giving the true position of the line of action of the resultant as well as its magnitude and direction.

In addition to finding resultants and antiresultants, a process that is referred to as the *composition of forces*, the parallelogram law allows us to *resolve* a single force into two or more *components* whose combined action is identical to that of the original force. To simplify structural calculations, we often do this to replace an inclined force with two components, one vertical

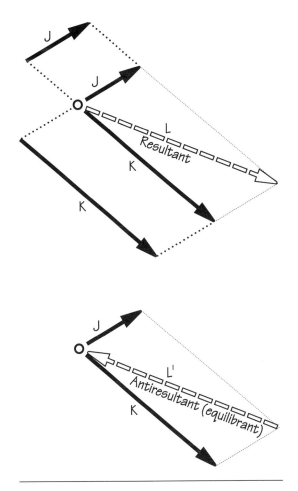

▲ *Figure 3.8*
Using the parallelogram law to find a resultant and an antiresultant (equilibrant).

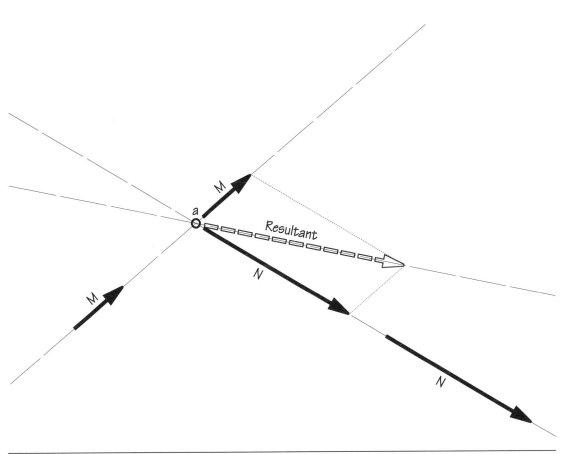

▲ *Figure 3.9*
Finding the position of the line of action of a resultant.

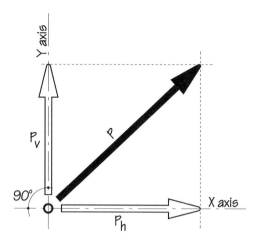

P_v is the vertical component of P.
P_h is the horizontal component of P.

▲ *Figure 3.10*
Resolving an inclined force into its horizontal and vertical components.

and one horizontal (Fig. 3.10). We accomplish this by projecting horizontally and vertically to Y- and X-axes from the ends of the vector, thus producing a level rectangle whose diagonal is the original vector. A vector on the left-hand vertical edge of the rectangle in this figure represents the vertical component of the inclined force, and a vector on the lower horizontal edge, the horizontal component. These two components, acting together, have the same effect as the single, inclined force from which they were resolved. When each inclined force in a free-body diagram has been replaced by its horizontal and vertical components, it becomes easy to add up the forces, no matter in how many different direc-

tions the inclined forces act. All the components in each of the two directions can be added directly as signed numbers. Then, if desired, the two sums can be composed into a single resultant force. Often it is more convenient to leave the answer as two component forces.

ADDING FORCE VECTORS NUMERICALLY

There are two general methods, graphical and numerical, of composing or resolving systems of forces. In a graphical solution, we construct the vectors and parallelogram accurately to scale on a drafting board, then measure the direction and length of the resultant. When solving numerically, we make a rough sketch of the parallelogram as an aid to visualization, but perform the vector addition by using numbers and trigonometric functions. We will demonstrate both these methods, starting with the numerical.

Returning to the problem of the 100-lb weight and ropes that is shown in Figures 3.1 and 3.2, we resolve the inclined force I into its horizontal and vertical components, I_h and I_v (Fig. 3.11). I_h is the projection of I onto a horizontal axis, and I_v, the projection onto a vertical axis. I lies at an angle of 30° from the vertical, which is 60° from the horizontal.

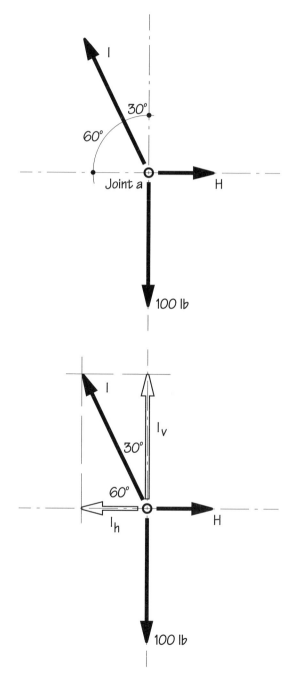

Figure 3.11 ▶
Rough sketches used in solving numerically for the forces in the simple suspended structure shown in Figure 3.1. The lengths of the vectors are not drawn to scale.

We know from trigonometry that the projection of the vector of an inclined force onto any axis is equal to the force times the cosine of the angle between the force and that axis. The horizontal component of force in this example is $I\cos 60°$, and the vertical component is $I\cos 30°$. We draw a new free-body diagram in which the inclined force has been entirely replaced by its horizontal and vertical components (Fig. 3.12).

At joint a, the sum of the forces that act in the vertical direction must be zero to prevent the movement of joint a in the vertical direction. In the horizontal direction, the same principle obviously applies: If joint a is not to move horizontally, the sum of the forces in the horizontal direction must be zero. This gives us a second equation of static equilibrium to go with the first:

$$\sum F_v = 0 \qquad [1\text{-}1]$$

$$\sum F_h = 0 \qquad [3\text{-}1]$$

It is evident that any system of concurrent forces that act in the same plane can be resolved entirely into horizontal and vertical components. Therefore, these two equations suffice for any such case, no matter how many forces or in what directions the forces act. (These two equations are often related to X and Y coordinates rather than horizontal and vertical directions, making them $\Sigma F_X = 0$ and $\Sigma F_Y = 0$. If a system of forces acts in a three-dimensional space rather than in a plane, we must also employ a third equation, $\Sigma F_Z = 0$.)

Having two equations to match the two unknowns, we are ready to solve numerically for the forces in the hanging structure. We substitute the magnitudes of the force components into the two equations of equilibrium, being careful to apply consistently a convention of using plus signs for downward forces and minus signs for upward ones. In addition, we establish arbitrarily a second convention that forces to the right are positive, and forces to the left are negative. (It does not matter what convention we establish in this regard, as long as we follow it consistently throughout the calculations.)

$$\sum F_v = 0$$

$$100\text{ lb} - I\cos 30° = 0$$

$$I = 115.5\text{ lb}$$

$$\sum F_h = 0$$

$$H - (115.5\text{ lb})\cos 60° = 0$$

$$H = 57.7\text{ lb}$$

We have found the magnitudes of all the forces in the hanging structure (Fig. 3.13). The positive signs of the answers mean that the directions of H and I were assumed correctly.

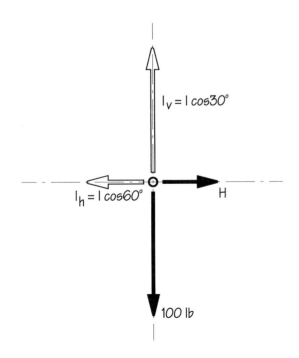

◀ *Figure 3.12*
Continuing the numerical solution.

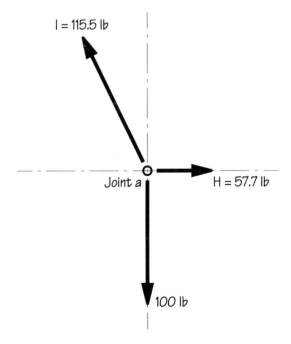

Figure 3.13 ▶
The completed numerical solution.

ADDING FORCE VECTORS GRAPHICALLY

It follows from the parallelogram law that **we can add two vectors graphically by connecting them tip to tail and constructing the resultant vector from the tail of the first vector to the tip of the second.** This is easily done at the drafting board to any scale that fits conveniently on the sheet of paper. The procedure inevitably involves moving at least one of the three vectors off its line of action, so it is important to remember that the lines of action of all three must intersect at the same point (Fig. 3.14).

In solving the rope-and-weight problem graphically, we know the magnitude of only one vector, but we know the directions of all three. We lay out first the vector that represents the 100-lb load, for which we know both the magnitude and the direction. We draw it as a vertical line segment that is exactly 100 lb long to the scale we have chosen, using horizontal ticks (short line segments) to delineate the ends of the vector as precisely as possible (Fig. 3.15[a]). It does not matter in which order we connect the other two vectors to the first one; the result will be the same. We choose to draw next a horizontal line representing the direction of force H from the lower end of the 100-lb vector, and a line at 30° from the vertical representing force I from the upper end of the 100-lb vector. The two lines intersect at a point that we label x, establishing the lengths of vectors H and I. We scale the lengths of the resulting line segments to arrive at values of 116 lb for I and 58 lb for H (Fig. 3.15[b]). These are not as precise as the values that we found numerically, but each is well within 1% of the exact value, which is sufficient for nearly all applications in structural design. If we need greater accuracy, we can do the construction at a larger scale.

In most graphical constructions, arrowheads are not used. They tend to obscure the precise locations of line intersections and interfere with accurate measurements. But it is often useful to prepare a sketch diagram with arrowheads to clarify the directions of the vectors. In this example (Fig. 3.15[c]), we show H pulling to the right, as we know it does from looking at our original diagram. The diagonal line I may be seen as indicating the resultant or sum of the 100-lb load and H, which therefore must act in a direction down and to the right. In our case, however, the diagonal line represents an antiresultant, a force that exactly balances the other two forces to maintain static equilibrium, so we indicate that its direction is upward and leftward by placing an arrowhead at its upper end. We add the letter t in parentheses to each of the numbers on our diagram to indicate that each is a tensile force.

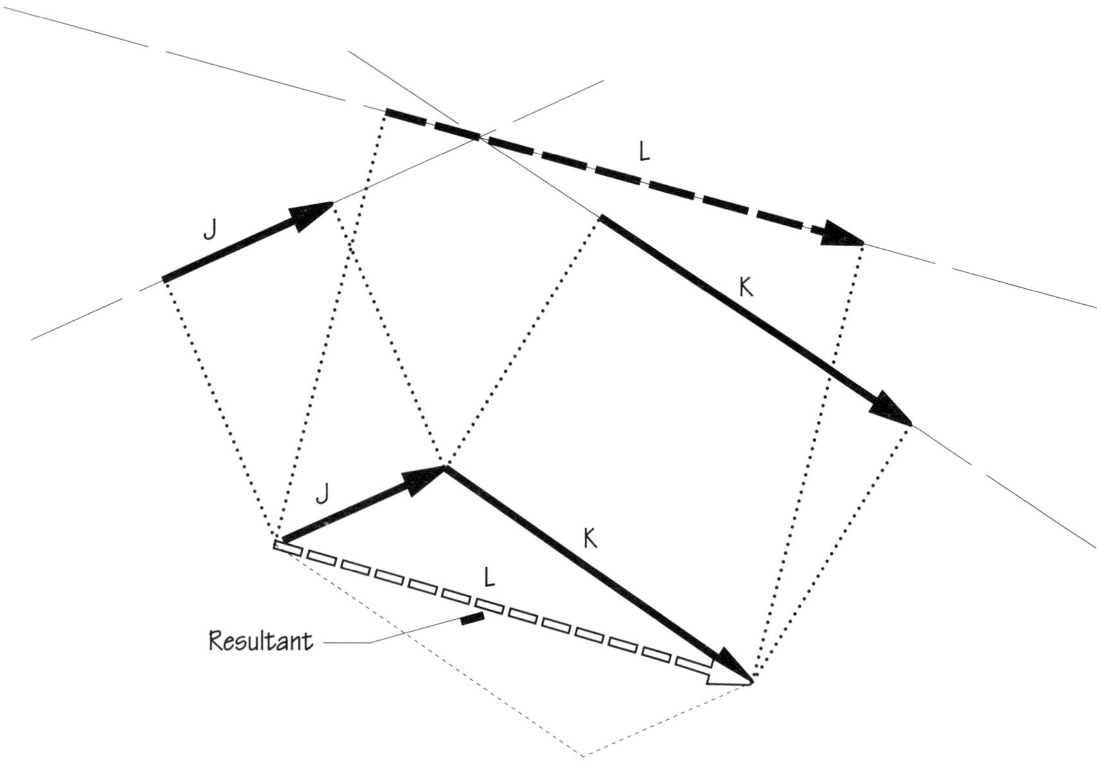

▲ *Figure 3.14*
Adding force vectors tip to tail.

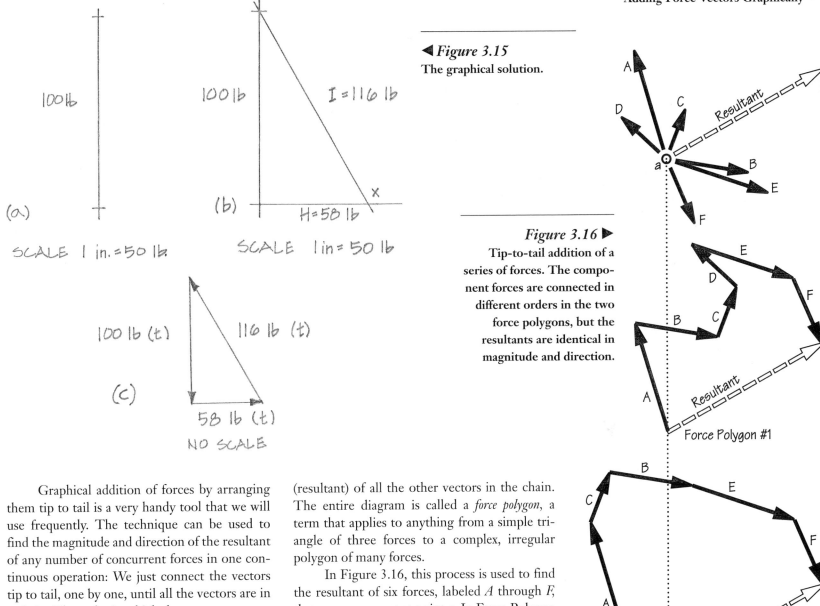

100 lb

(a)

SCALE 1 in. = 50 lb

100 lb   I = 116 lb

(b)

X

H = 58 lb

SCALE   1 in = 50 lb

100 lb (t)   116 lb (t)

(c)

58 lb (t)

NO SCALE

◄ *Figure 3.15*
The graphical solution.

Figure 3.16 ▶
Tip-to-tail addition of a series of forces. The component forces are connected in different orders in the two force polygons, but the resultants are identical in magnitude and direction.

Resultant

A   C   B   D   E   F   a

E   D   B   C   F   A   Resultant   Force Polygon #1

B   C   E   F   A   D   Resultant   Force Polygon #2

Graphical addition of forces by arranging them tip to tail is a very handy tool that we will use frequently. The technique can be used to find the magnitude and direction of the resultant of any number of concurrent forces in one continuous operation: We just connect the vectors tip to tail, one by one, until all the vectors are in a chain. The order in which the vectors are connected does not matter. After all the component vectors have been drawn, a vector that is constructed with its tail on the tail of the first vector and its head on the tip of the last, represents the direction and magnitude of the vector sum

(resultant) of all the other vectors in the chain. The entire diagram is called a *force polygon*, a term that applies to anything from a simple triangle of three forces to a complex, irregular polygon of many forces.

In Figure 3.16, this process is used to find the resultant of six forces, labeled A through F, that are concurrent at point a. In Force Polygon #1, the vectors of the forces are connected in alphabetical order. In Force Polygon #2, they are connected in clockwise order. The two different polygons, being made up of the same components, produce the same resultant. The line of action of the resultant in this example must pass through *a*, the point of concurrency of the component forces.

If we reverse the direction of a resultant, it becomes an antiresultant (equilibrant), and the force polygon represents a set of concurrent forces that are in static equilibrium. A force polygon is always a closed figure. Each vector in a closed polygon of forces is the antiresultant of all the remaining forces. If we reverse the direction of any vector in the polygon, as we did in the preceding paragraph, it becomes the resultant (vector sum) of all the remaining forces.

We have seen that when solving **numerically** a system of concurrent forces that all lie in the same plane, the forces are in static equilibrium when $F_v = 0$ and $F_h = 0$. When solving such a system of forces **graphically,** the forces are in static equilibrium when the force polygon closes exactly upon itself.

INVERTING THE STRUCTURE

The rope structure that we have just analyzed, like any other structure, can be inverted, with the accompanying reversal of the character of the force in each of the members (Fig. 3.17). The three tensile forces become compressive forces (indicated here by the letter *c* in parentheses), so that the three members will have to be converted from ropes to stiff members of wood, metal, or concrete. The magnitudes of the three forces remain the same, and the structure remains in equilibrium.

INCLINED HANGER STRAPS

In Chapter One, we analyzed vertical hanger straps for a 10-story building that is suspended

from a central core structure. Now we are prepared to examine what happens to the forces in the straps at the top of this building, where they are inclined so as to transmit their forces to the core. The initial design for the building indicates that the angle of the inclined hanger straps is 45°. If the force in a vertical strap just above the top floor is 2.4 MN, what is the magnitude of the force in the inclined strap, and how large must the strap be to carry this force safely?

From Figure 3.18, we select joint *y* as the subject of a free-body diagram with which to begin the solution, because this is the point at which the known force in the vertical strap intersects the unknown forces in the inclined strap and horizontal roof beam. We sketch the free-

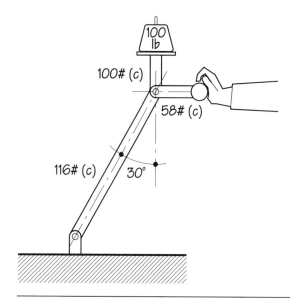

▲ *Figure 3.17*
An inversion of the structure shown in Figure 3.1.

body diagram in Figure 3.19. A roof beam joins the vertical hanger strap at joint *y* and adds a vertical roof load of 160 kN (0.16 MN), producing a total downward pull on the joint of 2.40 MN plus 0.16 MN, or 2.56 MN. After we have drawn the 2.56-MN vertical force and the 45° line of action of a force of the inclined strap, which we label *T*, our sense of equilibrium tells us that there must be at least one more force acting on this joint. The force in the inclined strap can be imagined as being resolved into two components, vertical and horizontal. The vertical component will balance the 2.56-MN vertical force, but there is not yet a vector on the diagram that will balance the horizontal component. Where will such a force come from? We reexamine the sketch of the structure and see that the roof beam must push to the left on joint *y*. We add an arrow representing this thrust to the free-body diagram and label it *C*.

Now we are ready to solve numerically for the axial forces in the inclined strap and the beam. We sketch a new free-body diagram, replacing the unknown inclined force, *T*, with its vertical and horizontal components (Fig. 3.20), and apply the two equations of static equilibrium:

$$\sum F_v = 0$$

$$2.56 \text{ MN} - T\cos45° = 0$$

$$T = \frac{2.56 \text{ MN}}{\cos45°} = 3.62 \text{ MN}$$

$$\sum F_h = 0$$

$$(3.62 \text{ MN})\cos45° - C = 0$$

$$C = \frac{3.62 \text{ MN}}{\cos45°} = 2.56 \text{ MN}$$

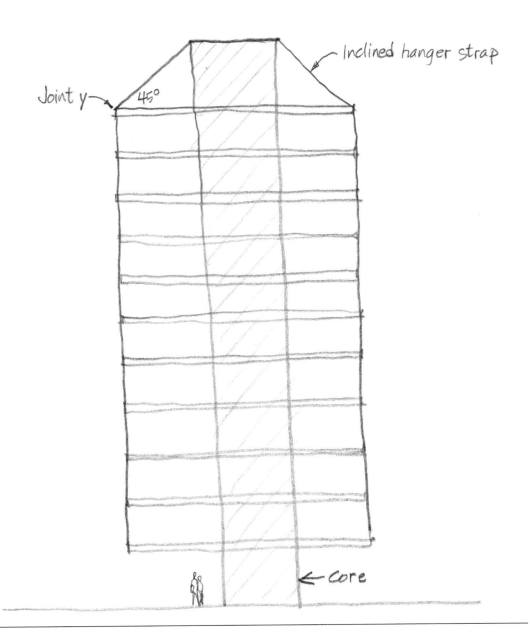

▲ *Figure 3.18*
Hanger straps for a high-rise office building.

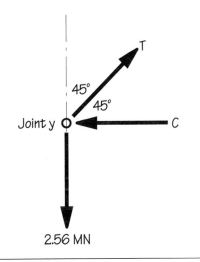

▲ *Figure 3.19*
Free-body diagram of joint *y*.

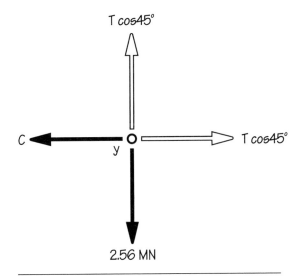

▲ *Figure 3.20*
Free-body diagram of joint *y* with the inclined
force replaced by its horizontal and vertical
components.

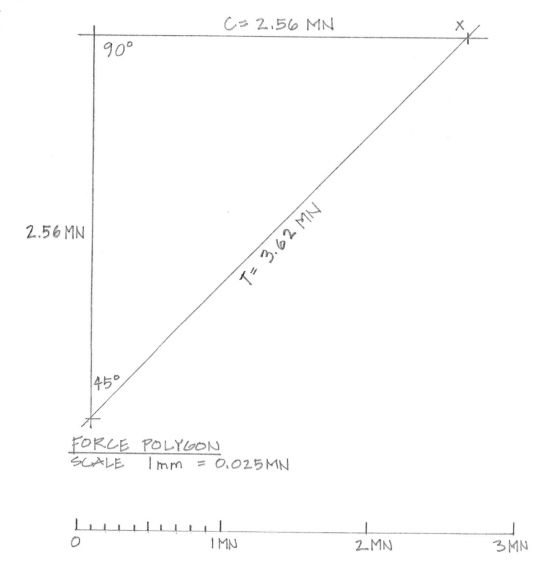

Figure 3.21 ▶
Graphical solution for the forces at joint y.

The graphical solution to the forces around joint y, comprising only three lines, is very simple and confirms the results of the numerical solution (Fig. 3.21).

We calculate the required size of the inclined portion of the hanger strap, using the given value of 150 MPa for the allowable stress of steel:

$$f_{\text{allow}} = \frac{P}{A_{\text{req}}}$$

$$A_{\text{req}} = \frac{P}{f_{\text{allow}}} = \frac{3.62 \text{ MN}}{150 \text{ MPa}} = 0.0241 \text{ m}^2$$

If we wish to make the inclined portion of the strap 150 mm (0.150 m) wide so as to match the vertical portion, we calculate its required thickness as follows, using t_r to represent the thickness of the strap above the roof level:

$$A_{\text{req}} = t_r(0.150 \text{ m})$$

$$t_r = \frac{A_{\text{req}}}{0.150 \text{ m}} = \frac{0.0241 \text{ m}^2}{0.150 \text{ m}} = 0.161 \text{ m} = 161 \text{ mm}$$

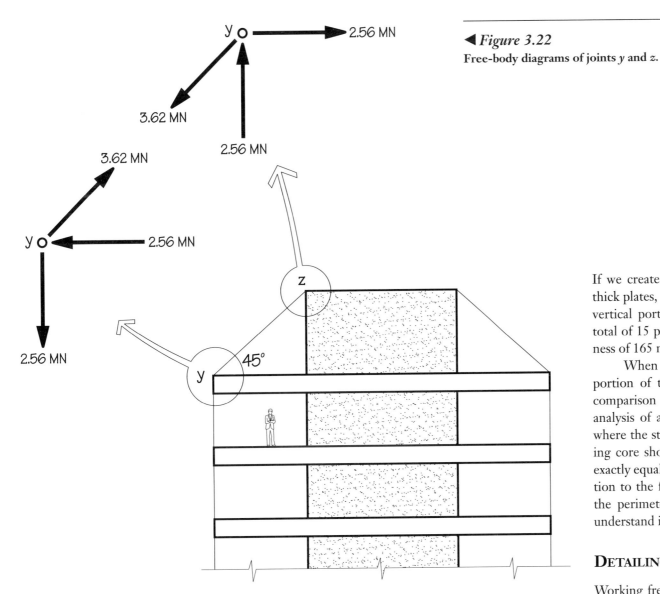

If we create the inclined strap out of 11-mm-thick plates, as we already have proposed for the vertical portions of the strap, it will require a total of 15 plates, giving it an actual total thickness of 165 mm.

When we ignore the weight of the inclined portion of the strap, which is insignificant in comparison to the loads that it supports, the analysis of a free-body diagram of the point *z* where the strap bears on a column in the building core shows that the force in the column is exactly equal in magnitude but opposite in direction to the force in the vertical hanger strap at the perimeter of the building (Fig. 3.22). We understand intuitively that this is correct.

DETAILING THE STRUCTURE

Working freehand, we draw preliminary details showing how the members of this structure join at the roof. The vertical loadbearing structure of the core consists of steel wide-flange columns. A simple, reliable way to detail the bearing of the

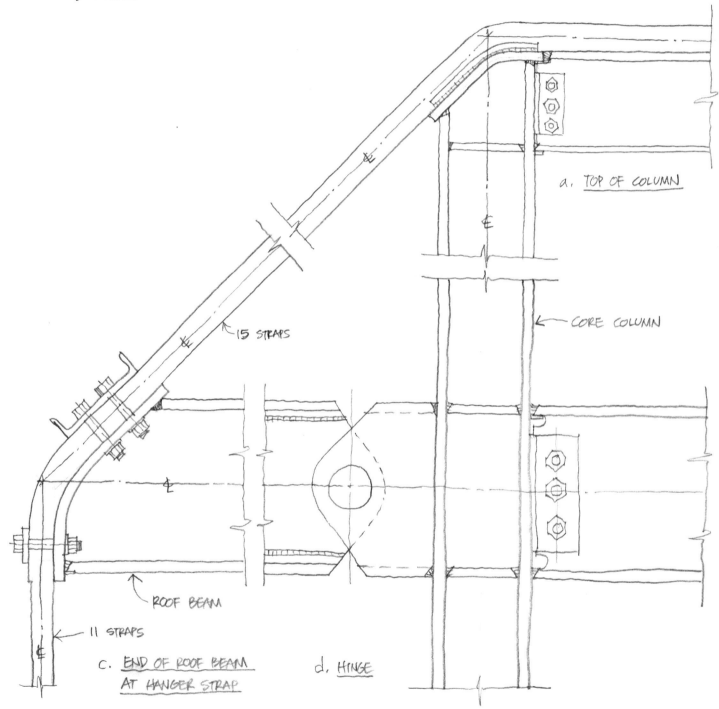

a. TOP OF COLUMN

CORE COLUMN

15 STRAPS

ROOF BEAM

11 STRAPS

c. END OF ROOF BEAM
AT HANGER STRAP

d. HINGE

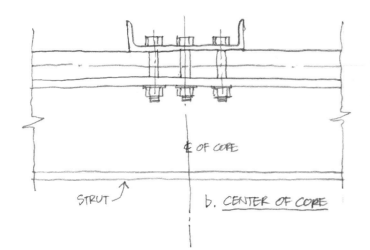

STRUT

℄ OF CORE

b. CENTER OF CORE

◄ *Figure 3.23*
Preliminary detail sketches for the structure at the roof.

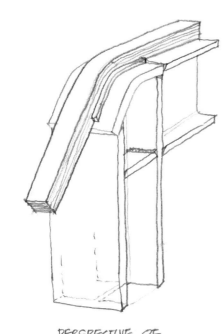

PERSPECTIVE OF
TOP OF COLUMN

strap on the top of the core would be to weld a steel saddle plate to the top of each column and let the strap run continuously across the saddle (Fig. 3.23[a]). The saddle is curved to avoid a sharp bend that might raise stresses in the strap and to transfer forces smoothly from the strap to the column. Small, square steel bars are welded to the top of the saddle to prevent the strap from slipping sideways. The force in the horizontal portion of the strap that passes over the top of the core is 2.56 MN. We could make the strap in this area thinner than the inclined portion, which carries 3.62 MN. This would complicate the detailing, however, and it would not save very much steel, so we decide to leave the strap constant in dimension where it passes over the core.

Notice that the saddle is designed so that the center lines of the inclined segment of the strap, the horizontal segment of the strap, and the vertical supporting column in the core intersect at the same point. Joints of intersecting structural members are designed in this way

whenever possible, because it eliminates troublesome secondary forces that might occur in a design that does not center on the point of concurrency of the forces in the members.

Although under the assumed loads on the building there is no net horizontal force exerted on the tops of the columns, it would be wise to connect the tops of the two columns that support each strap with a rigid steel strut made of a wide-flange shape. This will allow for some asymmetries in the actual floor loads in the building. A clamping plate made of a short piece of steel channel and high-strength bolts, located in the middle of this strut, secures the strap against slipping in its saddles should asymmetrical distribution of live loads, or wind or seismic forces, create unbalanced forces (Fig. 3.23[b]).

The detail at the end of the roof beam (Fig. 3.23[c]) is similar to the detail at the top of the column. At this joint, layers must be added to the strap to increase its thickness by more than 40% as it passes from a vertical orientation to an inclination of 45°. The outer end of the roof beam must exert a horizontal push against the point where the strap changes direction. Working around the point of concurrency of the center-lines of the three members that constitute the joint, we sketch another curved saddle of thick steel plate welded to the end of the beam, adding clamping plates and high-strength bolts to transmit the roof load into the strap. Because it is important to be sure that the heavy horizontal push of the roof beam is transmitted in a purely axial manner to the core structure, the beam is connected to the core by means of a hinge (Fig. 3.23[d]). The rotational capability of the hinge is provided by a cylindrical steel pin that joins the beam to a bracket that is welded to the side of the column.

OPTIMIZING THE STRUCTURE

Before leaving this problem, it is worthwhile to experiment with changing the inclination of the strap above the roof to observe the effect that this angle has on the force in the strap. We could do this numerically, but it is an ideal problem to tackle graphically because the graphical solution is faster, encourages exploration of more alternatives, and is easier to interpret (Fig. 3.24). It is readily apparent from the nested set of force polygons that as the strap assumes a progressively more horizontal orientation, the force in the strap rises rapidly and would approach infinity if the strap were to become horizontal. Conversely, we can reduce the force in the strap by inclining it more steeply than 45°. The penalty for the steeper inclination, however, is a taller and more costly core.

Other alternatives are suggested by this analysis. We could reduce the forces in the inclined straps by inclining the roof beams at some angle, such as 30°, while keeping the inclination of the straps at 45°, which we try in Figure 3.25. The accompanying force polygon shows that this reduces the force in the inclined strap to a value even lower than that of the vertical strap. However, this configuration would require a taller core structure, unless we widen the top of the core frame to compensate (Fig. 3.26).

Using simple graphical analysis, we can easily find an arrangement of inclined beams and

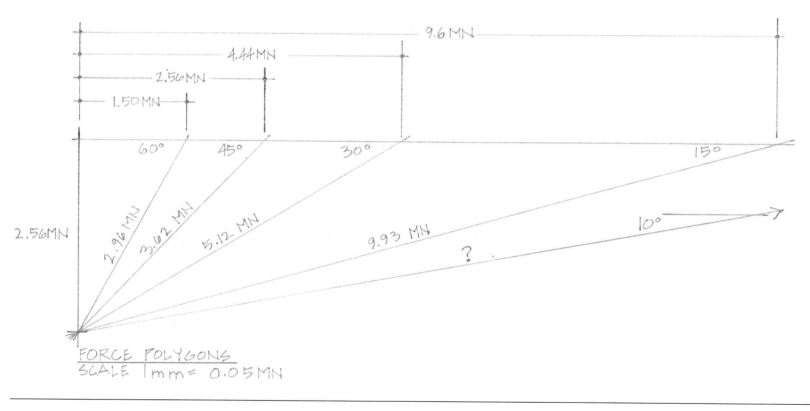

▲ *Figure 3.24*
The effect of changing the inclination of the strap.

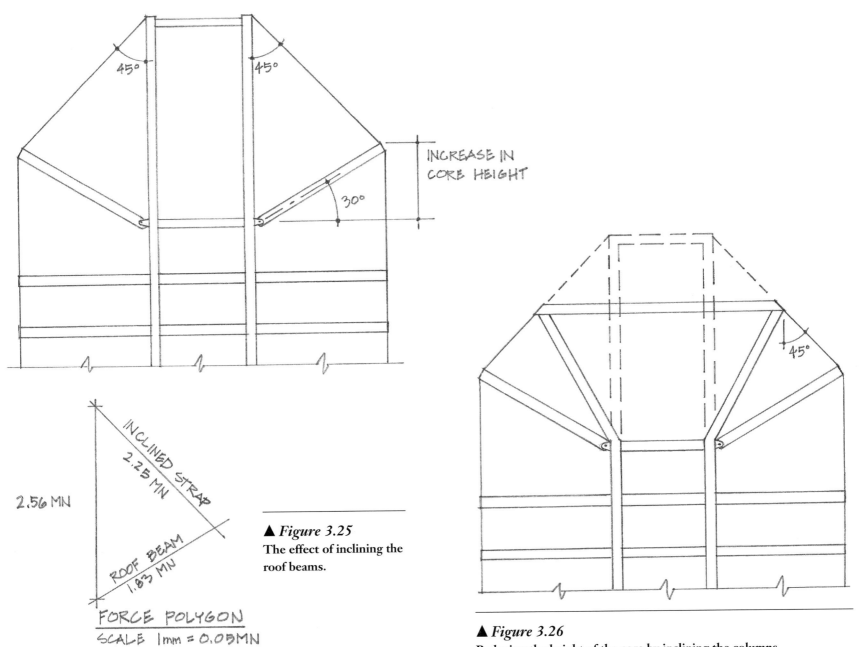

45° 45°

INCREASE IN
CORE HEIGHT

30°

2.56 MN

INCLINED STRAP
2.25 MN

ROOF BEAM
1.83 MN

FORCE POLYGON
SCALE 1mm = 0.03MN

▲ *Figure 3.25*
The effect of inclining the roof beams.

45°

▲ *Figure 3.26*
Reducing the height of the core by inclining the columns.

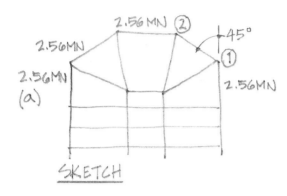

2.56 MN ②

2.56 MN

2.56 MN

2.56 MN

45°

①

2.56 MN

(a)

SKETCH

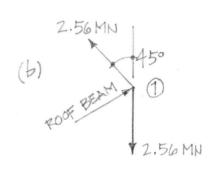

2.56 MN

45°

①

ROOF BEAM

2.56 MN

(b)

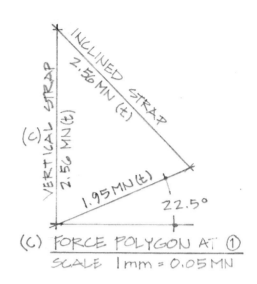

INCLINED STRAP 2.56 MN (t)

VERTICAL STRAP 2.56 MN (t)

1.95 MN (t)

22.5°

(c)

(c) FORCE POLYGON AT ①

SCALE 1 mm = 0.05 MN

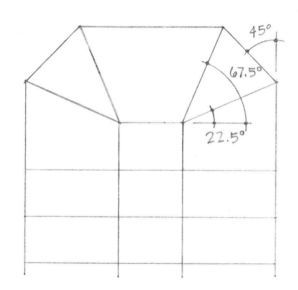

45°

67.5°

22.5°

(f) SCALED SECTION

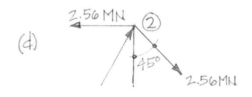

2.56 MN ②

45°

2.56 MN

(d)

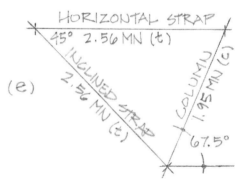

HORIZONTAL STRAP

45° 2.56 MN (t)

INCLINED STRAP 2.56 MN (t)

COLUMN 1.95 MN (c)

67.5°

(e)

FORCE POLYGON AT ②

SCALE 1 mm = 0.05 MN

◀ *Figure 3.27*

Shaping a rooftop structure that has constant force in all the segments of the strap.

columns that results in a constant tension in all portions of the strap that lie above the top floor. We make a rough sketch of the top of the building for reference (Fig. 3.27[a]), indicating on it the given quantities of 2.56 MN in each segment of the strap and an angle of 45° for the inclined portion of the strap. The inclinations of the roof beams and columns are not yet known. We label joints *1* and *2* on this sketch for reference.

The first step in the solution is to draw a free-body diagram of joint *1* (Fig. 3.27[b]). The directions and magnitudes of the forces in the two segments of the strap are given, and we draw them to scale to begin constructing the force polygon at joint *1* (Fig. 3.27[c]). The direction of

the roof beam and its axial force are represented by the line segment that closes this force polygon; we measure these quantities as 22.5° from horizontal and 1.95 MN, respectively. We repeat this process for joint *2* (Fig. 3.27 [d and e]), finding a 1.95 MN force in a column inclined 67.5° from the horizontal. In Figure 3.27(f), we draw the top portion of the frame of the building to scale, showing accurately the inclinations of the members.

The advantages of this design over the others that we are considering are twofold: the strap can be the same thickness at every point above the top floor, which saves money on the material and fabrication of the strap and its con-

nections; and the axial forces in the roof beams and columns are reduced from 2.56 MN to 1.95 MN, allowing the use of smaller members. These potential savings must be weighed against the increased cost of the more complex connections required by the inclined members and the expense of the additional wall area on the top floor. Also to be considered in this analysis are the appearances of the alternative designs and the spatial qualities of the top floor. This process of *optimization* is often a key part of a structural design project. Because it takes into account such disparate variables, it usually relies at least as much on judgment as on mathematics.

INVERTING THE STRUCTURAL CONCEPT

When the original design for this building is inverted, an interesting alternative emerges (Fig. 3.28). Inclined compression struts at the base of the building transmit forces from perimeter columns inward to the core columns, from which they pass to the foundations. We know intuitively that the forces in the struts, if they are inclined at 45°, are approximately equal in magnitude to the forces in the inclined hanger straps that we just analyzed, but they are a bit larger because of the dead load of the columns, and, of course, they are compressive rather than tensile. The effects of various strut angles on the forces in the structure can be judged from the earlier graphical analysis that we made of the inclinations of the hanger straps (Fig. 3.24).

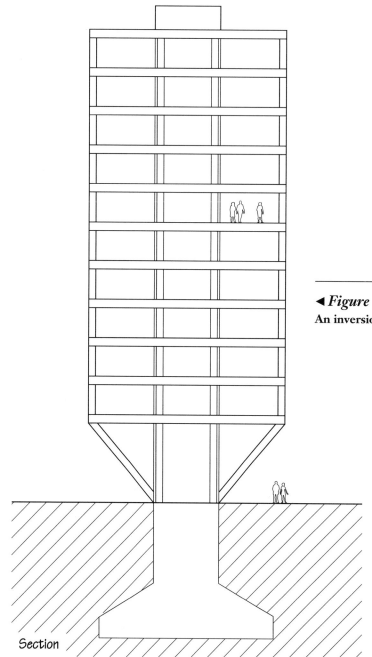

◄ *Figure 3.28*
An inversion of the hanging office building.

Key Terms and Concepts

concurrent forces   collinear forces   vector quantity   antiresultant   components

line of action of a force   scalar quantity   parallelogram law   equilibrant   force polygon

point of application   vector addition   resultant   composition of forces   optimization

Exercises

You may work numerically, graphically, or both, in solving these problems.

1. Assume that each inclined cable stay in the bridge shown in the drawing at the beginning of this chapter supports a portion of the bridge that weighs 5.6 MN. Assume also that the angle between the stay and the deck surface is 30° and that the effects of the small sags in the stay cables can be ignored.

  a. What is the force in the stay?

  b. Assuming that the central part of the span, between the lower ends of the stay cables, is mounted on rollers, is there any horizontal force in the portion of the deck that lies between the lower end of the stay and the tower? If so, how much?

  c. How much vertical force is exerted on the top of each tower by the four stay cables that bear on it?

  d. If the legs of the tower are inclined at 8° from the vertical, how much force do the cable stays create in each leg?

2. The forward portion of the building shown in Figure 3.29 is divided structurally into four tiers, each supported from above on hangers descend-

Figure 3.29 ▶

The Hongkong Bank building in Hong Kong (1986) is supported by eight column clusters of four columns each. These clusters, two of which are visible in this photograph, support triangular frameworks of struts and ties from which the floor structures of the building are suspended on vertical hangers. The columns and hangers are round steel tubes, and the struts and ties are square tubes. All these structural members are coated with fireproofing material and are enclosed in enameled aluminum cladding panels. The architect is Foster and Partners, and the structural engineer is Ove Arup and Partners. (Photo: Richard Bryant/Arcaid.)

ing from triangular frameworks. Assume that each hanger in the second tier from the ground in the center of the building supports seven floor loads of 550 kN each. Half this load is transmitted to each triangular framework at the top of the hanger, along with half the load of another floor of similar weight that lies directly behind the framework. The inclined members of the triangles are 25° from the horizontal.

a. What is the magnitude and character of the force in each member of the triangular framework?

b. At the outside corners of the building, another set of hangers supports the stair towers. Assuming that the load in the top of each hanger is 1.12 MN and that the angle of the inclined member in the supporting triangular framework is 36° to the horizontal, what are the magnitudes and characters of the forces in each of its members?

3. Four of the five forces that act on the joint of a truss are shown in Figure 3.30. Find the direction and magnitude of a fifth force that will bring this joint into equilibrium.

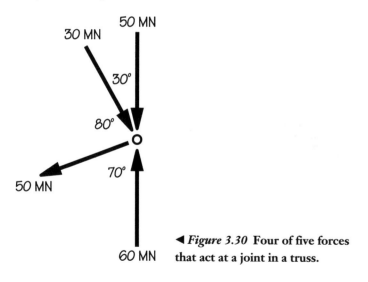

◀ *Figure 3.30* **Four of five forces that act at a joint in a truss.**

4. Each inclined stay of the cable-stayed bridge in Figure 3.31 supports a portion of the deck whose dead and live loads total 94,000 lb. Assuming as a simplification that the effects of the small sag in each cable can be ignored:

a. What is the tensile force in each cable?

b. What is the total axial compressive force caused by the cables in span 1 of the bridge deck?

c. What is the force in the backstay cable, *d?*

d. What is the compressive force in the tower, *e?*

e. What is the direction of the force exerted on the foundation at the foot of the tower?

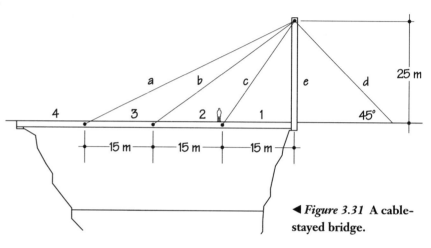

◀ *Figure 3.31* **A cable-stayed bridge.**

5. Bearing *b* exerts a total vertical reaction of 640 kN on the two inclined struts shown in Figure 3.32. What is the magnitude of the axial force in each strut?

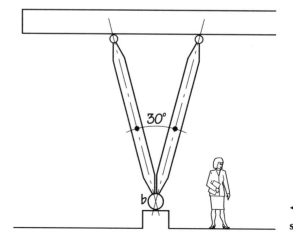

◀ *Figure 3.32* **Inclined struts supporting a roof.**

6. The derrick drawn in Figure 3.33 supports a block of granite that weighs 13,300 lb. Find the magnitudes and characters of the forces in the two cable segments and the mast.

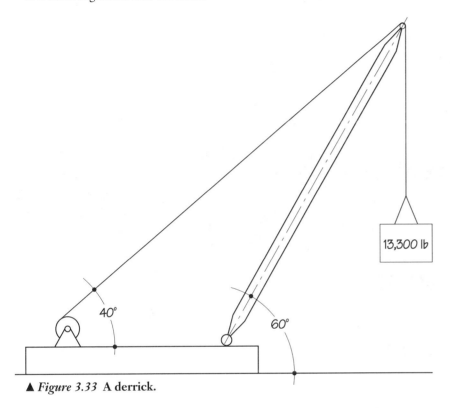

▲ *Figure 3.33* A derrick.

▲ *Figure 3.34* General view of the Lake Maracaibo Bridge, designed by Riccardo Morandi. The shorter spans of the approaches are accomplished with beams. The longer spans over the shipping channels are cable-stayed. (Photo: © R. Perron. Photo courtesy of Robert Perron.)

CHAPTER FOUR

MOMENTS OF FORCES

◀ **Hans Rudolph Manuel Deutsch created this woodcut illustration of a mineshaft windlass for Georgius Agricola's *De re metallica*, published in Basel in 1556. By pushing on the crank, the worker at the right exerts a moment of force on axle *A*, causing it to rotate. The magnitude of this moment is equal to the force exerted by the worker multiplied by the perpendicular distance of the crank handle from the centerline of the axle. The bucket of ore in the center of the picture hangs on a rope that exerts a moment on the axle by being wrapped around it. Because the moment arm of the rope is perhaps one-quarter as long as the moment arm of the crank, a single worker can raise a bucket that weighs about four times as much as the force he exerts on the crank. The two workers at the left are also able to exert moments on the axle by pushing or pulling on the projecting arms.**

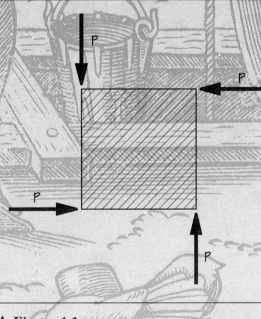

▲ *Figure 4.1*
A square body acted on by four nonconcurrent forces.

In previous chapters, we learned two conditions that must both be satisfied in order for a body to remain at rest in two-dimensional space:

$$\sum F_v = 0 \qquad\qquad [1\text{-}1]$$
$$\sum F_h = 0 \qquad\qquad [3\text{-}1]$$

Let us apply these expressions to the evaluation of the equilibrium of a square body that is acted on by four equal forces arranged so that the line of action of each force lies along one face of the body (Fig. 4.1). The computations are so simple that we can do them in our heads. The two forces in the horizontal (*X*) direction are equal in magnitude but opposite in direction. They add up to zero. So do the forces in the vertical (*Y*) direction. The body will not be displaced either horizontally or vertically. But will it remain motionless? No—we can readily imagine that the four forces will rotate it about its center, much as children pushing a playground merry-go-round cause it to spin (Fig. 4.2). This means that the two expressions of equilibrium that we have learned so far are not sufficient in themselves to assure that a body will not move.

Why does the body rotate? Although the opposing forces in each direction are equal to each other, they form a *moment* that tends to rotate the body. They do so because their lines of action do not pass through any common point. They are *nonconcurrent* forces. In previous chapters, we have considered only *concurrent* forces, forces whose lines of action all pass through a single point. As long as all the forces that act on a body are concurrent, the two conditions that we have already developed are sufficient to assure static equilibrium. But if the lines of action of all the forces do not pass through a single point, a moment may exist, and the two conditions alone are not sufficient.

WHAT IS A MOMENT?

The moment of a force is a measure of its ability to cause turning or twisting of a body about an axis of rotation. We quantify a moment, M, as the product of a force, P, and the perpendicular distance, d, from the line of action of the force to the axis of rotation about which we wish to find the moment:

$$M = Pd \qquad [4\text{-}1]$$

The perpendicular distance, d, which is also the shortest distance between the line of action of a force and an axis, is commonly referred to as the *moment arm* (Fig. 4.3). Force P creates the same moment Pd with respect to a given axis, regard-

▲ *Figure 4.2*
A simple playground merry-go-round.

less of its location on its line of action: Forces P, P', and P'' all exert the same moment about point a or any other point.

An axis of rotation may be thought of as being like the centerline of a rotating axle, or of the shaft of the machine shown in the woodcut at the beginning of this chapter. When we represent a system of forces on a sheet of paper, an axis of rotation is usually perpendicular to the sheet, and thus is drawn as a point. When we say we are taking moments about a "point," we understand that this point represents an axis of rotation.

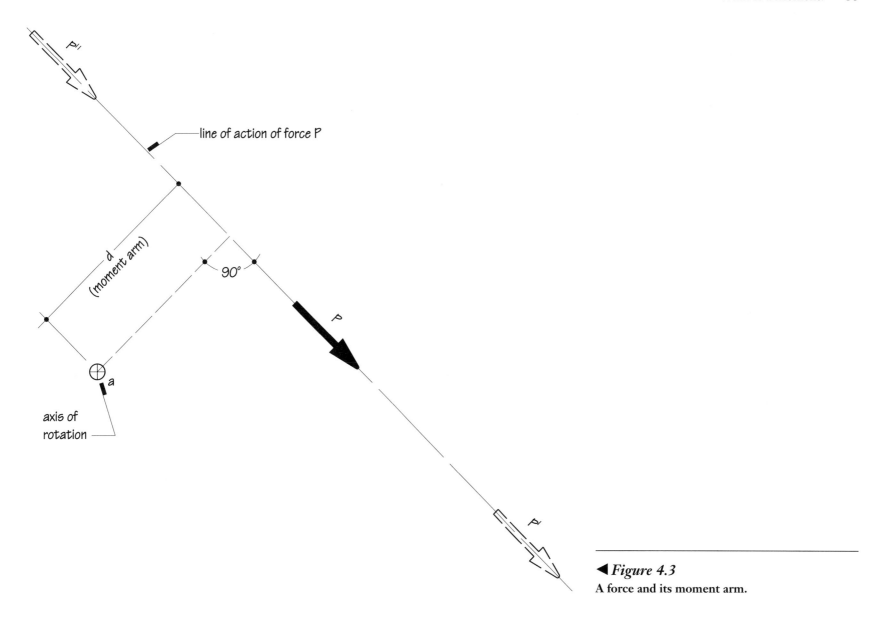

◀ *Figure 4.3*
A force and its moment arm.

Consider the force P shown in Figure 4.4. With respect to point a, the force exerts a clockwise moment, M_a, that is evaluated as follows:

$$M = Pd$$

$$M_a = (750 \text{ N})(3 \text{ m})$$

$$M_a = 2\ 250 \text{ N·m}$$

Notice that the moment arm is measured along a line through a that is perpendicular to the line of action of P, not to some point on the vector itself.

A moment is always expressed in units of force times distance, in this case newton·meters. Other common units for moments are lb-in., lb-ft, and kip-ft. (A *kip* is a kilopound, 1000 lb. In conventional units, liberties are often taken with the accepted practice of placing the force unit before the distance unit, so that lb-in., for example, are often called in.-lb). It does not make any difference which units we adopt in evaluating moments, as long as they remain consistent throughout a computation. It is customary to assign a positive sign to clockwise moments and a negative sign to counterclockwise moments. To keep track of the rotational sense of a moment, we may add a circular arrow above its term in a calculation, although the plus and minus signs are sufficient in themselves.

The force in Figure 4.4 exerts a different moment with respect to point b than it does with respect to point a:

$$M_b = -(750 \text{ N})(4.5 \text{ m}) = -3\ 375 \text{ N·m}$$

The sign is negative because the moment is counterclockwise about point b. We could also evaluate the moment of this force about point c, point d, or any other point we might choose. Points e, f, and g, as well as any other points that

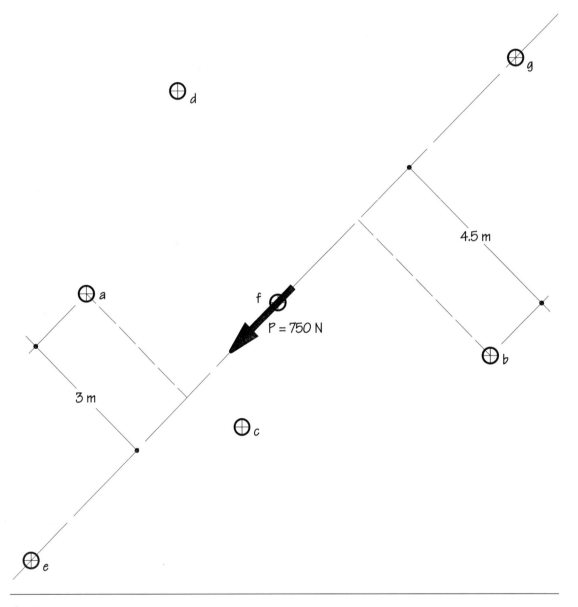

▲ *Figure 4.4*

Evaluating moments of a force about various axes of rotation.

lie on the line of action of the force, are of particular interest, because the moment arm of the force with respect to each of them is zero. This means that the force exerts no moment about any of these points, a phenomenon that we will put to good use shortly.

EQUILIBRIUM OF MOMENTS

Experimentation has shown that a body does not rotate if the sum of the moments of force that act upon it equals zero:

$$\sum M = 0 \qquad [4\text{-}2]$$

This is the third and final expression of static equilibrium for forces that act in a plane. To summarize all three expressions in a single sentence, a body is in equilibrium if the sum of the forces in the horizontal direction is zero, the sum of the forces in the vertical direction is zero, and the sum of the moments of force about any axis of rotation is zero.

In evaluating the equilibrium of any structure or part of a structure in which the external forces are nonconcurrent, we must employ all three expressions. The moments of force that we use in eq. [4-2] may be evaluated about any point or axis that we wish to adopt, but, within any single computation, all the moments for a given body must be evaluated about the **same** point or axis. It turns out, conveniently, that, for any set of forces in equilibrium, if the sum of the moments about any one axis is zero, the sum of the moments about any other axis is also zero.

FINDING THE REACTIONS ON A BEAM

A wooden beam 12 ft long is subjected to a single load of 150 lb at a distance of 4 ft from its right support. The beam is supported by two vertical reactions at its ends (Fig. 4.5). What is the magnitude of each reaction, assuming for the sake of simplicity that the beam itself is weightless?

We have three expressions that we can use to find these reactions. First, the sum of the horizontal forces must be zero. There are no forces in the horizontal direction, so this condition is satisfied automatically. Second, the sum of the vertical forces must be zero. This means that the

downward force of 150 lb must be balanced by upward forces that total 150 lb:

$$\sum F_v = 0$$

$$150 \text{ lb} - R_1 - R_2 = 0$$

$$R_1 + R_2 = 150 \text{ lb}$$

This is as far as this expression will take us. Now we must turn to the third expression to complete our solution: The sum of the moments about any axis must be zero. If we chose to take moments about a point that does not lie on the line of action of one of the reactions, we would have to solve two simultaneous equations for two unknowns, R_1 and R_2. There is a much easier way

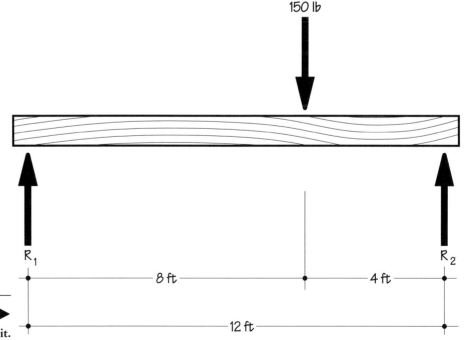

Figure 4.5 ▶
A wooden beam and the forces that act on it.

to achieve the same result. It involves selecting an axis about which to take moments in such a way that one of the unknowns is eliminated from the computation. To do this, we select a point that lies on the line of action of one of the unknown reactions. As we learned earlier in this chapter, a force whose line of action passes through the point about which a moment is taken has a zero moment arm, and therefore a zero moment, with respect to that point. Applying this knowledge to solution of the same problem of finding beam reactions (Fig. 4.6), we take moments about point *1*, which results in an equation with only one unknown, R_2:

$$\sum M_1 = 0$$

$$(150 \text{ lb})(8 \text{ ft}) - R_2(12 \text{ ft}) = 0$$

$$R_2 = 100 \text{ lb}$$

Having found the value of R_2 so directly, we may find the value of R_1 with equal ease, either by taking moments about R_2 or by substituting into the expression $\Sigma F_v = 0$.

Selecting the most advantageous axis about which to evaluate moments is the key to efficient solution of any problem involving two or more unknown forces. It is always possible to locate an axis on the line of action of at least one unknown force, thus eliminating that force from the initial computation, as we did in the preceding example. In a problem that involves three unknowns, it is often possible to find an axis that lies at the intersection of the lines of action of two of them; this reduces the evaluation of the remaining unknown to a single, simple equation.

THE SEESAW ANALOGY

In childhood, each of us learned about the equilibrium of moments while playing on a seesaw or teeter-totter. If we invert the diagram of the beam that we have been analyzing, we can visualize the analogy clearly (Fig. 4.7): A larger child and a smaller one can seesaw on equal terms by placing the smaller child farther from the axis. The larger child exerts a larger force at a shorter distance from the axis, and the smaller child achieves an equal moment by exerting a smaller force at a greater distance.

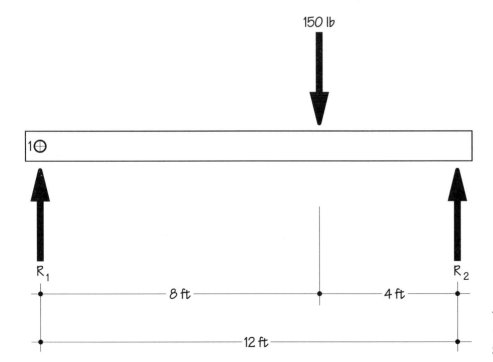

◀ *Figure 4.6*
Selecting an axis of moments that eliminates one of the unknowns.

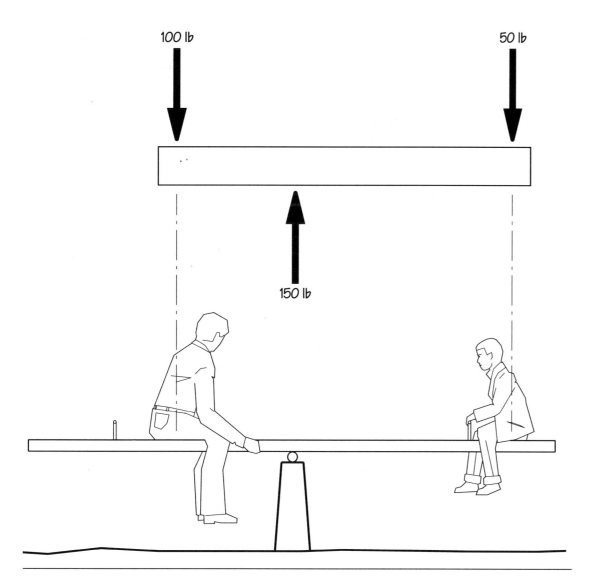

▲ *Figure 4.*7
The seesaw analogy.

FINDING THE REACTIONS ON A BEAM WITH A COMPLEX LOADING

Beam loadings in real structures are often complex. Consider a beam that supports a mass of 200 kg that is concentrated at the end of an overhang and a mass of 600 kg whose action is distributed over two-thirds of the main span (Fig. 4.8). The beam must also support its own uniformly distributed mass of 160 kg. What are the values of the two reactions, R_a and R_b?

The loads on this beam are given in kilograms, which are units of mass. We convert them to units of force (kilonewtons) by multiplying each load by the acceleration of gravity, which is 9.8 m/s², and dividing by 1 000. For the purpose of finding the reactions, we may replace each distributed load with its resultant, a single force of equal magnitude that is located at the center of the distributed load (Fig. 4.9).

We can find the solution to this seemingly messy problem with two simple equations, each

Figure 4.9 ▶

A free-body diagram of the beam with a complex loading.

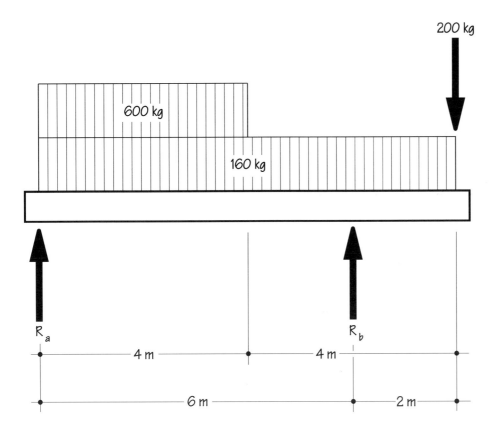

◀ *Figure 4.8*
A beam with a complex loading.

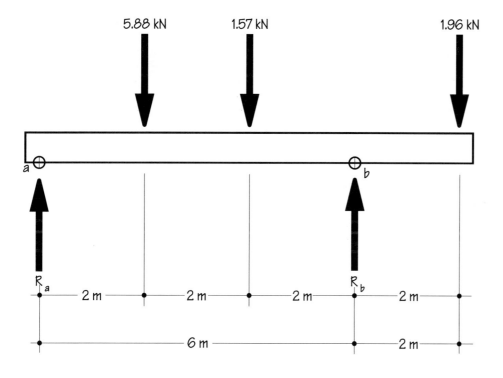

of which contains only one unknown quantity. We set up each equation by summing moments about an axis that lies on the line of action of one of the reactions, thus eliminating one of the unknowns:

$$\sum M_a = 0$$

$$(5.88 \text{ kN})(2 \text{ m}) + (1.57 \text{ kN})(4 \text{ m})$$
$$+ (1.96 \text{ kN})(8 \text{ m}) - R_b(6 \text{ m}) = 0$$

$$R_b = 5.62 \text{ kN}$$

$$\sum M_b = 0$$

$$- (5.88 \text{ kN})(4 \text{ m}) - (1.57 \text{ kN})(2 \text{ m})$$
$$+ (1.96 \text{ kN})(2 \text{ m}) + R_a(6 \text{ m}) = 0$$

$$R_a = 3.79 \text{ kN}$$

Check for accuracy:

$$\sum F_v = 0$$

$$- 3.79 \text{ kN} + 5.88 \text{ kN} + 1.57 \text{ kN} - 5.62 \text{ kN}$$
$$+ 1.96 \text{ kN} \stackrel{?}{=} 0$$

$$0 \equiv 0$$

Our work is correct.

FINDING REACTIONS ON A BEAM WITH INCLINED LOADS

Figure 4.10 depicts a beam that supports two inclined loads. One load is applied to the top of the beam, and the other to the bottom. The beam is 12 in. deep. One reaction is furnished by a roller, which can transmit force only in a vertical direction. The other reaction is through a hinge, which can transmit force at any angle.

To find the reactions, we must sum the moments of the inclined loads. There are two ways of doing this: one is to find the lengths of

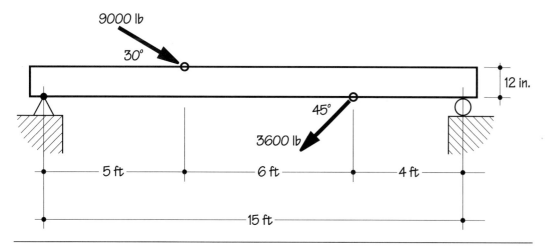

▲ *Figure 4.10*
A beam with inclined loads.

the inclined moment arms of these loads with respect to a selected point; the other is to resolve each inclined load into its vertical and horizontal components, and then to sum the moments of the components of the loads. Either method will yield the same result, a fact that was first proved by Varignon (1654–1722). For this example, we choose to resolve the forces into components because it makes the determination of the lengths of the moment arms much easier.

Figure 4.11 shows a free-body diagram in which the inclined loads are resolved into their horizontal and vertical components. The horizontal component of the 9000-lb load was found by multiplying 9000 lb by the cosine of 30°. The vertical component is equal to 9000 lb times the

cosine of 60°. The components of the 3600-lb load were determined in a similar way. The left-hand reaction has been resolved into horizontal and vertical components whose magnitudes are unknown.

We begin by summing moments about point *a* in the lower left corner of the beam. This point is a good axis about which to take moments, because the lines of action of three force components of unknown magnitudes pass through it and are thus eliminated from the first step of the computation, leaving only one unknown force for which to solve. We are careful to include an expression for the moment caused by the 7794-lb horizontal component of the top load:

$$\sum M_a = 0$$

$$(4500 \text{ lb})(5 \text{ ft}) + (7794 \text{ lb})(1 \text{ ft})$$
$$+ (2546 \text{ lb})(11 \text{ ft}) - R_b(15 \text{ ft}) = 0$$

$$R_b = 3887 \text{ lb}$$

$$\sum M_b = 0$$

$$- (4500 \text{ lb})(10 \text{ ft}) + (7794 \text{ lb})(1 \text{ ft})$$
$$- (2546 \text{ lb})(4 \text{ ft}) + R_{a_v}(15 \text{ ft}) = 0$$

$$R_{a_v} = 3159 \text{ lb}$$

The remaining unknown quantity, R_{a_h}, is found by summing forces in the horizontal direction. It is 5248 lb, acting leftward on the beam. We may check the accuracy of our moment calculations by summing forces in the vertical direction:

$$\sum F_v = -3159 \text{ lb} + 4500 \text{ lb} + 2546 \text{ lb}$$
$$- 3887 \text{ lb} = 0 \quad \text{O.K.}$$

APPLYING MOMENT ANALYSIS TO A PORTION OF A STRUCTURE

If a structure is in static equilibrium, then any portion or segment of it must also be in equilibrium. To illustrate the usefulness of this principle, let us apply what we know about moments to find the force in member *m* of the steel bridge truss shown in Figure 4.12.

We make an imaginary cut that passes completely through the truss in such a way that it intersects member *m*. We discard the portion of the truss to one side of the cut (we could pick the portion to the right of the cut line or the one to the left; it does not matter which). Then we construct a free-body diagram of the remaining portion of the truss (Fig. 4.13). On this diagram, we show the forces in the cut members as vectors of unknown magnitude but known lines of action.

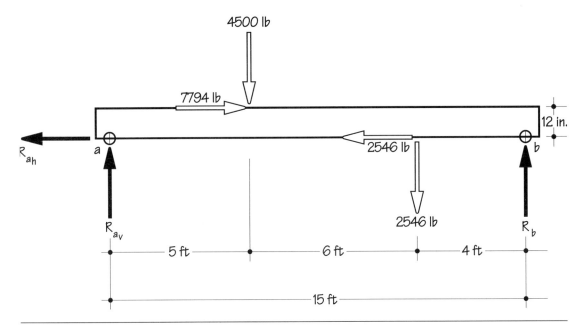

▲ *Figure 4.11*
Resolving the inclined loads into their components.

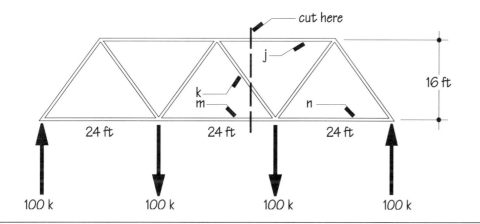

▲ Figure 4.12

A steel bridge truss.

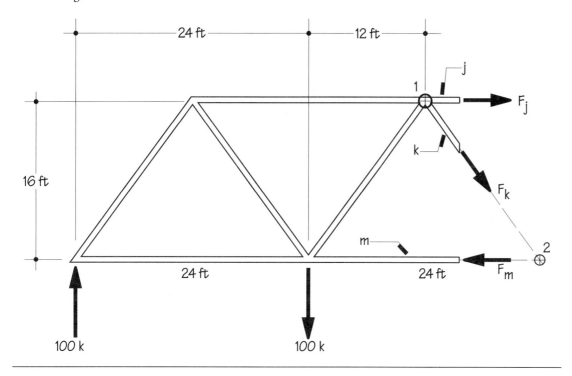

▲ Figure 4.13

A free-body diagram of a portion of the truss.

We assume a character, tensile or compressive, for each of them. There are three of these vectors, and a solution may appear at first glance to require fairly involved calculations. But the lines of action of two of the vectors, F_j and F_k, pass through joint *1*, so we will sum moments about this point, leaving as the only unknown in this expression F_m, the force in member *m*:

$$\sum M_1 = 0$$

$$(100,000 \text{ lb})(36 \text{ ft}) - (100,000 \text{ lb})(12 \text{ ft})$$
$$+ F_m(16 \text{ ft}) = 0$$

$$F_m = -150,000 \text{ lb}$$

We had assumed initially that F_m pushed to the left. The minus sign of the answer tells us that it pulls to the right instead. Member *m* is a tension member rather than a compression member.

We can use the same free-body diagram (Fig. 4.13) to find force F_j in member *j*. To do so in a single step, we must take moments about the point through which the lines of action of the other two unknown forces pass, thus eliminating them from the computation. This point of intersection, *2*, lies in the empty space to the right of the diagram. From the dimensions on Fig. 4.12, we know that it lies at a distance of 24 ft from the adjacent 100-kip load, which makes it easy to set up the solution:

$$\sum M_2 = 0$$

$$(100,000 \text{ lb})(48 \text{ ft}) - (100,000 \text{ lb})(24 \text{ ft})$$
$$+ F_j(16 \text{ ft}) = 0$$

$$F_j = -150,000 \text{ lb}$$

The minus sign tells us that we assumed the wrong direction for F_j, as we did for F_m; *j* is compressed.

DRAWING FREE-BODY DIAGRAMS

The construction of a clear, complete free-body diagram (FBD) is the first, crucial step in solving any problem in structural analysis. If there is an error in the free-body diagram, there is certain to be an error in the solution. To draw a free-body diagram correctly, follow these steps:

1. **Isolate the body that you wish to study from the bodies that surround it.** Draw a diagram of the body as if it were floating in space all alone, not touching anything else.

2. **Determine all the forces that act *upon* the body that you have isolated. Do not** consider forces that the body exerts on other bodies, only forces that are exerted **on it** by other bodies and external actions.

3. **Draw arrows to represent the positions, directions, and distributions of all the loads and forces that act upon the body.** Forces exerted by other bodies act at the point or area where the two bodies touch. For many types of analyses, a distributed load may be represented by one or more simple forces that act at the centroids of the corresponding portions of the load. Weights are always represented by downward-pointing arrows.

4. **Label each arrow with its magnitude.** Use numbers to give magnitudes of known forces. Use letter symbols such as P, Q, and W for forces of unknown magnitude, and R with a subscript for a reaction. A subscript H or h denotes a horizontal component of a force, and V or v a vertical component.

5. **Check the diagram for equilibrium.** First, inspect the diagram and apply com-

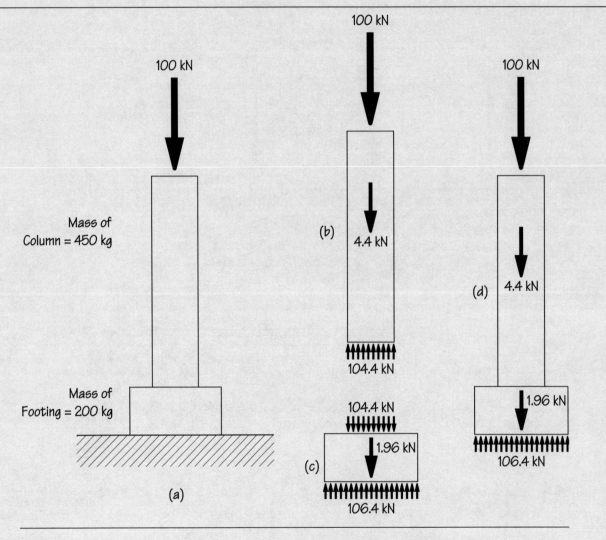

▲ *Figure A*

mon sense to see whether there are any obvious errors. Then apply the three expressions of static equilibrium to determine whether any forces are missing and whether any arrows or moments are drawn in the wrong direction.

Part (a) of Figure A is a picture of a column and footing that transmit a force of 100 kN from the top of the column to the ground. The masses of the column and footing are also given; these must be converted to forces before adding them to the FBD. Part (b) is a free-body diagram of the column alone; notice especially that the force at the bottom is an **upward force exerted by the footing on the column,** and that it is equal to the sum of the applied force at the top plus the weight of the column. Part (c) is a free-body diagram of the footing alone, in which the force from the bottom of the column is represented as a **downward action of the column on the top of the footing.** Part (d) is a free-body diagram of the column and footing together; it tells us nothing about the interaction between the column and the footing, but it does represent the external forces on the entire column-footing system without requiring us to examine its parts separately. What these three free-body diagrams have in common is that in each of them we show only forces that act on the body, not forces exerted by the body.

We will often find use for such FBDs of assemblies of structural parts. A careful review of these examples should clear up any points of confusion about how to draw an accurate free-body diagram. ■

It is apparent that we could find the force in any other member by cutting completely through the truss along a line that intersects the member, selecting a point about which to take moments in such a way that only the member force we wish to find remains as an unknown, and following a similar procedure to a solution. This method of finding the forces in the members of a truss is known as the *method of sections.* The method of sections may be applied to finding internal forces in other types of structures as well, as we will often do in succeeding chapters.

COUPLES

Two parallel, nonconcurrent forces that are equal in magnitude but opposite in direction are known as a *couple* (Fig. 4.14). It is easily demonstrated, by taking moments about a point on the line of action of one of the forces, that a couple exerts a moment that is equal to one of the forces times the perpendicular distance between the forces:

$$M = Pd \qquad [4\text{-}3]$$

Because the forces in a couple are equal and opposite, the couple does not cause linear displacement of a body as a whole, only rotation. We will encounter couples from time to time in following chapters as we examine the internal behavior of various structural devices.

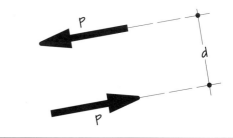

▲ *Figure 4.14*
A couple.

Key Terms and Concepts

moment of force

nonconcurrent forces

concurrent forces

$M = Pd$

moment arm

kip

$\Sigma M = 0$

FBD

method of sections

couple

Exercises

1. The free-body diagram in Figure 4.15 is a cross section that represents the forces that act on a garden toolshed. The downward vector of 2250 lb represents the weight of the shed. The horizontal vector of 1600 lb represents the resultant of the estimated force of the wind. How much downward force is required at point *a* to keep the shed from overturning? What are the components of the reaction at the other corner of the shed?

2. Find the force in member *n* of the truss shown in Figure 4.12.

3. Find the reactions at roller *a* and hinge *b* in Figure 4.16.

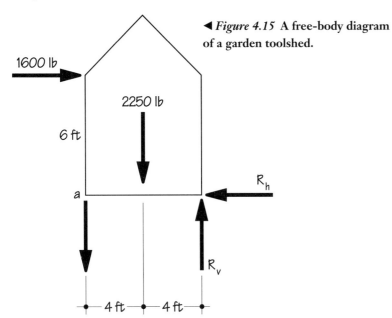

◀ *Figure 4.15* **A free-body diagram of a garden toolshed.**

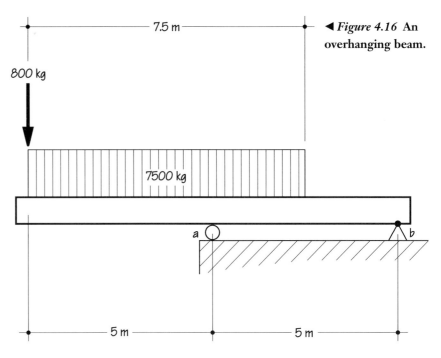

◀ *Figure 4.16* **An overhanging beam.**

4. Assuming that the beam in Figure 4.17 is weightless, find force P and the force at hinge H.

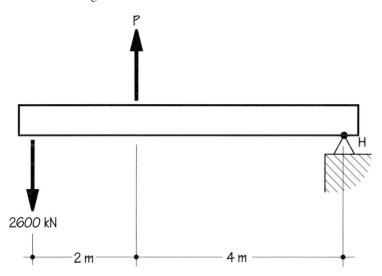

▲ *Figure 4.17* **A beam subjected to two pulls.**

P

H

2600 kN

2 m   4 m

5. The cantilever beam in Figure 4.18 is embedded in a rectangular block of concrete that weighs 30,000 lb. At what load W will the block begin to tip over?

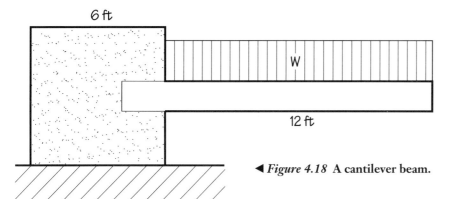

6 ft

W

12 ft

◀ *Figure 4.18* **A cantilever beam.**

6. The tower in Figure 4.19 has a mass of 3360 kg and is subjected to a horizontal pull of 1000 kN at the top. Find the magnitudes and directions of the reactions at a and b.

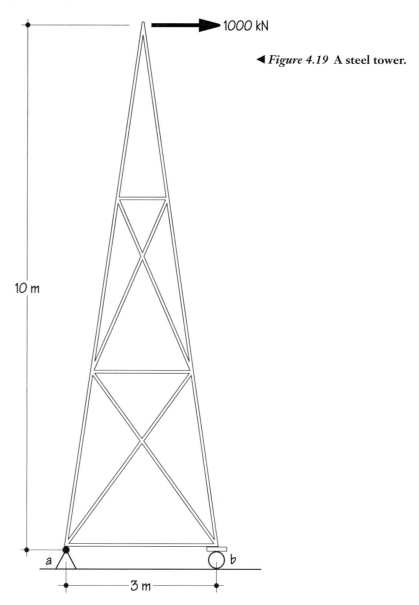

1000 kN

◀ *Figure 4.19* **A steel tower.**

10 m

a   b

3 m

7. The beam in Figure 4.20 supports both a uniformly distributed load of 1500 lb/ft and a load that varies linearly from zero at one end to 4000 lb/ft at the other end. Find the reactions.

8. Find the reactions at *a* and *b* on the welded steel frame in Figure 4.21. Ignore the weight of the frame.

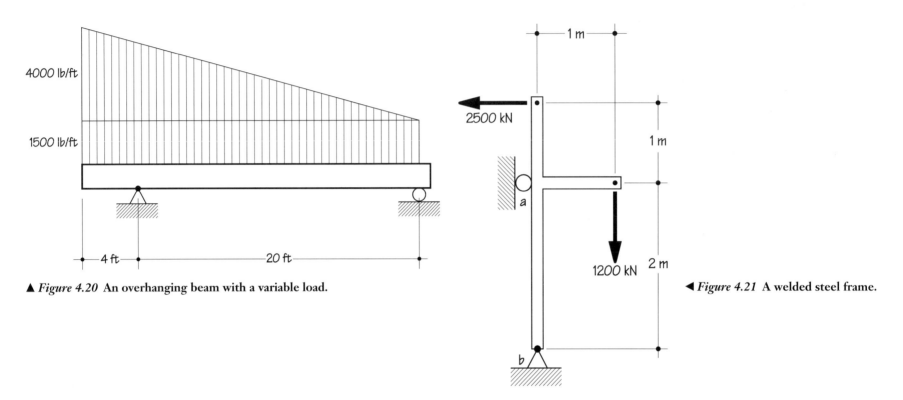

▲ *Figure 4.20* **An overhanging beam with a variable load.**

◄ *Figure 4.21* **A welded steel frame.**

Figure 4.22 ▶
Each roof beam in this automobile parts warehouse in Swindon, England, is supported at midspan by a sloping steel tie rod that is connected to the top of a tubular steel column. The pull of the tie rod exerts a moment on the top of the column that is balanced by an opposing moment created by the pull of another tie rod that passes over a projecting strut on the right and is anchored vertically to the ground. The moments of force of the ties and struts balance one another so that there is no net moment exerted on the column. The architect is Foster and Partners, and the structural engineer is Ove Arup and Partners. (Photo: Richard Davies.)

The ridge beam of this primitive, stone-walled dwelling is supported by simple triangular trusses made of heavy timbers. (Drawing by Edward Allen.)

CHAPTER FIVE

FINDING FORCES IN A SIMPLE TRUSS

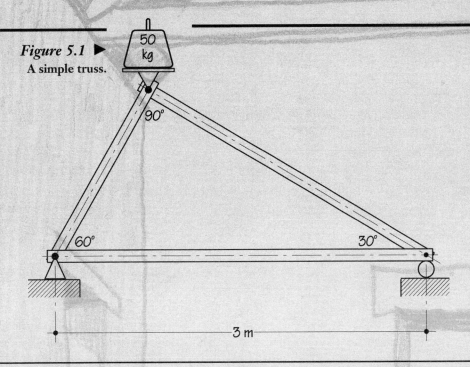

Figure 5.1 ▶
A simple truss.

A body whose mass is 50 kilograms is supported at the top of a triangular framework of wooden members that is pinned together by a single bolt at each joint (Fig. 5.1). The framework takes the shape of a 30°–60° right triangle with its hypotenuse placed in a horizontal orientation. It is held up by reactions at its two lower corners, 3 m apart. One of its lower corners is supported by a hinge that allows free rotation; the other sits on a roller that allows free horizontal motion. This framework is a simple *truss*. A truss is a collection of members arranged in a triangle or connected triangles so that the forces that act on its joints cause only axial tensile or compressive forces to occur within its members. What is the character and magnitude of the force in each member of this simple truss? First we will find these forces numerically, then graphically.

FINDING FORCES NUMERICALLY

We begin the numerical solution by drawing a free-body diagram of the truss and the external forces that act on it, representing each member of the truss with a single line (Fig. 5.2). The force exerted by the 50-kg mass is indicated by a downward-pointing arrow. Two upward-pointing arrows denote the reactions at the two lower corners of the truss. The roller support at the lower right can exert a force only in the upward direction, so we know that the arrow on the free-body diagram that represents the reaction at this point must be vertical. The hinge support at the lower left could exert an inclined force or even a horizontal force, but, because the only other two external forces on the truss are vertical, the force through the hinge must also be vertical; otherwise, the truss would move in a horizontal direction.

The 50-kg load is a mass. How much force does gravity exert on this mass?

$$P = (50 \text{ kg})(9.8 \text{ m/}s^2) = 490 \text{ N}$$

We need a system of notation to keep track of the various members, forces, and joints in the truss. There are several such systems in general use. The simplest of these suffices for a numerical solution. We label the joints of the truss with the letters A, B, and C. We label the left reaction R_B as an abbreviation for "reaction at joint B", and the right one R_C. AB will refer both to the left-hand sloping member in the truss and to the force in that member.

We begin by determining the values of the reactions, R_B and R_C. To do this, we need to know the lengths of the moment arms of the 490 kN force in respect to points B and C. The line of action of the 490 KN force is perpendicular to

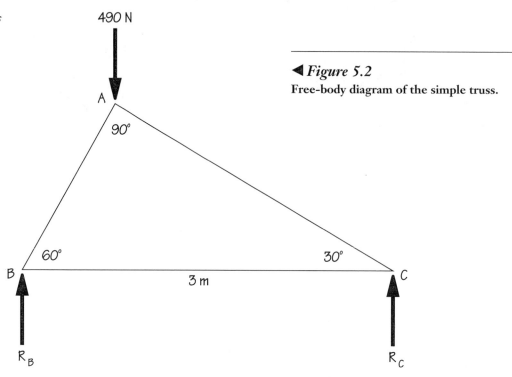

490 N

◀ *Figure 5.2*
Free-body diagram of the simple truss.

BC at *D* (Fig. 5.3). In a 30°–60° right triangle, the length of the short leg is half the length of the hypotenuse. This means that *AB* is 1.5 m long. Triangle *ADB* is also a 30°–60° right triangle, so *BD* is 0.75 m, half the length of *AB*. Taking clockwise moments as positive, we solve for the reactions, keeping only three digits of each answer, and check our work:

$$\sum M_B = 0 = (490 \text{ kN})(0.75 \text{ m}) - R_C(3 \text{ m})$$

$$R_C = 122.5 \text{ N}, \textit{say } 123 \text{ N}$$

$$\sum M_C = 0 = -(490 \text{ N})(2.25 \text{ m}) + R_B(3 \text{ m})$$

$$R_B = 367.5 \text{ N}, \textit{say } 367 \text{ N}$$

$$\sum F_V = (490 \text{ N}) - (123 \text{ N}) - (367 \text{ N}) = 0 \quad \text{O.K.}$$

It is customary to begin finding the member forces of a truss at the left reaction. We draw

a free-body diagram of joint B (Fig. 5.4). We do not need to know the characters of forces AB and BC to solve for the forces at this joint; if we assume a wrong direction for a vector, the calculation will yield a negative answer, which tells us that its character is the opposite of what we had assumed. Still, it is useful to develop the ability to deduce the characters of member forces in advance of calculations. AB must push downward and to the left so that its vertical component will equilibrate the reaction, R_B. BC must pull to the right to balance the horizontal component of AB. We adopt a convention that downward and rightward forces are positive. To resolve AB into its orthogonal components, we use a simple trigonometric relationship: The component of an inclined force along any axis is equal to the force times the cosine of the angle

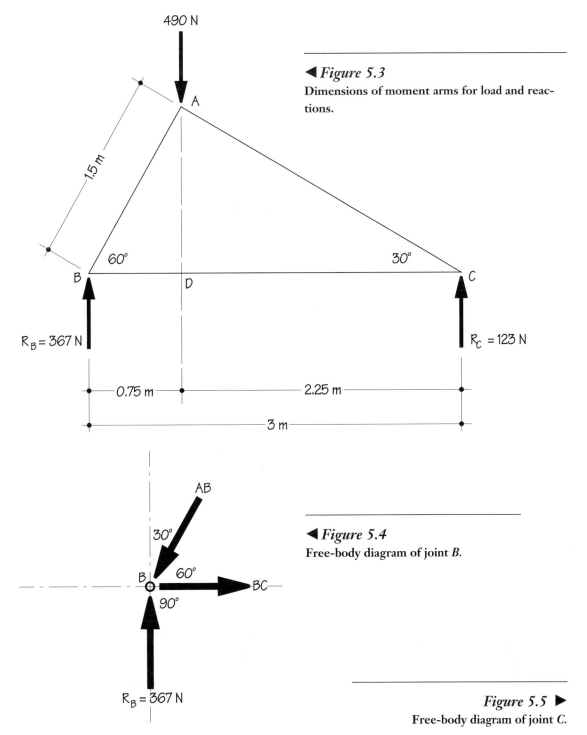

490 N

◄ Figure 5.3
Dimensions of moment arms for load and reactions.

1.5 m

A

60°   D   30°   C

B

$R_B = 367$ N $R_C = 123$ N

0.75 m   2.25 m

3 m

◄ Figure 5.4
Free-body diagram of joint B.

AB

30°

B   60°   BC

90°

$R_B = 367$ N

between the axis and the line of action of the force:

$$\sum F_V = 0 = AB \cos 30° - 367 \text{ N}$$
$$= 0.866 AB - 367 \text{ N}$$

$$AB = 424 \text{ N}$$

$$\sum F_H = 0 = BC - AB \cos 60° = BC - 0.5 AB$$

$$BC = 212 \text{ N}$$

The answers are both positive, confirming our deductions regarding the characters of the member forces. At this point, we know the forces in two of the three members of the truss, allowing us to solve next for the forces at either of the two remaining joints, each of which has just one unknown force, AC. We choose joint C and draw its free-body diagram (Fig. 5.5). AC must act down and to the right so that its vertical component can equilibrate R_C, and BC must act to the left to equilibrate the horizontal component of

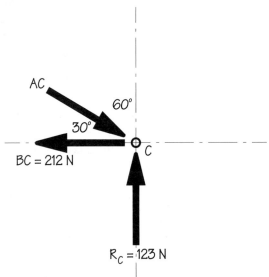

AC

60°

30°

$BC = 212$ N   C

$R_C = 123$ N

Figure 5.5 ►
Free-body diagram of joint C.

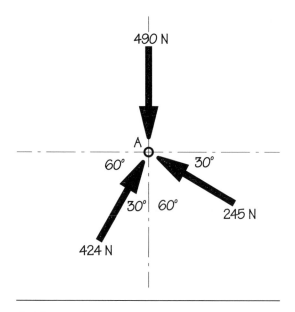

▲ *Figure 5.6*
Free-body diagram of joint *A*.

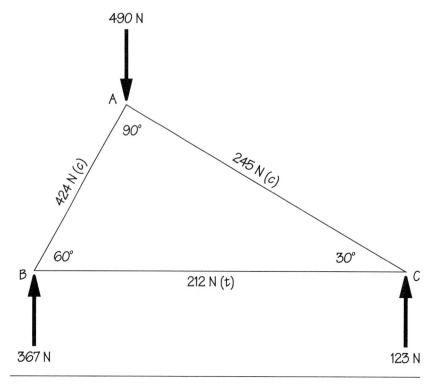

▲ *Figure 5.7*
Summary diagram of member forces in the simple truss.

AC. We can sum forces in either direction to find *AC*:

$$\sum F_H = 0 = AC\cos 30° - 212 \text{ N}$$

$$AC = 245 \text{ N}$$

Again, the positive answer tells us that we assumed the correct sense for this force. Now we know the forces in all the members of the truss, but we sum the vertical components of the forces at joint *A* as a check (Fig. 5.6):

$$\sum F_V = 490 \text{ N} - (424 \text{ N})\cos 30°$$
$$- (245 \text{ N})\cos 60° = 0 \quad \text{O.K.}$$

We draw a summary diagram that shows all the forces on and within the truss (Fig. 5.7). We indicate compressive forces with a (*c*) and tensile forces with a (*t*).

FINDING FORCES GRAPHICALLY

A graphical analysis of a truss is carried out at a drafting board and requires the construction of precise diagrams with a sharp pencil. It yields the same result as a numerical analysis, but it does so without using any arithmetic, algebra, or trigonometry.

We begin a graphical analysis of the simple triangular truss by drawing an accurate picture of it (Fig. 5.8). We do this to any convenient scale of length to length; we adopt a metric scale of 1:25 (one-twenty-fifth full size) in this case. (In conventional units of measurement, the closest equivalent scale is ½ in. equals 1 ft, which is

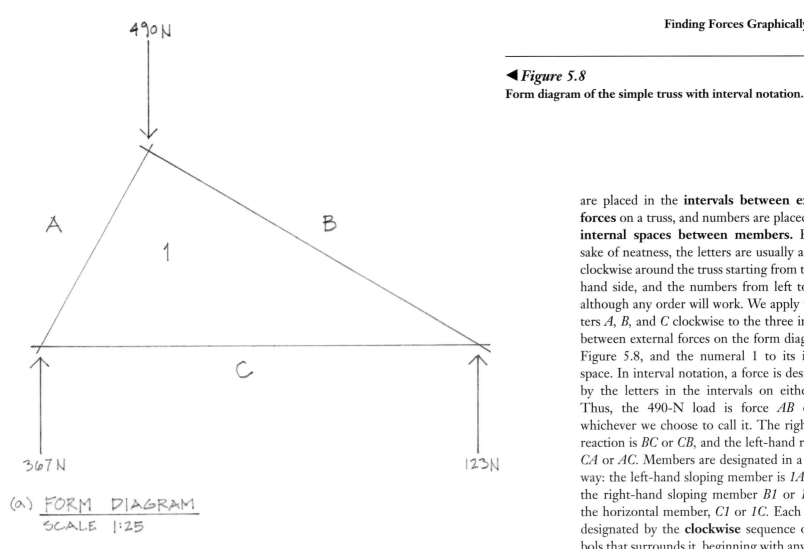

490 N

A

B

1

C

367 N

123 N

(a) FORM DIAGRAM
SCALE 1:25

◀ *Figure 5.8*
Form diagram of the simple truss with interval notation.

are placed in the **intervals between external forces** on a truss, and numbers are placed in the **internal spaces between members.** For the sake of neatness, the letters are usually assigned clockwise around the truss starting from the left-hand side, and the numbers from left to right, although any order will work. We apply the letters *A*, *B*, and *C* clockwise to the three intervals between external forces on the form diagram in Figure 5.8, and the numeral 1 to its interior space. In interval notation, a force is designated by the letters in the intervals on either side. Thus, the 490-N load is force *AB* or *BA*, whichever we choose to call it. The right-hand reaction is *BC* or *CB*, and the left-hand reaction *CA* or *AC*. Members are designated in a similar way: the left-hand sloping member is *1A* or *A1*, the right-hand sloping member *B1* or *1B*, and the horizontal member, *C1* or *1C*. Each joint is designated by the **clockwise** sequence of symbols that surrounds it, beginning with any one of the symbols. Thus, the top joint in the truss is *AB1*, or *B1A*, or *1AB*. Interval notation may appear cumbersome at this juncture, but it will greatly facilitate our work later on, especially as we undertake the analysis of more complex structures, and with a bit of practice it will become easy and comfortable.

To the right of the form diagram, we construct a force polygon, beginning with a load line

1:24.) By working to scale, we represent the shape of the truss accurately, with all its members sloping at the correct inclinations. We call this picture a *form diagram*, because it is an accurate representation of the form of the truss. We add vectors to the form diagram to represent the directions and magnitudes of all the external forces, using for the reactions the numbers that we calculated earlier in this chapter. In so doing,

we make the form diagram into a free-body diagram of the truss.

To facilitate various aspects of the analysis, we will label the joints of the truss on the form diagram with a system that was designed especially for graphical solutions. This system is often called *Bow's notation*, after Robert H. Bow, who introduced it in Britain in the 1870s. We will call it *interval notation*, because capital letters

(Fig. 5.9). Working to a convenient scale of length to force—in this case 1 mm equals 5 N—we plot a vertical line segment 98 mm long to represent the 490 N vertical load, *AB*. (This is done most easily by using the 1:50 scale on a standard metric drafting rule.) We indicate the ends of this line segment, as precisely as we can, with horizontal tick marks. As we read clockwise around joint *AB1* on the form diagram, moving from *A* to *B*, the force *AB* acts downward. To identify this force on the load line, we apply a lowercase *a* to the upper tick mark, and a lowercase *b* to the lower one, the downward sequence from *a* to *b* indicating the downward sense of the force. This convention is perhaps the hardest thing to grasp at first about interval notation: Capital letters that designate **intervals** on the form diagram correspond to lowercase letters that designate **points** on the load line, with the order of the letters on the load line indicating the directional sense of the force.

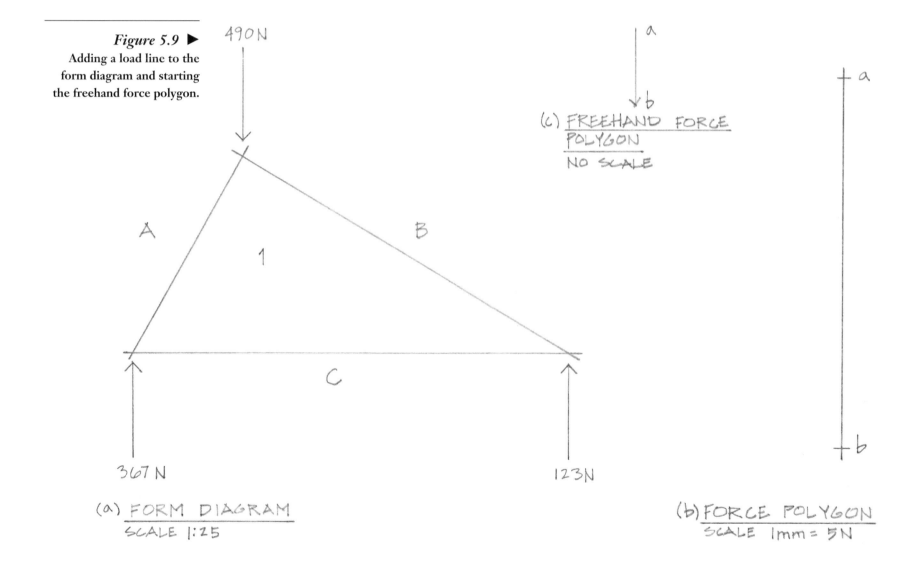

Figure 5.9 ▶

Adding a load line to the form diagram and starting the freehand force polygon.

In graphical analysis of forces, arrowheads are not usually applied to line segments in the force polygon. One reason for this is that they tend to obscure points of intersection and reduce the accuracy of the construction. Another reason is that a line in a force polygon usually ends up representing forces that act in two opposing directions, which would require arrowheads at both ends, leading to considerable confusion. Because this is our first exploration of graphical analysis of trusses, we will keep track of the directions of forces by drawing a freehand force polygon, Figure 5.9(c), on which we apply an arrowhead at *b* to indicate the direction in which *ab* acts. This diagram is not to scale; its only function is to keep track of the senses of forces.

In Figure 5.10, we add the two reactions to the load line. Reading clockwise, the right-hand reaction is *BC*. It acts upward. This means that on the load line, we plot its length beginning at *b* and finishing 123 N above at *c*, indicating its

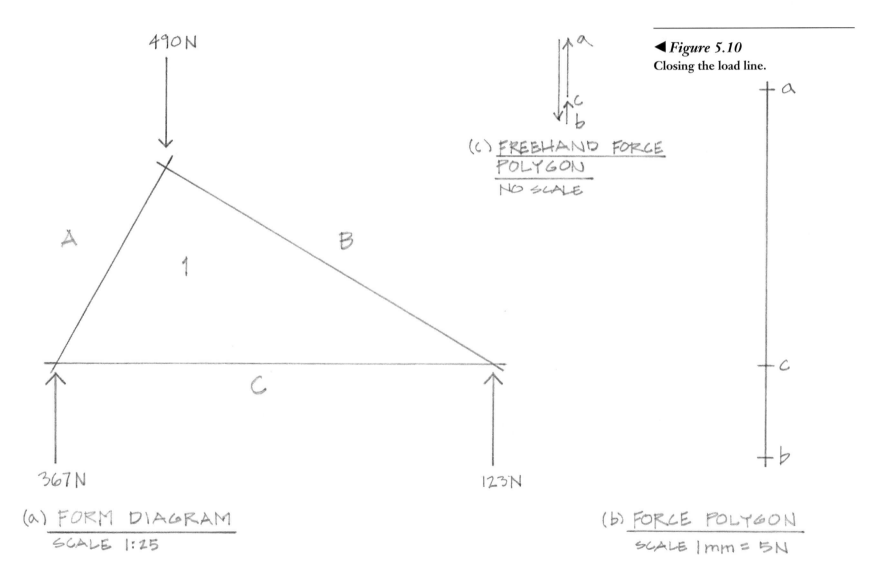

490 N

A

1

B

C

367 N

123 N

(a) FORM DIAGRAM

SCALE 1:25

(c) FREEHAND FORCE POLYGON

NO SCALE

◀ *Figure 5.10*
Closing the load line.

a

c

b

(b) FORCE POLYGON

SCALE 1mm = 5N

upward sense. Reading clockwise, the left-hand reaction, which also acts upward, is *CA*. We add it to the load line beginning at *c* and measuring upward a distance of 367 N to arrive precisely at *a*, which we located earlier on the load line. The load line has *closed* accurately, indicating that our work so far is correct. If a load line does not close when all the external loads and reactions have been drawn on it, a mistake has been made that must be found and corrected before proceeding.

We sketch upward-pointing vectors *bc* and *ca* on the freehand force polygon, Figure 5.10(c), and find that, to avoid confusion, we must draw them alongside *ab*. The load line is an example of a line in a force polygon that represents forces that act in both directions.

In Figure 5.11, we begin the process of finding the forces in the members of the truss. We start at the left reaction, as is customary. Two members, *A1* and *C1*, meet here. Their two forces must be in equilibrium with the left reaction, *CA*. Force *ca*, the 367 N reaction, is already plotted on the load line. We represent *a1*, the force in member *A1*, by a line through *a* parallel to *A1*. We do not know its length. The force *c1*, in horizontal member *C1*, is represented by a horizontal line through *c*. The two lines that we have just drawn intersect. Their intersection is point *1* on the force polygon, making one of the line segments *a1* and the other *c1*. The triangle *a1c* on the force polygon is an equilibrium polygon for the forces at joint *A1C* of the truss. We scale *a1* and *c1* to find that the forces in the two members are approximately 422 N and 210 N. Each of these values is within 1% of the values found in our earlier numerical analysis. We write

the measured values next to the two members on the form diagram.

FINDING THE CHARACTERS OF FORCES IN A GRAPHICAL SOLUTION

What are the characters of these two forces—are they tensile or compressive? Remember that for a set of forces to be in equilibrium, their corresponding vectors must be connected **tip to tail** in a closed polygon, which in this case is the triangle *a1c* that we have just drawn. Reaction *CA* acts in an upward direction, as we have indicated by the arrowhead at *a* on vector *ca* in the freehand force polygon (Fig. 5.11(c)). If *a* is the tip of *ca*, then it must be the tail of *a1*, and *1* must be the head. This tells us that member *A1* acts downward and leftward on joint *A1C*; it is in compression. We add a (c) to the 422 N quantity on the form diagram to indicate compression. Similarly, *1* must be the tail of vector *1c*. Member *1C* pulls to the right on joint *A1C*; it is in tension.

Using interval notation, this commonsense approach becomes a generalized method for determining quickly and accurately the character of any force in the polygon. It works like this: The joint is named by reading the letters and numbers that surround it in any **clockwise** sequence (Fig. 5.12). Thus, we may call the joint that we are examining *A1C*, *CA1*, or *1CA*, all of which are clockwise readings. We may **not** call it *C1A*, *1AC*, or *AC1*, because these are in counterclockwise order. To find the character of the force in member *1C* with respect to joint *1CA*, we note that its name in clockwise order is *1C*,

Figure 5.11 ▶
Finding the forces in the first two members.

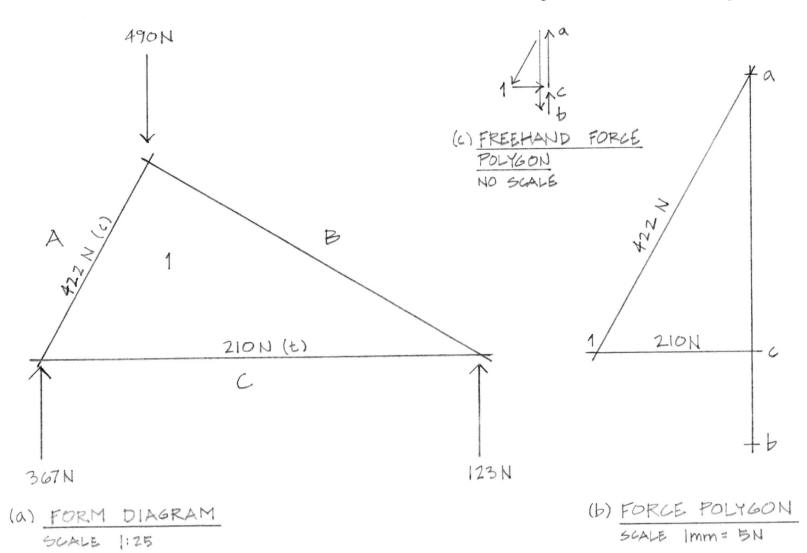

490 N

A

422 N (c)

1

B

210 N (t)

C

367 N

123 N

(a) FORM DIAGRAM
SCALE 1:25

(c) FREEHAND FORCE
POLYGON
NO SCALE

a

c

b

1

a

422 N

210 N

c

b

(b) FORCE POLYGON
SCALE 1mm = 5N

DRAWING PARALLEL LINES

Graphical analysis techniques require the drawing of many lines that are accurately parallel to other lines. The construction of a force polygon for a truss, as we have seen, involves drawing lines that are parallel to all of the truss members. For a large truss, this may amount to several dozen such operations. What are some efficient, precise ways of constructing parallel lines on a drawing?

The traditional method is to use two drafting triangles, placing the hypotenuse of one tightly against the hypotenuse of the other (Fig. A). A leg of the upper triangle is aligned with the original line. Then the lower triangle is held firmly against the paper while the upper triangle is slid to a new location that allows a parallel line to be constructed through the desired point. It often takes a bit of experimentation to find the best way of arranging the triangles for a particular pair of lines. If the operation must occur over a long distance, it sometimes works better to substitute a long straightedge for the lower triangle (Fig. B).

An adjustable triangle (Fig. C), used in conjunction with a T square or parallel rule, offers a means of drawing parallel lines that many designers find more convenient and secure than two triangles.

A drafting machine is an ideal instrument for graphical constructions, because it facilitates rapid, very accurate construction of parallel lines at any location on a sheet (Fig. D).

A rolling ruler offers a simple, easy way of ruling parallel lines, even if the paper is not fastened to a drawing board (Fig. E).

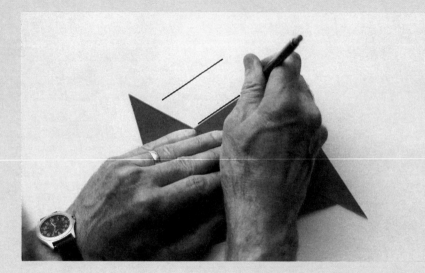

◀ *Figure A*

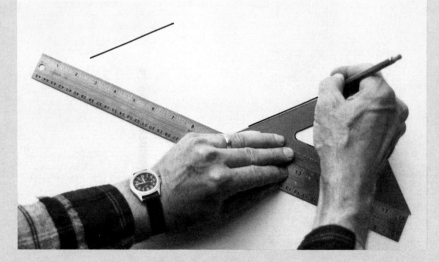

◀ *Figure B*

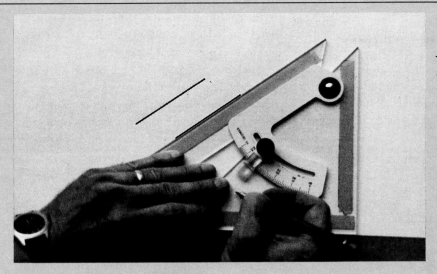

◀ *Figure C*

Computer-aided drafting (CAD) offers graphical constructions that give results identical to those of numerical computations that are carried to the same number of decimal places. Every CAD program has a simple routine for drawing parallel lines, as well as another routine for scaling the lengths of line segments with extreme precision. As we noted earlier, however, extreme numerical accuracy is not usually required, and CAD construction of a force polygon is generally appropriate only when the entire process of designing a truss is being carried out by computer. If the truss is being designed on paper, it is easiest and more natural to analyze it on the same sheet of paper. (Photos: Gregory D. Thomson) ■

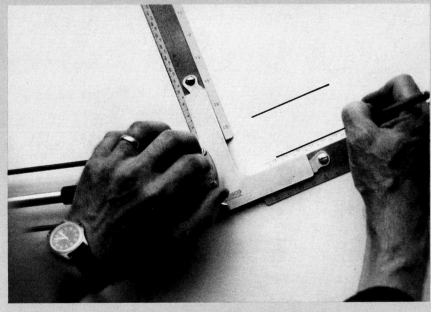

▲ *Figure D*

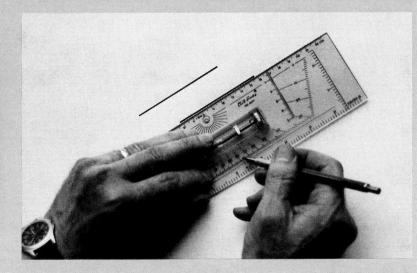

▲ *Figure E*

not *C1*. Reading from *1* to *c* on the force polygon, the line moves from left to right, meaning that the force in member *1C* pulls in that direction on joint *1CA*. Member *1C* acts in tension. The other member whose force we have just determined is named *A1* as we read in clockwise order around joint *1CA*. Reading from *a* to *1* on the force polygon, the line moves from upper right to lower left, meaning that the force in

member *A1* pushes in that direction on joint *1CA*. Member *A1* acts in compression.

FINISHING THE FORCE POLYGON

Continuing the graphical solution, we plot another triangle of forces, *bc1*, on the force polygon to represent the equilibrium of forces at joint *BC1* of the truss (Fig. 5.13). This construc-

tion begins with segment *bc* of the load line. We draw a line through *b*, parallel to member *B1*, to represent the direction of the force in that member. Point *1* has already been located on the force polygon. If our work is accurate, the line through *b* parallel to *B1* passes through this point, *closing the force polygon*. We measure *b1* as being 244 N in length, just 1 N different from the calculated value. To find its character, we read clockwise

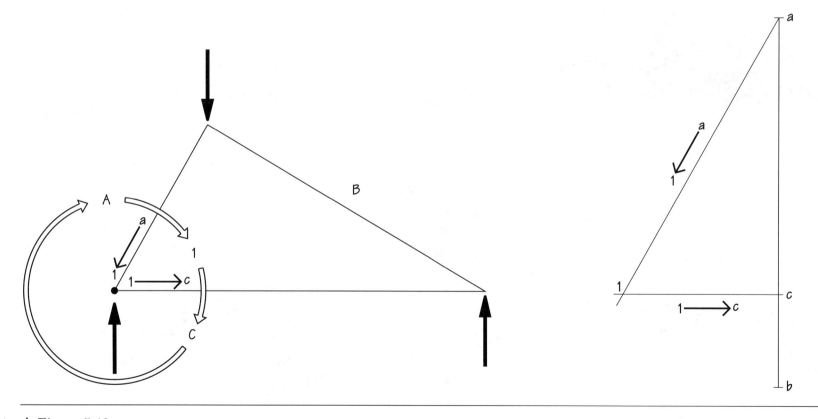

▲ *Figure 5.12*
Finding the characters of the member forces with interval notation.

around the lower right-hand joint on the form diagram to find that with respect to this joint, the member is called *1b*. Moving from *1* to *b* on the force polygon, we move from upper left to lower right, toward the joint. Member *1b* pushes on the joint; it is in compression.

We verify this determination by drawing vectors *1b* and *c1* tip to tail to the freehand force polygon (Fig. 5.13[c]). Because vector *bc* on the load line acts upward, *c1* must pull to the left, and *1b* must push down to the right, in order for the tips and tails to be in proper order.

We have not set out to draw the equilibrium triangle for load *AB* and the forces in members *B1* and *1A* at the top joint of the truss, *AB1*. But corresponding line segments *b1* and *1a* are already in place on the force polygon, products of our earlier analyses of the other two joints,

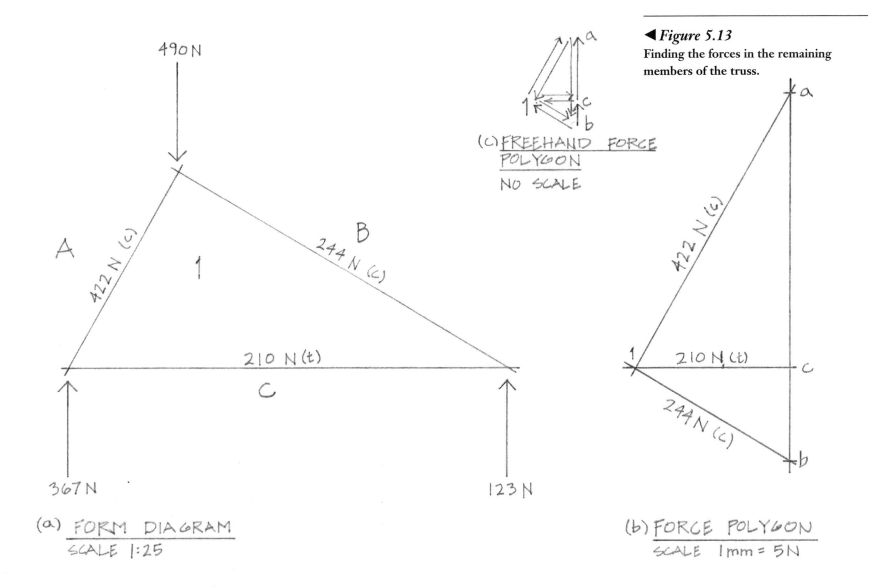

◀ *Figure 5.13*
Finding the forces in the remaining members of the truss.

and we already know that the forces are compressive in both these members. As a check, let us determine the sense of each force with respect to the top joint, using the clockwise protocol. The right-hand sloping member reads clockwise as *B1*. Moving from *b* to *1* on the force polygon, we move upward and leftward, toward the joint. This confirms our earlier finding that *b1* is in compression. We repeat the operation to verify that *1a* is also in compression. (If you read the name of each of these members in clockwise order at its lower joint, you will see that the letters in its name reverse to indicate that it presses downward on that joint.)

On the freehand force polygon, Figure 5.13(c), we add two last vectors, *b1* and *1a*, alongside *1b* and *a1* to represent the forces at the top joint of the truss. These must be oriented tip to tail with vector *ab*, the 490-N load. Looking more closely in Figure 5.14 at the completed freehand force polygon, we observe that it consists in actuality of four equilibrium polygons nested together. The first of these is the load line, which is made up of three vectors that connect tip to tail, verifying the equilibrium of the external forces. The second and third are *ac1* and *cb1*, which represent the forces at the lower joints of the truss. The fourth is *ab1*, the polygon for the top joint. Because of the nesting of these four partially congruent polygons, every line in Figure 5.14 consists of vectors of equal length that act in opposite directions to cancel each other's effects. This indicates that all the external and internal forces of the truss are in a state of equilibrium.

We will see in the next chapter that this graphical method of analysis in a single force

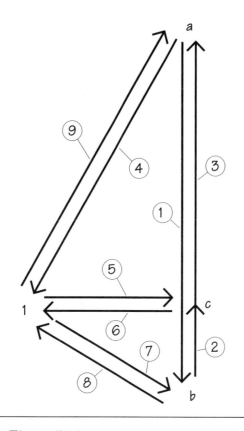

▲ *Figure 5.14*

The freehand force polygon. The circled numbers indicate the order in which the vectors were added to the diagram.

polygon works well for even the most complex trusses. It was developed independently in the nineteenth century by James Clerk Maxwell in Britain and Luigi Cremona in Italy. The single force polygon for a truss is often called a *Maxwell diagram* or a *Cremona plan*. We will call it simply a force polygon.

The force polygon that we have constructed closed accurately. What if a force polygon for a truss does not close? Often the last line misses its intended point by a small distance. In this case, we must judge how large the dimensional error is. If it is no more than 2 or 3% of the length of the line, it is due to an accumulation of small drafting errors and is not worth worrying about under most circumstances. If the last line does not come close to closing, a major mistake has been made. The entire construction of the force polygon should then be reviewed from the beginning.

THE METHOD OF JOINTS

We have found the forces in the members of this simple truss by working systematically, joint by joint, from one side of the truss to the other. We have done this twice, the first time numerically and the second time graphically. This general technique for finding the forces in a truss, whether numerically or graphically, is called the *method of joints*. In the numerical version of the method of joints, we sketch a free-body diagram of each joint in turn and apply the expressions of equilibrium in the vertical and horizontal directions to the forces in each free-body diagram. In the graphical version, we construct first a form diagram, which is an accurately shaped free-body diagram. Then we draw a succession of linked triangles in a single force polygon to represent the interactions of the forces in the truss, then scale the sides of these triangles to determine the magnitudes of the forces. In either version, we can solve for no more than two unknown forces at each joint, so we must start analyzing a truss at a joint that has only two unknowns, usually the lower left-hand joint.

The numerical method is as accurate as the number of decimal places that we wish to carry through our calculations, whereas the graphical method is inherently less accurate. There are several disadvantages to the numerical method, however: one is that it is often laborious and slow, especially if the truss is highly irregular in form. Another is that its purely numerical character does little to help us visualize what is actually happening within a truss, or to show us how to make improvements in the configuration of the members in order to regulate the forces within them. Moreover, the extreme precision in determining member forces that is made possible by the numerical method gives the illusion of a very accurate analysis, when in fact the calculations are invariably based on external loads that are only rough estimates of the forces that will be applied to the truss during the life of the building.

If a large enough scale is chosen for a graphical solution, and if the drafting of the force polygon is done with reasonable care, the results will agree with the results of a numerical solution to within 1% and will be considerably more accurate than the assumptions we are able to make about the applied loads. A graphical analysis is usually much faster and easier than a

numerical one, especially if the truss contains many different angles. As we shall see in Chapter Fourteen, a graphical analysis can also give strong clues to the designer concerning how to modify the form of the truss so as to minimize the forces in its members.

TRUSSES

At the beginning of this chapter, we defined a truss as a framework of members connected together to form a triangle or triangles that converts all external forces, no matter what their directions, into axial compression or tension in its members. The joints of a truss are usually assumed to behave as frictionless hinges. This allows us to treat the members as being subjected only to axial forces. Usually we associate the term *truss* with a framework that contains a number of connected triangles, but the simple truss that is made up of a single triangle is found in most wood frame houses in the form of the tied *rafter* pairs that hold up the roof (Fig. 5.15). Two sloping rafters that act in compression lean against each other at the ridge of the roof. They are tied together by a horizontal *ceiling joist* acting in tension at the base. The tied rafter pair differs from the truss that we have just analyzed in one important particular, however: each rafter supports a load of sheathing boards, shingles, snow, and wind along its entire length, whereas we have analyzed a similar shape that is loaded only at its apex. Thus, the rafter is subjected to the combined actions of both axial compression and bending. The analysis of a rafter pair is done in three stages. It begins by substituting for the loads that are actually distributed along the

lengths of the rafters equivalent pairs of forces that are concentrated at the joints. This allows us to perform the type of analysis that we have just carried out, either numerically or graphically, to find the axial forces and stresses in the rafters and ceiling joist. Then another analysis is made of the bending stresses in the rafters and joist that are caused by distribution of the loads over their lengths. Finally, the two sets of stresses are added together to determine the total stresses in the members.

Most trusses, including the one that we have just studied, are *planar trusses* whose members lie essentially in a single plane. *Space trusses* that are fully three-dimensional are also in common use (Fig. 5.16). The analysis of space trusses is more complex than that of planar trusses, but comes down to the same basic operations: the three-dimensional action of the members in space is resolved into a series of two-dimensional force components to which the equations of equilibrium can be applied.

TRUSS DETAILING

Laying out its shape and finding the forces in its members are only the first steps in the process of designing a truss. Once the forces are known, each member must be given an appropriate size and shape based on stress calculations of the type we have already done in earlier chapters. An analysis must also be made of the potential for buckling in compression members. Simultaneously, a method of connecting the members of the truss must be worked out, and all the joints must be designed so that they can transmit safely

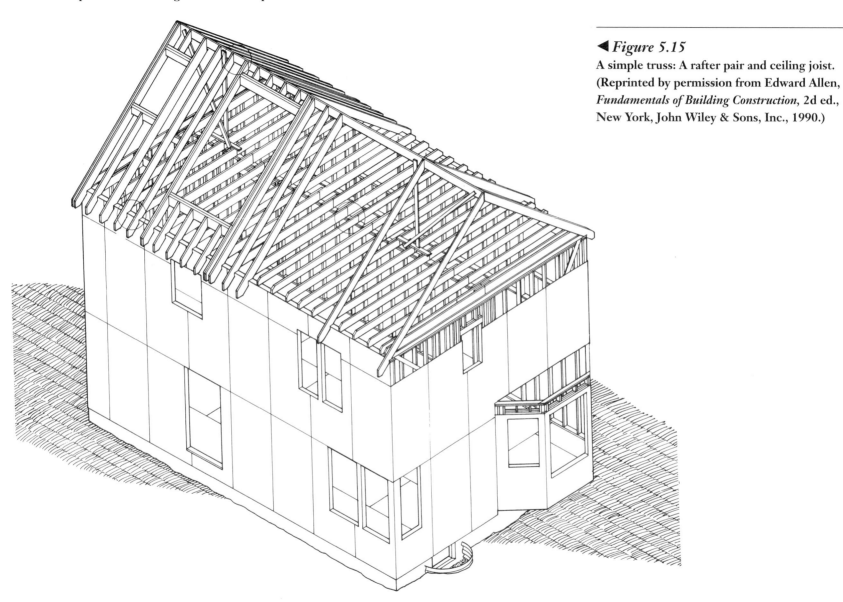

◀ *Figure 5.15*
A simple truss: A rafter pair and ceiling joist.
(Reprinted by permission from Edward Allen,
Fundamentals of Building Construction, 2d ed.,
New York, John Wiley & Sons, Inc., 1990.)

▲ *Figure 5.16*
A space truss. (Courtesy of Unistrut® Space Frame Systems.)

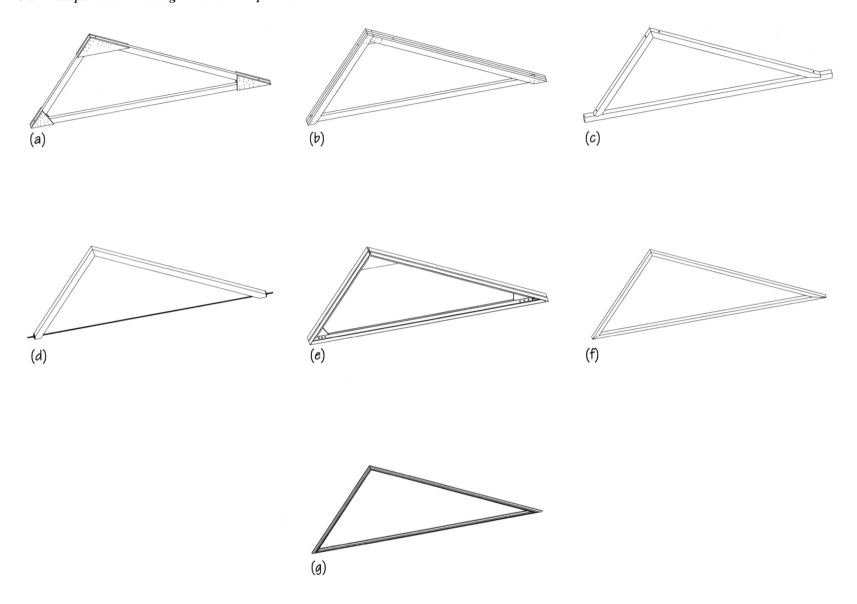

◀ *Figure 5.17*

Some ways of assembling the simple truss that we have analyzed.
(a) A single layer of wood members with side plates of plywood or steel,
connected with nails, screws, or bolts. (b) Three layers of wood mem-
bers that overlap, connected with nails or bolts. (c) Heavy timber mem-
bers notched and bolted. (d) Heavy timber top members with a steel rod
bottom member. (e) Two layers of steel angles bolted or welded to steel
gusset plates between the layers. (f) Square tubular members welded
together. (g) Round tubular members welded together.

from one member to another the forces that have been found. This includes a determination of the number, size, and exact placement of the bolts, nails, welds, plates, or other fasteners. Figure 5.17 suggests some ways in which our simple triangular truss might be assembled from wood and steel members. Notice that most of the joints in these constructions do not act strictly as hinges, but have some tendency to prevent rotation of the members. This tendency usually has little practical effect on the forces in the members.

CHANGING THE SPAN

The graphical method of analysis offers a quick, easy way of doing some experiments with our simple triangular truss to develop a sense of how trusses behave. First we will see what happens to the forces in the truss members if we double its *span* (the distance between its supports) from 3 m to 6 m, increasing its height proportionally so

that its shape remains the same. As we review the analyses that we have done, both numerical and graphical, we find that the span of the truss never played a part in them. Regardless of the scale of the truss, whether it spans one meter or a hundred, the member forces will remain the same as long as the external forces and the relative proportions of the truss remain the same. There are factors, however, that complicate this simple conclusion. Trusses with longer spans tend to have to carry heavier loads. If a roof truss, for example, spans 100 ft rather than 50 ft, it will generally have to carry twice as much load, and its own weight will increase by more than a factor of 2, because as a truss grows larger, its members grow longer. This has little practical effect on tension members, but as compression members grow longer, their slenderness ratios rise and the members often must be thickened accordingly to prevent buckling. Consider, too, that the member forces remain constant only if

the height of the truss increases in direct proportion to the increase in span. If the height is held constant as the span increases, the shape of the truss changes and member forces rise.

CHANGING THE MAGNITUDES OF THE LOADS

If we double the supported mass to 100 kg without changing the dimensions or geometry of the truss, what happens to the forces in its members? We can answer this question with a simple "thought experiment." We do not have to redraw the force polygon; we just imagine changing its scale to 1 mm = 10 N, instead of 1 mm = 5 N. If we do this, all the member forces will become double what they were under the original loading. We can deduce from this experiment that member forces in a truss vary in direct proportion to the magnitudes of the exterior forces.

CHANGING THE DEPTH OF THE TRUSS

In Figure 5.18, we experiment with four different depths for the simple truss. We construct the force polygons for all the options off the same load line so that we can make comparisons more easily. Even without taking measurements, the differences are clear: the deeper the truss is, the lower its member forces are. As the depth of the truss approaches zero, the member forces approach infinity. A good way to keep member forces low in a truss is to make the truss as deep as possible. The same general principle holds true for any spanning device, whether it is a beam, a slab, an arch, or a hanging cable: Increased depth results in lower internal forces.

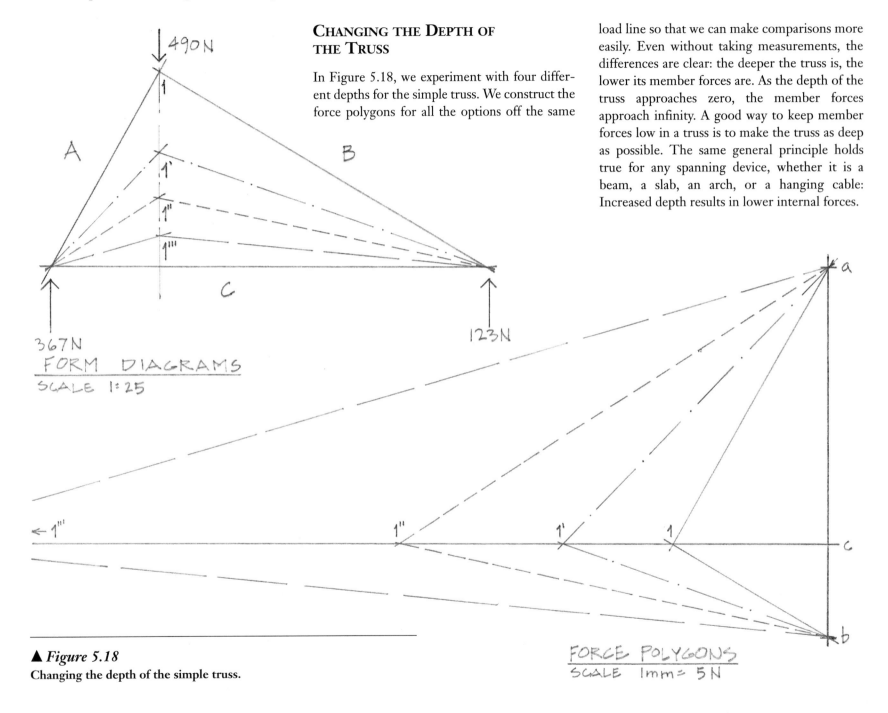

▲ *Figure 5.18*

Changing the depth of the simple truss.

As a truss becomes deeper, however, its members grow longer, which generally results in an increase of the weight and cost of the structure. We need to be able to find a depth that is optimal for a given set of conditions. For example, suppose that we have two pieces of lumber on hand to use for the sloping members of this truss, and we know that each of these pieces can carry safely an axial compressive force of 600 N. Can we regulate the depth of this truss so that its more heavily loaded sloping member carries exactly 600 N under a 50 kg external load, while keeping the reactions of 367 N and 123 N constant? This is easily done with the graphical method by constructing the force polygon first, and then the form diagram of the truss (Fig. 5.19). We begin with the load line, which we divide into the two known reactions, *bc* and *ca*, which are unaffected by a change in height of the truss. Then we set a compass for a radius of 600 N and swing an arc around *a* until it intersects the horizontal line that passes through *c*. This point of intersection determines the slopes of lines *a1* and *b1*, and therefore the slopes of members *A1* and *B1* on the form diagram, for a truss that meets our specification. The same result

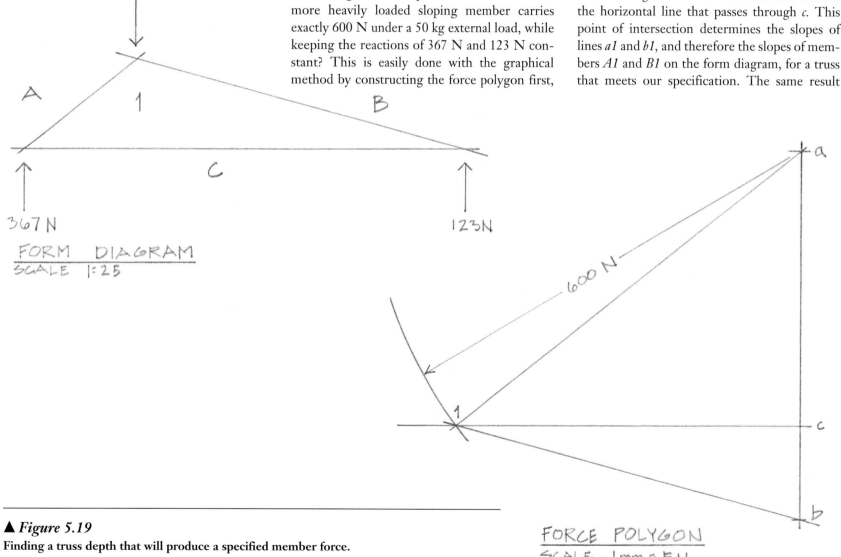

▲ Figure 5.19
Finding a truss depth that will produce a specified member force.

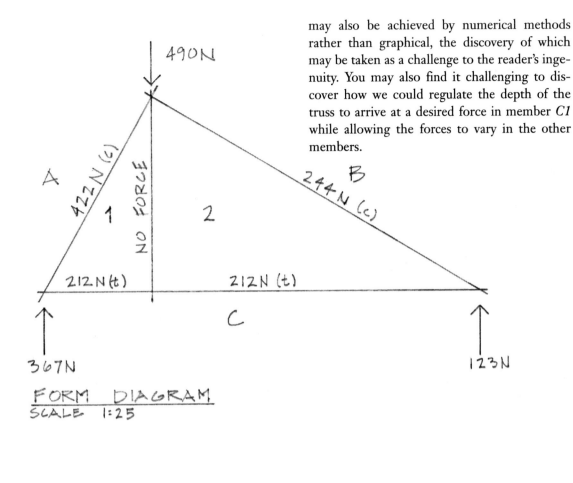

FORM DIAGRAM
SCALE 1:25

▲ *Figure 5.20*
Adding a kingpost to the truss.

may also be achieved by numerical methods rather than graphical, the discovery of which may be taken as a challenge to the reader's ingenuity. You may also find it challenging to discover how we could regulate the depth of the truss to arrive at a desired force in member *C1* while allowing the forces to vary in the other members.

ADDING A KINGPOST TO THE TRUSS

A simple triangular truss is often constructed with a vertical *kingpost* at its center. What is the role of this member? Figure 5.20 is a graphical analysis of a modified design that adds a kingpost to a simple triangular truss. It shows that the kingpost carries no force whatever, because points *1* and *2* on the force polygon occupy the same location. We should have been able to predict this before performing the analysis, because the two horizontal members, *C1* and *C2*, lie in the same line and are perpendicular to the king-

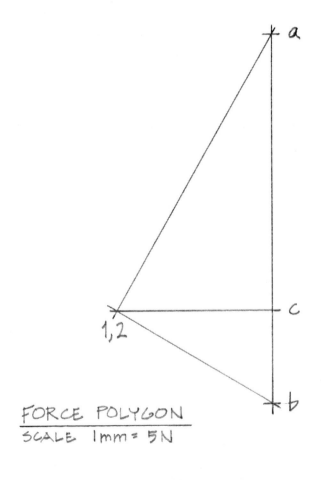

FORCE POLYGON
SCALE 1mm = 5N

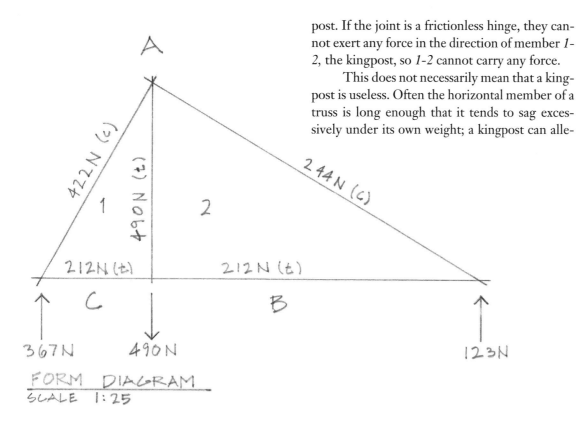

post. If the joint is a frictionless hinge, they cannot exert any force in the direction of member *1-2*, the kingpost, so *1-2* cannot carry any force.

This does not necessarily mean that a kingpost is useless. Often the horizontal member of a truss is long enough that it tends to sag excessively under its own weight; a kingpost can alleviate this situation. It can also allow a load to be hung from the bottom middle joint of the truss, which results, as you might expect, in a tensile force in the kingpost itself (Fig. 5.21). Notice all the changes that occur in the analysis when the load is moved from the top of the truss to the bottom. In the form diagram, the letter *A* now indicates the whole space over the top of the truss, from one reaction to the other, because no external load is applied anywhere in this interval. The space beneath the horizontal member is divided into *B* and *C* by the external load. The force polygon looks entirely different from those

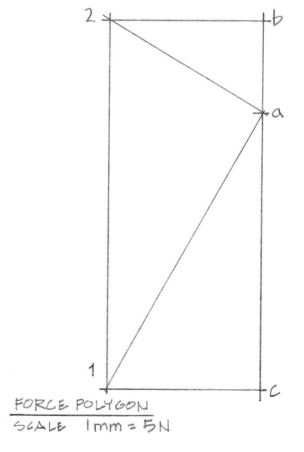

▲ *Figure 5.21*
Hanging the load from the bottom of a king post truss.

we constructed earlier, with a different layout for the load line and a different overall geometry. On the load line, *bc* represents the 490 N load, *ca* the left reaction, and *ab* the right reaction. To locate point *1*, *a1* and *c1* were plotted first. To locate point *2*, *1-2* and *b2* were drawn next. Then *a2* was added to close the diagram.

INVERTING THE TRUSS

If the external, vertical forces on the original top-loaded truss without kingpost are held constant in magnitude, direction, and point of application, and the triangular form of the truss is inverted, the characters of all the member forces reverse (Fig. 5.22). Tension becomes compression, and vice versa. The absolute values of the member forces remain constant. This is true of all trusses, as long as the external forces are all vertical.

APPLYING AN INCLINED LOAD TO THE TRUSS

Trusses are often subjected to nonvertical loads. A common example of this is the pressure exerted by wind on a sloping roof, which is assumed to act perpendicular to the surface, applying inclined loads to the supporting structure. The effect of inclined loads on member forces in a truss may be assessed by either numerical or graphical means; the graphical assessment is especially easy.

Figure 5.23 shows our original triangular truss subjected to a single load at its apex that is inclined at an angle of 15° to the vertical. In this example, referring back to Fig. 5.1, the hinge and roller connections at the two reactions take

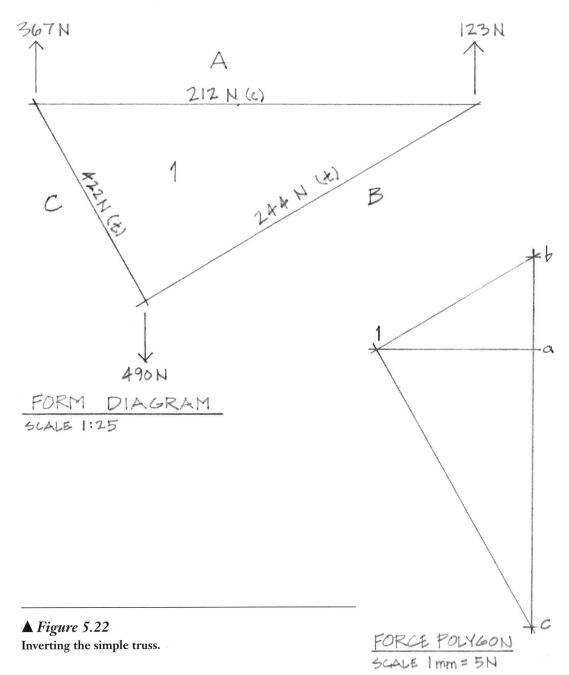

▲ *Figure 5.22*
Inverting the simple truss.

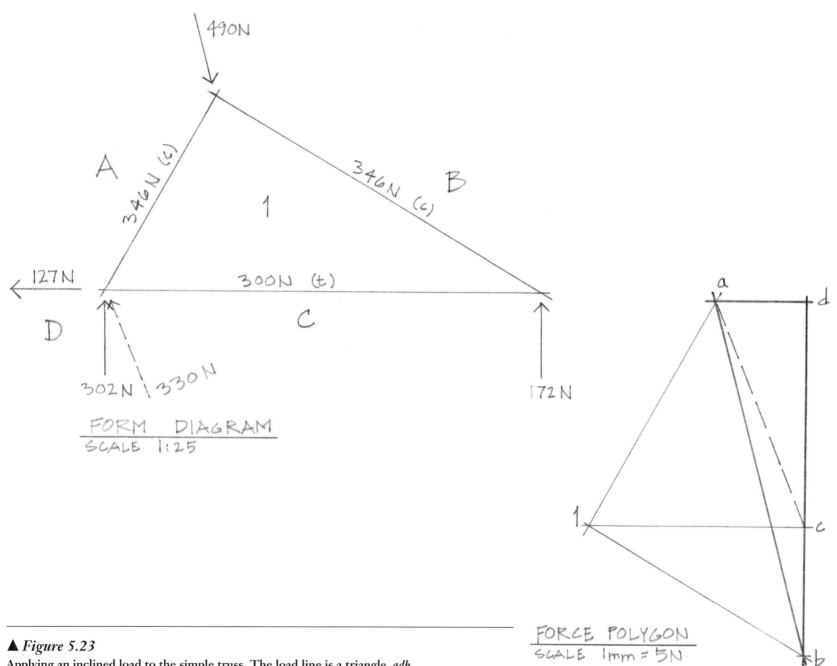

490N

A

346N (c)

B

346N (c)

1

127N

300N (t)

D

C

302N 330N

172N

FORM   DIAGRAM
SCALE 1:25

a   d

1   c

b

FORCE POLYGON
SCALE 1mm = 5N

▲ *Figure 5.23*
Applying an inclined load to the simple truss. The load line is a triangle, *adb*.

on particular significance, because an inclined load has a horizontal component as well as a vertical one. The roller to the right can transmit only a vertical reaction, which means that the entire horizontal component of the load will be resisted by the hinge at the lower left. We choose to represent the lower left reaction in the form of its horizontal and vertical components. Thus, a letter, *D* in this case, is placed between these two components when we assign letters to the spaces between forces on the outside of the truss.

Construction of the load line begins with *ab*, which is 490 N long and inclined at 15° to the vertical. At this point, we do not know the magnitudes of the reactions, only their directions. We know that *bc* and *cd* are vertical and that *da* is horizontal. This allows us to draw a vertical line through *b* and a horizontal one through *a* to complete the load line, although we do not know where *c* lies on line segment *bd*. The load line is a triangle rather than a single line. We can scale the magnitude of *da*, 127 N, which is clearly depicted on the load line as being the horizontal component of the 490-N load.

The only joint with fewer than three unknowns is *AB1*, so we begin the analysis there, drawing *a1* and *b1* on the force polygon to locate point *1*. Next we move to the lower right joint, drawing *1c* horizontally to find point *c*. This completes the force polygon, from which we can scale all the reactions and member forces. Both *b1* and *1a* scale at 346 N. Is this a coincidence? No—the angle at which the 490-N load is applied to the truss in this example is such that each of these forces is exerted at the same angle to the applied load, so that they share the load equally. In other words, the line of action of load *AB* bisects the angle between members *A1* and *B1*.

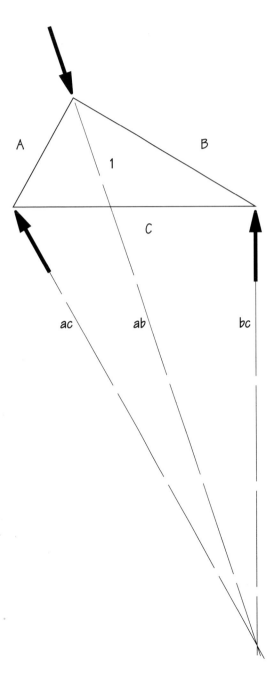

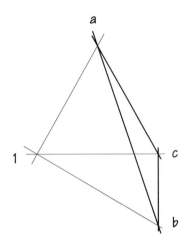

◄ *Figure 5.24*
Equilibrium of the external forces on the truss under an inclined load.

The force polygon gives us the horizontal and vertical components of the left reaction, *ad* and *dc*. We find the direction and magnitude of the reaction itself by drawing line *ca*, which represents the resultant of *ad* and *dc*. The direction and magnitude of *ca* are those of the reaction. This makes sense: if we remove the two components of the reaction and the letter between them from the form diagram and replace them with a single force, the name of this force is *CA*.

If the lines of action of the 490-N load and the two reactions are extended downward, the three meet at a single point, as they must do if the truss is in equilibrium (Fig. 5.24). This serves as a check on the accuracy of our work.

WHAT WE HAVE LEARNED SO FAR ABOUT TRUSSES

We have expended considerable time and effort on the examination of some very simple trusses. It has been worth doing because we have learned how to find the forces in the members of a truss by both numerical and graphical means. We have learned that changing the span of a truss has no effect on its member forces if its loads and geometry remain constant. We know that if we change the external loads on a truss by proportional amounts, the member forces change in the same proportion. We know that member forces decrease if the depth of a truss is increased, and increase if the depth decreases. If a vertically loaded truss is inverted but its loads and reactions are unchanged in magnitude and direction, we know that the characters of the forces in all its members are reversed. We have learned that we can solve for forces in a truss with inclined loads just as we can for one with only vertical loads. And we have a beginning understanding of some common ways in which trusses may be assembled from wood or metal. Thus, we have already developed a broad, fundamental understanding of truss behavior that will serve us well as we study more complex trusses in the next chapter.

Key Terms and Concepts

truss
form diagram
Bow's notation
interval notation
closing of load line

closing of force polygon
Maxwell diagram
Cremona plan
method of joints
planar truss

space truss
span
kingpost
rafter
ceiling joist

Exercises

You may develop solutions to these exercises numerically or graphically, or you may use one to check the other.

1. At the base of a building, a vertical load of 1500 kips is redirected from a single column above to two columns below by using a triangular truss (Fig. 5.25). Find a height for this truss such that each compressive member carries a load of 1250 kips. What is the force in the horizontal member?

Figure 5.25 ▶
Redirecting a load from one column to two.

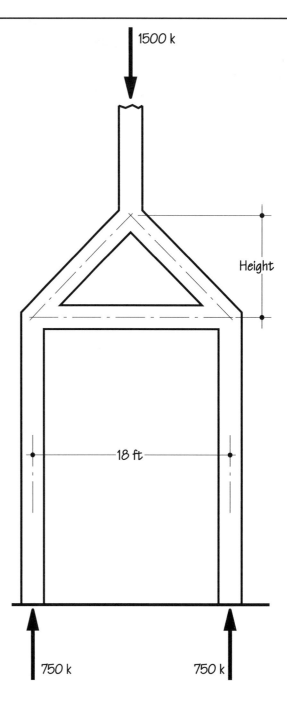

2. A hanging cable supports a single mass of 27,000 kg (Fig. 5.26). Assuming that the weight of the cable is negligible, what is the force in the compression member that holds the ends of the cable apart? What is the force in each segment of the cable?

▼ *Figure 5.26* **A hanging cable structure.**

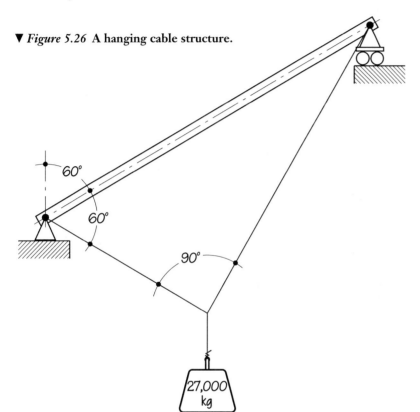

3. The solid lines in Figure 5.27 show a kingpost truss whose bottom member is level. Find the forces in the members of this truss as drawn. What happens to the forces in the members if the center of the bottom member is raised so that the inclination of its two halves is 15° to the horizontal? 30°? What happens to the forces if the center of the bottom member is depressed to an angle of 15° below the horizontal?

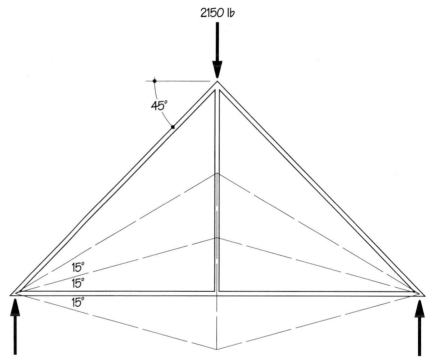

▲ *Figure 5.27* **Kingpost trusses with various bottom chord angles.**

4. A pair of rafters span a house that is 7 m wide (Fig. 5.28). The slope of the rafters is 1 m of vertical rise for each 2 m of horizontal distance. The rafters support a load of 700 N per meter of horizontal span. The lower end of each rafter rests directly on the top of the supporting wall. How many nails are needed to connect each end of the ceiling joist to the rafter if each nail can transmit safely a force of 420 N?

5. Assume that the shortest diagonals in the truss pictured in Figure 5.29 have an inclination of 45°. A man stands on the rear platform of the caboose, which is the second car behind the engine. If the wheels nearest him apply a load of 10 kips to the top of the vertical strut below, trace the path by which this load is transmitted to the two stone supports. Find the force that this load creates in each member of the truss.

Figure 5.29 ▶

A nineteenth-century Fink truss carries a train across a river. The highway bridge in the background is supported by wooden arches; it is covered by walls and a roof to keep the wooden structure dry and free from decay. (Smithsonian Institution Photo No. 41,436.)

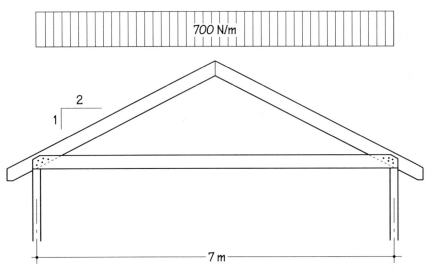

▲ *Figure 5.28* **A rafter pair and ceiling joist.**

CHAPTER SIX

MULTIPANEL TRUSSES

The roof of the Sainsbury Centre, an art museum and studio building in Norwich, England, is supported by Warren trusses welded together from round steel tubing. The span is 34 m (112 ft). Trusses are paired in an inverted delta arrangement that creates excellent stability against out-of-plane forces such as buckling of the top chords. If you lay a straightedge along the truss, you will see that the designers have given it a substantial camber by making the bottom chord segments slightly shorter than the top chord segments. The camber compensates for any deflection of the truss and imparts to the viewer a sense that the truss carries its load with ease. Slip joints and a floppy rubber airseal gasket were installed between the lower chord of the truss and the top of the glass wall to deal with anticipated deflections of up to 84 mm (3.3 in.) at midspan. Architects: Foster and Partners. Structural engineer: Anthony Hunt Associates. (Photo: Ken Kirkwood AFAEP.)

In the preceding chapter, we learned some secrets of the behavior of trusses in general by examining some very simple trusses, each of which consisted of a single triangle of members, or a single triangle with a kingpost. Now we will extend this knowledge to larger, more complex trusses. Figure 6.1 illustrates the terminology that is applied to trusses. The top and bottom members of a truss are the *chords*. The members that connect the top and bottom chords are the *web members*. The web members can be further identified as *verticals* and *diagonals*. Compression members of trusses are often called *struts*, and tension members, *ties*. The portion of a truss that is bounded by adjacent verticals is called a *panel*. The points at which members converge may be termed *joints*, *panel points*, or, less commonly, *nodes*.

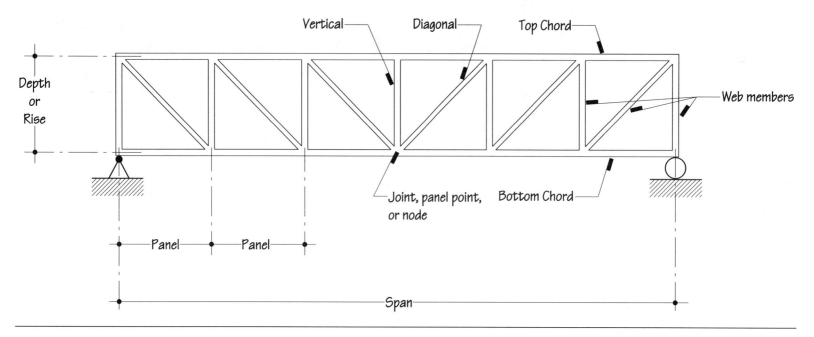

▲ *Figure 6.1*
Truss terminology.

GRAPHICAL ANALYSIS OF A SIX-PANEL FLAT TRUSS

We begin our examination of multipanel trusses by finding the forces in the members of a simply supported six-panel *flat truss* (also called a *parallel chord truss*) with 45° diagonals that slope downward toward the center of the truss. A vertical load of 1600 lb is applied to each panel point along the top chord. The span is 48 ft.

Our analysis will follow the graphical procedure that we developed in the Chapter Five. First, we draw an accurate form diagram of the truss at the upper left corner of the sheet (Fig. 6.2). This is constructed to a convenient scale of length to length, ⅛ inch to the foot in this example, so as to represent accurately the shape of the truss and the slopes of its members. We draw vectors to represent the loads on the truss.

Next we find the two reactions on the truss and add their vectors to the force diagram. Because the loading is symmetrical in this case, we simply assign half the total load to each reaction. The form diagram is now a complete free-body diagram of the truss (Fig. 6.3). Working clockwise and from left to right, we apply inter-

val notation to the diagram, assigning capital letters to the spaces between external forces and numbers to internal spaces. (The letter *I* has been omitted to avoid confusion with the numeral *1*.)

To the right of the form diagram, we begin the construction of a force polygon by plotting a load line to a convenient scale of length to force; here 1 in. equals 2500 lb. Using interval notation and working clockwise around the truss from the upper left, we tick off carefully measured increments of vertical length on the load line to represent each of the applied loads. This brings us

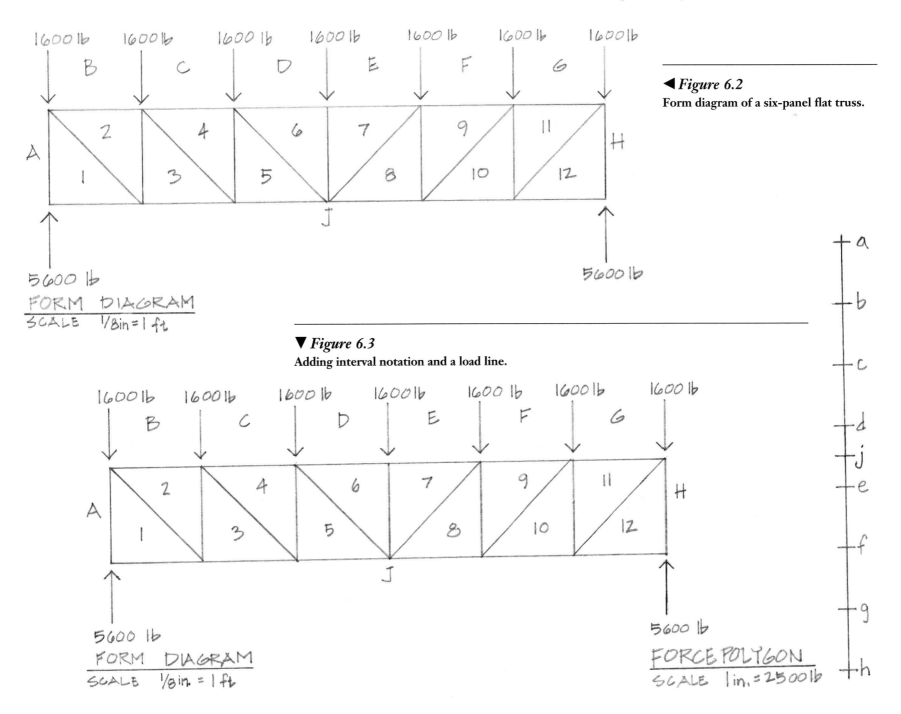

▼ *Figure 6.3*
Adding interval notation and a load line.

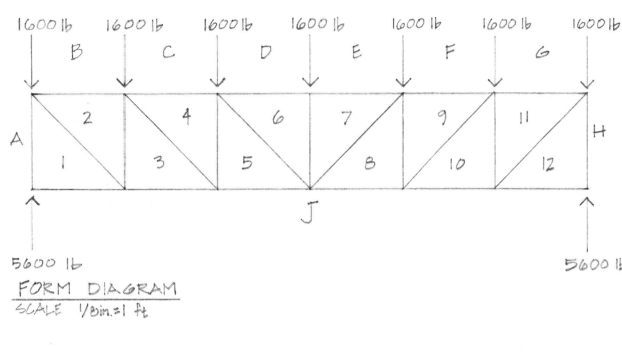

FORM DIAGRAM
SCALE 1/8in.=1 ft

▲ *Figure 6.4*
Starting construction of the force polygon.

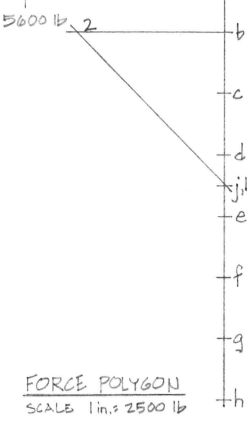

FORCE POLYGON
SCALE 1 in.= 2500 lb

to *h* at the bottom. The right-hand reaction is *HJ*, an upward-acting force that we plot on the load line as a segment that begins at *h* and extends upward to *j* at a location that is 5600 lb above. Finally, we plot the left-hand reaction as *ja*, another upward force that closes the load line back to its point of origin. This completes our clockwise tour of the external forces. If *ja* does not scale to 5600 lb, we have made an error somewhere in laying out the load line and must find and correct this error before proceeding. (A good way to avoid cumulative errors of measurement in the load line is to measure each of the loads from the end of the line rather than from

the previous tick mark: measure and mark *ab* as 1600 lb, then *ac* as 3200 lb, *ad* as 4800 lb, and so on.)

Examining the left end of the truss, we find that the only joint with fewer than three unknown forces is *A1J*, so this is where we begin our analysis of the members of the truss (Fig. 6.4). On the force polygon, the forces in the two members that meet at *A1J* are represented by a vertical line segment, *a1*, that intersects a horizontal line segment *j1* at point *1*. Line segment *a1* must pass vertically through *a*, which means that it lies along the load line, and *j1* must pass horizontally through *j*. These conditions can be satisfied only if point *1* lies precisely at *j*. Because

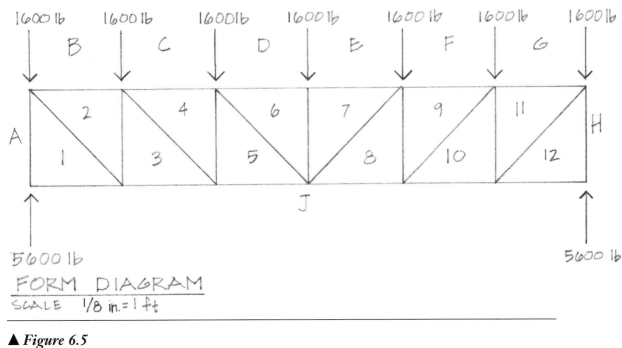

▲ Figure 6.5

Continuing construction of the force polygon.

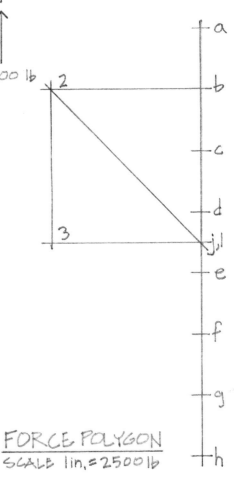

it has zero length, *j1* is a point rather than a line, which means that *J1* is a zero-force member.

Now that we have determined the length of *a1*, we are ready to solve for the forces at the upper left-hand joint, *AB2-1*. The two remaining unknown forces at this joint are in members *B2* and *2-1*. We construct lines *b2* and *2-1* parallel to these members on the force polygon. Thus, *b2* is a horizontal line through *b* on the load line, and *2-1* is a diagonal line through *1*. The point of intersection of these lines is the location of point *2*.

In Figure 6.5, we continue to find the forces in the truss by moving to the next joint

that has only two unknown forces, which is *1-2-3J*. The unknown forces are in members *2-3* and *3J*; we plot lines *2-3* and *3j* on the force polygon parallel to these members to find point *3*.

We repeat this process, moving joint by joint across the truss. We move each time to an adjacent joint that has only two unknown forces. **The second number in the name of the web member is always the same as the number in the name of the chord member that is considered at the same time.** If the numbers were applied systematically left to right on the form diagram, **the common number at each step is always one higher than the number that was**

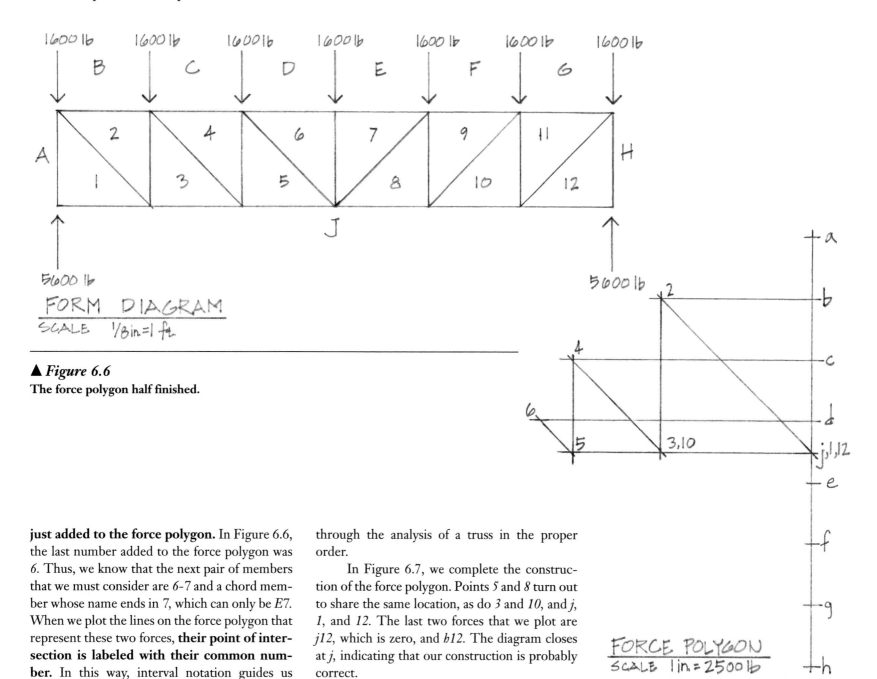

▲ Figure 6.6
The force polygon half finished.

just added to the force polygon. In Figure 6.6, the last number added to the force polygon was 6. Thus, we know that the next pair of members that we must consider are 6-7 and a chord member whose name ends in 7, which can only be E7. When we plot the lines on the force polygon that represent these two forces, **their point of intersection is labeled with their common number.** In this way, interval notation guides us

through the analysis of a truss in the proper order.

In Figure 6.7, we complete the construction of the force polygon. Points *5* and *8* turn out to share the same location, as do *3* and *10*, and *j*, *1*, and *12*. The last two forces that we plot are *j12*, which is zero, and *h12*. The diagram closes at *j*, indicating that our construction is probably correct.

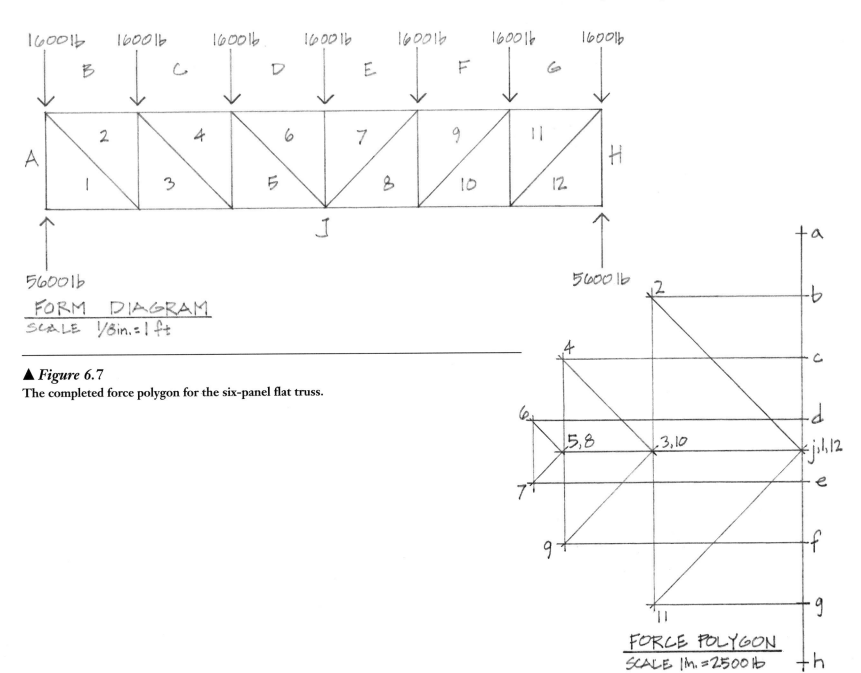

1600 lb   1600 lb   1600 lb   1600 lb   1600 lb   1600 lb   1600 lb

B   C   D   E   F   G

A   H

2   4   6   7   9   11

1   3   5   8   10   12

J

5600 lb   5600 lb

FORM   DIAGRAM
SCALE ⅛ in. = 1 ft

▲ *Figure 6.7*
The completed force polygon for the six-panel flat truss.

a
2   b
4   c
6   d
5,8   3,10   j,1,12
7   e
9   f
11   g
h

FORCE POLYGON
SCALE 1 in. = 2500 lb

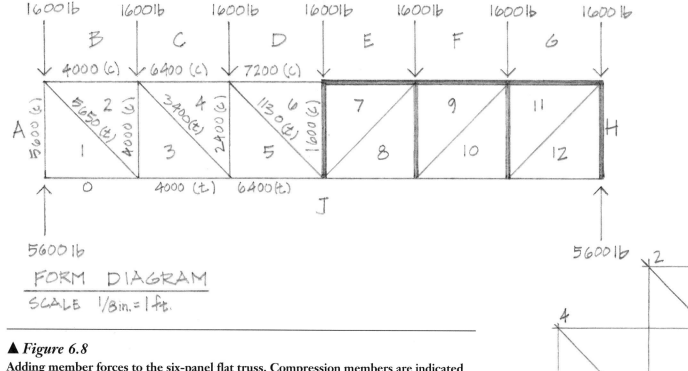

FORM DIAGRAM
SCALE 1/8 in. = 1 ft.

▲ *Figure 6.8*
Adding member forces to the six-panel flat truss. Compression members are indicated by heavy lines on the right half of the form diagram.

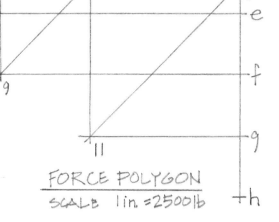

FORCE POLYGON
SCALE 1 in. = 2500 lb

The last steps in the analysis are to measure the line segments in the force polygon to find their magnitudes, and to apply interval notation to determine their characters. Figure 6.8 shows the resulting information applied to half the truss. The values for the other half are mirror images of these values.

To review the method of finding the character of the forces in the members, let us examine the joint just to the right of center on the top chord of the truss, which is named *EF9-8-7* in clockwise order (Fig. 6.8). It helps to place the index finger of the left hand on this joint on the form diagram and to keep it there while proceeding. The top chord segment to the right of the joint, named in clockwise order, is *F9*. On the force polygon, a motion of the right index finger from *f* to *9* is leftward, meaning that member *F9* presses to the left on the joint where our left index finger lies, and is therefore in compression. Similarly, moving from *9* to *8* on the force polygon, we move upward, toward the left index finger, indicating a compressive force, and so on.

UNDERSTANDING THE BEHAVIOR OF THE SIX-PANEL TRUSS

Examination of the magnitudes of the forces in this truss shows that the forces in the top and bottom chords are least in the end panels of the truss and rise panel by panel to maximum values at the center. The forces in the web members vary in just the opposite manner: they are least in

the center panels and reach their maxima in the end panels. This pattern is typical of uniformly loaded, simply supported trusses. Later on, when we study beam behavior, we will find that the forces inside solid beams follow a very similar pattern.

Figure 6.9 shows a way of visualizing the paths that loads take through this truss. At the center of this model is an inverted kingpost truss

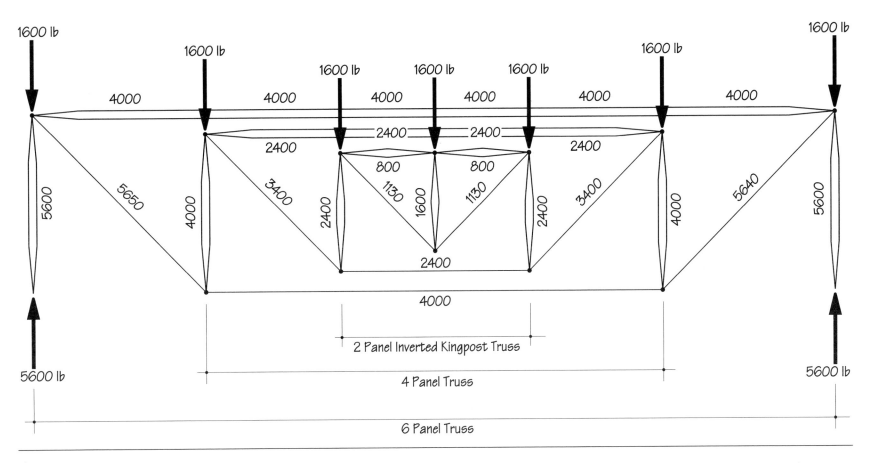

▲ *Figure 6.9*
Visualizing load paths through the six-panel truss.

of two panels that supports a single load of 1600 lb at midspan. The member forces in this truss are indicated on it. Each thick, tapered member is a compressive strut, and each single-line member is a tensile tie.

Each end of the two-panel inverted king-post truss is supported on a vertical strut that also bears an additional 1600-lb load. These two struts are supported by a tie whose two sloping ends are held apart by a long horizontal strut. Taken together, all these members make up a four-panel truss. The four-panel truss is supported in turn by a construction made up of two more vertical struts that are held up by a long tie and a horizontal strut, thus arriving at the full six-panel configuration.

The forces in the web members of these nested trusses are identical to those that we found for the original six-panel truss. The forces in the top and bottom chords of the three nested trusses can be added to arrive at the magnitude of the chord forces in the original truss. Thus, the bottom chord forces in the center panels of the original truss are 2400 lb plus 4000 lb, or 6400 lb. The top chord forces for the center panels are 4000 lb plus 2400 lb plus 800 lb, or 7200 lb. The chord forces for the remaining panels may be found similarly.

The center joint in the bottom chord, in addition to being pulled horizontally in each direction with a force of 6400 lb, is also acted upon by two diagonal pulls of 1130 lb each. The horizontal component of the 1130-lb force is a pull of 800 lb. Added to the force in the lower chord, the total horizontal pull on the joint is 7200 lb, which is equal to the maximum compression in the top chord.

Figure 6.10 ▶

Reversing the direction of the diagonal members: a flat Pratt truss above, a flat Howe truss below.

REVERSING THE DIRECTION OF THE DIAGONAL MEMBERS

What happens if the diagonals of this truss, instead of sloping downward toward the middle, slope upward instead? Figure 6.10 tells the answer. In each form diagram, the compressive members are shown as thick lines, tensile members as thin lines, and zero-force members as broken lines. When the direction of the diagonal members is reversed, the character of the forces in all the web members, both diagonal and vertical, reverses. The magnitudes of the forces, however, stay the same.

The truss with the tensile diagonals is called a flat *Pratt truss*, after its inventor. The Pratt design is an excellent choice for a steel truss, whose members tend to be very slender, because its long diagonal members are in tension and therefore are not subject to buckling. The vertical members are less likely to buckle because they are shorter than the diagonals and experience lower forces. The truss design with the compressive diagonals, called a flat *Howe truss*, is often preferred for heavy timber trusses. Whereas steel tensile members may be joined strongly with bolts or welds, bolted tensile joints in timber are relatively weak. The Howe configuration allows the diagonal members to transfer their forces to the vertical and horizontal members by bearing directly against them, and timber members tend to be thick enough that buckling is less likely to be a problem than in steel members.

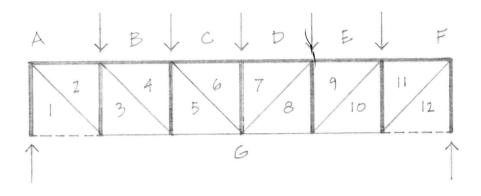

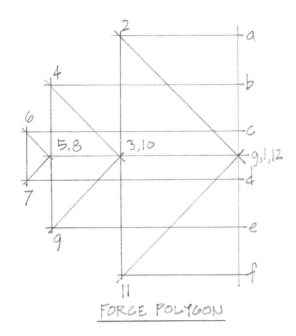

FORCE POLYGON

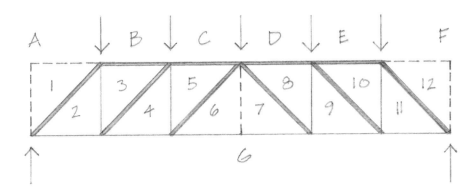

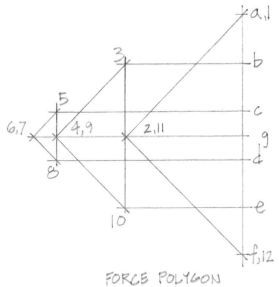

FORCE POLYGON

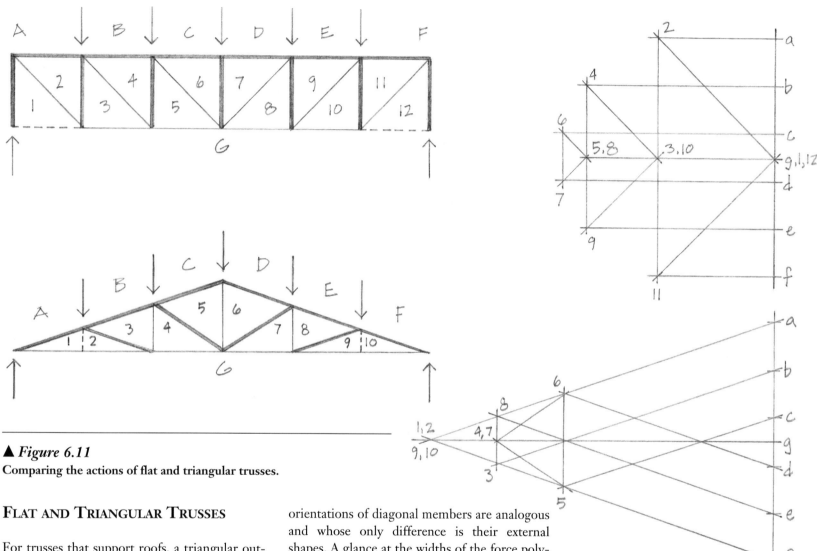

▲ *Figure 6.11*
Comparing the actions of flat and triangular trusses.

FLAT AND TRIANGULAR TRUSSES

For trusses that support roofs, a triangular out-line is often used, with the slope of the roof establishing the slope of the top chords of the truss. Triangular trusses are sometimes called *gable* trusses, after the double-sloped gable roofs that they support. Does a triangular truss behave differently from a rectangular one? Figure 6.11 compares two trusses whose depth, loads, and orientations of diagonal members are analogous and whose only difference is their external shapes. A glance at the widths of the force polygons tells us that member forces are substantially higher in the triangular truss, a situation that can be overcome by increasing its depth. The indications of tensile and compressive members on the form diagrams tell us that the characters of the forces in the web members are opposite in the two trusses, even though the direction of inclina-tion of the diagonals is the same. This leads to a somewhat confusing situation in the naming of trusses. Whereas the parallel-chord truss shown in this figure is a flat Pratt truss, the triangular

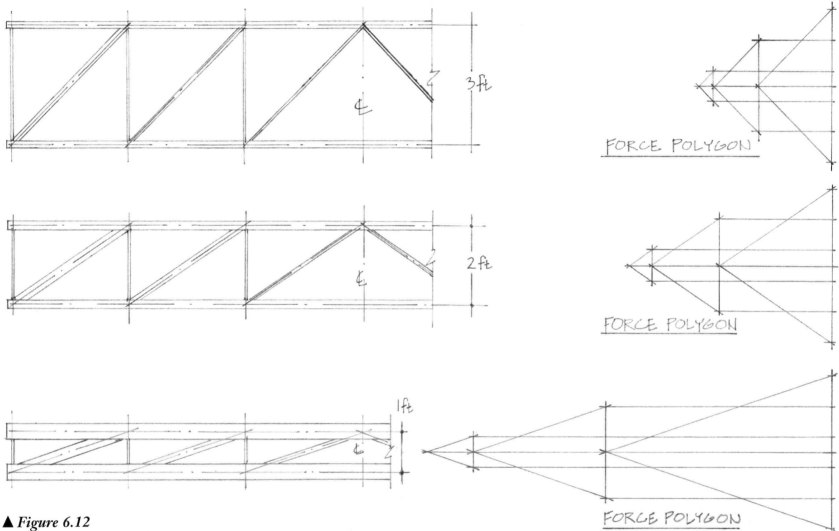

▲ *Figure 6.12*
The effect on member sizes of reducing the depth of a truss.

truss with the analogous inclination of diagonals is a triangular Howe truss. For a triangular truss to be a Pratt, which by definition has tensile diagonals, its diagonals must be inclined in the opposite direction from those in a flat Pratt truss.

REDUCING THE DEPTH OF A FLAT TRUSS

Figure 6.12 depicts the left halves of three six-panel flat Howe trusses, each made of laminated wood members. All three trusses support identi-

cal loads of 1600 lb at each panel point. The top truss is 3 ft deep, the middle one is 2 ft deep, and the bottom one is only 1 ft deep, as measured between the centerlines of the top and bottom chords. The forces in the members of each truss have been found by constructing its force polygon to the right, and each member has been given a thickness based purely on the magnitude of the force it must carry, assuming a uniform stress in all members of 1500 psi and disregarding any potential for buckling of compression members. As is the usual practice in detailing trusses, the center axes of the members are made to coincide with the lines of the form diagrams of the three trusses.

It is apparent from the force polygons that the forces in the members of the shallowest truss are several times higher than in the members of the deepest one. In fact, as the depth of the truss approaches zero, the member forces rise more and more rapidly. If the chords of the shallowest truss were forced to lie entirely within the 1-ft depth rather than being centered on it, the truss would have to be solid wood. It would become, in other words, a wooden beam rather than a truss.

This demonstration illustrates two important lessons. The first is that a truss needs sufficient depth to operate efficiently. In general, a truss must be deeper than a beam to carry the same load over the same span. (In exchange for this disadvantage, however, a truss offers brilliant advantages: it uses much less material than a beam, and trusses in general can span much, much farther than beams.) The second lesson is that the internal behavior of a solid beam is strikingly similar to that of a truss, a phenomenon that we will study in a subsequent volume.

A Truss with an Odd Number of Panels

So far, we have examined only trusses with an even number of panels. Figure 6.13 shows an analysis of member forces in a five-panel truss

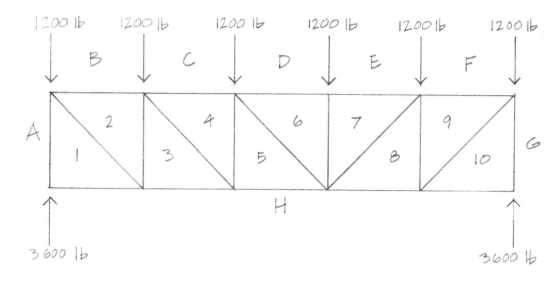

▲ *Figure 6.13*
A truss with an odd number of panels.

that has identical loads of 1200 lb at its panel points. The unique feature of this truss proves to be that its middle diagonal, 5-6, is a zero-force member. If the uniform character of the loading is reliably constant, and if the truss is assembled in such a way that it derives significant stiffness from its joints (as it does when the top and bottom chords are single pieces that are as long as the truss), the diagonal may be omitted from the center panel. This is the basis for floor truss designs in both wood and steel in which the diagonal is omitted in the center panels to allow for the passage of large air-conditioning ductwork. It also suggests that any web members in the center panel of an exposed truss could be designed more for visual delight than for structural function.

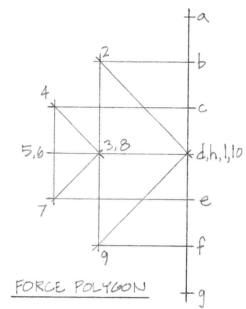

FORCE POLYGON

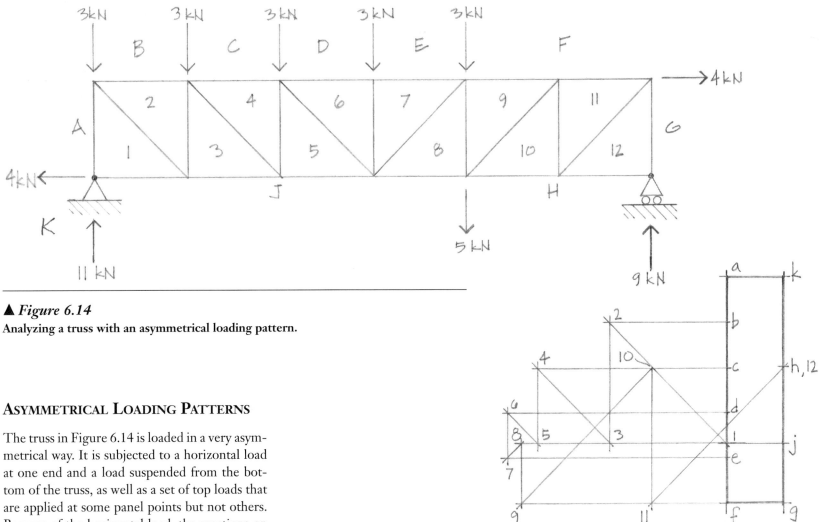

▲ *Figure 6.14*
Analyzing a truss with an asymmetrical loading pattern.

ASYMMETRICAL LOADING PATTERNS

The truss in Figure 6.14 is loaded in a very asymmetrical way. It is subjected to a horizontal load at one end and a load suspended from the bottom of the truss, as well as a set of top loads that are applied at some panel points but not others. Because of the horizontal load, the reactions on this truss must be found by assuming that one of them passes through a roller and therefore must be vertical. This assumption having been made, the reactions are readily found by taking moments about each support. The resulting load line is a rectangle, *akgf*. The force polygon is asymmetrical but is easily constructed and closes with segment *12g*. This example demonstrates that the graphical method of truss analysis is general and applies to any combination of loads. Inclined loads can be included either by resolving each of them into horizontal and vertical components or, as is more commonly done, by including them as inclined segments in the load line, as we did in the preceding chapter.

HINGES AND ROLLERS

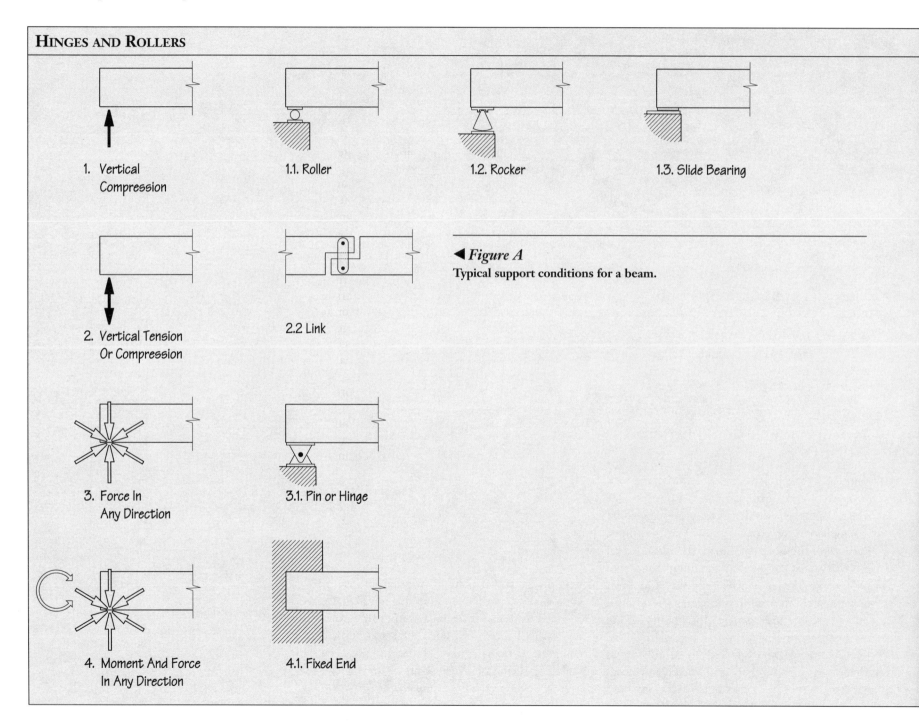

1. Vertical Compression

1.1. Roller

1.2. Rocker

1.3. Slide Bearing

2. Vertical Tension Or Compression

2.2 Link

◀ *Figure A*
Typical support conditions for a beam.

3. Force In Any Direction

3.1. Pin or Hinge

4. Moment And Force In Any Direction

4.1. Fixed End

The type of support that is provided at each reaction of a truss, arch, or beam has an important effect on the distribution of forces throughout the member (Fig. A).

- A **roller** or **rocker** (1.1, 1.2) cannot transmit moment. It can transmit only compressive force, and it can do so only in a direction that is perpendicular to the surface on which it bears. The same effect can be achieved with a **slide bearing** (1.3), which depends on petroleum grease or slippery Teflon plastic between two metal plates to avoid transmission of lateral forces.
- A **link** (2.1), like a roller or a rocker, cannot transmit moment. It can transmit either tensile or compressive force along its axis.
- A **pin** or **hinge** (3.1) also cannot transmit moment, but it can transmit a force in any direction.
- A **fixed end** (4.1) can transmit any direction and character of force, as well as moment.

When analyzing a simply supported spanning element such as a truss or beam, we usually show diagrammatically on the free-body diagram a hinge support at one reaction and a roller support at the other (Fig. B). This enables us to assume with confidence that the reaction at the roller is vertical. Any lateral component of the reactions must pass through the hinge. A hinge-and-roller support condition also assures that there will be no forces placed on the structural element by thermal expansion and contraction, material shrinkage, or small movements in foundations.

To be certain that the conditions for which a beam or truss is designed are those that it will actually experience, rollers, slide bearings, hinges, and rockers are often translated literally into support hardware in bridge construction and in the longer-spanning elements of large buildings (Fig. C). Because of the high concentrations of forces that pass through very small areas of their material, these elements are invariably made of steel, regardless of the predominant material of the structure of which they are a part. By keeping an eye out as you pass under bridges and walk through very large enclosed spaces, you will discover a surprising variety of practical ways of creating these details.

▲ *Figure C*
This large hinge beneath a bridge transmits a reaction from a foundation to a steel plate girder that spans more than 200 ft (60 m). The pin is about 6 in. (150 mm) in diameter, and the whole assembly is about 5 ft (1.5 m) high. (Photo by Edward Allen.)

▲ *Figure B*
Diagrammatic representation of a simply supported beam.

HINGES AND ROLLERS *(continued)*

The famous concrete hinges in Maillart's arch bridges function mainly through the flexing action of steel reinforcing bars (Fig. D). The crossing of the bars at the hinge point reduces their resistance to bending almost to zero.

A fixed-end condition for a beam of any material may be created by embedding it deeply into a large, inert mass of masonry or concrete (Fig. E[a]). In steel construction, a beam whose flanges are fully welded to a stiff steel column is considered to have a fixed end (b). In concrete construction, fixed ends are easily created by placing steel reinforcing bars continuously through the connections (c). Except for cantilevers, structural elements with one or more fixed ends are statically indeterminate, which makes them somewhat more difficult to analyze than those with ends that are free to rotate. However, fixed ends usually create a much more efficient utilization of the material in a beam, which results in a lower overall cost for a structure.

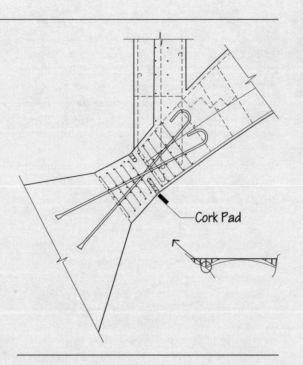

Cork Pad

▲ *Figure D*

Detail of the concrete and steel hinge at the end of Robert Maillart's Salginatobel Bridge in Switzerland. The rotations of a hinge in a structure are so minute that the concrete in the hinge is not subjected to tensile stress.

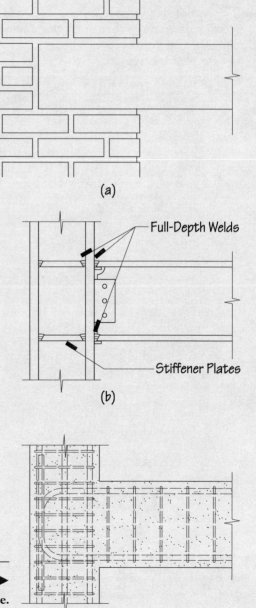

(a)

Full-Depth Welds

Stiffener Plates

(b)

(c)

Figure E ▶

Fixed-end conditions in masonry, steel, and concrete.

It is helpful in understanding various support conditions to imagine that each is made up entirely of links (Fig. F). A roller, rocker, slide bearing, or link is equivalent to a single link. A pin is equivalent to two links. A fixed end is equivalent to three links. A stable support condition cannot be created with a total of only one or two links. If the total number of links that support a single span is three, the support is both stable and statically determinate. A support condition that totals four or more links is statically indeterminate.

Most beams, joists, rafters, and purlins in buildings span modest distances and are bolted, nailed, or welded to their supporting members with simple connections that, strictly speaking, are neither hinges nor rollers. Yet these common connections offer little restraint against rotation and act almost as hinges, thus avoiding any significant level of incidental forces in the members. ■

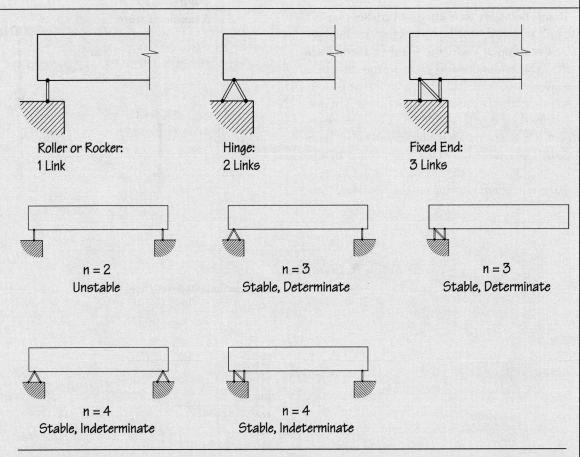

▲ *Figure F*
Visualizing support devices as being made up of links.

A Cantilever Truss

To this point, we have examined trusses that are *simply supported*, that is, trusses that are held up by a reaction at each end. Figure 6.15 shows a truss that is designed to carry a projecting balcony of a concert hall. This is referred to as a *cantilever* truss because it is supported only at one end by a rigid wall or column. The upper support is a horizontal link that is hinged at both ends. The lower support is a hinge. What are the member forces in this truss, and what are the magnitudes and directions of the reactions?

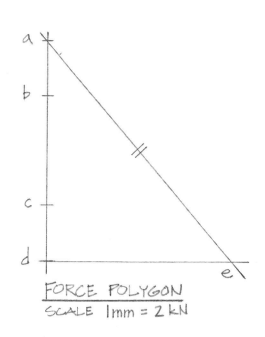

Figure 6.15 ▶
A cantilever truss.

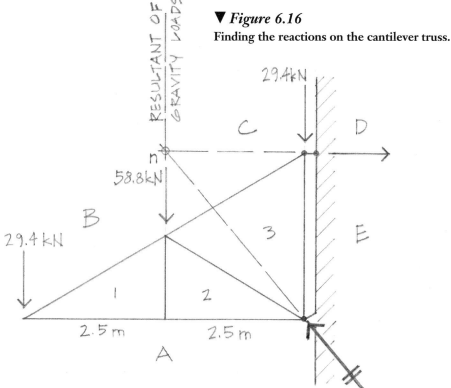

▼ **Figure 6.16**
Finding the reactions on the cantilever truss.

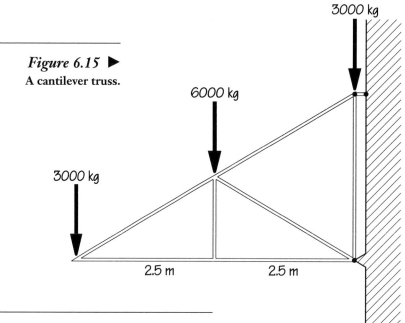

We convert the loads in kilograms to forces in kilonewtons and construct a combined form diagram and free-body diagram of the truss, on which we indicate all the external forces that act on it (Fig. 6.16). Interval notation helps us to identify these forces. *AB*, *BC*, and *CD* are the loads from the longitudinal floor beams of the balcony. *DE* is the top reaction. Because it occurs through a hinged link, it must act horizontally, but we do not know its magnitude. *EA*, the bottom reaction, can occur in any direction through the hinged connection, so we know neither its direction nor its magnitude.

We could find the magnitude and direction of the reactions by taking numerical moments, but let us pursue instead a graphical solution. We begin by plotting the external loads on a load line at a convenient scale. We see that *ab*, *bc*, and *cd* are vertical line segments. We know *de* to be a horizontal force, so we lay out a horizontal line through *d*, but we do not know how long segment *de* should be, so we cannot locate point *e*. Because we cannot locate point *e*, we are also unable to draw line segment *ea*, which will terminate at point *a* at the top of the load line. We recognize now that the load line, rather than being just a vertical line, will be a triangle.

We complete the load line by means of a simple graphical operation. The line of action of the resultant of the three gravity loads passes through the central vertical member of the truss. The line of action of the horizontal reaction, *DE*, intersects the line of action of the resultant at a point that we label *n*. Because the truss is in equilibrium, the line of action of the remaining external force, *EA*, must also pass through *n*. This construction gives us the direction of line segment *ea* on the force polygon, which allows us to complete the load line, *ade*.

The rest of the force polygon is easily drawn (Fig. 6.17). We scale the diagram and use the clockwise convention of interval notation to assign magnitudes and characters of forces to all the members and reactions.

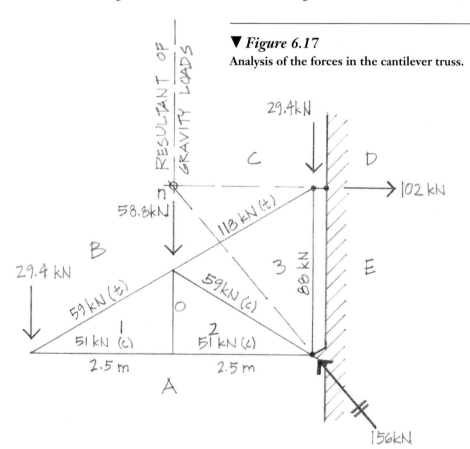

▼ *Figure 6.17*
Analysis of the forces in the cantilever truss.

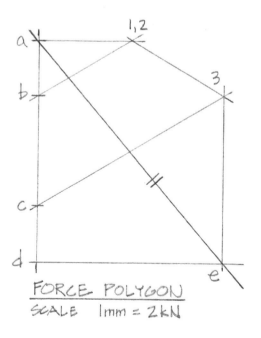

You may find it intriguing to investigate what happens to the reactions and the member forces if the upper support becomes a hinge, and the lower support, a link. If both supports become hinges, the truss cannot be analyzed by the methods we have learned, because we have no way of discovering how the vertical force is divided between the supports unless member *3E* is removed.

An Overhanging Truss

Figure 6.18 illustrates the analysis of an *overhanging* truss, one that projects beyond one of its supports. The force polygon projects both to the right and to the left from the load line. The con-

struction crosses the load line along diagonal *7-8*. It is no coincidence that panel *7-8* on the space diagram is unique in being surrounded on all four sides by compression members, as indicated by thick lines. The panels to its right have a tensile chord along the bottom, and those to its left have a tensile chord along the top. In panel *7-8*, there is a reversal of the direction in which the truss bends under load. The force polygon is very compact, indicating in a general way that this is a truss with low member forces. This efficiency stems partly from the fact that the truss is relatively deep in relation to its span, but it also indicates that the overhang has the effect of decreasing the forces in the members of the panels that lie between the two supports.

Common Truss Configurations

Figure 6.19 illustrates a range of common truss configurations. Each has its particular advantages and disadvantages. We have already discussed how a Pratt design, with its tensile diagonals, is advantageous for a steel truss because its compressive members are short and therefore less susceptible to buckling. The Howe design is often preferable for a timber truss, despite its long compressive members, because of the ease of making compressive connections between heavily loaded wood members. A *Warren truss* and its triangular equivalent, the *simple Fink truss*, offer large apertures for the passage of ductwork. The Warren configuration also offers

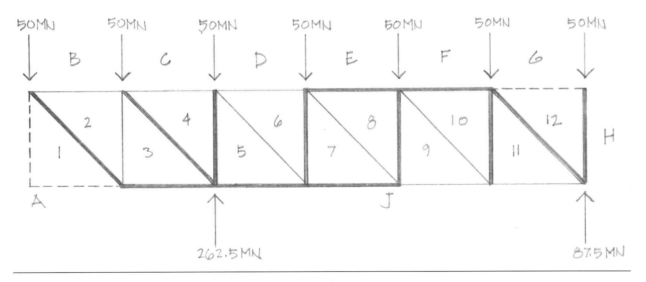

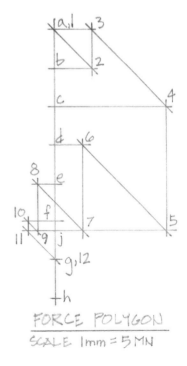

▲ *Figure 6.18*
An overhanging truss.

FORCE POLYGON
SCALE 1mm = 5MN

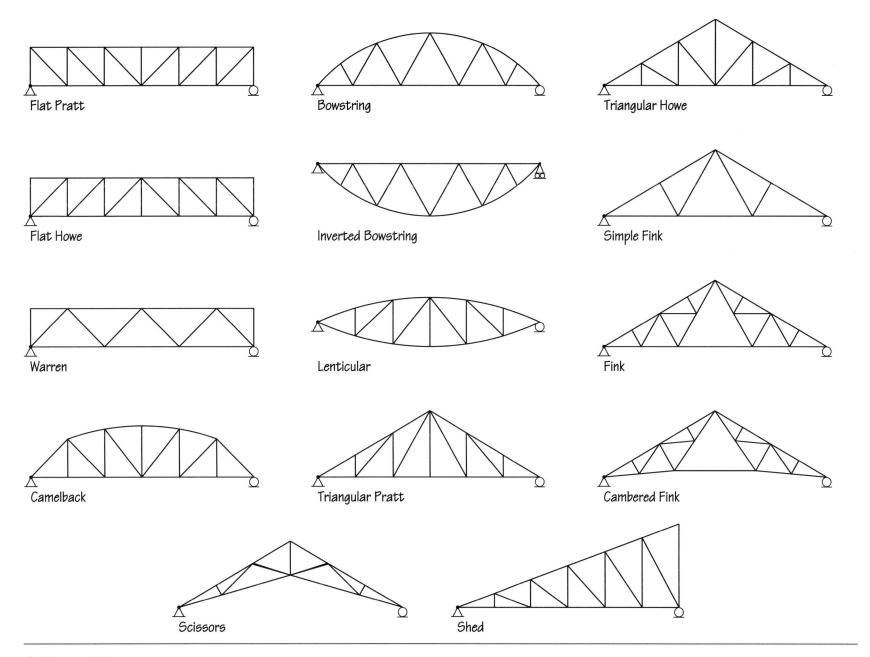

▲ Figure 6.19
Common truss configurations.

a pleasing appearance and a simplicity of fabrication that stems from the fact that its web members are all the same size and shape and are joined in the same way. The Fink truss allows roof purlins to bear on the truss at close intervals along the top chords. The *cambered Fink* design experiences somewhat higher internal forces than the regular Fink truss, in exchange for which it imparts a more gracious shape to the interior space of the building. The *scissors truss* is much beloved by architects for its agreeable spatial qualities, but the very acute angles between the chords at the supports create very high chord forces, which can lead to a heavy appearance and great difficulty in designing the joints. The *bowstring, inverted bowstring, lenticular,* and *camelback trusses* are all shapes that result in highly efficient structural performance. Under ideal loading conditions, the web members in these four designs carry little or no force, and the top and bottom chords experience uniform or nearly uniform forces throughout their length. We will learn how to derive the shapes of these efficient trusses in Chapter Fourteen.

DEFORMATIONS IN TRUSSES

When a truss assumes a load, its compression members grow shorter and its tensile members grow longer. When the triangular truss in Figure 6.20(a) is loaded, its top chords grow shorter, causing the apex of the truss to drop slightly. This effect is increased by the lengthening of the bottom chord, which also causes the truss to grow slightly longer. The lengthening of the truss must be accommodated either by a slight pushing apart of the tops of the supporting walls or columns, or by the movement of a roller or slide bearing at one reaction. The inversion of this design (Fig. 6.20[b]) grows shorter and deeper under load instead of longer and shallower.

In a more complex truss, the deformations of the individual members accumulate in intricate ways to create an overall sagging and lengthening effect. Most trusses, because of their high ratio of depth to span, do not deflect enough to cause physical problems, but even a tiny sag is often exaggerated by the eye to create a disturbing psychological impression of instability. Thus, even a truss with an apparently level bottom chord is often *cambered*, which is to say that it is fabricated with a slight upward curvature (see the photograph at the beginning of this chapter). The amount of camber is often calculated to allow for expected deformations under load, plus a residual upward curvature that creates an appearance of lightness and ease in the structure.

Planar trusses are not strictly planar in the Euclidian sense, but have a finite thickness that is generally small in relationship to their spans; a truss that is only a fraction of a meter thick often supports a floor or roof across a span many meters in length. Thus, although a truss is very stiff against forces exerted in its plane, it has little stiffness against forces exerted perpendicular to its plane, and its long, slender compression chord is apt to buckle laterally. This tendency must be overcome by bracing the truss laterally. Most trusses are fastened securely to a floor or roof deck at close intervals along their compressive chords, which effectively prevents their buckling. If the load is suspended beneath a truss, however, either the top chord will have to be made thicker or it will have to be supported in the lateral direction by lateral bracing that stiffens the entire truss. Lateral bracing is often provided to prevent *out-of-plane movement* of the lower, tensile members of trusses, although in many cases this is not strictly necessary. Another way of avoiding buckling and out-of-plane movement of planar trusses is to combine three or four trusses into a single, long member that is no longer planar, but has a triangular or rectangular cross section that is self bracing. The trusses shown in the photograph at the beginning of this chapter are arranged in triangular fashion according to this principle.

DESIGNING A TRUSS

We will return to truss design and analysis from time to time in succeeding chapters, both because of the importance of trusses in buildings and bridges and because the notion of the truss is very helpful to us in modeling and understanding the internal behavior of solid structural devices such as beams and loadbearing walls. In the meantime, you may wish to begin using trusses in your design work. Trusses are useful at spans ranging from normal residential dimensions up to hundreds of feet or meters in long-span roofs and bridges.

Most trusses are made of steel or wood because these materials are economical, easily fabricated, and can resist both tension and compression. Often the two materials are combined in a truss, with wood generally used for the compressive members and steel for the tensile members. Aluminum works well for trusses, being lighter and less susceptible to corrosion than steel, but it is more expensive than steel and is not as strong or stiff. Trusses may also be made

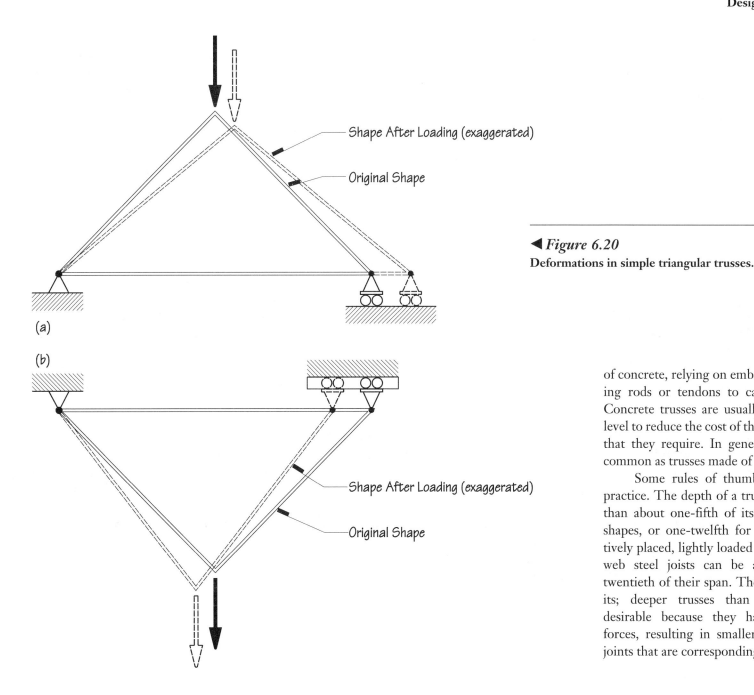

Shape After Loading (exaggerated)

Original Shape

(a)

(b)

Shape After Loading (exaggerated)

Original Shape

◀*Figure 6.20*
Deformations in simple triangular trusses.

of concrete, relying on embedded steel reinforcing rods or tendons to carry tensile stresses. Concrete trusses are usually precast at ground level to reduce the cost of the complex formwork that they require. In general, they are not as common as trusses made of other materials.

Some rules of thumb work out well in practice. The depth of a truss should be no less than about one-fifth of its span for triangular shapes, or one-twelfth for flat shapes. Repetitively placed, lightly loaded trusses such as open web steel joists can be as shallow as one-twentieth of their span. These are extreme limits; deeper trusses than these are usually desirable because they have lower member forces, resulting in smaller member sizes and joints that are correspondingly easier to make.

Figure 6.21 illustrates early steps in designing a wood roof truss for a summer camp assembly building in a snowy climate. The shape of the truss has been determined largely by the architecture of the building. The top chord segments follow the planes of the roof, and the bottom chord is shaped to create the desired volume for the interior of the room. The truss is made up entirely of connected triangles, so although it does not conform to any of the configurations drawn in Figure 6.19, we know that it is structurally stable. What we would like to learn through an early analysis of this truss is whether its shape and proportions are feasible in structural terms. We would also like to have a more detailed picture of what the truss will look like, including a sense of how thick its members will be. To do this, we will make a rough estimate of the loads on the truss, determine the member forces, and from these forces, estimate the sizes of the most heavily loaded members and joints.

The shape of the truss is taken directly from a section drawing on the developing architectural design. A numerical analysis of the forces in this truss would be arduous, because it would require a fairly precise determination of all the angles between members. A graphical analysis is easier because it requires no such determination, and it can be carried out on the same sheet of paper as the architectural section, using the section as the form diagram.

We estimate the total load on the truss by multiplying an approximate total figure for snow load and dead load (50 lb/ft²) by the area of roof that the truss supports. This area, measured as if it were projected on a horizontal surface, is equal to the gross span of the truss (30 ft) times the spacing between trusses (15 ft). The resulting total load is estimated at 22,500 lb per truss.

This load must be apportioned as discrete loads concentrated at the panel points of the truss. We scale the horizontal intervals between the panel points and use these as a basis for this apportionment. The proportion assignable to force *AB*, for example, is calculated by adding half of the 3.4 ft interval on one side to half of the 6.6 ft interval on the other side, for a total of 5.0 ft. Then we divide this sum by the net span of the truss, 29.6 ft, which is the distance from the center of one support to the center of the other, to determine that force *AB* is 17% of the total load, or 3825 lb. When the total load has been fully apportioned in this manner, 9% is assigned directly to the two supports and does not affect the member forces in the truss.

The reactions are determined by taking moments about each of the supports. Then a load line is plotted at a convenient scale, and a force polygon is constructed. We can conclude immediately from the relative compactness of this diagram, even before we measure any of the forces, that the configuration of the truss is quite reasonable. Member forces are not excessively large as compared to the length of the load line, and member forces are relatively uniform. This first quick reading is a crucial and useful one; if the force polygon had included long spikes extending great distances from the load line, we would have known that member forces were excessively high and that the truss configuration should probably be reworked to reduce these forces.

The largest member forces in the truss scale at about 14,000 lb. We assume that we will use a species and grade of wood that can safely resist a stress of about 1000 psi, a value that allows for the buckling potential in compression members of moderate length. Assuming also that these truss members are 3.5 in. thick, we can determine their approximate depth:

$$f = \frac{P}{A} = \frac{14,000 \text{ lb}}{(3.5 \text{ in.})d} = 1000 \text{ psi}$$

$$d = 4 \text{ in.}$$

The smallest standard size of lumber that will suffice for these members is a 4 by 6, whose actual dimensions are 3.5 in. by 5.5 in.

This rough analysis has ignored several factors. It is based on a uniform vertical live load from snow and does not include loads for wind and earthquake. Furthermore, it assumes that all the roof loads are applied only at panel points, rather than continuously along the top chord, where they would cause bending and increase stresses. Experience has shown, however, that although these additional factors are likely to add somewhat to the required sizes of some of the truss members, our simple gravity-load analysis that includes the effects of both dead and live loads gives results that are sufficiently close to final member sizes to establish the feasibility of the configuration. This is especially true in the case of this design, because in rounding up the size of the largest members to the nearest standard lumber dimension, we have already increased member sizes by 38%.

Assuming that we would like the truss to consist of a single layer of nominal 4-in. lumber sandwiched between steel side plates and bolted at the connections, another look at the force

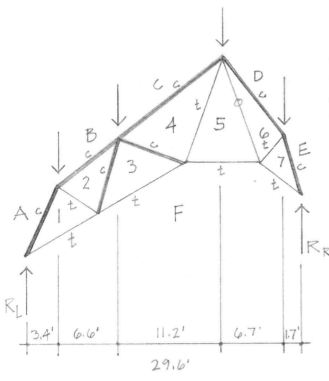

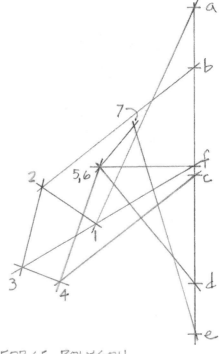

◀ *Figure 6.21*
Analyzing a roof truss for a summer camp assembly building.

FORCE POLYGON
SCALE 1 in. = 6000 lb

50 lb) - 29.6 R_R

AB: 17% = 3825 lb

BC: 30% = 6750 lb

CD: 30% = 6750 lb

DE: 14% = 3150 lb

91% 20,475 lb

(9% DIRECT TO SUPPORTS)

TOTAL LOAD = (30')(15')(50 lb/ft²) = 22,500 lb

$\Sigma M_{RL} = 0 = 3.4 ft(3825 lb) + 10 ft(6750 lb) + 21.2 ft(6750 lb) + 27.9 ft(3150 lb) - 29.6 R_R$

$R_R = 10,523 lb = EF$

$\Sigma M_{RR} = 0 = -1.7 ft(3150 lb) - 8.4 ft(6750 lb) - 19.6 ft(6750 lb) - 26.2 ft(3825 lb) + 29.6 R_L$

$R_L = 9,952 lb = FA$

$R_R + R_L = 20,475 lb$ CHECK

▼ *Figure 6.22*
A preliminary detail elevation of the roof truss.

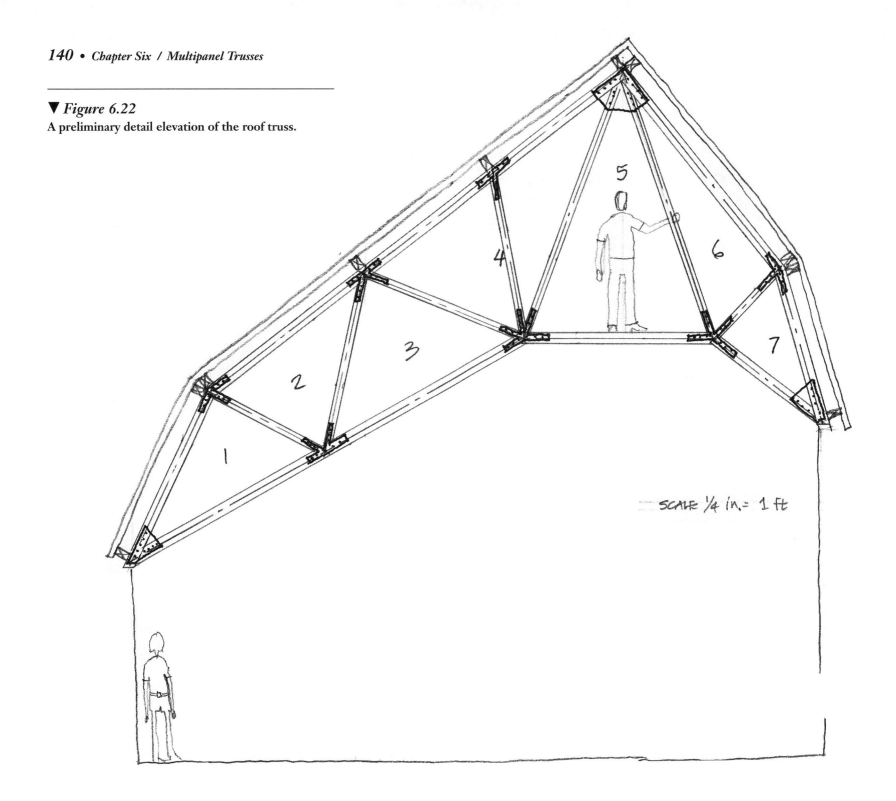

SCALE ¼ in.= 1 ft

▲ *Figure 6.23*
Light roof trusses for small wood frame buildings are made of lengths of nominal 2-in. lumber (38 mm thick) joined with spiked metal plates that are pressed into the wood. (Photo courtesy of Gang-Nail Systems, Inc.)

▲ *Figure 6.24*
Each member of the roof trusses of this shopping mall consists of two steel angle shapes. Joints are made by welding the angles to steel plates that are sandwiched between the paired angles. (Photo courtesy of American Institute of Steel Construction.)

polygon tells us that the forces in the web of the truss are small enough that 4 × 4s will probably suffice for these members. We decide to adopt 4 × 6s for all segments of the top and bottom chords, and 4 × 4s for all the web members. With this information, we can draw a preliminary elevation of the truss (Fig. 6.22). We conclude that

its proportions are quite graceful. The form diagram of the truss furnishes the centerlines for the members on this drawing. We consider adding a web member in space *4* to reduce the length of top chord member *C4* and give a more uniform spacing of roof purlins. Perhaps we will adjust the spacing of the joints along the left slope of the top chord to make it completely uniform. If we make either of these changes, we will have to do a new analysis of the truss; but this can be put off until the next stage of structural design, because it will not have a very large effect on member forces. We sketch shapes for the steel connector plates, though we do not yet know exactly how large they will have to be or how many bolts will be needed. We think about lateral bracing of the trusses; perhaps we will brace all three of the joints in the bottom chord. We sketch ourselves to scale on the drawing, because this helps us understand the scale and feel of the design. The truss is already showing a strong personality of its own that we find very satisfying. We have established its feasibility, and we know enough about it to proceed with the preliminary design of the building. When the building design has developed more fully, we will be able bring the process of analyzing and detailing the truss to completion.

▼ *Figure 6.25*

The floors and roof of the Centre Georges Pompidou in Paris are supported by Warren trusses 2.5 m (8.2 ft) deep that span 45 m (148 ft). Each top chord is a pair of 419 mm (16.5 in.) diameter steel tubes. A pair of 225 mm (9 in.) solid steel rods make up the bottom chord. Inverted vees of inclined struts between the trusses at midspan and near each support impart lateral stability to the entire frame in the short direction of the building. Stability in the long direction of the building is created by external cross bracing made of steel rods. Architect: Piano and Rogers. Structural engineer: Ove Arup and Partners. (Photo by Edward Allen.)

Key Terms and Concepts

chord

web member

vertical

diagonal

strut

tie

panel

joint

panel point

node

flat truss

parallel chord truss

Pratt truss

Howe truss

triangular or gable truss

simply supported truss

cantilever truss

overhanging truss

Warren truss

simple Fink truss

cambered Fink truss

scissors truss

bowstring truss

inverted bowstring truss

lenticular truss

camelback truss

shed truss

camber

out-of-plane movement

Exercises

1. Find and compare the forces in the members of the gable trusses in Figure 6.26.

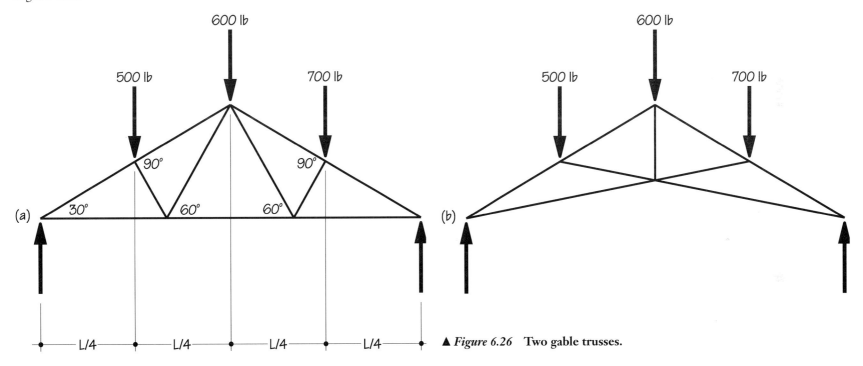

▲ *Figure 6.26* **Two gable trusses.**

2. Figure 6.27 depicts a steel truss for a sloping footbridge. Find the forces in its members.

Figure 6.27 **A steel truss for a sloping footbridge.** ▶

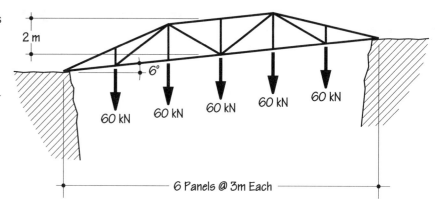

3. Find the forces in the members of the overhanging truss in Figure 6.28.

Figure 6.28 **An overhanging truss.** ▶

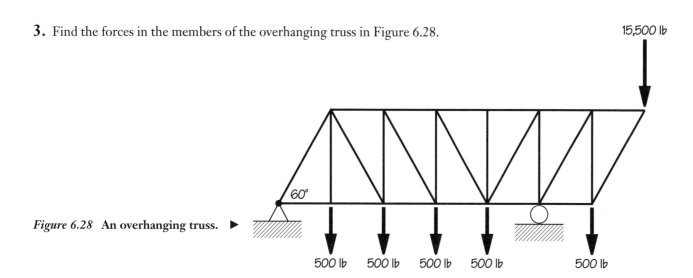

4. Determine the effects of the horizontal and vertical loads on the Warren truss in Figure 6.29.

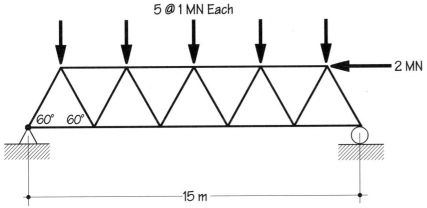

◀ *Figure 6.29* **A Warren truss.**

5. Find the forces in the cantilever truss in Figure 6.30.

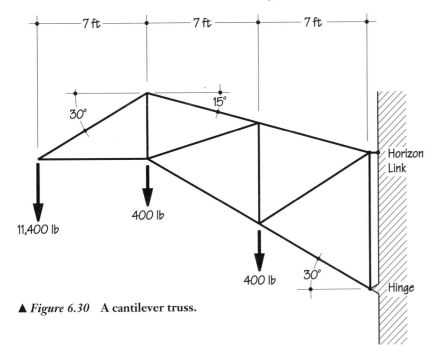

▲ *Figure 6.30* **A cantilever truss.**

6. Prepare a preliminary design for a footbridge to span a distance of 11.4 m between abutments on either side of a stream. The bridge will have an inside clear width of 1.0 m. Total live and dead loads have been estimated at 400 kg per meter of span. With the aid of a handbook of standard steel shapes, assign approximate sizes to the members, using square steel tubing with welded joints.

7. Design a trussed roof for an art exhibition room that is 24 ft wide and 36 ft long with walls that are uniformly 11 ft tall. Shape the wooden trusses in such a way that clerestory windows admit light to the space from one direction only. Assume that the total of live and dead loads is 50 lb per square ft of horizontal projection.

The roof of the ▶ Inmos Microprocessor Factory in Wales is framed with shallow steel trusses. Stay rods fan out from central columns of steel tubing to support the trusses at the third points of their spans. The architects are Richard Rogers and Partners, and the engineers are Anthony Hunt Associates. (Photo: Pat Hunt.)

CHAPTER SEVEN

FANLIKE STRUCTURES

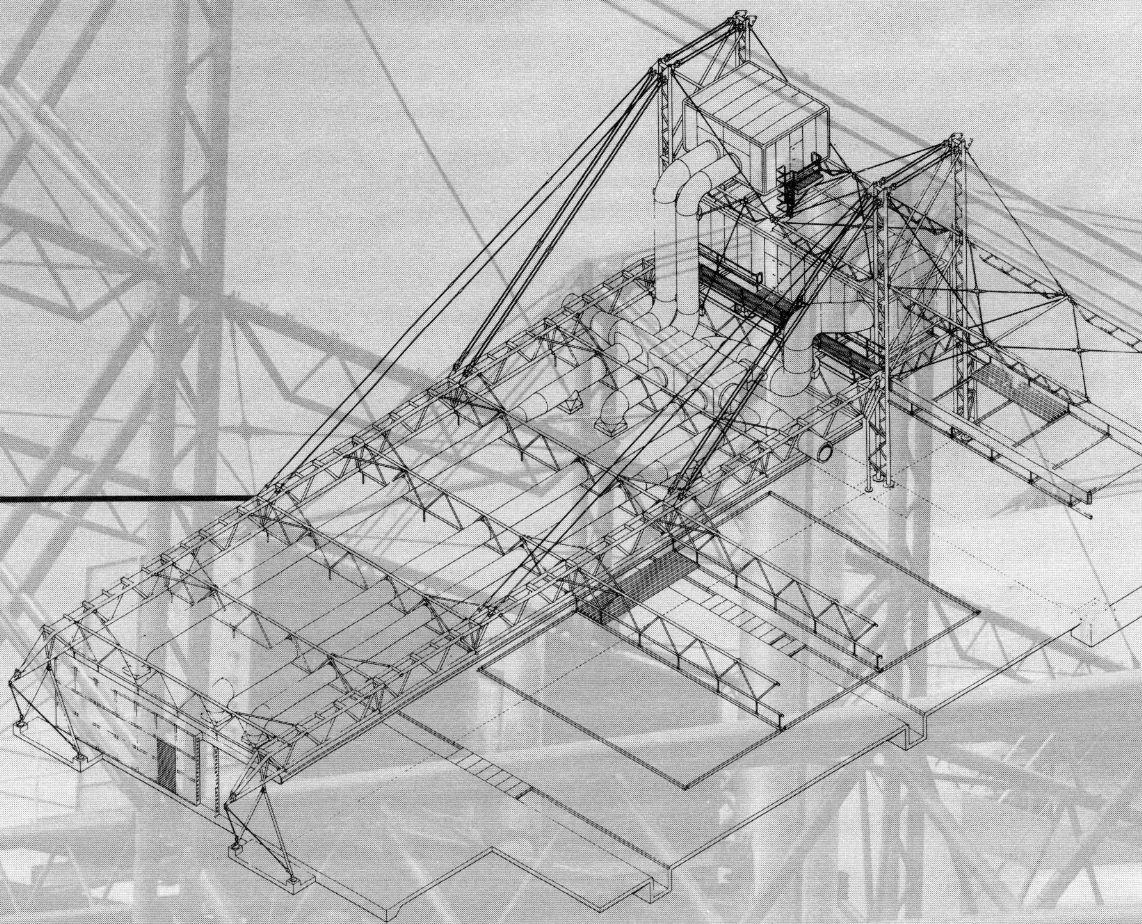

The methods that we have learned in the last two chapters for finding the forces in truss members can be applied readily to the analysis of fanlike structures that fall into two general classifications. *Cable-stayed* structures support roof or bridge decks on inclined cables or tension rods. Their inversion, which is characterized by fanlike arrangements of struts, is less common and has no collective name.

CABLE-STAYED STRUCTURES

The photograph on the facing page and Figures 7.1 and 7.2 illustrate a roof and a bridge that are cable-stayed. Very long spans are feasible, though not nearly as long as those of *suspension* structures, which use continuous, curving cables. The longest span for a cable-stayed bridge at this

▲ *Figure 7.1*
A diagram of the Inmos roof discloses that each main truss is supported at four points. One end bears on a pair of inclined struts, the other end on a trussed column, and the two interior supports are provided by inclined stays. (From Chris Wilkinson, *Supersheds,* reproduced by permission of the publisher, Butterworth-Heinemann.)

▲ *Figure 7.2*

The semifans of cables of the Normandy Bridge in France, completed in 1995, support the longest cable-stayed span in the world, 856 m, which is a little over half a mile. (Photo courtesy of Michel Virlogeux, Designer. Photographer: Gérard Forquet–SETRA.)

writing is 856 m (2808 ft), about half the longest span for a suspension bridge. Cable-stayed construction is economical for bridge spans as short as 150 m (500 ft) and is often practical for much shorter spans in both bridges and buildings. The most economical height for the *tower* that supports the cables is between 0.2 and 0.25 of the span. It is usually assumed for purposes of preliminary design that a cable-stayed structure is supported completely by its inclined *stays*, with little or no vertical force being transferred from the end of the span to its adjacent abutment or column. This is a simplification, because in actu-

ality the ends of the bridge or roof must be restrained so that they remain aligned with adjacent construction. Thus, as the design develops, forces must also be taken into account at these junctions. The stays for a roof or bridge are usually arranged in one of three patterns: the *fan*, the *harp*, or the *semifan* or *half-harp* (Fig. 7.3). The fan pattern is easily analyzed by means of a force polygon that gives the forces in each of the stays, the *tower* (sometimes called a *pylon*), and each segment of the deck or roof beam. We see in the force polygons of Figure 7.3 that the compressive forces in the deck can be very large in

the vicinity of the tower, especially if the stays fan out at very flat angles. The deck structures of the longer cable-stayed bridges are generally hollow box girders of steel or concrete, because the box shape is highly resistant to buckling. Steel or concrete box beams are also used in cable-stayed roofs, although ordinary beams of steel, concrete, or wood may be used if the axial compression in the beams is not too high.

A practical disadvantage of the fan pattern is that it is difficult to connect all the stays to the tower in the same place. The other two patterns avoid this problem. The choice between them is often purely visual, but it is evident in comparing the force polygons in Figure 7.3 that the nearer the pattern is to a true fan, the lower the forces are in the stays and deck. On the other hand, the total length of the stays in a fan pattern is higher than in the other arrangements, which can lead to higher costs. The semifan pattern of stays is usually the best compromise between structural efficiency and ease of construction.

Although these overall analyses of the forces in the stays, tower, and deck are simple and straightforward, the full design process for a cable-stayed structure is complicated by a number of factors. Each stay stretches under load in an amount that is proportional to its stress and its length. Because the stays vary considerably in length, a heavy vehicle, when crossing a cable-stayed bridge, tends to cause a much larger deflection in the deck when it is distant from a tower than it does when it is near one, and a cable-stayed roof that is subjected to a uniform snow load tends to sag more at points distant from the towers than at points closer in. Each stay also sags slightly under its own weight, a factor that can be ignored during the early stages of design but must be taken into account as the

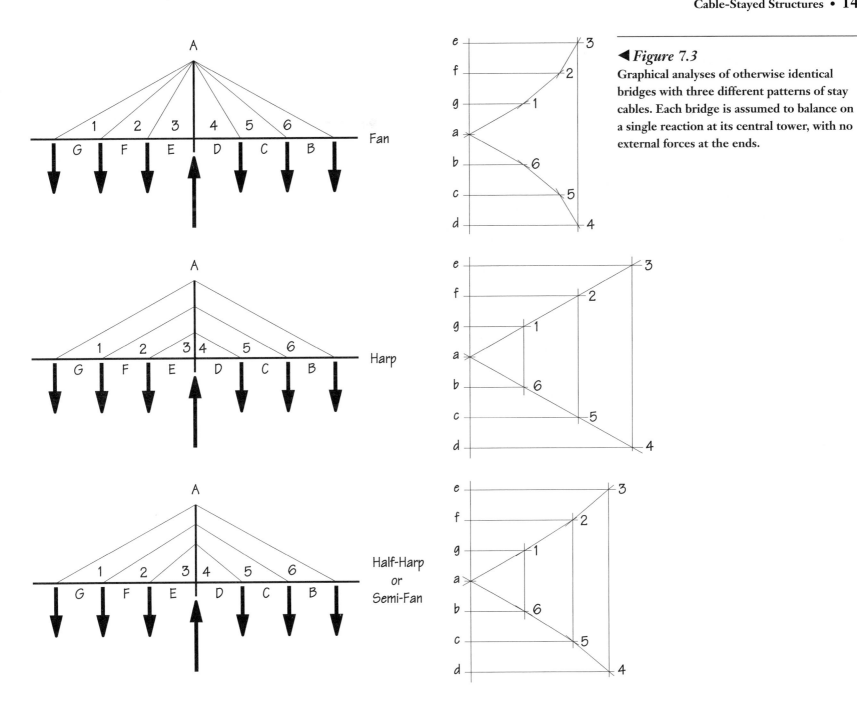

Fan

Harp

Half-Harp
or
Semi-Fan

◄ *Figure* 7.3
Graphical analyses of otherwise identical
bridges with three different patterns of stay
cables. Each bridge is assumed to balance on
a single reaction at its central tower, with no
external forces at the ends.

design develops. A cable-stayed structure should be designed to support its load safely even if any single stay is ruptured; this allows for accidental breakage and for maintenance replacement of cables. Oscillations of the structure under moving traffic loads or wind loads must also be predicted and designed for.

A cable-stayed roof generally employs as many planes of stays as it requires to keep the spans of the roof deck within reasonable limits. A cable-stayed bridge may be supported on one, two, or three planes of stays, depending on its width and the judgment of its designer. Often, only a single plane is used. It is placed along the center of the deck, between the opposing lanes of traffic, reducing the number of towers and

◀ *Figure 7.4*

A diagrammatic view from below of the deck of the Chesapeake and Delaware Canal Bridge, constructed in 1994 to the design of the Figg Engineering Group. The main span is 750 ft (230 m). The single central plane of cables supports a roadway that is 127 ft (39 m) wide. Two box girders, each 12 ft (3.7 m) deep, are made up of precast concrete segments that are held together longitudinally with posttensioned cables. Precast concrete triangulated frameworks work together with diagonal struts inside the box girders to form transverse trusses that bring the loads of the roadway to the stay cables.

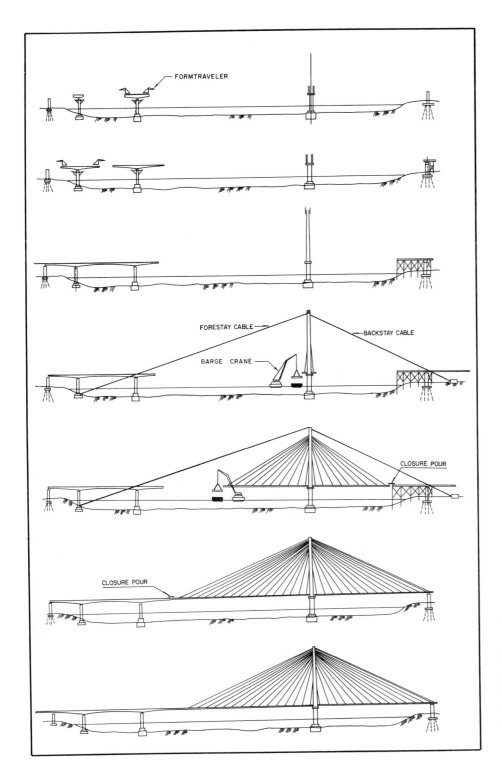

cables and producing a bridge that often appears quite slender and daring. Bridge decks more than 120 ft (36 m) wide have been supported successfully by a single central plane of cables. At this width, the roadway must cantilever more than 60 ft (18 m) in each direction from the plane of the stays (Fig. 7.4). If the lanes on one side of the plane are loaded with stalled rush-hour traffic while the lanes on the other side are clear, the deck structure will tend to twist in the direction of the loaded lanes. The boxlike configuration of the girders that works best to prevent buckling of the deck under the high compressions it experiences near the towers is also ideal for resisting this twisting tendency, which is called *torsion*. The longitudinal and torsional rigidity of the *box girder* are important factors in distributing among the stays nonuniform loads such as the weights of moving trucks, and in resisting the forces that result from the structural continuity of the deck from one span to another and from a cable-stayed span to a rigid abutment or column at the end of the roof or bridge. In a bridge, the depth of a box girder that is supported by a single plane of cables is typically about one-tenth of the width of the deck.

Most cable-stayed structures can support themselves throughout the construction process. The *balanced cantilever method* of erection, illustrated in Figures 7.5 and 7.6, is most common.

◀ *Figure 7.5*
The balanced cantilever method as applied to erection of the East Huntington Bridge in West Virginia and Ohio, built in 1987 to the design of Arvid Grant and Associates, engineers. The main span is 900 ft (275 m). (PCI Journal, Precast/Prestressed Concrete Institute, Chicago, Illinois.)

◀ *Figure 7.6*
Balanced cantilever construction of the Alex Fraser (formerly Annacis) Bridge, near Vancouver, B.C. (1986). The main span is 1526 ft (465 m). The engineer of record was CBA-Buckland & Taylor. (Photo courtesy of Buckland & Taylor, Ltd.)

Deck sections, typically 6 to 8 m (20 to 25 ft) long and coordinated in length with the spacing of the stays, must be added symmetrically on both sides of the tower to maintain equilibrium at each stage of construction. The tower must have sufficient rigidity to resist overturning and torsion that may be caused by high winds and unbalanced loads during construction.

Figure 7.7 shows some typical details for a cable-stayed bridge. The tower and deck in these details are made of reinforced concrete. The deck is often precast in segments at a nearby casting yard. The segments are hoisted into place and joined with prestressing tendons that are threaded through longitudinal openings that are made during casting of the concrete. Alternatively, the deck sections may be cast in place. The stays are high-strength steel cables, usually encased in a plastic or steel covering that is filled with *grout*, a fine-grained form of concrete, for protection against corrosion. After erection, small adjustments of stay lengths may be made at their anchorages on or in the tower, as provided for by the designer.

Every cable-stayed roof tends to be a highly customized design; thus, there are no "typical" details. Figures 7.8–7.10 illustrate the major details of the roof shown in the photograph at the beginning of this chapter.

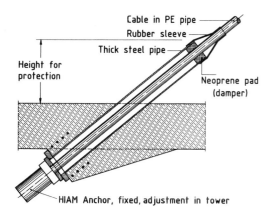

Cable in PE pipe
Rubber sleeve
Thick steel pipe

Height for protection

Neoprene pad (damper)

HIAM Anchor, fixed, adjustment in tower

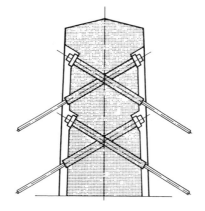

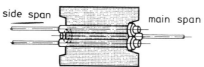

side span   main span

easy access

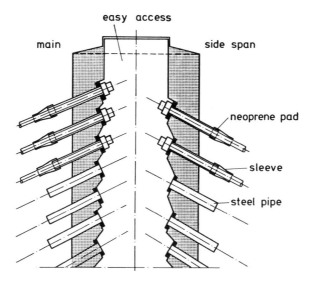

main   side span

neoprene pad

sleeve

steel pipe

cross section

prestress – bars or loops

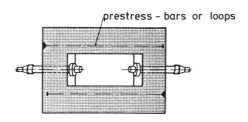

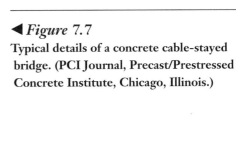

◀ *Figure* 7.7
Typical details of a concrete cable-stayed bridge. (PCI Journal, Precast/Prestressed Concrete Institute, Chicago, Illinois.)

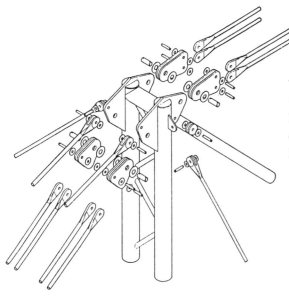

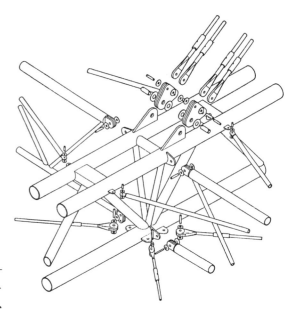

◀ *Figure 7.8*
Details of the attachment of stay rods to the top of a tower in the Inmos Factory. (Credit: © 1988 Deutsche Verlags-Anstalt GmbH, Stuttgart.)

Figure 7.9 ▶
Details of the attachment of stay rods to the roof trusses in the Inmos Factory. (Credit: © 1988 Deutsche Verlags-Anstalt GmbH, Stuttgart.)

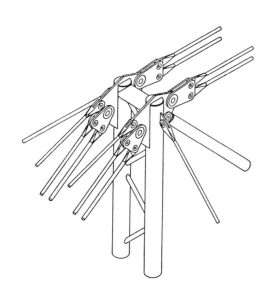

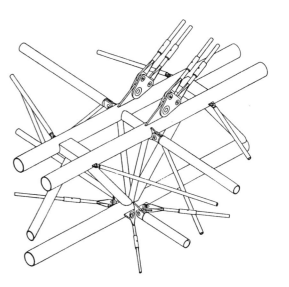

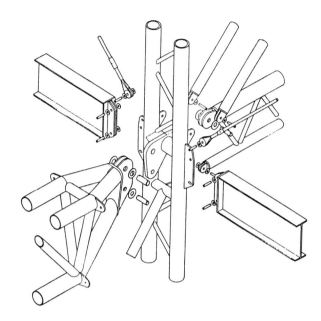

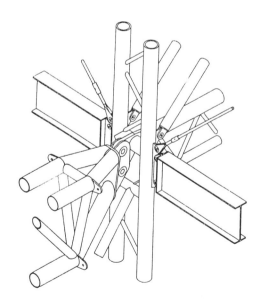

◀ *Figure* 7.10
Details of the attachment of the roof trusses to the center tower in the Inmos Factory. (Credit: © 1988 Deutsche Verlags-Anstalt GmbH, Stuttgart.)

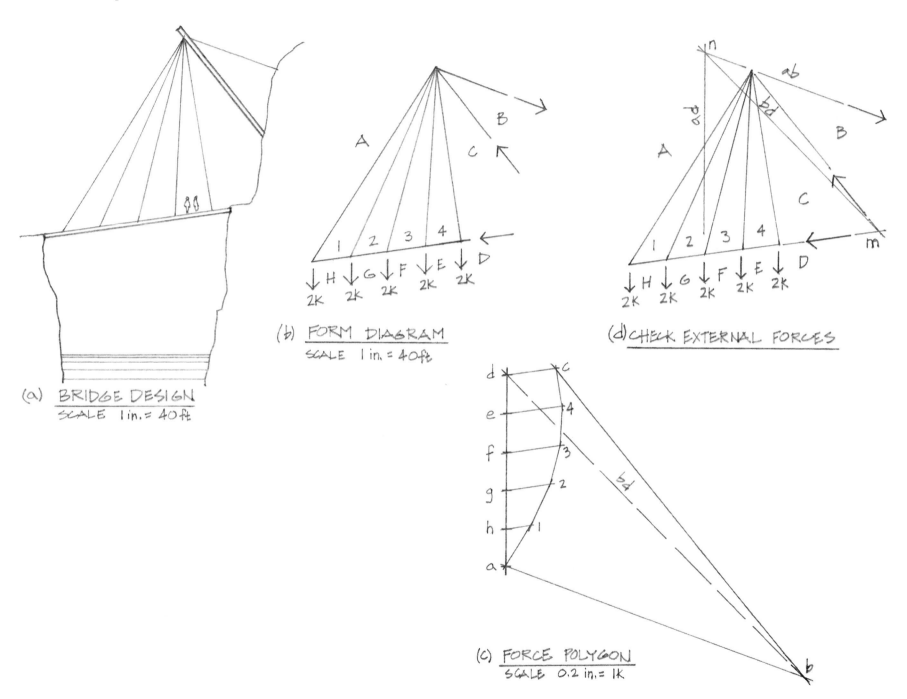

(a) BRIDGE DESIGN
SCALE 1 in.= 40 ft

(b) FORM DIAGRAM
SCALE 1 in. = 40 ft

(d) CHECK EXTERNAL FORCES

(c) FORCE POLYGON
SCALE 0.2 in.= 1k

DESIGNING A CABLE-STAYED FOOTBRIDGE

Figure 7.11(a) shows a sketch of an idea for a cable-stayed footbridge on a mountain path. The topography dictates an inclined deck. The inclinations of the steel pipe tower and cable *backstay* that pulls to the right have been drawn rather arbitrarily. In (b), we construct a combined form diagram and free-body diagram of the bridge, which we label carefully with interval notation. For purposes of analysis, we assume that there is a force *CD* that acts in the plane of the bridge deck at the end nearest the tower, but that no external vertical forces act on either end of the deck.

There are three unknown external forces, *AB, BC,* and *CD,* that act on this bridge. We could calculate these forces by means of the three equations of equilibrium, but this would be fairly laborious. Instead, we will analyze the system graphically, finding the external forces in the process, and check the equilibrium of the forces with a simple graphical construction. In Figure 7.11(c), we construct a partial load line, *ad,* that represents all the gravity loads. We begin the analysis from the left end of the bridge by constructing *a1* and *b1,* then *g2* and *1-2*. By the time the construction reaches the upper end of the partial load line, we know the forces in each of the stays and each segment of the deck. We also know external force *CD,* another segment of the still-unfinished load line, through the plotting of *4c* and *cd.* We complete the load line and the solution by drawing *cb* and *ab* parallel to their respective members. These last two segments represent the forces in the tower and backstay, respectively.

As a check on the accuracy of our work, we construct the lines of action of three forces that represent all the external forces on the bridge. Normally this operation is done on the form diagram, but for clarity, it is presented separately here as Figure 7.11(d). The line of action of the first of the three forces, the resultant of all the gravity loads, *ab* through *ed,* is *ad.* The line of action of the second force, the tension in the backstay, is *ab.* Line segments *ad* and *ab* intersect at *n.* The third force is *bd,* the resultant of the two forces exerted by the foundations, *bc* and *cd.* Its direction is found by constructing broken line *bd* on the force polygon, (c). When the line of action of *bd* is drawn through *m,* the intersection of the lines of action of the foundation forces, it, too, passes through *n,* confirming that the external forces that we have found are in equilibrium.

The line segments in the force polygon that represent the forces in the tower and backstay, *cb* and *ab,* seem very long in relation to the line segments that represent the other forces in the bridge, which means that their corresponding members carry very high forces. Is there any way to reduce these forces without compromising the design of the bridge?

If line *cb* were rotated in a clockwise direction about *c,* or if *ab* were rotated counterclockwise about *a,* the lengths of both lines would diminish rapidly. We see in the form diagram that these rotations represent changes in the inclinations of the tower and backstay. Inspecting the original design sketch, we see that we have some leeway to experiment with such

◀ *Figure 7.11*
Analysis of a design for a cable-stayed footbridge.

changes. Figure 7.12 shows the result: the forces in both tower and backstay are reduced to about half of those in the original design, and the visual composition of the bridge is somehow more relaxed and satisfying. The tower has grown about 20 ft taller, however, and its base may interfere with the path on which it sits. Further experimentation is needed to find a compromise solution that will keep the path clear and give a tower of feasible height and diameter. The eventual solution will come from a process that includes a determination of the required diameter and wall thickness of the tower for each alternative bridge configuration.

We use interval notation to check the characters of all the member forces in the bridge. This process confirms that all the deck segments are in compression and all the cables in tension. You may find it interesting to discover from experimentation with the force polygon how the compressive forces in the deck segments may be minimized by further changes in the geometry of the bridge.

FANLIKE COMPRESSIVE STRUCTURES

The nineteenth-century English engineer Isambard Kingdom Brunel built a number of railway bridges in which the track is supported by fanlike arrangements of timbers on top of stone piers (Fig. 7.13). These represent the inversion of the cable-stayed bridge concept. Their action is analyzed in Figure 7.14. Clockwise reading of joint names in interval notation confirms that all the timbers in the fan are in compression.

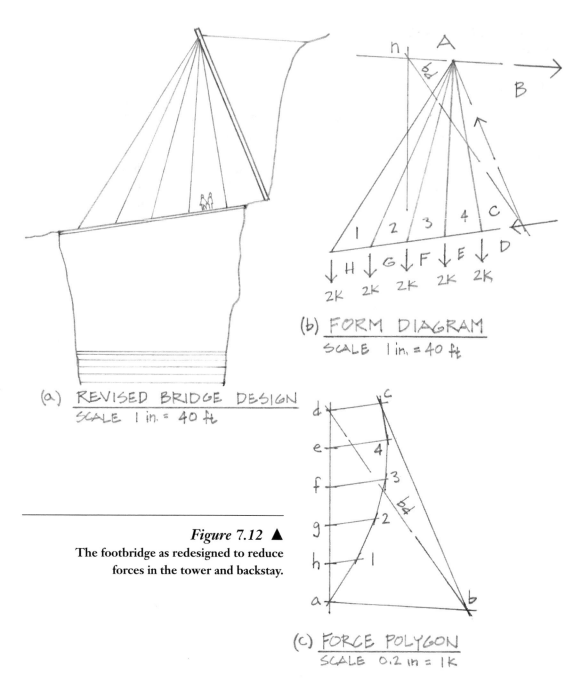

(a) REVISED BRIDGE DESIGN
SCALE 1 in. = 40 ft

(b) FORM DIAGRAM
SCALE 1 in. = 40 ft

(c) FORCE POLYGON
SCALE 0.2 in = 1K

Figure 7.12 ▲
The footbridge as redesigned to reduce forces in the tower and backstay.

A nineteenth-century timber railway bridge in Britain, designed by engineer I. K. Brunel. The cables below the timber fans were apparently added later in an attempt to stabilize the bridge against the effects of decay or poor construction. (Photo courtesy of Great Western Railway Museum, Swindon, England.)

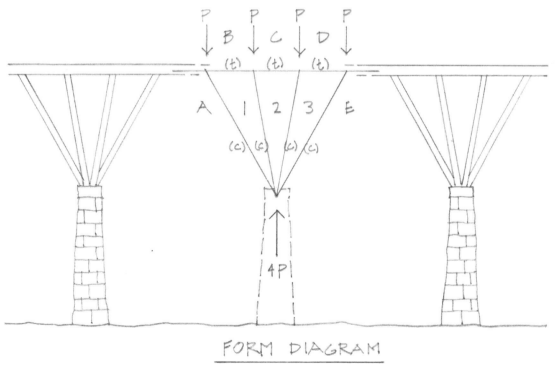

FORM DIAGRAM

◀ *Figure 7.14*
Analysis of the timber bridge in Figure 7.13.

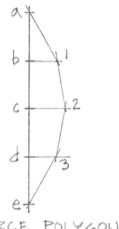

FORCE POLYGON

◄ *Figure 7.15*
Model of a roof structure designed by architect Jørn Utzon. (Photo: Strüwing Reklamefoto.)

Figure 7.15 is a photograph of a structure for the roof of a swimming hall in Denmark. Each pier supports two rafters by means of two diverging fans of timbers. Because the pier sits well outside the center of the rafter span, each rafter tends to tip inward. This tendency is resisted by the direct bearing of each rafter end against its mirror-image partner at the ridge of the roof. In analyzing this roof (Fig. 7.16), we apportion gravity loads to each of the panel points, including a partial load *EF* at the ridge.

FG is the horizontal thrust at the ridge. This must be balanced by an opposing thrust, *HA*, at the top of the supporting pier. We can find the magnitudes of these thrusts as we solve for the forces in the members. We begin the force polygon, (c), by laying out the gravity loads on partial load line *af*. Then we draw the lines that represent the components of the member forces that lie in a vertical plane, starting with *a1* and ending with *eg*, which gives us the magnitude of the horizontal thrust, *fg*. With *gh* and *ha*, we complete

the load line, which is a rectangle. The struts do not lie in a vertical plane: they reach outward from the pier in two sloping planes to the rafters on either side (Fig. 7.16[b]). The true forces in the struts, *a1′* through *3g′*, are found by drawing simple triangles of forces on line segments *a1* through *3g* of the force polygon, the acute angle in each triangle being the inclination from the vertical of the sloping plane.

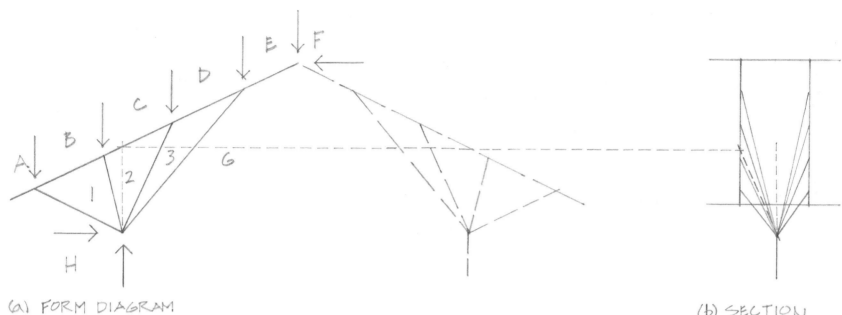

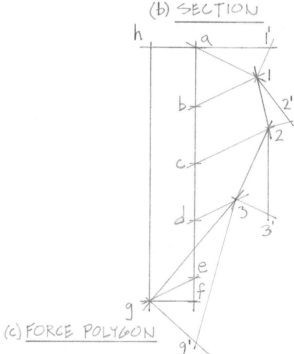

(a) FORM DIAGRAM

(b) SECTION

(c) FORCE POLYGON

▲ *Figure* 7.16

Analysis of the roof structure in Figure 7.15. The vertical broken line in panel 2 of the form diagram, (a), represents a vertical plane. The projection to the section, (b), of the intersection of this plane with member C2 establishes an inclined broken line whose slope is exactly the inclination from the vertical of a plane of struts. This inclination is then used to find points 1', 2', 3', and g' on the force polygon, (c).

A CABLE-STAYED BRIDGE WITH NO BACKSTAY

The Alamillo Bridge in Seville, Spain, resists the pull of its single harp of stays not with a backstay or a balancing set of stays on the other side of its tower, but with the weight of a backward-leaning tower (Figs. 7.17 and 7.18). Just how heavy does this tower have to be? In Figure 7.19 we concep-

tualize a graphical answer to this question. The form diagram, (a), is based on the geometry of the actual bridge, but for the moment we simplify the analysis by assuming that there are only four stay cables. We divide the load of the deck into four equal segments, one at the lower end of each cable. We assume that the roller at the right end of the span bears no load.

The force polygon, (b), begins with the partial load line, *ae*, that represents the deck loads. Starting with *ab4* and finishing with *de1-2*, we draw equilibrium polygons for the four nodes in the deck. The four segments of the sloping line represent the equal tensile forces in the four stays. The horizontal lines represent the axial compressive forces in the deck segments.

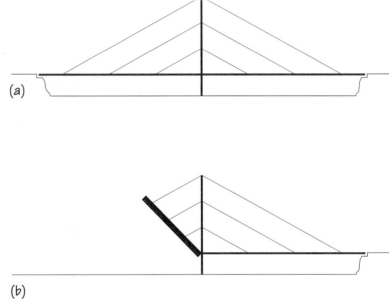

(a)

(b)

▲ *Figure 7.17*
**The Alamillo Bridge, Seville, Spain, designed by Santiago Calatrava.
(Photo: Edward Allen.)**

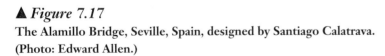

Figure 7.18 ▶
**Understanding the Alamillo Bridge: In a symmetrical cable-stayed bridge
(a), the weights of the two spans balance each other. If one span is tilted
up and shortened to become a counterweight (b), its weight must increase
to compensate for its reduction of moment arm. In the actual bridge (c),
the tower and counterweight merge to become a single member.**

(c)

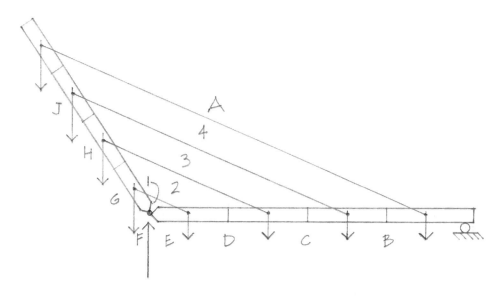

(a) FORM DIAGRAM

▲ *Figure 7.19*
Simplified analysis of the Alamillo Bridge: Part 1.

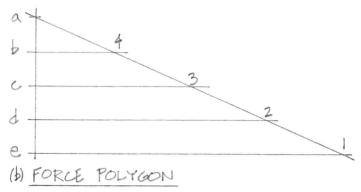

(b) FORCE POLYGON

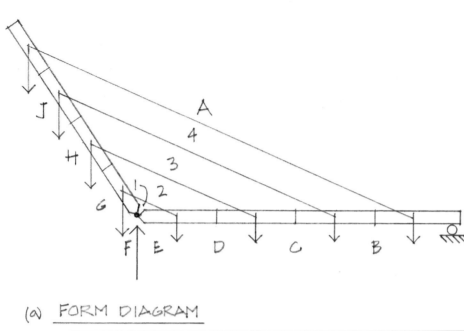

(a) FORM DIAGRAM

▲ *Figure 7.20*
Simplified analysis of the Alamillo Bridge: Part 2.

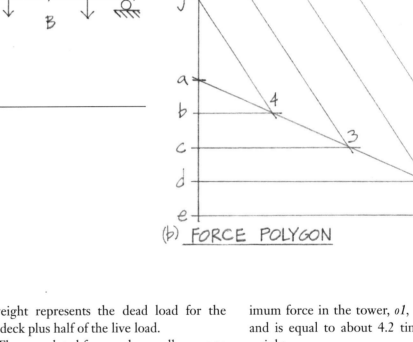

(b) FORCE POLYGON

We complete this simplified analysis in Figure 7.20 by examining the forces that act on the sloping tower. Steeply sloping lines $f1$ through $j4$ are drawn parallel to the slope of the tower; they represent the magnitudes of the axial compressive forces in the four segments of the tower. They intersect a vertical extension of the load line at points f through j, dividing it into the weights that are required in each segment of the tower to maintain the equilibrium of the bridge.

In Figure 7.21, we carry out a more detailed analysis that is based on the actual configuration of 13 stays. Segment an of the load line is constructed first to represent the weight of the deck. For reasons that we will discuss shortly,

this weight represents the dead load for the entire deck plus half of the live load.

The completed force polygon allows us to quantify the forces in the bridge. The maximum compressive force in the deck, $n1$, is about 2.2 times the deck weight, an. Each stay experiences a tension that is equal to about one-fifth of the total deck weight. The total weight of the tower, oa, is about 2.5 times the deck weight. The max-

imum force in the tower, $o1$, occurs at the base and is equal to about 4.2 times the total deck weight.

All these conclusions are based on the theoretical assumption that the entire bridge is delicately balanced on a hinge at point *1-N-O* when it carries traffic uniformly distributed across its span at half the maximum intensity. The reality, however, is more complicated. The right-hand

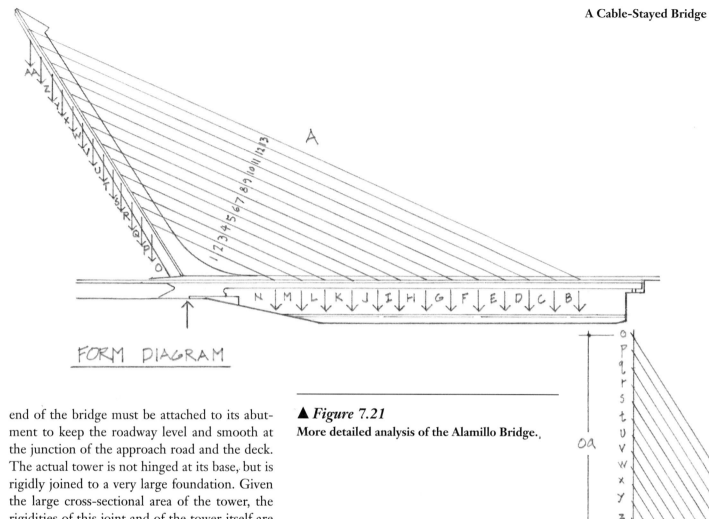

FORM DIAGRAM

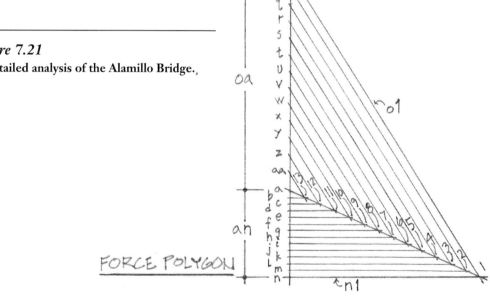

FORCE POLYGON

end of the bridge must be attached to its abutment to keep the roadway level and smooth at the junction of the approach road and the deck. The actual tower is not hinged at its base, but is rigidly joined to a very large foundation. Given the large cross-sectional area of the tower, the rigidities of this joint and of the tower itself are able to play major roles in stabilizing the bridge under varying live loads. If the weight of the tower was designed to balance the full dead load plus half of the maximum live load, the tower will experience moderate bending in one direction when the bridge is free of traffic, and in the other direction when traffic is bumper-to-bumper. The graphical approach allows us, if we wish, to experiment freely with different loading assumptions, and with different angles, heights, and weights of towers.

▲ *Figure 7.21*
More detailed analysis of the Alamillo Bridge.

TWO ALPINE BRIDGES

The bridge in Figure 7.22, high in the Swiss Alps, uses fans of cables encased in triangular concrete walls to support the roadway. The concrete encasement protects the cables from the weather. The tall, slender towers and the graceful curvature of the underside of the deck combine with the palpable tautness of the cables to give this bridge an extraordinarily light, soaring appearance.

Figure 7.23 is a photograph of another, older Swiss bridge that is supported by fanlike compressive members of reinforced concrete below the deck. If you hold this picture upside down, you will see that this structure is essentially the inverse of the bridge in the preceding photograph. The compressive version cannot be used for so long a span as the tensile version because of the tendency of long compressive members to buckle, but the principles on which the two designs are based are much the same.

MORE COMPLEX CABLE-STAYED ROOFS

The roof of the Patscenter manufacturing facility in Princeton, New Jersey, is suspended on steel rods from a linear series of steel pipe A-frames (Fig. 7.24). The junctions of the rods and pipes are expressively detailed with circular steel plates. In studying the section drawing of the

▼ *Figure 7.22*

Two photographs of the Ganter Bridge, Simplon Pass, Switzerland (1980), designed by Christian Menn. The main span is 174 m (571 ft), and the higher tower is 150 m (490 ft) tall. (Photos: Professor Dr. Chris H. Luebkeman.)

▲ *Figure 7.23*
The Simme River Bridge, Garstatt, Switzerland, constructed in 1940 to the design of Robert Maillart. (Photo: ETH-Bibliothek, Zurich.)

▲ *Figure 7.24*
The Patscenter manufacturing facility, Princeton, New Jersey. The architect is Richard Rogers, and the architect of record, Kelbaugh and Lee. The engineer is Ove Arup Partners, Peter Rice, lead designer. (Photo: Kelbaugh and Lee.)

building (Fig. 7.25), we notice that of the four rods that connect to each span of roof, the two longest are attached to points that are already supported by columns. We infer from this observation that only the two short rods near midspan actually support the roof beam, a conclusion that is borne out by the much smaller diameters of the two longer rods in the photograph. The function of the longer rods is to keep the suspended circular plate, and therefore the roof beam, from moving excessively if snow or wind should load the span unevenly.

In the analysis shown in Figure 7.26, we designate the outermost rods (*A1* and *A9*) as zero-force members. The compactness of the force polygon may be attributed to the generous height of the A-frame, which helps keep member forces low. The innermost tensile members, *3-4* and *6-7*, carry very little force. They, like the outermost members, serve primarily as stabilizers in the event of nonuniform loadings. The

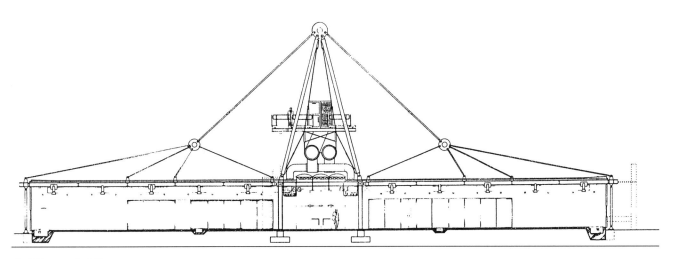

▲ *Figure 7.25*
A cross section of the Patscenter roof. (From Chris Wilkinson, *Supersheds*, reproduced by permission of the publisher, Butterworth-Heinemann.)

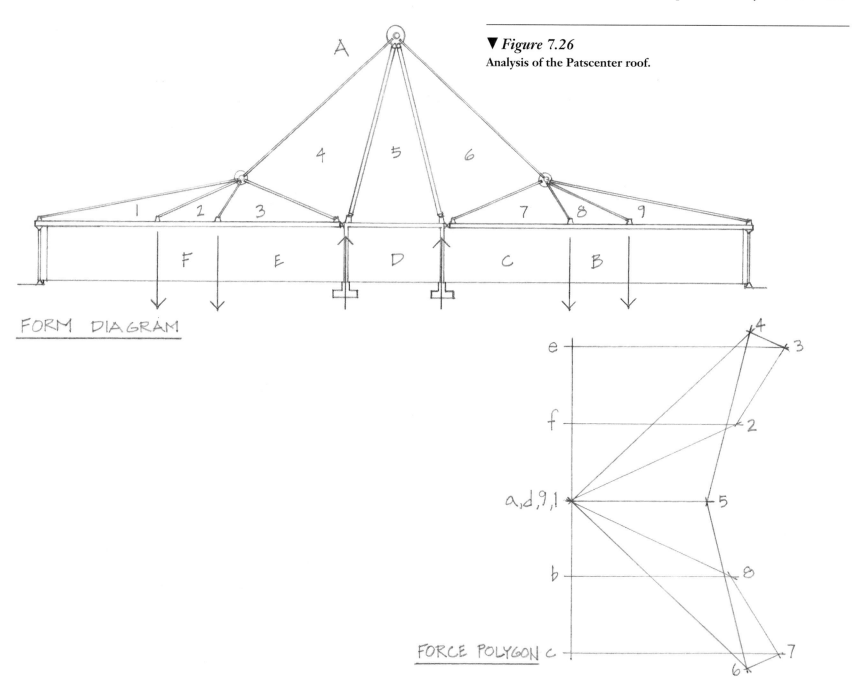

▼ *Figure* 7.26
Analysis of the Patscenter roof.

FORM DIAGRAM

FORCE POLYGON

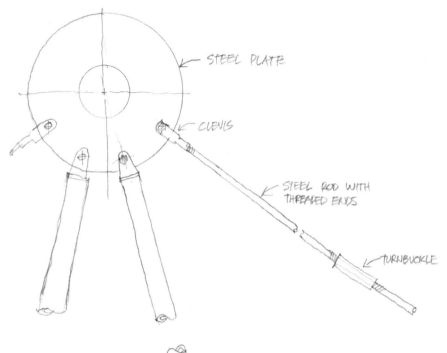

connections are based on thin steel plates that are straddled by *clevises* (Fig. 7.27). Rod tensions may be adjusted by turning threaded *turnbuckles*.

Stay cables need not be confined to planes. The roof diagrammed in Fig. 7.28 shelters a hall for 1000 diners, yet it is supported from only two columns by three-dimensional arrays of stay cables. The roof plane is framed with a grid of steel beams. Interior cable stays and perimeter columns stabilize the structure against wind uplift and asymmetrical loads.

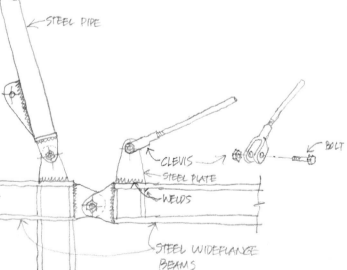

◀ *Figure* 7.27
Sketches of typical details of the Patscenter roof.

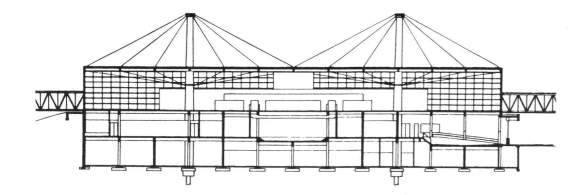

◄ *Figure 7.28*
Diagram of the Baxter Laboratories dining hall, Deerfield, Illinois. The architects and engineers are Skidmore, Owings, and Merrill. (From Andrew Orton, *The Way We Build Now*, reproduced by permission of the publisher, Chapman and Hall.)

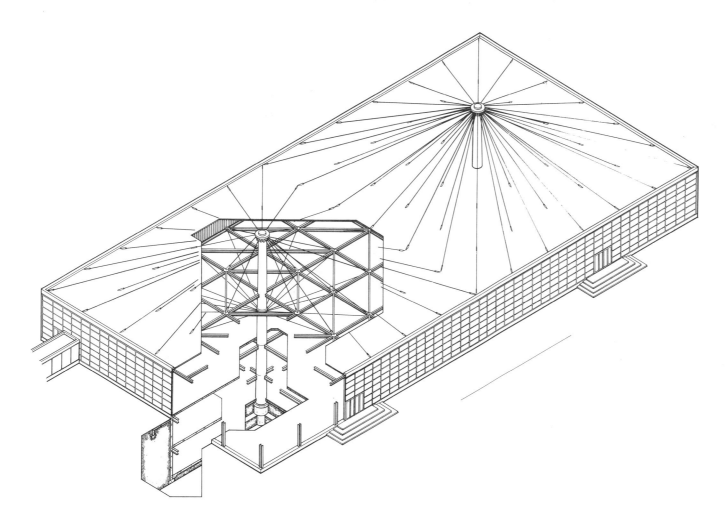

TAKING CABLE STAYS TO THE LIMIT

The Ruck-a-Chucky Bridge is an unbuilt design for a California river crossing in rugged terrain. Jammed into a tight canyon, the road makes a U-turn on the bridge itself (Figs. 7.29 and 7.30). The steep rock cliffs on either bank offer anchorages for numerous cables without the need for towers. In this virtuoso performance, engineer T. Y. Lin has designed the locations and inclinations of the stays so that they produce longitudinal forces in the deck that are carried along the curved axis of the bridge to its abutments. Because no two cables lie in the same plane, we would not even attempt an analysis of this bridge by graphical means, but our prior experience with graphical analyses of fanlike structures helps us understand how this graceful bridge works.

Fanlike structures reveal their behavior to us through their forms; their cables and towers are visible conduits of forces, resulting in highly expressive shapes that most people find pleasing and satisfying (Fig. 7.31). They share these desirable traits with trusses, which we have already begun to study, and with suspended and arched structures, whose study we will take up in the next chapter.

▲ *Figure 7.29*
Aerial view of the Ruck-a-Chucky Bridge project.

▲ *Figure 7.30*
View from the river of the Ruck-a-Chucky Bridge project. (Photos courtesy of the designer, T. Y. Lin.)

Figure 7.31 ▶

Cable stays being installed in the roof structure of Bartle Hall, a convention center in Kansas City, Missouri. Each stay is a length of high-strength bridge strand that is 3 in. (76 mm) in diameter. Each plane of stays supports a steel box girder that is 3 ft wide and 5 ft deep (0.9 m by 1.5 m); the spool of cable sits atop the free end of one box girder, and the open end of another box girder is prominently visible near the right side of the picture. Steel trusses 10 ft (3 m) apart span between the box girders and support corrugated steel roof decking. The architects and engineers are HNTB Corporation. (Photo courtesy of Vulcraft Division of Nucor Corporation.)

Key Terms and Concepts

cable-stayed structures   pylon
suspension structures   box girder
stays   torsion
fan   balanced cantilever method
harp   grout
semifan   backstay
half-harp   clevis
tower   turnbuckle

Exercises

1. Redesign the footbridge shown in Figure 7.11 so that it is supported by a tower on the left side rather than the right. Find the forces in all its members, and experiment with various ways of reducing these forces.

2. Estimate loads and dimensions for the cable-stayed roof shown in the photograph at the beginning of this chapter and in Figure 7.1. Based on these estimates, find the forces in all its members.

3. Design a different arrangement of tensile members to support the roof shown in Figures 7.24–7.26. Compare the member forces in your design with those in the original design.

4. Imagine that, for an elevated footbridge that you are designing, you are reinterpreting Brunel's timber bridges (Figs. 7.13 and 7.14), using steel pipes rather than heavy timbers. The deck beams are rectangular steel tubes, 100 mm wide and 200 mm deep. Struts of 80-mm-diameter pipe join these beams at 3 m intervals. At their lower ends, the fans of pipes are supported by reinforced concrete piers that are 500 mm square. Sketch a set of details that shows how all these members might be joined.

5. Reconfigure the Alamillo Bridge (Figs. 7.17–7.21) so that it is supported by a single vertical tower in the center of the span but maintains the same harp pattern and inclination of cables as in the original design. Compare the member forces in this design with those in the original design.

6. Work out a simple method for finding the force in any stay cable of the roof shown in Figure 7.28. How would you find the axial force(s) that this cable induces in the roof beam(s)?

A construction ▶ photograph of the suspended roof of Dulles Airport, Chantilly, Virginia, designed by architect Eero Saarinen and engineers Ammann and Whitney in 1959. (Photo courtesy of Ammann and Whitney.)

CHAPTER EIGHT

FINDING FORMS AND FORCES FOR FUNICULAR STRUCTURES

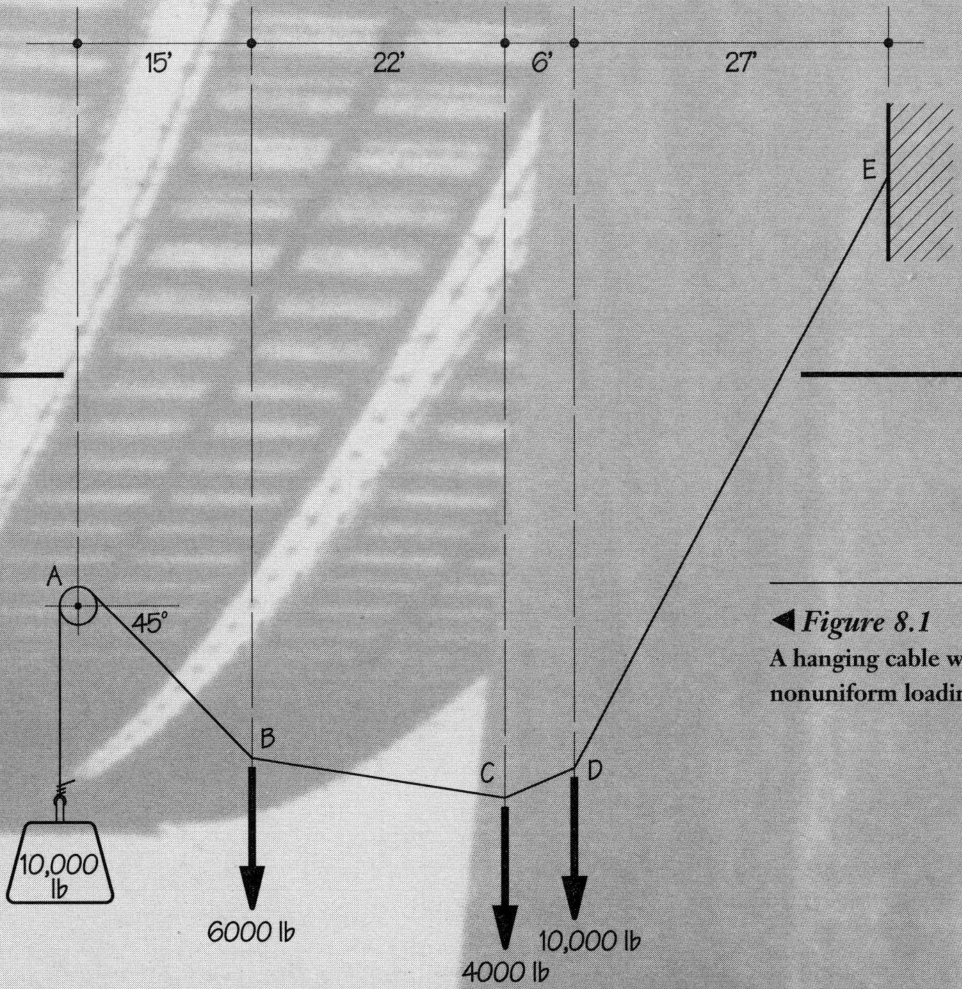

◀ Figure 8.1
A hanging cable with a nonuniform loading.

Relative to its length, a cable is a very thin, flexible member. It has no significant resistance to bending, so it transmits only axial tensile forces. Therefore, a hanging cable assumes automatically a shape that brings its applied loads and its internal forces into equilibrium. In so doing, it becomes a clear diagram of the effects of the forces that act on it. In order to design hanging structures such as suspension bridges and cable-supported roofs, we must be able to predict the form that a cable will take under any set of loads that may act on these structures. We must also be able to find the magnitudes of the tensile forces that will be produced by these loads in all parts of the cable.

As an example, consider the cable in Figure 8.1. It supports three different concentrated loads that are applied to it at irregular intervals.

Its right support is higher than its left. At its left support it runs over a frictionless pulley to a 10,000-lb weight. When the system is at rest, the leftmost segment of cable lies at an angle of 45° to the horizontal. What are the forces in each segment, and what is the direction of each segment? First we will find the answers numerically, then graphically. We will simplify the solutions by assuming with negligible error that the cable is weightless and perfectly flexible.

FINDING FORM AND FORCES NUMERICALLY

To begin a numerical solution to this problem, we assign a letter to each *node* (point of application of a force) in the cable. We know that the left-hand segment of the cable, *AB*, lies at an angle of 45°, and we know that the force in this segment is 10,000 lb because of the weight and the pulley. For the rest of the cable, although we know the horizontal dimensions between the loads, we do not know the exact form the cable will take, and we do not know its internal forces.

We draw free-body diagrams of each of the interior nodes of the cable (Fig. 8.2). We know the angles and forces at *A*, the left-hand support. Each of the interior nodes has three or four unknowns, except for node *B*, at which there are only two unknowns, the angle β and the force *BC*. We will solve for these quantities, then work our way node by node from left to right until we know all the forces and angles in the cable. We apply the equations of equilibrium in the horizontal and vertical directions to the forces at *B*, assuming upward and rightward forces as positive (Fig. 8.2[b]).

$$\sum F_v = 0$$

$$(10{,}000 \text{ lb})\cos 45° - 6000 \text{ lb} - BC\cos(90° - \beta) = 0$$

By definition, $\cos(90° - \beta) = \sin \beta$. Substituting and simplifying,

$$BC\sin\beta = 1071 \text{ lb}$$

$$\sum F_h = 0$$

$$(-10{,}000 \text{ lb})\cos 45° + BC\cos\beta = 0$$

$$BC\cos\beta = 7071 \text{ lb}$$

$$\tan\beta = \frac{BC\sin\beta}{BC\cos\beta} = \frac{1071 \text{ lb}}{7071 \text{ lb}} = 0.1515$$

$$\beta = 8.61°$$

$$BC = 7150 \text{ lb}$$

Now that *BC* and β are known, two unknowns remain at *C*: angle γ and force *CD* (Fig. 8.2[c]). The solution for node *C* parallels that for node *B*, after which we can complete our finding of form and forces by solving for the remaining angle and force at node *D* (Fig. 8.2[d]). We summarize the findings:

$$\beta = 8.61°$$

$$\gamma = -22.5°$$

$$\delta = -61.36°$$

$$AB = 10{,}000 \text{ lb}$$

$$BC = 7150 \text{ lb}$$

$$CD = 7640 \text{ lb}$$

$$DE = 14{,}726 \text{ lb}$$

This information enables us to plot an accurate shape for the cable on drawings of the structure,

to calculate lengths of cable segments between nodes and the forces in each segment, and to select a cable of suitable strength.

An interesting property of hanging cables is revealed in this analysis. Examining the forces at node *B* in Figure 8.2(b), we see that in order for this node to be in equilibrium, the horizontal components of forces *AB* and *BC* must be equal. Moving to node *C*, we note by the same logic that the horizontal components of *BC* and *CD* must be identical. Because *BC* is common to both of the nodes we have examined so far, this means that the horizontal components of the forces in cable segments *AB*, *BC*, and *CD* are all the same. Extending this process to the last node, we conclude that in fact **the horizontal component of force is constant throughout the length of any hanging cable that carries only vertical loads.** In the example that we are considering, the magnitude of this horizontal component is equal to the force in any segment of the cable times the cosine of the angle between that segment and the horizontal. This comes out to 7071 lb.

We will take up numerical methods for finding the form and forces of cables again in Chapter Nine. In the meantime, we will explore some powerful graphical methods that pertain to hanging cables.

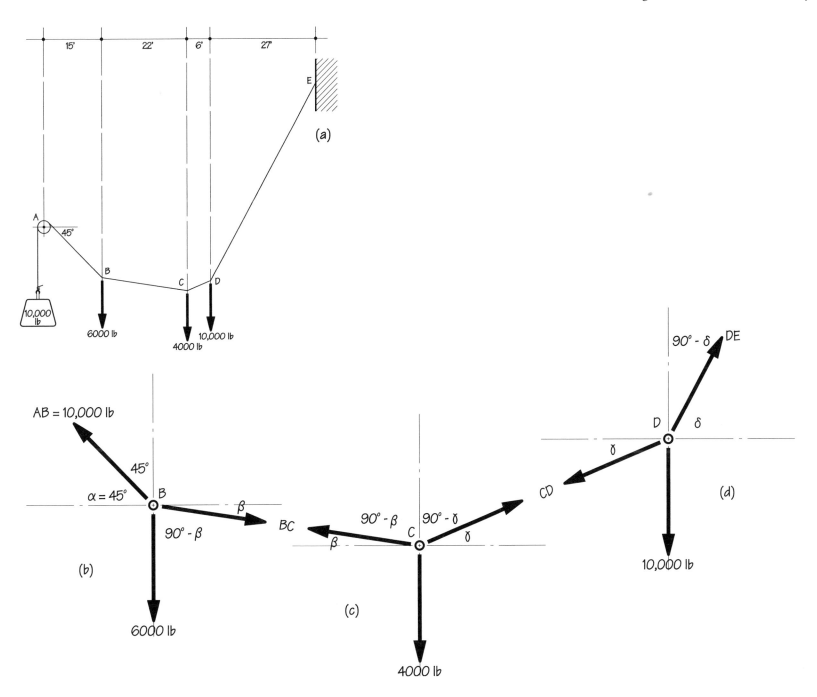

FINDING FORM AND FORCES GRAPHICALLY

In Figure 8.3, we begin a graphical solution to the same problem. The *loading diagram* (Fig. 8.3[a]) is a device that we will use for hanging cables and arches to facilitate a consistent application of interval notation. On it, we represent the horizontal projection of the cable as a line whose length is equal to the span. Along this line, we show the distances between the lines of action of the loads. We show the loads and reactions as vectors. We apply capital letters to the spaces between the loads, using the letter *O* to denote the space below the horizontal line. Projecting downward along the lines of action of the loads, we will construct the *funicular polygon*, which is the form that the cable takes under the given loading. At the moment, we are able to draw only the leftmost segment of the funicular polygon, *oa*, whose direction is given as 45° to the horizontal (Fig. 8.3[b]).

The sequence of the graphical solution parallels that of the numerical solution. We begin in Figure 8.4(c) by constructing a force polygon for the first node, *ABO*. To represent the load *AB* at this node, we plot a vertical vector, *ab*, that is exactly 6000 lb long to our chosen scale of 1 in. = 4000 lb. Next, we draw *oa*, the vector that represents the known direction and magnitude of the force in cable segment *OA*. Segment *oa*, which joins *ab* at point *a*, starts at point *o*, downward and to the right from point *a* at a distance of 10,000 lb. A vector from *o* to *b* completes the force polygon and represents the direction and magnitude of the force in cable segment *OB*. The length of *ob* scales as 7100 lb. The direction of vector *ob* may be transferred directly to the funicular polygon (Fig. 8.4[b]),

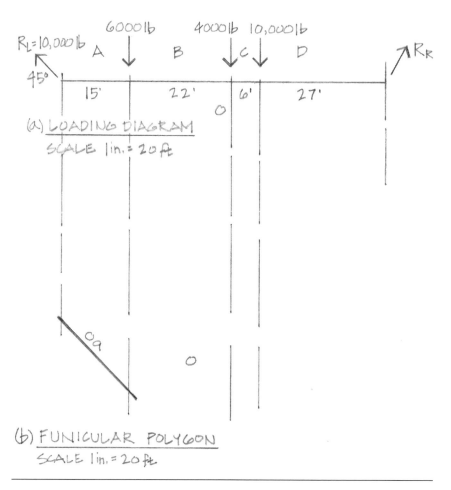

▲ *Figure 8.3*
A graphical analysis of the cable: Step 1.

where it represents the direction and length of segment *ob* of the cable. By convention, each line segment that passes through *o* on the force polygon is labeled with the lowercase letter *o* first, then the lowercase letter at its other end, which is *b* in this case (Fig. 8.4[c]). The line segment on

the funicular polygon that is drawn parallel to this segment on the force polygon is given the same label, *ob* (Fig. 8.4[b]). Notice that the lowercase *b* in *ob* on the funicular polygon corresponds to the capital letter *B* in the space directly above on the loading diagram.

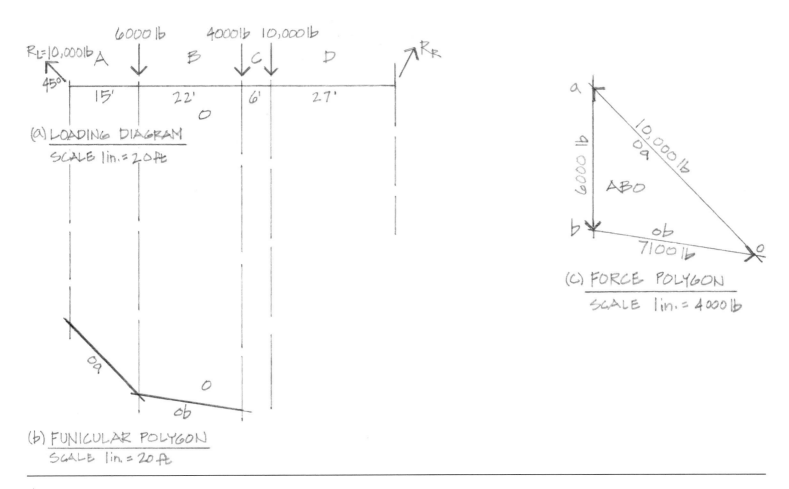

▲ *Figure 8.4*
A graphical analysis of the cable: Step 2.

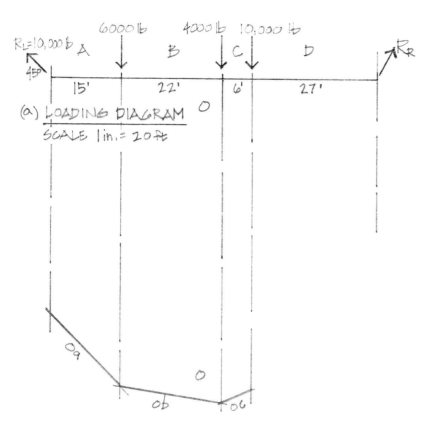

(a) LOADING DIAGRAM
SCALE 1 in. = 20 ft

(b) FUNICULAR POLYGON
SCALE 1 in. = 20 ft

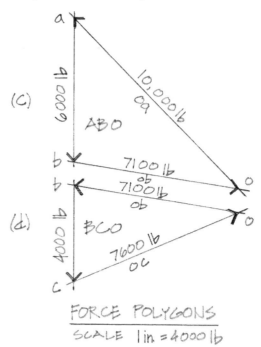

◄ *Figure 8.5*
A graphical analysis of the cable: Step 3.

FORCE POLYGONS
SCALE 1 in. = 4000 lb

Moving to node *BCO* (Fig. 8.5[a]), we are able to plot a second triangular force polygon, (d), whose known sides are *ob*, which we found a moment ago in completing the first triangle, (c), and *bc*, which represents the vertical load *BC*. The third vector, *oc*, has a magnitude that scales at 7600 lb. We draw *oc* on the funicular polygon, (b), parallel to *oc* on the force polygon.

A third triangle, *cdo*, in Figure 8.6(e), completes the graphical solution, giving the magni-

tude of force *DO* and allowing us to plot *od* on the funicular polygon (Fig. 8.6[b]).

It is evident in looking at the three triangular force polygons, (c), (d), and (e), that vectors *ob* and *oc* are each common to two triangles. It would be advantageous to merge all the triangles into a single, unified diagram. This would eliminate any errors that might stem from having to replot each of the repeated vectors, and it would save time and effort. We construct this unified diagram to the right of the three triangles (Fig. 8.6[f]). The three vertical load vectors now lie

end to end, creating a load line that is identical in concept and construction to the load lines that we used to find forces in trusses. Lowercase letters on the load line correspond to capital letters on the loading diagram, just as they did for trusses. The vectors that represent the form and forces for the four segments of the cable are represented by line segments that meet at point *o*. What we have constructed is a unified force polygon for the cable structure that is exactly analogous to the force polygon that we used for trusses.

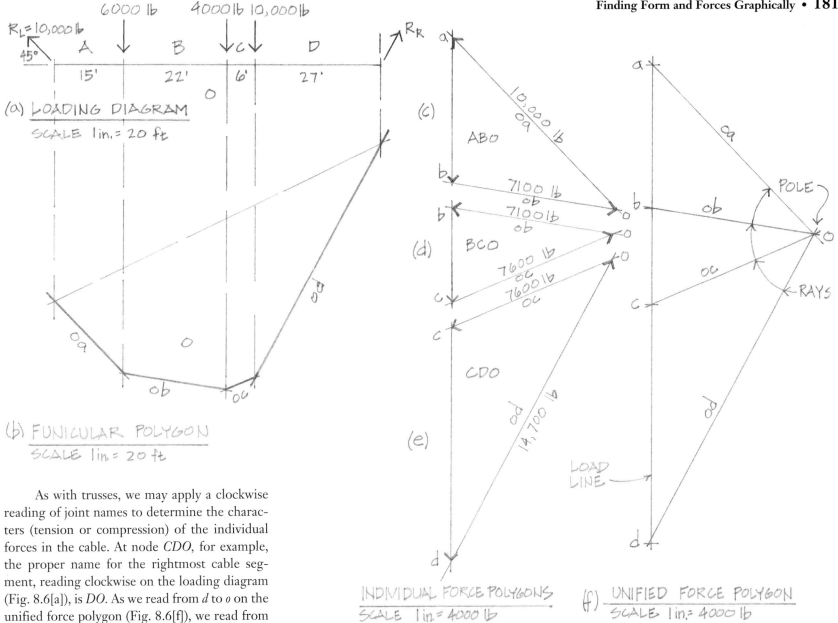

(a) LOADING DIAGRAM
SCALE 1 in. = 20 ft

$R_L = 10,000$ lb
45°
6000 lb
4000 lb 10,000 lb
A   B   C   D
15'   22'   6'   27'
R_R
O

(b) FUNICULAR POLYGON
SCALE 1 in. = 20 ft

(c) ABO
10,000 lb
oa

(d) BCO
7100 lb
ob
7600 lb
oc

(e) CDO
14,700 lb
od

INDIVIDUAL FORCE POLYGONS
SCALE 1 in. = 4000 lb

(f) UNIFIED FORCE POLYGON
SCALE 1 in. = 4000 lb
POLE
RAYS
LOAD LINE

▲ *Figure 8.6*
A graphical analysis of the cable: Step 4.

As with trusses, we may apply a clockwise reading of joint names to determine the characters (tension or compression) of the individual forces in the cable. At node *CDO*, for example, the proper name for the rightmost cable segment, reading clockwise on the loading diagram (Fig. 8.6[a]), is *DO*. As we read from *d* to *o* on the unified force polygon (Fig. 8.6[f]), we read from lower left to upper right. The force in this segment acts upward and rightward on node *CDO*, pulling on it. Segment *od* on the funicular polygon is in tension.

The cable structure that we have just examined is irregular in almost every respect: its ends lie at different elevations, and it is loaded with dissimilar forces placed at irregular intervals. It illustrates the general case of a hanging structure with any support condition and any group of vertical loads. Its force polygon (Fig. 8.6[f]) is also typical for any vertically loaded cable structure. The vectors *oa* through *od* that represent the directions and magnitudes of the segments of the cable all meet at a point. This point is known as the *pole*, and it is customarily assigned the lowercase letter *o*. (This is why we selected *O* to represent the space below the line in the loading diagram in Figure 8.6[a]). The vectors that radiate from the pole are called *rays*. We find the form of the cable (Fig. 8.6[b]) by plotting line segments parallel to each of the rays between the lines of action of the forces on the loading diagram. Interval notation assists us in determining where each of these line segments belongs: *oa* lies in space *A*, *ob* in space *B*, and so on.

The form of the cable that we have plotted in Figure 8.6(b) is known as a *funicular polygon* or *string polygon* for this group of forces. The word *funicular* comes from the Latin *funiculus*, meaning "string." A funicular polygon is a form that a piece of string (or rope, cable, or chain) would assume under a given pattern of loads. When we refer to the shape of a structure as being *funicular*, we mean that it has the same shape that a string or cable would take under the loadings on the structure, or, if it is a compressive structure, the inversion of this shape. Structures with funicular shapes have the advantage that they experience an axial flow of internal forces, either

tension or compression, under the assumed loading condition. This means that they utilize material very efficiently. In general, structures with funicular shapes can span much longer distances than structures with nonfunicular shapes, because structures with nonfunicular shapes, which experience nonaxial flows of internal forces, do not utilize material as efficiently.

LEARNING MORE FROM THE GRAPHICAL SOLUTION

The graphical solution in Figure 8.6 yields additional information beyond the forces and directions that we originally sought. At its supports, the cable produces inclined reactions. We can find the vertical and horizontal components of each reaction by drawing and scaling vertical and horizontal projections from the corresponding rays of the force polygon (Fig. 8.7). In Figure 8.7(b), od_v represents the vertical component of the right-hand reaction; it measures 12,900 lb in length. The horizontal pull of the cable on the support is represented by od_h, which scales at 7100 lb. It is apparent that od_h also represents the horizontal components of all the rays in the force polygon, which tells us graphically that the horizontal components of the forces throughout the cable are exactly the same, as we discovered in the numerical analysis earlier in this chapter. Only the vertical components vary.

Looking back and comparing Figure 8.6(c), (d), and (e) with Figure 8.6(f), we see that each of the two internal rays in the unified force polygon, *ob* and *oc*, represents a pair of vectors that are equal in magnitude but opposite in direction. In seeking to find the net **external**

forces that act on the structure as represented in the unified force polygon, each internal ray can be seen as having a value of zero, because the opposing vectors of which it is composed cancel each other. Thus, the net external forces on this cable structure comprise the vertical loads, represented by the load line, *ad*, and the two reactions, represented by the top and bottom rays, *oa* and *od*. These three line segments form a triangular equilibrium polygon. Therefore, on the funicular polygon, the lines of action of the forces that they represent must intersect at a point. It follows that on the funicular polygon, Figure 8.7(a), the lines of action of the two reactions, *oa* and *od*, intersect at a point that lies on the line of action of the resultant of all the external loads on the cable. This is a useful fact that we will have occasion to employ a bit later on in several types of solutions to common structural problems.

If any point on a hanging cable is pinned in place, restrained from moving horizontally or vertically but free to rotate, the cable on one side of the point may be cut without affecting the form or forces of the cable on the other side. In

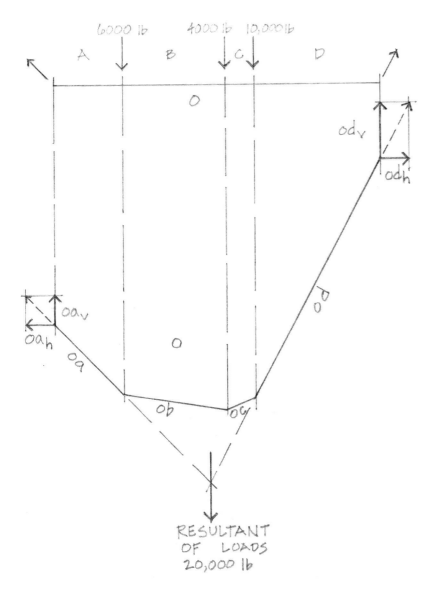

6000 lb   4000 lb   10,000 lb

A   B   C   D

O

O

oa_v

oa_h   oa

ob   oc

od

od_v

od_h

RESULTANT
OF LOADS
20,000 lb

(a) FUNICULAR POLYGON
SCALE 1 in. = 20 ft

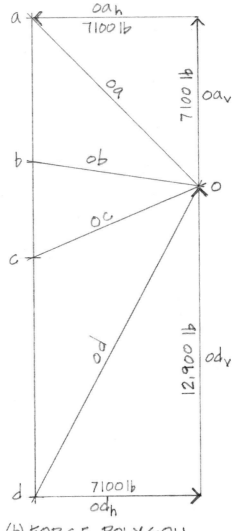

a   oa_h
7100 lb

7100 lb   oa_v

oa

b   ob

O

c   oc

od

12,900 lb   od_v

d   7100 lb
od_h

(b) FORCE POLYGON
SCALE 1 in. = 4000 lb

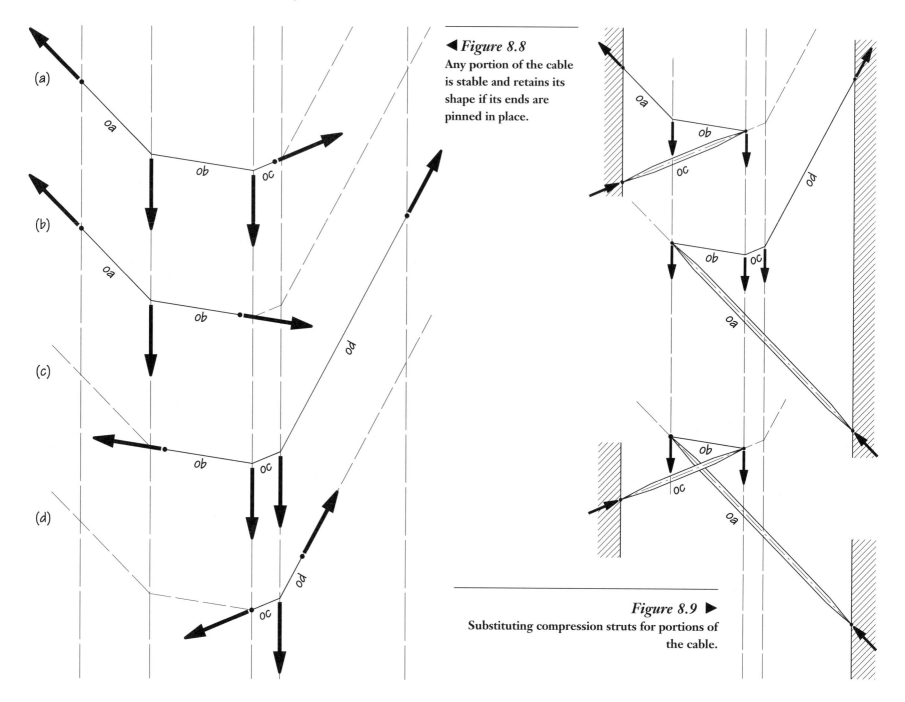

◀ Figure 8.8
Any portion of the cable is stable and retains its shape if its ends are pinned in place.

Figure 8.9 ▶
Substituting compression struts for portions of the cable.

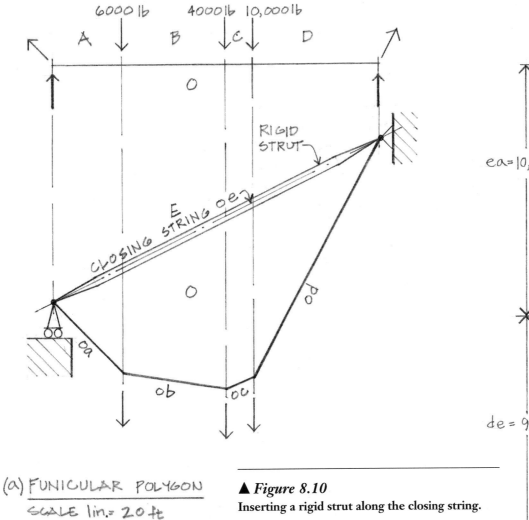

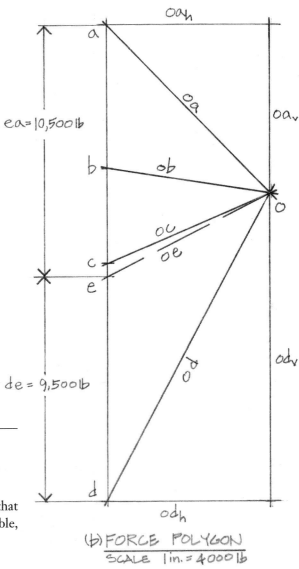

(a) FUNICULAR POLYGON
SCALE 1 in.= 20 ft

▲ *Figure 8.10*
Inserting a rigid strut along the closing string.

(b) FORCE POLYGON
SCALE 1 in. = 4000 lb

Figure 8.8(a), a point on segment *oc* is pinned and the cable to the right is cut, leaving the portion to the left in its original form. Figures 8.8(b), (c), and (d) illustrate further examples of this principle.

A compression strut may be substituted for any segment of the cable with which it shares an axis, without affecting the form or forces of the remaining cable segments (Fig. 8.9). The compressive force in the strut is identical in magni-

tude to the tensile force in the cable segment that it replaces, and the entire system of strut, cable, and loads remains in equilibrium.

THE CLOSING STRING

In Figure 8.10, we insert a rigid strut between the two ends of the cable. To be sure that the resulting structure applies only vertical forces to its supports, we support one end of it on a hinge

and the other, on a horizontal roller. The forces in the cable do not change, but the strut absorbs the horizontal pull of the cable, leaving only vertical reactions at the two supports. What is the magnitude of each of these reactions?

To answer this question, we construct two new force polygons to represent the forces that act at each of the supports. For efficiency, we do this directly on the unified force polygon in Figure 8.10(b) by simply adding vector *oe* through the pole *o*, parallel to the axis of the strut. The polygon for the right-hand support includes the vectors *od*, representing the force in the cable, *oe*, representing the force in the strut, and *de*, representing the right-hand vertical reaction. By similar logic we can show that vector *ea* represents the left-hand vertical reaction.

The axis of the strut is a line segment that connects the two ends of the funicular polygon. This line segment is called the *closing string*. A useful fact to remember is that **a line parallel to the closing string through the pole of the force polygon divides the load line into segments whose respective lengths can be scaled to give the magnitude of the vertical reactions of a thrust-free structure that supports the given pattern of loads.** The term "thrust-free" should be noted carefully; without the strut, the cable structure pulls inward on the two supports. This pull may be thought of as a negative thrust. The vertical components of the inwardly thrusting reactions of a freely hanging cable are not the same as the vertical reactions for the same cable with the strut added unless the closing string is level. This is evident in Figure 8.10(b): the vertical component of the left-hand reaction of the freely hanging cable, oa_v, is not equal to *ea*, the vertical reaction on the cable with strut, and od_v does not equal *de*. If the closing string were level, *e* would remain in the same place, but *o* would move down to the same elevation, making $oa_v = ea$ and $od_v = de$.

FAMILIES OF FUNICULAR LINES

How many forms can a cable take under a given set of loads? In other words, how many shapes are there that are funicular for a given loading condition? Looking back at the force polygon for the cable structure we have been examining, we see that the rays converge at a single point, the pole. What would happen if we were to assume some other point as the pole? In Figure 8.11(b), we add two randomly chosen pole locations, *o'* and *o''*, to the original pole, *o*, and superimpose the three force polygons on one another. We then generate a new funicular polygon from each new force polygon, starting arbitrarily from the identical left support location in each case (Fig. 8.11[a]). It is obvious that we could continue this exercise for as many repetitions as we wish by continuing to select pole locations at random. For this loading pattern, there is an infinite number of funicular polygons. By tightening or slackening the cable, and by raising and lowering its ends, we can make as many shapes as we wish, all of them funicular for this loading. Though the shapes are different, they are not random. They resemble one another as brothers and sisters resemble one another, and for this reason we refer to these shapes as belonging to a *family of funicular lines.* For any set of loads, there is an infinitely large family of funicular lines, any one of which can be the basis for a structure that experiences only axial internal forces under this loading.

It is worth our while to become more familiar with the properties of the various members of a family of funicular lines. Detailed study of Figure 8.11 reveals that as the pole moves far-ther from the load line, the corresponding funicular polygon becomes shallower, and its horizontal pull and the forces in its segments rise. As the pole moves closer to the load line, a deeper funicular polygon with a lower horizontal pull and lower internal forces results. If we were to construct a set of funicular polygons from force polygons whose poles all lie at the same distance from the load line, we would discover that corresponding points in the force polygons would lie at identical vertical distances from their closing strings, and that the horizontal pulls in all the force polygons would be the same.

We also see in Figure 8.11 that if the pole moves up or down in relation to the load line, the right-hand end of the funicular polygon moves up or down in response. If we draw the closing strings of the three funicular polygons (Fig. 8.11[a]), the corresponding rays *oe*, *o'e*, and *o''e* in the force polygon (Fig. 8.11[b]) all intersect the load line at point *e*. This confirms the conclusion we reached from the construction in Figure 8.10.

Figure 8.11 ▶
A family of funicular lines.

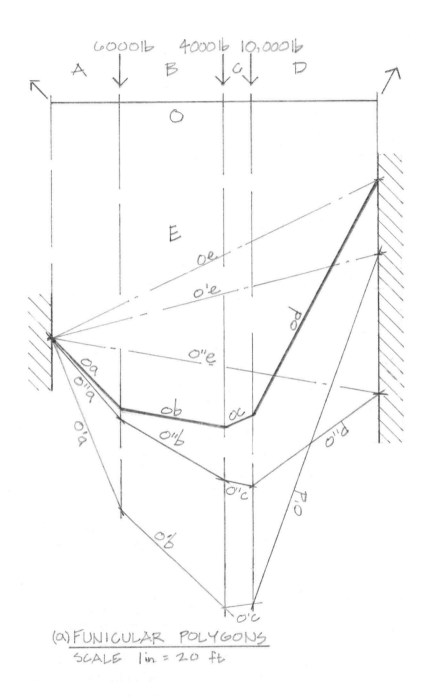

6000 lb   4000 lb   10,000 lb

(a) FUNICULAR POLYGONS
SCALE 1 in. = 20 ft

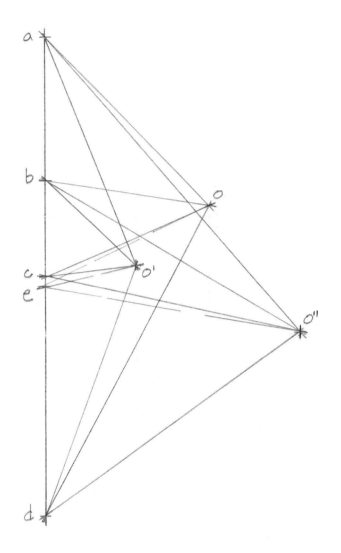

(b) FORCE POLYGONS
SCALE 1 in. = 4000 lb

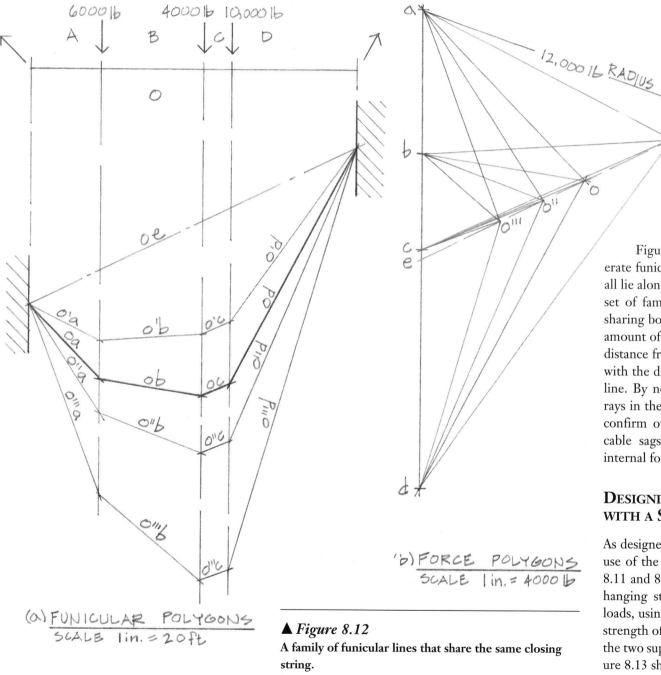

(a) FUNICULAR POLYGONS
SCALE 1 in. = 20 ft

6000 lb   4000 lb 10,000 lb

A   B   C   D

O

▲ *Figure 8.12*

A family of funicular lines that share the same closing string.

'b) FORCE POLYGONS
SCALE 1 in. = 4000 lb

12,000 lb RADIUS

Figure 8.13 ▶
Finding the form for a cable between level supports and with a predetermined maximum force.

Figure 8.12 shows what happens if we generate funicular polygons from a set of poles that all lie along the same line through point *e*: a new set of family members emerges, each of them sharing both its end points with the others. The amount of *sag* in the cable, its maximum vertical distance from the closing string, varies inversely with the distance between the pole and the load line. By noting the comparative lengths of the rays in the force polygons in Figure 8.12(b), we confirm our earlier finding that the more the cable sags, the lower its horizontal pull and internal forces are.

DESIGNING A FUNICULAR STRUCTURE WITH A SPECIFIED MAXIMUM FORCE

As designers of structures, we can make creative use of the discoveries we have made in Figures 8.11 and 8.12. Suppose that we wish to design a hanging structure to support this same set of loads, using a cable that has an allowable tensile strength of 12,000 lb. Suppose also that we want the two supports to be level with each other. Figure 8.13 shows how this may be done. From any

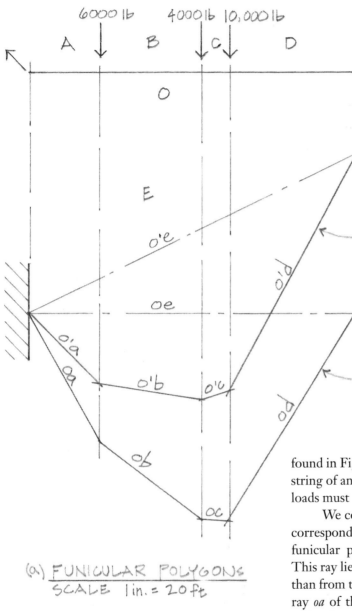

6000 lb   4000 lb 10,000 lb

A   B   C   D

O

E

o'e

oe

o'a

oa

o'b   o'o

ob

oc

TRIAL FUNICULAR POLYGON

FINAL FUNICULAR POLYGON

o'd

od

(a) FUNICULAR POLYGONS
SCALE 1 in. = 20 ft

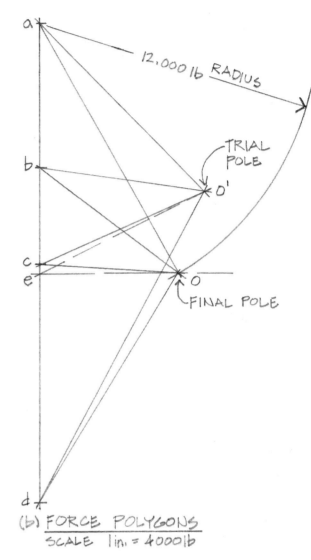

12,000 lb RADIUS

a

b

c
e

d

TRIAL POLE
o'

FINAL POLE
o

(b) FORCE POLYGONS
SCALE 1 in. = 4000 lb

arbitrarily located *trial pole*, *o′*, we construct a set of rays (Fig. 8.13[b]). Drawing cable segments parallel to these rays, we construct the corresponding *trial funicular polygon* and its closing string *o′e* (Fig. 8.13[a]). We draw ray *o′e* parallel to this closing string on the force polygon. As we

found in Figure 8.11, a ray parallel to the closing string of any cable that is funicular for this set of loads must pass through *e* on the load line.

We construct a horizontal ray through *e* to correspond to the level closing string of the funicular polygon that we seek (Fig. 8.13[b]). This ray lies farther from the top of the load line than from the bottom, meaning that the topmost ray *oa* of the force polygon will be the longest and will represent the force in the most heavily loaded segment of the cable. It is therefore ray *oa* that must be limited to a length of 12,000 lb. We set a compass to a radius of 12,000 lb at the given scale and swing an arc around point *a* that intersects the horizontal ray through *e*. This point of

intersection is the *final pole*, *o*. We construct a set of rays through *o* and, parallel to these, plot the segments of the *final funicular polygon* (Fig. 8.13[a]), which is the shape of a cable structure that will support the given loading pattern across level supports with a maximum cable force of 12,000 lb.

CONSTRUCTING A FUNICULAR POLYGON FOR A UNIFORMLY DISTRIBUTED LOAD

Figure 8.14 illustrates the design of another hanging structure across level supports, this one to carry a mass of 9000 kg that is distributed uniformly along the horizontal projection of the cable, using a cable whose safe capacity is 55 kilonewtons (kN). Because the graphical method offers no way of dealing directly with a distributed load, we must approximate it as a series of small, concentrated loads. We divide the uniform mass into a series of nine smaller masses. (Nine is an arbitrary number; it was chosen in this case to take advantage of the fact that the total mass, 9000 kg, is easily divisible by 9. The more divisions we create, the more accurate the approximation will be, but more divisions also create more labor and more opportunities for drafting errors to accumulate). Each of the nine masses is 1000 kg. Multiplying 1000 kg times 9.8 m/s^2, the acceleration of gravity, we convert each mass to its corresponding force of 9.8 kN. At the center of each of the nine masses we indicate a downward vector with the value of 9.8 kN. We extend a vertical construction line down the sheet of paper from each of these vectors.

To the right, we draw, to any convenient scale, a vertical load line that consists of nine segments of 9.8 kN each (Fig. 8.14[b]). We choose a trial pole location arbitrarily and construct a set of rays. Parallel to these rays we plot the trial funicular polygon and its closing string, $o'x$.

Drawn parallel to this closing string, ray $o'x$ on the trial force polygon locates point x on the load line, the point through which lines par-

allel to the closing strings of all the members of this family of funicular curves must pass. We find that x lies at the midpoint of the load line, as it does for any uniform loading. Because we want our structure to have level supports, we draw a horizontal line through x, knowing that the final pole must lie somewhere on this line.

To locate the final pole, we set a compass for a radius of 55 kN, the maximum force the cable can carry. We draw an arc about either end of the load line until it intersects the level line through x (Fig. 8.14[b]). This intersection is o, the final pole. We construct a set of rays from o, and from these plot the final funicular polygon (Fig. 8.14[d]), which is a close approximation of the form the cable will take under a uniform loading while experiencing a maximum internal force of 55 kN. The actual shape is a smooth curve that passes through the end points and is tangent to the centers of segments ob through oj. It is a parabola, which is the shape a cable always takes under a load that is uniformly distributed on its **horizontal projection.** A cable hanging under only its own weight has its load distributed uniformly over its **length** and takes a slightly different shape, called a *catenary*.

ANALYZING AN EXISTING CABLE ROOF STRUCTURE

The roof of Dulles Airport in Chantilly, Virginia (shown in the photograph at the beginning of this chapter) is a curving concrete deck that is supported by pairs of hanging cables spaced 10 ft apart, spanning 200 ft between stiff edge beams. Working from a published section drawing of the building, we will verify the form of the roof

Figure 8.14 ▶

Finding the form for a cable with a uniform loading and with a predetermined maximum force.

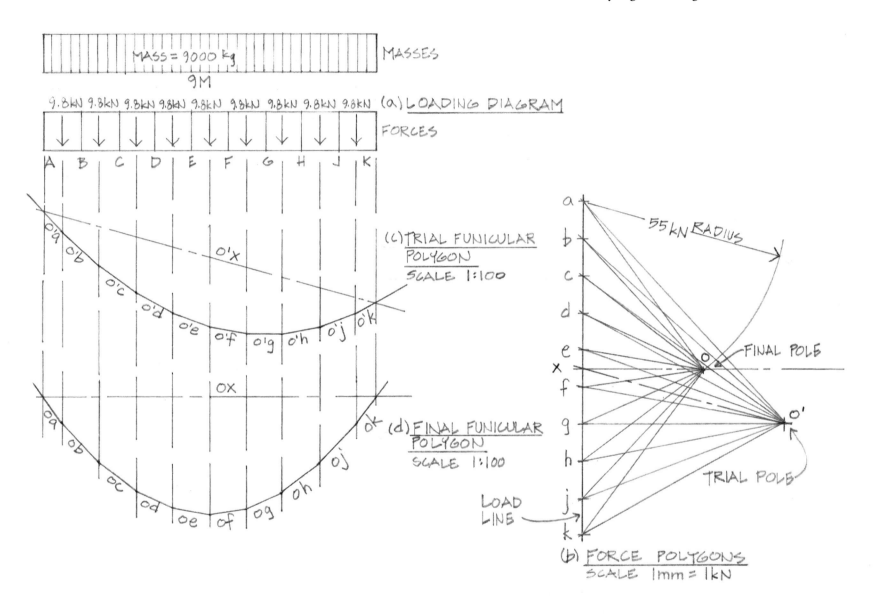

MASSES

MASS = 9000 kg

9M

9.8kN 9.8kN 9.8kN 9.8kN 9.8kN 9.8kN 9.8kN 9.8kN 9.8kN (a) LOADING DIAGRAM

FORCES

A   B   C   D   E   F   G   H   J   K

(c) TRIAL FUNICULAR POLYGON
SCALE 1:100

O'x

OX

(d) FINAL FUNICULAR POLYGON
SCALE 1:100

55 kN RADIUS

a
b
c
d
e
x
f
g
h
j
k

O FINAL POLE

O' TRIAL POLE

LOAD LINE

(b) FORCE POLYGONS
SCALE 1mm = 1kN

and find the forces in the cables (Fig. 8.15). Because the deck follows the curve of the cables, the form of this roof is a catenary rather than a parabola. As a practical matter, however, for a cable whose sag does not exceed a quarter of its span, there is little difference between a parabola and a catenary. We divide the span of the roof arbitrarily into 10 equal segments, each 20 ft long in horizontal projection. We place a load at the center of each segment. Assuming that the dead and live loads on the roof reach a maximum total of 80 lb/ft², we can estimate the load on each segment of the roof:

$$w = (20 \text{ ft})(10 \text{ ft})(80 \text{ } lb/ft^2) = 16,000 \text{ lb}$$

We construct a load line accordingly.

We draw our funicular polygon at a constant distance above the curve of the roof on the space diagram; this allows us to compare the shapes easily while doing our construction on clean paper. Working with as much precision as

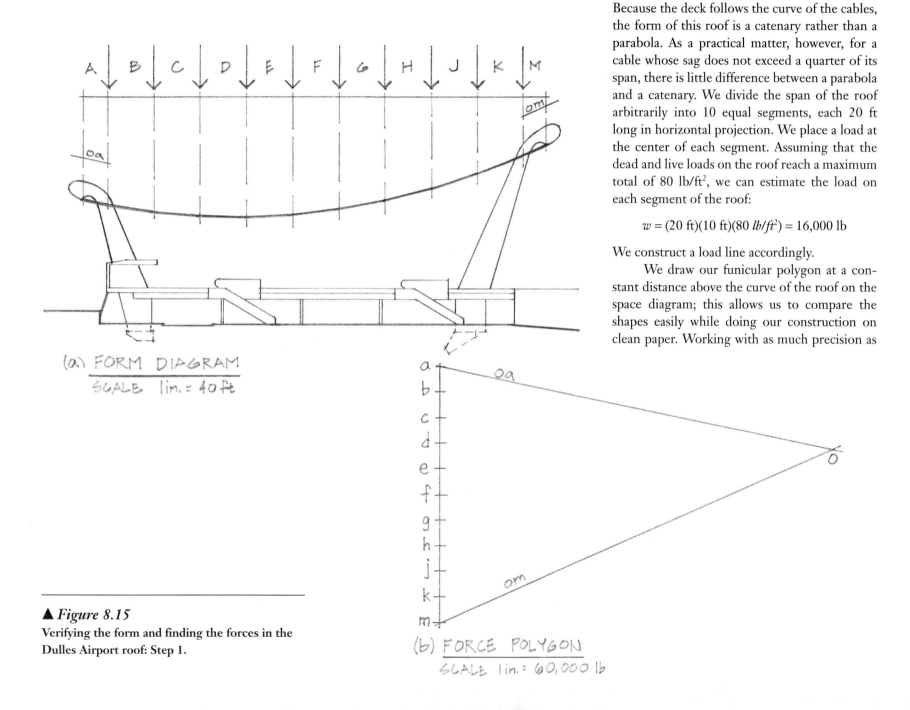

(a) FORM DIAGRAM
SCALE 1 in. = 40 ft

(b) FORCE POLYGON
SCALE 1 in. = 60,000 lb

▲ *Figure 8.15*
Verifying the form and finding the forces in the Dulles Airport roof: Step 1.

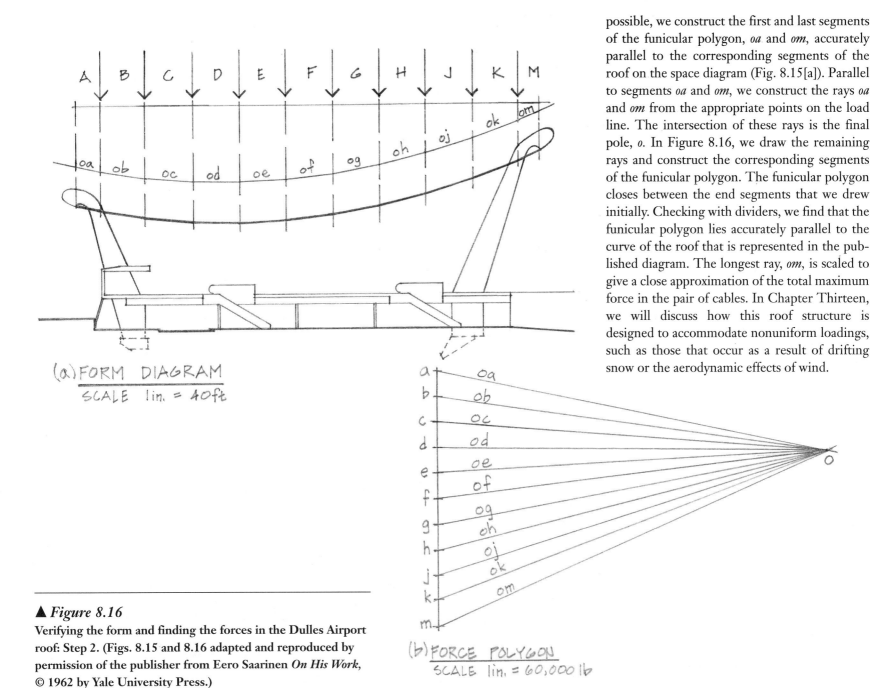

(a) FORM DIAGRAM
SCALE 1 in. = 40 ft

(b) FORCE POLYGON
SCALE 1 in. = 60,000 lb

possible, we construct the first and last segments of the funicular polygon, *oa* and *om*, accurately parallel to the corresponding segments of the roof on the space diagram (Fig. 8.15[a]). Parallel to segments *oa* and *om*, we construct the rays *oa* and *om* from the appropriate points on the load line. The intersection of these rays is the final pole, *o*. In Figure 8.16, we draw the remaining rays and construct the corresponding segments of the funicular polygon. The funicular polygon closes between the end segments that we drew initially. Checking with dividers, we find that the funicular polygon lies accurately parallel to the curve of the roof that is represented in the published diagram. The longest ray, *om*, is scaled to give a close approximation of the total maximum force in the pair of cables. In Chapter Thirteen, we will discuss how this roof structure is designed to accommodate nonuniform loadings, such as those that occur as a result of drifting snow or the aerodynamic effects of wind.

▲ *Figure 8.16*
Verifying the form and finding the forces in the Dulles Airport roof: Step 2. (Figs. 8.15 and 8.16 adapted and reproduced by permission of the publisher from Eero Saarinen *On His Work*, © 1962 by Yale University Press.)

ESTIMATING LOADS

In order to design any structure, we must estimate the magnitude of the forces that act upon it. These include gravity loads, which are vertical, and loads that are assumed to act laterally, such as wind forces, seismic forces, and hydrostatic pressures.

Gravity loads are usually classified as dead loads and live loads. Dead loads include the self-weight of the structure—decking, purlins, rafters, joists, beams, girders, columns, load-bearing walls, arches, cables, and trusses. Dead loads also include fixed nonstructural components such as windows, ceilings, flooring, partitions, and stairs. Dead loads can usually be estimated fairly closely and with reasonable certainty, although self-weight estimates for structural members must be based initially on estimated sizes of the members and later adjusted to correspond to calculated sizes. The following densities are useful in calculating dead loads:

Material	lb/ft³	kg/m³
Earth, average	125	2000
Wood, average	35	560
Brick masonry, average	125	2000
Building stone, average	165	2640
Concrete, reinforced	150	2400
Steel	490	7850
Aluminum	165	2645
Glass	156	2500
Water, fresh	62.4	1000
Seawater	64	1025

Live gravity loads include the changing weights of people, furniture, goods, vehicles, snow, and rainwater that act on a structure. We are unable to estimate these loads with certainty, so we try to be somewhat conservative. However, a structure can become very bulky and expensive if its design is based on a too conservative estimate of live loads. For most structures, live load estimates are based on minimum values mandated by building codes. These are assumed to be applied to every square foot or square meter of a floor or roof surface. Building codes permit reductions in these loads for structural members that support more than a certain minimum area, usually 150 ft² (14 m²); the percentage of reduction increases with the area the member supports. In addition to complying with code minima, the designer of a structure must exercise good judgment in estimating live loads. The following are typical live load figures from a building code:

Floors Occupancy	lb/ft²	kg/m²
Residences, apartments, hotels, hospitals	40	200
Offices, schools, auditoriums	50	250
Retail stores, museums, grandstands, bleachers	100	500
Manufacturing	75 and up	375 and up
Storage	125 and up	600 and up
Parking garages	50	250
Service or storage garages	100	500
Pedestrian bridges	100	500

Roofs		
Roofs with snow	Typically 20–40 lb/ft² (100–200 kg/m²), depending on location, but two to four times as much in high mountains	
Roofs without snow	12–20	60–100

Loads on vehicular bridges must be addressed according to the type and weight of the vehicle, the distribution of the load among the wheels of the vehicle, and the positions of the wheels. A road bridge that is jammed bumper-to-bumper with fully loaded trucks experiences an average load of about 180 lb/ft² (900 kg/m²), which is concentrated under the wheels. Surprisingly, average loads from automobiles are not especially great; a typical car loaded with passengers results in an **average** floor loading of only about 20 lb/ft² (100 kg/m²), although a typical front wheel applies a concentrated load of 800 lb (360 kg).

Wind and seismic loads are the most difficult of all to estimate. Building codes estimate wind loads through a combination of factors that include the geographic area, surrounding trees or structures that offer wind protection, the shape of the building, and height above the ground. Wind loads based on building code estimates are generally apportioned with a certain percentage as pressures on windward surfaces of walls and roofs and the remaining percentage as suctions on leeward surfaces. For tall buildings, wind tunnel testing is a more accurate way of predicting wind loads and their variation in intensity from one part of a building to another.

Seismic load estimates are based on code-mandated formulas that take into account the mass, rigidity, and period of vibration of the building, the character of the soil around the foundations, and the expected maximum severity of an earthquake in the geographic area where the building is located. The formulas convert the dynamic loads that would result from these complex factors during an earthquake to equivalent static load figures that are easy to use in structural calculations. ■

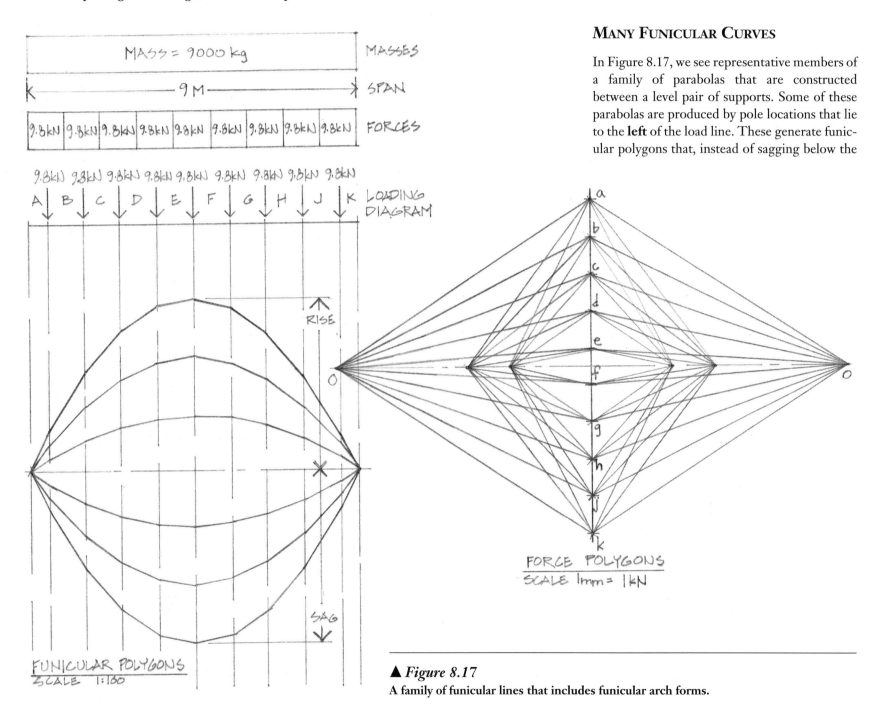

MASS = 9000 kg — MASSES

9 M — SPAN

| 9.8kN | 9.8kN | 9.8kN | 9.8kN | 9.8kN | 9.8kN | 9.8kN | 9.8kN | 9.8kN | FORCES |

9.8kN 9.8kN 9.8kN 9.8kN 9.8kN 9.8kN 9.8kN 9.8kN 9.8kN

A B C D E F G H J K LOADING DIAGRAM

RISE

O

SAG

FUNICULAR POLYGONS
SCALE 1:100

FORCE POLYGONS
SCALE 1mm = 1kN

MANY FUNICULAR CURVES

In Figure 8.17, we see representative members of a family of parabolas that are constructed between a level pair of supports. Some of these parabolas are produced by pole locations that lie to the **left** of the load line. These generate funicular polygons that, instead of sagging below the

▲ *Figure 8.17*
A family of funicular lines that includes funicular arch forms.

horizontal, arch gracefully above it. These curves represent the centerlines of funicular *arches*, structures that would experience only axial **compressive** forces under a uniform loading. This is another example of the principle that every structural shape can be inverted. If a funicular cable is inverted, it defines the centerline of an arch that can carry the same pattern of loads by acting in axial compression. If we wish to design a funicular arch, we can follow the method that we have been using for hanging structures, but we must look to the left of the load line for a final pole location. In a hanging structure, the greater the sag is, the lower the forces are in the cable are. Similarly, in an arch, the greater the *rise*, its maximum height above the closing string, the lower the forces are.

DESIGNING AN ARCH WITH A GIVEN MAXIMUM COMPRESSIVE FORCE

Figure 8.18 is a photograph of a bridge whose supporting arch does not curve smoothly, but is made up of concrete slab segments with straight-line axes. It is evident that this shape is a funicular polygon for the concentrated loads that are brought to the arch by the eight vertical concrete walls that support the deck. The arch does not taper to match the variations in its internal forces from one segment to another, but is constant in thickness. In this small bridge, although the constant thickness results in a small waste of concrete, it saves considerable money by simplifying the formwork for the arch.

Suppose that we want to design a bridge of this type to span 27 m across level supports, as sketched in Figure 8.19. The elevation of the roadway above the river is given. The bridge deck is 8 m wide, and its weight is carried down

▲ *Figure 8.18*
The Schwandbach Bridge near Hinterfultigen, Switzerland, constructed in 1933, typifies the deck-stiffened concrete arch design that was pioneered in the 1920s and 1930s by Robert Maillart. The span is 37.4 m (123 ft). (Photo: ETH-Bibliothek, Zürich.)

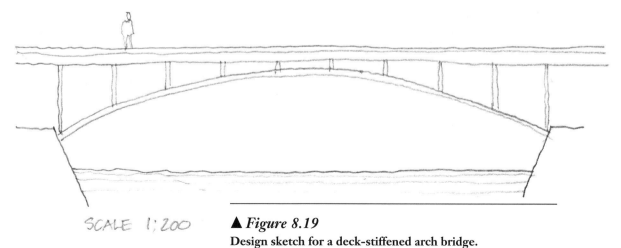

SCALE 1:200

▲ *Figure 8.19*
Design sketch for a deck-stiffened arch bridge.

to the arch by eight walls, each 0.3 m thick, that divide the arch into nine segments, each 3 m long as measured in horizontal projection. The average thickness of the concrete in the deck is 400 mm. The live load is assumed to be 900

kg/m^2. We would like the arch to be 200 mm thick and 5 m wide. Though we will specify a concrete mixture whose ultimate strength is 30 MPa, we will design the arch for a maximum compressive stress of 5.0 MPa. This will leave

ample reserves of strength to withstand the effects of asymmetrical loads, change of temperature, yielding of supports, creep and shrinkage of concrete, and the tendency of the arch to buckle.

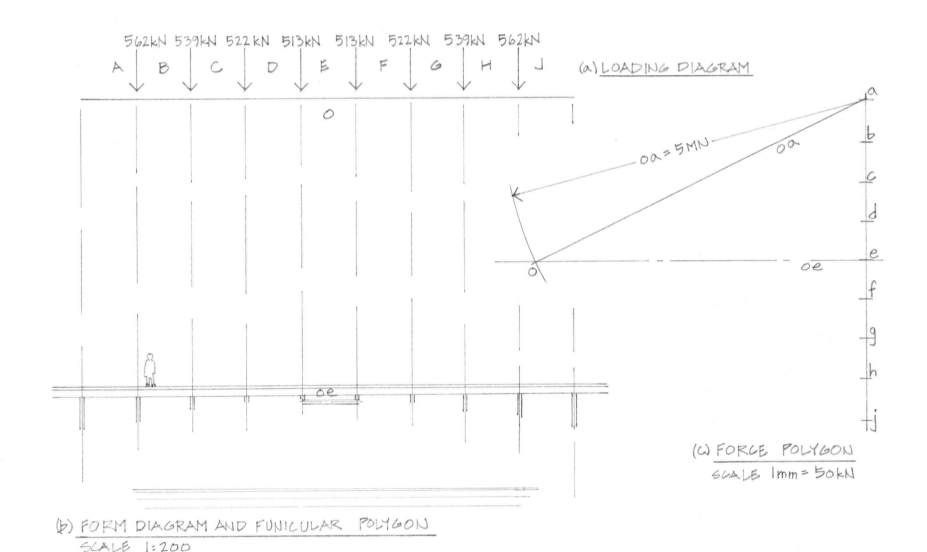

(a) LOADING DIAGRAM

(b) FORM DIAGRAM AND FUNICULAR POLYGON
SCALE 1:200

(c) FORCE POLYGON
SCALE 1mm = 50kN

Our task is to find a shape for the arch that will result in a maximum stress in the concrete of 5.0 MPa. The first step is to estimate the dead and live loads that the arch must support. For the most part, this a simple numerical exercise, but we cannot calculate accurately the dead loads of the vertical walls and the arch segments until the polygon of the arch has been determined. We must guess as closely as we can, taking measurements from the freehand design sketch for the approximate heights of the walls and lengths of the arch segments. We estimate that the outer arch segments will each be about 3.1 m long, and that the segments near the crown will be closer

to 3.0 m. We calculate dead loads accordingly, based on the density of concrete, which is 2400 kg/m³. We do the load estimates in tabular form, relating them to interval notations for the forces on the loading diagram in Figure 8.20.

We enter these forces as numbers on the loading diagram, (a), and plot them to scale on a load line, (c). We want to find the form of an arch 5 m wide and 0.2 m thick that will support this loading pattern while experiencing a maximum compressive stress, F_c, of 5.0 MPa. We calculate the maximum allowable force, P, in the arch:

$$F_C = \frac{P}{A}$$

$$P = F_C A$$

$$P = (5.0 \text{ MPa})(5 \text{ m})(0.2 \text{ m}) = 5.0 \text{ MN}$$

Because the arch is symmetrically loaded and spans between level supports, we know that the pole for its force polygon will lie on a horizontal line through the center of the load line, point e. We draw this line, oe. The center segment of the arch, also labeled oe, will be parallel to it. We establish an elevation on the space diagram for the center segment of the arch, oe, that places it at a minimal but constructible distance below the deck, and draw both the axis and the thickness of this segment.

We set a compass for a radius of 5.0 MN, the maximum allowable force in the arch. On the force polygon, Figure 8.20(c), we draw an arc of radius 5.0 MN around point a intersecting horizontal ray oe to locate the final pole, o. It is then an easy matter to draw the rays of the force polygon and the parallel segments of the funicular

◀ *Figure 8.20*
Designing the bridge: Step 1.
▼

	AB, HJ	BC, GH	CD, FG	DE, EF
Live Load Estimate				
(3 m)(8 m)(900 kg/m²)	21 600 kg	21 600 kg	21 600 kg	21 600 kg
Dead Load Estimate				
Deck: (3 m)(8 m)(0.4 m)(2 400 kg/m³)	23 040	23 040	23 040	23 040
Arch: (3.1 m)(5 m)(0.2 m)(2 400 kg/m³)	7 440	7 440		
(3.0 m)(5 m)(0.2 m)(2 400 kg/m³)			7 200	7 200
Wall: h×(5 m)(0.3 m)(2 400 kg/m³)	5 280	2 880	1 450	500
Total Estimated Mass	**57 360 kg**	**54 960 kg**	**53 290 kg**	**52 340 kg**
Total Estimated Force (mass × 9.8 m/s²)	**562 kN**	**539 kN**	**522 kN**	**513 kN**

polygon. We use these segments as centerlines for drawing the segments of the arch, working from the center toward the supports (Fig. 8.21).

In Figure 8.22, we complete the scale drawing of the preliminary design for the bridge. The line of the arch, although not precisely a parabola

▼ *Figure 8.21*
Designing the bridge: Step 2.

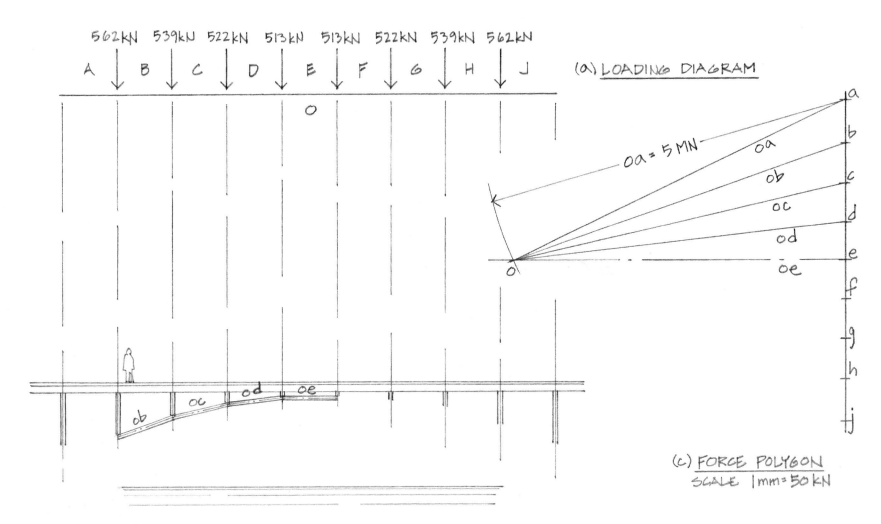

(a) LOADING DIAGRAM

(b) FORM DIAGRAM AND FUNICULAR POLYGON
SCALE 1:200

(c) FORCE POLYGON
SCALE 1mm=50 kN

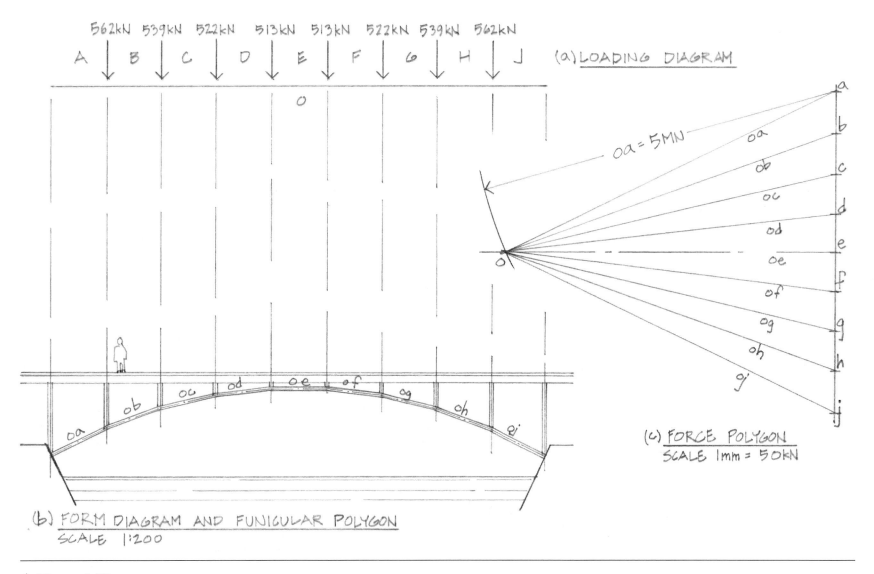

562kN 539kN 522kN 513kN 513kN 522kN 539kN 562kN

A   B   C   D   E   F   G   H   J   (a) LOADING DIAGRAM

O

oa = 5MN

(c) FORCE POLYGON
SCALE 1mm = 50kN

(b) FORM DIAGRAM AND FUNICULAR POLYGON
SCALE 1:200

▲ *Figure 8.22*
Completing the preliminary design of the bridge.

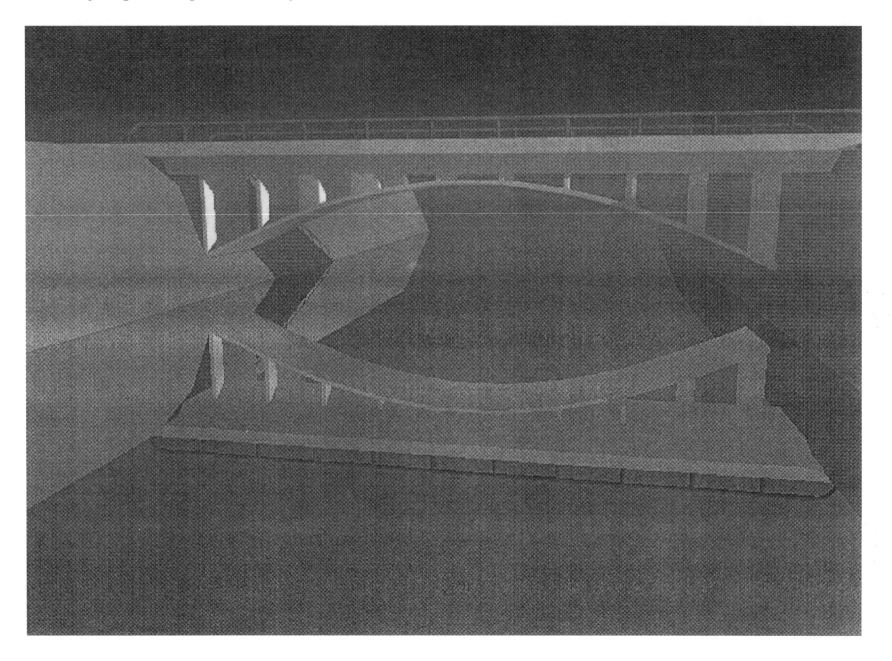

◀ *Figure 8.23*
The finished appearance of the bridge.

because of the nonuniformity of the loads, is nevertheless graceful (Fig. 8.23).

Another iteration of this procedure using more precise dead load estimates would give us the basic form of the arch with considerable accuracy, but it would by no means end our design work. The arch shape would have been derived for a live load that is applied uniformly to the entire deck. If a heavy truck rolls across an otherwise deserted bridge, its moving load, together with the dead load, will generate a very large number of new funicular polygons, none of which matches the polygon of the arch we have designed. If the left half of the bridge is jammed with vehicles but the right half is empty, still another funicular polygon will be produced. Yet the arch cannot change shape to match these new and ever-changing polygons. The arch slab will be reinforced with steel bars, of course, which will permit it to resist forces that lie slightly outside its axis, but further measures are required to accommodate the more extreme loading conditions. We could make the arch much thicker, so that the funicular polygons for all possible loading conditions would lie well within it. This is often done in conventional masonry arches, which tend to be thick anyway, but the thin concrete arch that we have designed would grow fat and appear quite clumsy if this

were done. The various options for solving this dilemma are discussed more fully in Chapter Thirteen. The designer of the bridge in Figure 8.18 chose to confront this problem by making the deck of the bridge deep and stiff, which is readily apparent in the photograph. The stiff deck absorbs the effects of the nonsymmetrical components of loading, allowing the arch to remain as a slender, elegant expression of the funicular polygon for a symmetrical loading.

SOME COMMON FUNICULAR FORMS

Figure 8.24 depicts the tensile and compressive funicular forms that are associated with four common, symmetrical loading patterns. Alongside each form is the force polygon from which it may be generated. We must remember that each of these forms represents only one of an infinite family of forms that are funicular for that loading. We can visualize the rest of each family by imagining a range of sags or rises, and by imagining one of the two supports being raised and lowered by different distances. We can begin to envisage the full range of funicular forms by imagining further that the loads are unequal to one another and irregularly spaced across the span, as they were in the example with which this chapter began.

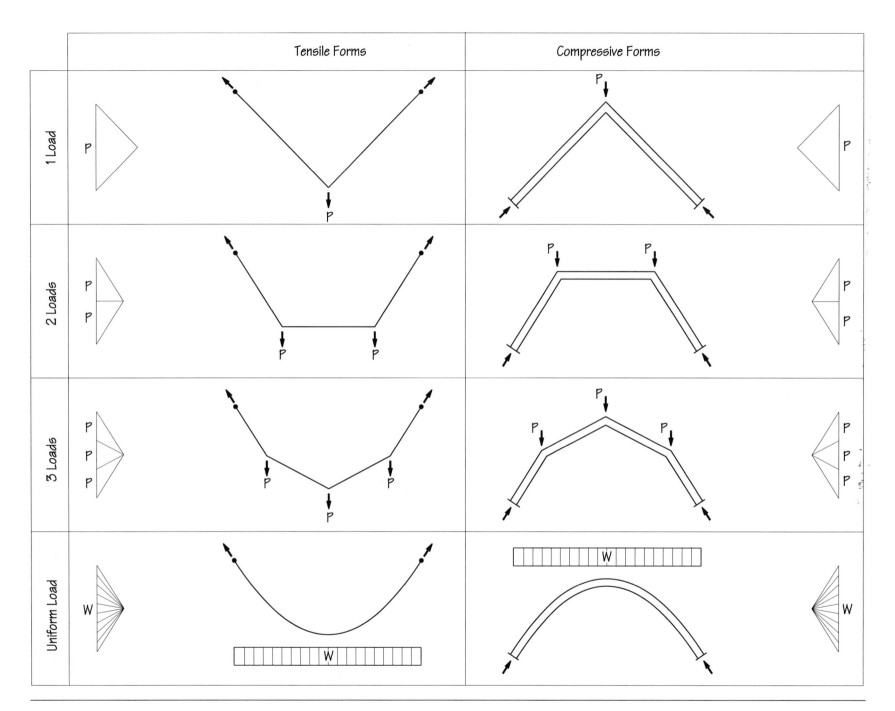

▲ *Figure 8.24*
Funicular forms for four common loading patterns.

◀ *Figure 8.25*
The Brooklyn Bridge, completed in 1883 after 14 years of construction, has a main span of nearly 1600 ft (487 m), which was the longest in the world at the time. The side spans are 930 ft (283 m) each. Its original designer was engineer John Roebling, who died as a result of a construction accident as construction began, leaving the work to his son, Washington Roebling. Washington Roebling was later disabled in another construction accident and had to pass on much of the responsibility for supervision of the work to his wife, Emily Roebling. The width of the roadway is 85 ft (26 m). Each cable is made of 5440 parallel wires of zinc-coated steel, wrapped tightly into a bundle 15.75 in (400 mm) in diameter. (Smithsonian Institution Photo No. 94-3829.)

Key Terms and Concepts

node
loading diagram
funicular polygon
pole
rays
string polygon

funicular
closing string
family of funicular lines
sag
trial pole
trial funicular polygon

final pole
final funicular polygon
catenary
rise
arch

Exercises

1. Without doing any computations, either numerical or graphical, sketch approximate funicular forms for concrete arches to support the six loading patterns shown in Figure 8.26 (*facing page*). Ignore the dead loads of the arches themselves. The axis of each arch must pass through the two supports and the black dot. The relative magnitudes of the loads are indicated by the lengths of the vectors. (*Hint:* You may find it easier to visualize first the shape that would be taken by a cable that is subjected to each of the loading patterns. Invert this shape to arrive at the appropriate arch form.)

2. Figure 8.27 is a designer's first rough sketch of a section through the roof of an outdoor concert hall. The main span of the roof transmits the weights of four masses, estimated at 40,000 kg each, to a suspension cable through vertical hangers. The towers project identical distances above the plane of the roof, which slopes at an angle of 1:5 (11.3°). Find the form of a suspension cable that will support this set of loads while not experiencing tensile force greater than 2.5 MN. How far must each tower project above the roof?

3. For the live loads shown in Figure 8.28, find the form and forces of a funicular concrete arch on level supports whose maximum axial force is 200,000 lb. Include a distributed dead load of 2000 lb per foot of horizontal projection for the estimated self-weight of the arch itself. Find the vertical and horizontal components of each reaction. (*Suggestion:* Apportion the self-weight of the arch as concentrated loads at 5-ft intervals.)

4. Assume that each cable of the Brooklyn Bridge (Fig. 8.25) spans 1600 ft between towers of identical height and supports a horizontal deck whose live and dead loads total 3000 lb per linear foot. Assume also that each cable has a maximum safe tensile capacity of 6.4 million lb. Plot the shape of the cable and find the required height of the towers above the deck. (*Suggestion:* Divide the span into 16 increments of 100 ft each.)

5. Find a funicular shape for a cylindrical vaulted concrete roof with a span of 66 m and a uniformly distributed dead and live load of 400 kg/m² (Fig. 8.29). Assume that the vault is 100 mm thick, and design for a maximum compressive stress of 4.0 MPa. (*Suggestion:* Base your calculations on a strip of the roof that is an arch 1 m wide and 100 mm thick that spans 66 m.) Suggest some ways of stiffening this thin vault so that it is able to resist asym-

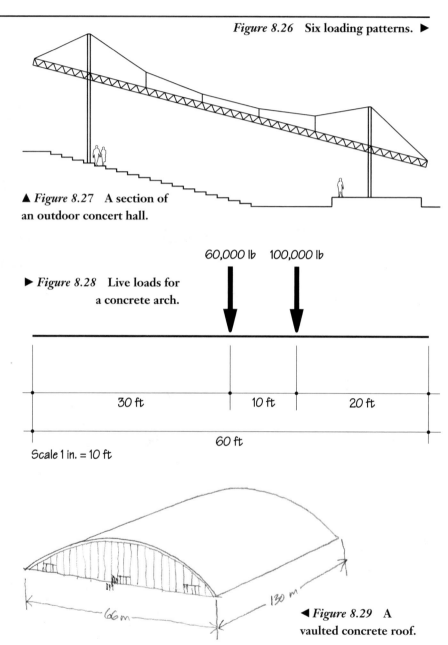

Figure 8.26 **Six loading patterns.** ▶

▲ *Figure 8.27* **A section of an outdoor concert hall.**

60,000 lb   100,000 lb

▶ *Figure 8.28* **Live loads for a concrete arch.**

30 ft   10 ft   20 ft

60 ft

Scale 1 in. = 10 ft

66 m   130 m

◀ *Figure 8.29* **A vaulted concrete roof.**

metrical loads from wind and drifting snow, while still keeping its average thickness to 100 mm.

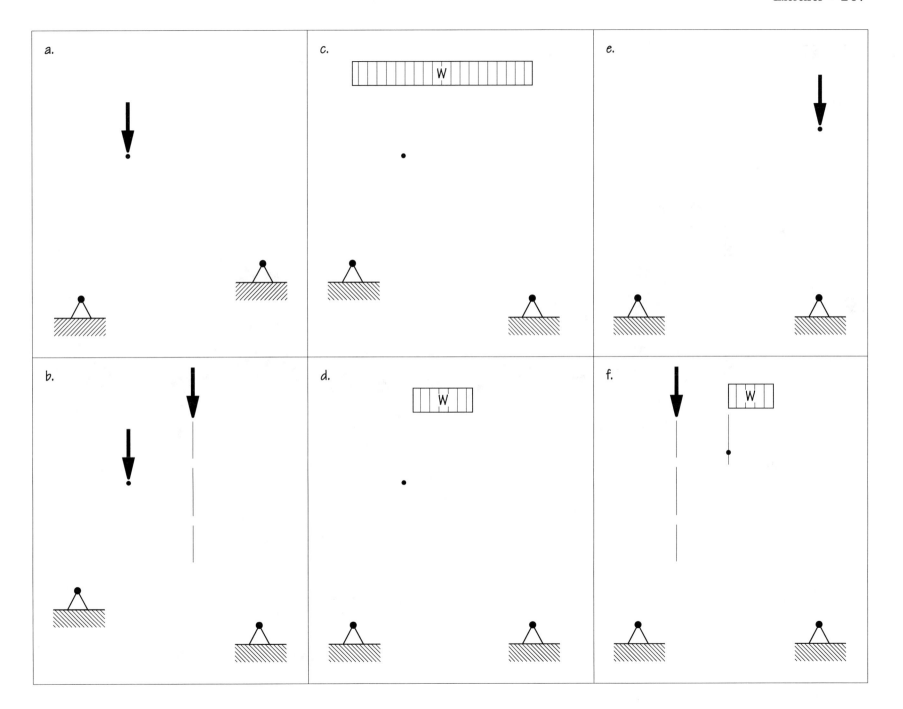

CHAPTER NINE

FURTHER DESIGN TOOLS FOR FUNICULAR STRUCTURES

◀ **The Burgo Paper Mill in Mantua, Italy (1961–1963) was designed by engineer Pier Luigi Nervi. The forms of the parabolic cables that support its roof and the forces in the cables can be found by any of the graphical or numerical methods that are developed in this chapter. (Photo: Professor Dr. Chris H. Luebkeman.)**

The funicular polygon is a powerful, versatile tool for designing structures. In this chapter, we explore additional graphical operations and introduce numerical tools relating to funicular polygons.

GRAPHICAL CONSTRUCTION OF A FUNICULAR POLYGON THROUGH THREE POINTS

For any loading pattern, there is an infinite family of funicular polygons that pass through two specified points. There is only one polygon of that family, however, that passes through three specified points.

A museum director wishes to display five large models of flying dinosaurs overhead in a gallery by hanging them at intervals from a sin-gle suspension cable. As seen in section (Fig. 9.1[c]), the cable will be anchored to supports at points *1* and *3*. The largest, heaviest model hangs near the center of the span, at which point the cable must pass through point *2*. We need to find the form that the cable will take and the largest force in the cable.

From the weights of the models that are shown on the loading diagram, Figure 9.1(a), we construct a load line, (d). Adopting any convenient location for a trial pole, o', we draw a trial force polygon and, from this, a trial funicular polygon, (b). Parallel to the closing string, $o'g$, we draw ray $o'g$ through the trial pole, intersecting the load line at g and dividing it into two segments, ga and fg. A ray parallel to the closing string of any polygon that is funicular for this loading must pass through g.

Continuing the solution in Figure 9.2(c), we draw the closing string, *1-3*, of the final funicular polygon. Parallel to this line, we construct ray *1-3* through *g* on the load line. The final pole must lie somewhere along this ray. Locating points *1′*, *2′*, and *3′* on the trial funicular polygon, (b), to correspond to the numbered

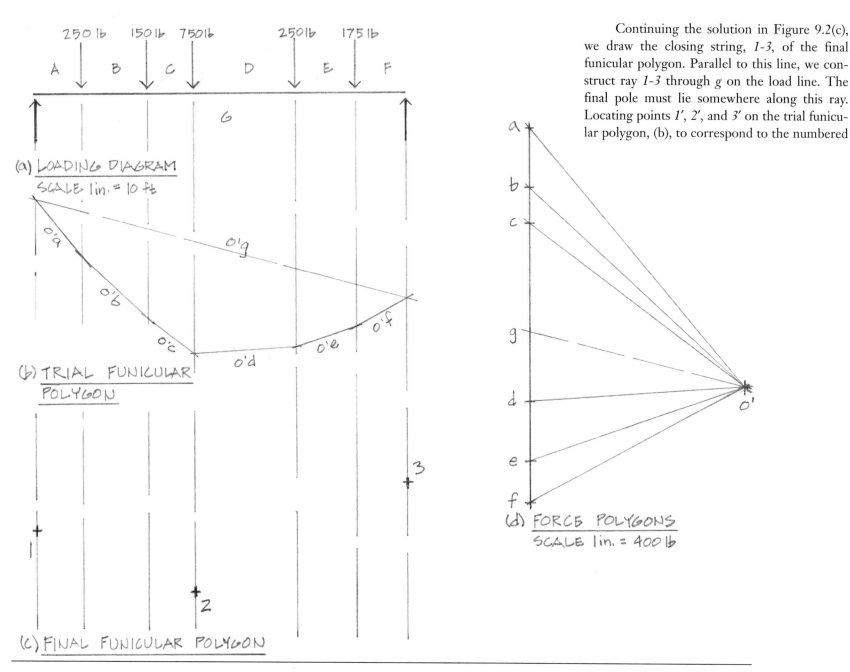

(a) LOADING DIAGRAM
SCALE 1 in. = 10 ft

(b) TRIAL FUNICULAR POLYGON

(c) FINAL FUNICULAR POLYGON

(d) FORCE POLYGONS
SCALE 1 in. = 400 lb

▲ *Figure 9.1*
Finding form and forces for a cable that passes through three designated points: First steps.

points on the final funicular polygon, we draw two *partial closing strings, 1'-2'* and *2'-3'*. We draw a ray through *o'* parallel to each of these strings on the force polygon. Each of these two rays intersects the load line at a point, *m* or *n*, that must lie on the corresponding partial closing string of any polygon that is funicular for this loading.

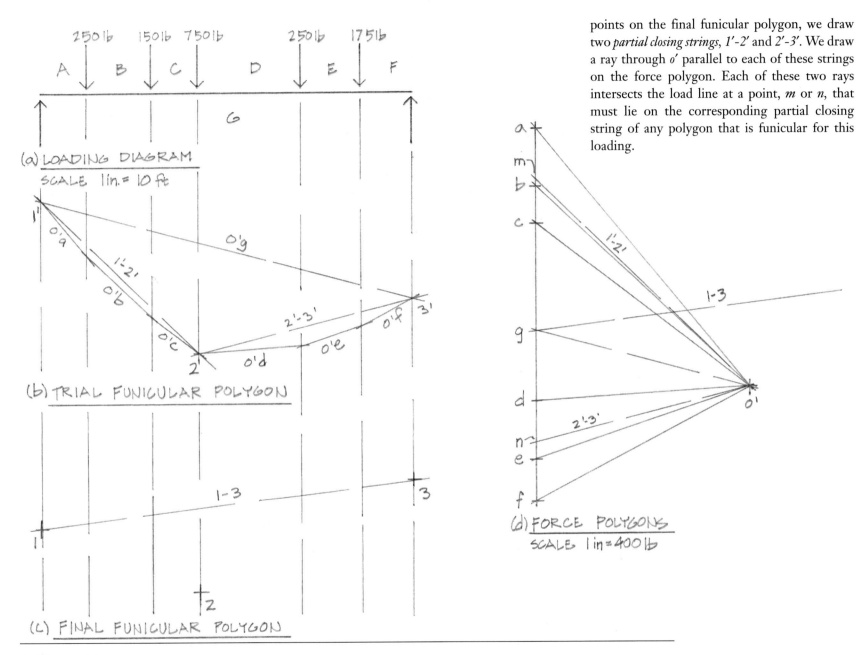

▲ *Figure 9.2*

Finding form and forces for a cable that passes through three designated points: Continued.

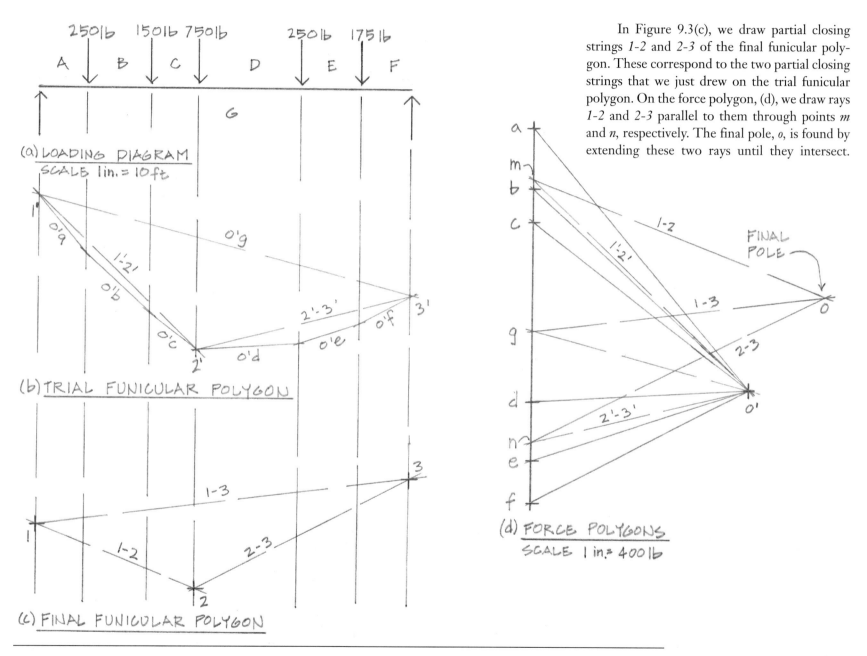

(a) LOADING DIAGRAM
SCALE 1 in. = 10 ft

(b) TRIAL FUNICULAR POLYGON

(c) FINAL FUNICULAR POLYGON

(d) FORCE POLYGONS
SCALE 1 in. = 400 lb

In Figure 9.3(c), we draw partial closing strings *1-2* and *2-3* of the final funicular polygon. These correspond to the two partial closing strings that we just drew on the trial funicular polygon. On the force polygon, (d), we draw rays *1-2* and *2-3* parallel to them through points *m* and *n*, respectively. The final pole, *o*, is found by extending these two rays until they intersect.

▲ *Figure 9.3*
Finding form and forces for a cable that passes through three designated points: Continued.

They do so on ray *1-3*, which confirms that our work is accurate.

In Figure 9.4(d), rays are drawn through *o* to construct the final force polygon, from which the final funicular polygon is plotted in (c). This polygon can be scaled to determine the lengths of the cable segments. The maximum force in the cable is ascertained by scaling the longest ray, *of*.

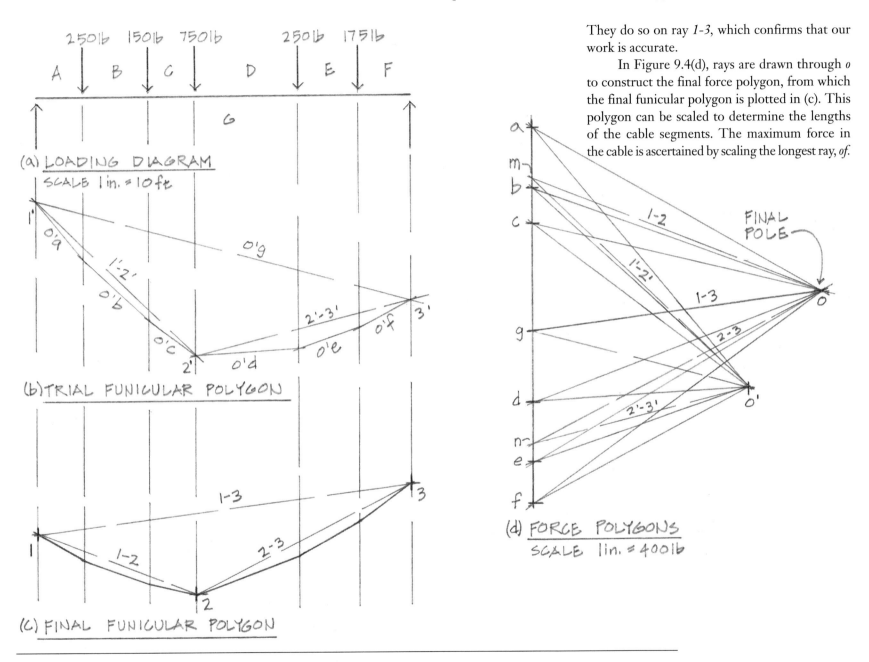

(a) LOADING DIAGRAM
SCALE 1 in. = 10 ft

(b) TRIAL FUNICULAR POLYGON

(c) FINAL FUNICULAR POLYGON

(d) FORCE POLYGONS
SCALE 1 in. = 400 lb

▲ *Figure 9.4*
Finding form and forces for a cable that passes through three designated points: Completion.

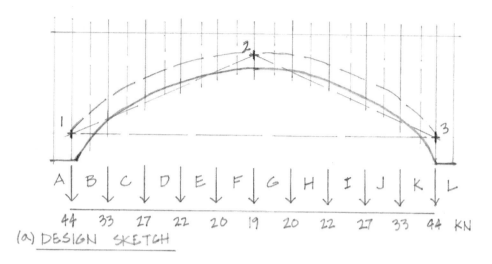

(a) DESIGN SKETCH

A | B | C | D | E | F | G | H | I | J | K | L

44 33 27 22 20 19 20 22 27 33 44 KN

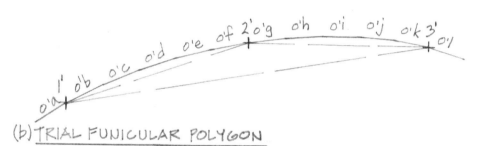

(b) TRIAL FUNICULAR POLYGON

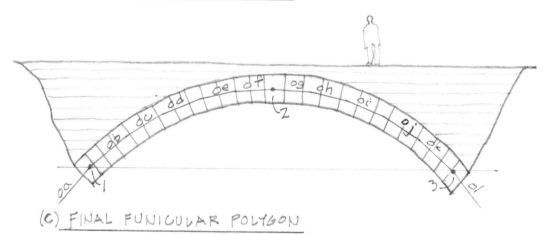

(c) FINAL FUNICULAR POLYGON

SHAPING THE ARCH OF A MASONRY BRIDGE

Figure 9.5(a) is a freehand design sketch of the elevation of a footbridge. The walls and arch will be constructed of stone masonry, and the interior will be filled with compacted earth to create a level path. We would like the *pressure line* of the arch, the curved axis along which its compressive forces act, to pass through points *1*, *2*, and *3*. The self-weight of the walls and earth fill constitutes the major portion of the loads. We estimate this

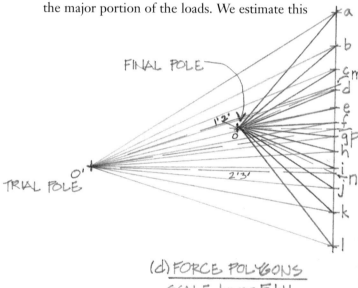

(d) FORCE POLYGONS

SCALE 1mm = 5kN

◄ *Figure 9.5*
Finding the pressure line of a masonry arch bridge.

self-weight by superimposing vertical strips on the sketch and scaling the approximate volume that is represented by each strip. Because the height of the material in the bridge changes with the rise and fall of the arch, the loads vary considerably, from 44 kN for the vertical strip over the supports to 19 kN for the midspan strip. Thus, the pressure line will not be a regular parabola and cannot be designed using standard formulas or shortcut graphical methods.

In Figure 9.5(d), we construct a load line and adopt a convenient trial pole, o'. In (b), we plot a trial funicular polygon, its closing string $1'$-$3'$, and its partial closing strings $1'$-$2'$ and $2'$-$3'$. Rays parallel to these three strings locate points p, m, and n on the load line.

On Figure 9.5(a), we draw the corresponding strings of the final funicular polygon, 1-3, 1-2, and 2-3, respectively. Rays constructed parallel to these three strings through points p, m, and n on the load line intersect at o, the final pole. The final funicular polygon is plotted in (c). This represents the pressure line of the arch, which we use for the axis of the arch as we sketch freehand the graceful profile of the bridge. The forces in the arch may be scaled from the rays of the final force polygon.

In both these design examples, the stone bridge and the hanging cable for the dinosaur display, the final pole was located by means of the intersection of three concurrent rays. To save time, any two of these rays may be plotted rather than all three. If the loading is symmetrical in respect to the center of span of the arch or cable, further efficiency may be gained by drawing only half of the trial funicular polygon. These shortcuts eliminate the check of accuracy that is furnished by plotting the third ray, but any error

GRAPHIC STATICS

This book is based on the science of *statics*, which is the study of the effects and distribution of forces on bodies that remain at rest. The body of graphical methods that we are studying is called *graphic statics*. The roots of graphic statics go back to early studies of the composition of forces by Italians Leonardo da Vinci and Galileo Galilei. Dutch mathematician Simon Stevin (1548–1620) was the first person to represent force as a vector. In a 1608 publication, Stevin also presented a correct interpretation of the parallelogram of forces. The Englishman Isaac Newton (1642–1727) formulated the laws of force and motion upon which statics and its sister science of moving bodies, *dynamics*, are based. The Frenchman Varignon (1654–1722) presented the force polygon and the funicular polygon in a work published in 1725. In 1748, Giovanni Poleni published a graphical analysis of the structural action of the masonry dome of St. Peter's Basilica in Rome. Early nineteenth-century French and German texts presented many of the rudiments of graphic statics at about the same time as Louis Navier published in Paris the first comprehensive text on numerical methods of structural analysis (1826). In 1864, Britons James Clerk Maxwell and W. P. Taylor published a graphical method for analyzing forces in trusses, but this method was not widely known or accepted until Robert H. Bow explained and elaborated it in a book of 1873. Bow also introduced the system of interval notation that we use today. In Milan, in 1872, Luigi Cremona published a volume in which, independently of the Britons, he demonstrated the graphical analysis of trusses.

The German engineer Karl Culmann (1821–1881) is generally acknowledged as the father of graphic statics. In *Die Graphische Statik*, first published in Zürich in 1866, Culmann presented the first consistent, comprehensive body of graphical techniques. He introduced many of the fundamental graphical methods that we use today and demonstrated how they could be used to solve a wide variety of structural problems. Culmann's work was further developed by his pupil and the successor to his teaching post at the Swiss Federal Technical Institute in Zürich, Wilhelm Ritter (1847–1906). The German Otto Mohr (1835–1918) introduced many additional innovations and improvements.

The influence of the pioneers of graphic statics on the shape of modern structures is enormous. Maurice Koechlin, the co-designer of the Eiffel Tower, was Culmann's student. Robert Maillart studied under Ritter. Christian Menn became acquainted with Maillart's structures while still a child and studied structures in Zürich with Ritter's pupil, Pierre Lardy. Pier Luigi Nervi and Riccardo Morandi were heirs to the legacy of Cremona. In Spain, Antoni Gaudí, Gaudí's structural engineer Mariano Rubió y Bellvé, vault builder Rafael Guastavino, and engineers Eduardo Torroja and Felix Candela were schooled in graphic statics. Santiago Calatrava journeyed from Spain in the 1970s to study engineering at Karl Culmann's school, the Swiss Federal Technical Institute in Zürich, where he learned graphic statics and studied bridge design under Christian Menn. ∎

will be apparent if the final funicular polygon does not pass through the three specified points.

In both these examples, we located the middle point of the three specified points at what we assumed would be the high or low point of the structure, and in both examples we were right. In cases in which the magnitudes and spacings of the loads are complex, it is often difficult to discern in advance exactly where the high or low point will be. If the construction is correct, the final funicular polygon will indeed pass through any three points that are specified, but the high or low point will not necessarily lie on any of the specified points.

FINDING THE RESULTANT OF A GROUP OF FORCES

Shown in Figure 9.6(a) are the vectors of four forces for which we wish to find the resultant. In the first step of the graphical solution, the magnitude and direction of the resultant are easily found in (b) by connecting the vectors tip to tail and drawing vector *ae*.

Because the component forces are nearly parallel, the location of the line of action of the resultant would be difficult to find by plotting their intersections. Continuing the solution in Figure 9.7, we locate the line of action with the aid of a funicular polygon. We treat the force polygon as a load line, adopt any pole location, *o*, and draw rays *oa* through *oe*. Parallel to these rays, over the lines of action of the force vectors, we construct a funicular polygon. The intersection of the first and last strings, *oa* and *oe*, lies on the line of action of resultant *ae*. Any pole location and any location of the funicular polygon

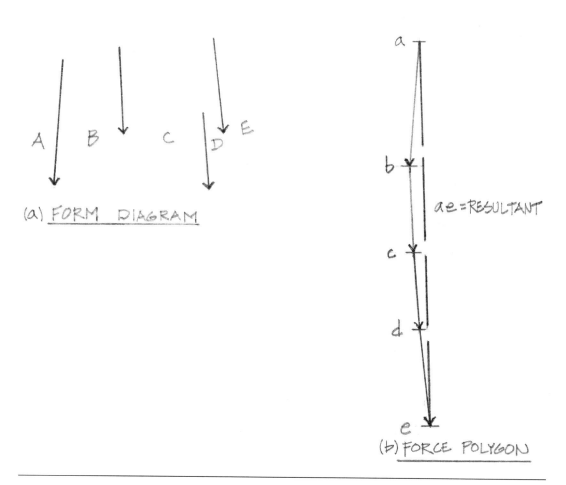

▲ *Figure 9.6*
Finding the resultant of a group of forces: First steps.

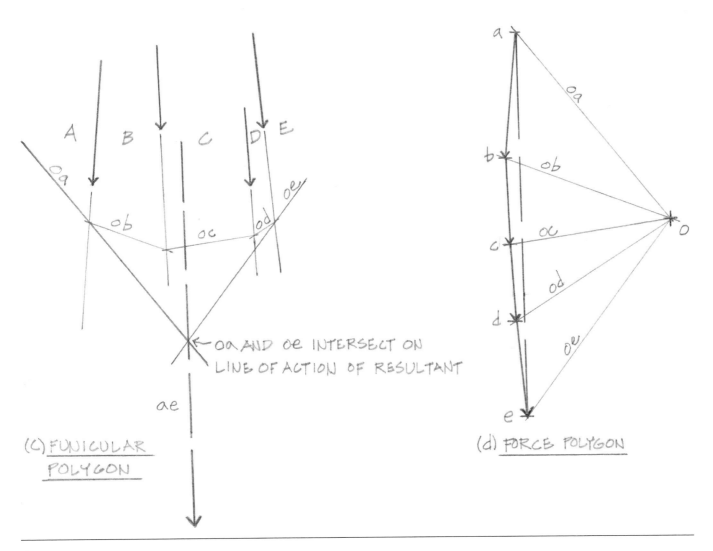

A   B   C   D   E

Oa

ob

oc

od

oe

Oa AND oe INTERSECT ON
LINE OF ACTION OF RESULTANT

ae

(c) FUNICULAR
POLYGON

a

Oa

b   ob

c   oc

od

d

oe

e

O

(d) FORCE POLYGON

▲ *Figure 9.7*
Finding the resultant of a group of forces: Completion.

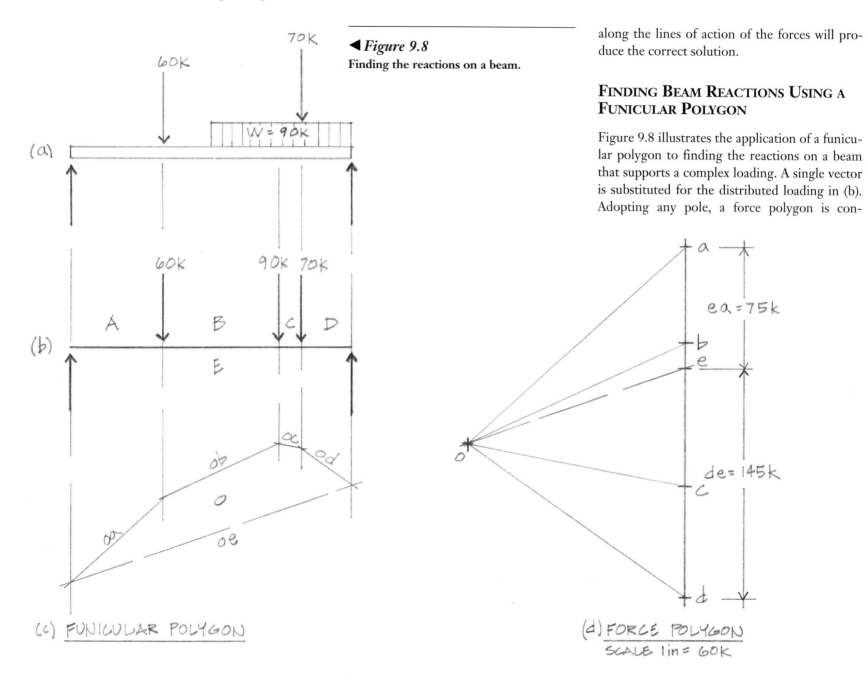

◀ *Figure 9.8*

Finding the reactions on a beam.

along the lines of action of the forces will produce the correct solution.

FINDING BEAM REACTIONS USING A FUNICULAR POLYGON

Figure 9.8 illustrates the application of a funicular polygon to finding the reactions on a beam that supports a complex loading. A single vector is substituted for the distributed loading in (b). Adopting any pole, a force polygon is constructed from the load vectors in (d). The corresponding funicular polygon, (c), has closing string *oe*. Ray *oe* on the force polygon divides the load line into the two reactions, *ae* and *de*, which are scaled to determine their magnitudes.

This solution demonstrates that a funicular polygon may be used to locate the line of action of the resultant of a group of parallel forces, which cannot be done by plotting intersections of the lines of action of the forces themselves. The funicular polygon acts to assure that the sum of the moments in the force system is zero, and the force polygon assures that the sums of the vertical and horizontal components are zero.

In most cases, it is faster and easier to find reactions on spanning devices by taking numerical moments about each of the supports rather than by using a funicular polygon. However, if the loading is very complex, if some of the loads are inclined, or if numerical dimensions have not yet been assigned to a structure that exists only in the form of a scaled drawing, the funicular polygon may provide a more efficient route to a solution than numerical moments.

NUMERICAL CONSTRUCTION OF A FUNICULAR POLYGON THROUGH THREE POINTS

The example with which we began this chapter, the cable that supports the flying dinosaur models, is representative of the general case of the three-point funicular problem: its loads are random in spacing and magnitude, and the ends of the cable do not lie on the same level. Thus, this example will serve to illustrate the numerical approach to the same problem.

The numerical method grows out of the concept of the *bending moment*, so named because its most common use is in finding the stresses in beams that are subjected to bending action, a function that we will explore in a subsequent volume of this series. **The bending moment at any vertical section through a structural element is the summation of moments about a point on the axis of the element at that section of all the forces and reactions that act to the left of it.** Figure 9.9 illustrates this: The bending moment at section *x-x* is found as follows, taking clockwise moments as positive:

$$M = R_L x_L - P_1 x_1 - P_2 x_2$$

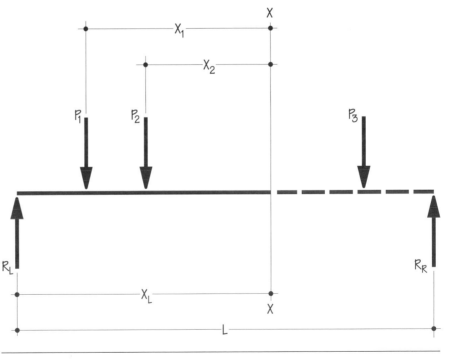

▲ *Figure 9.9*
Finding the bending moment at section *x-x*.

Applying this concept to the problem at hand, we begin in Figure 9.10(a) by treating the loading diagram of the hanging cable as if it were a beam, taking moments about each support to find the reaction at the other support. (If the two supports of the cable were at the same elevation, these reactions would represent the vertical components of the forces in the first and last segments of the cable. Because the cable supports in our problem are not at the same elevation, the vertical components of the first and last segments do not match these reactions, but that is immaterial to this method of solution.)

In Figure 9.10 (b) through (f), we evaluate the bending moments at each of the nodes of the cable. At node *C*, for example, the bending moment of all the forces to the left of the section is the sum of 859 lb, the left reaction, times a moment arm of 11.8 ft, minus 250 lb times 7.0 ft, which is 8386 lb-ft. The 150-lb load at *C* does not enter the calculation, because its line of action passes through the axis of moments. The bending moments at the supports are zero, as we understood when we took moments about each of them to find the reactions.

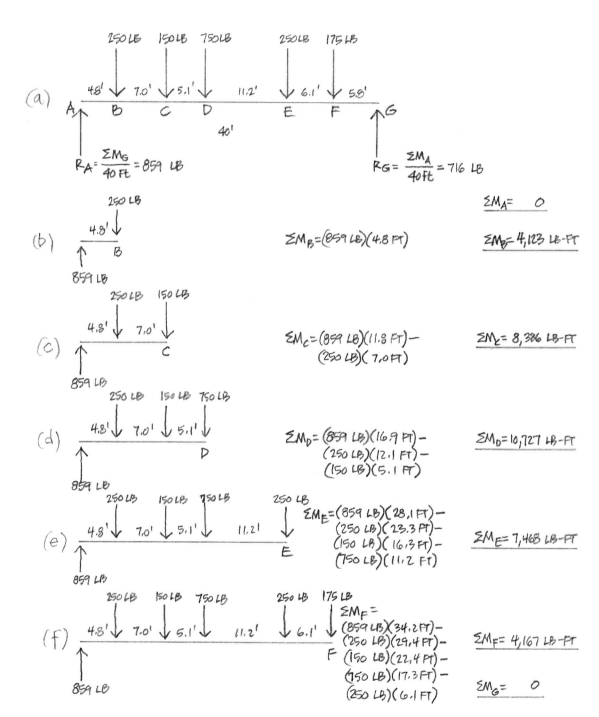

Figure 9.10 ▶
Finding the bending moments in every segment of the structure.

There is a simple, important relationship between the bending moment and the horizontal component of force in a cable or funicular arch, which is illustrated in Figure 9.11. A vertical section has been cut through the cable at node C, and the portion of the structure to the left of that point is represented as a free body. Summing moments about point n:

$$\sum M_n = O = R_L x_2 + Hd - P_1 x_1 - Hy_c$$

All the terms of this expression except Hy_c are equal by definition to the bending moment at C. Therefore Hy_c is equal to the bending moment. Putting this into words, **the bending moment at any point in a vertically loaded funicular structure is equal to the horizontal component of the force in the structure multiplied by the vertical distance from that point to the closing string.**

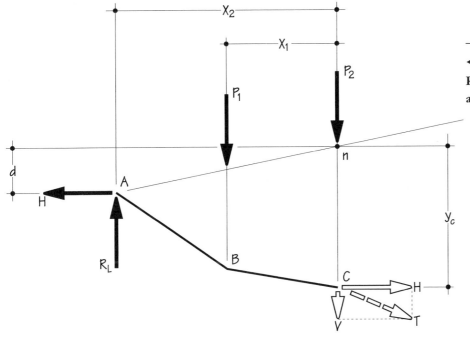

◀ *Figure 9.11*
Relating the ordinates of the cable nodes to bending moments and the horizontal component of the force in the cable.

Figure 9.12 shows how the bending moments that we found in Figure 9.10 are used to find the form of the cable. The locations of points *A*, *D*, and *G* in the diagram, (a), were specified in the problem statement by the dimensions shown on the drawing. We draw level baseline *HG*, closing string *AG*, and vertical coordinate y_D on the basis of the given points. In (b), we calculate the length of y_D as being equal to the 6.6-ft difference in height from *D* to *A*, plus a fraction of the 4.9-ft dimension that is proportional to the horizontal coordinate of point *D* divided by the length of the span; this comes to 8.67 ft.

In line (c), we calculate the horizontal component of the force in the cable by dividing M_D, the bending moment at node *D*, by y_D, the *y* coordinate of that point; the horizontal component is 1237 lb.

In lines (d) through (g) of Figure 9.12, we calculate the vertical distance of each node from the closing string. Because *H*, the horizontal component of force, is constant throughout a cable that supports only vertical loads, each vertical distance is easily calculated as being equal to the bending moment at that node divided by *H*.

The forces in the segments of the cable are found in Figure 9.13. The dimensions in feet are carefully entered on the form diagram, (a). In line (b), these dimensions are used to calculate the tangent of the angle to the horizontal of each segment of the cable. In line (c), the tan^{-1} function of the electronic calculator has been used to find the angle of each segment, and in line (d), the cosine of each angle is entered. Finally, in line (e), the tension in each cable segment is calculated as the horizontal component, 1237 lb, divided by the cosine of the angle of inclination. These numbers may be compared to quantities

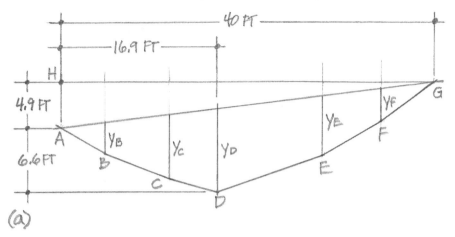

(a)

POINTS A, D, AND G ARE GIVEN.

(b) $\quad y_D = 6.6 \text{ FT} + (4.9 \text{ FT})\left(\dfrac{16.9 \text{ FT}}{40.0 \text{ FT}}\right) = \underline{8.67 \text{ FT}}$

(c) $\quad H = \dfrac{M_D}{y_D} = \dfrac{10,727 \text{ LB-FT}}{8.67 \text{ FT}} = \underline{1237 \text{ LB}}$

(d) $\quad y_B = \dfrac{M_B}{H} = \dfrac{4,123 \text{ LB-FT}}{1237 \text{ LB}} = \underline{3.33 \text{ FT}}$

(e) $\quad y_C = \dfrac{M_C}{H} = \dfrac{8,386 \text{ LB-FT}}{1237 \text{ LB}} = \underline{6.78 \text{ FT}}$

(f) $\quad y_E = \dfrac{M_E}{H} = \dfrac{7,468 \text{ LB-FT}}{1237 \text{ LB}} = \underline{6.04 \text{ FT}}$

(g) $\quad y_F = \dfrac{M_F}{H} = \dfrac{4,167 \text{ LB-FT}}{1237 \text{ LB}} = \underline{3.37 \text{ FT}}$

▲ *Figure 9.12*
Finding the ordinates of the cable nodes.

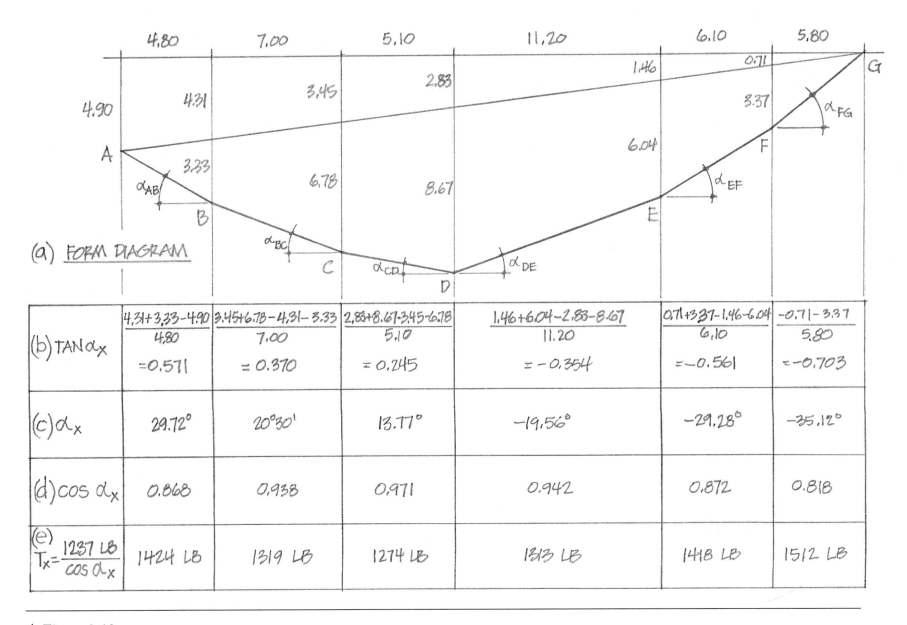

4.80	7.00	5.10	11.20	6.10	5.80

(a) FORM DIAGRAM

(b) TAN α_x	$\dfrac{4.31+3.33-4.90}{4.80}$ $=0.571$	$\dfrac{3.45+6.78-4.31-3.33}{7.00}$ $=0.370$	$\dfrac{2.83+8.67-3.45-6.78}{5.10}$ $=0.245$	$\dfrac{1.46+6.04-2.83-8.67}{11.20}$ $=-0.354$	$\dfrac{0.71+3.37-1.46-6.04}{6.10}$ $=-0.561$	$\dfrac{-0.71-3.37}{5.80}$ $=-0.703$
(c) α_x	29.72°	20°30'	13.77°	-19.56°	-29.28°	-35.12°
(d) cos α_x	0.868	0.938	0.971	0.942	0.872	0.818
(e) $T_x = \dfrac{1237\ LB}{\cos \alpha_x}$	1424 LB	1319 LB	1274 LB	1313 LB	1418 LB	1512 LB

▲ *Figure 9.13*

Finding the forces in the cable segments.

scaled from the rays of the final force polygon in Figure 9.4.

The method that we have followed in solving numerically for the form and forces of this hanging cable is generally applicable to any funicular structure with any set of vertical loads. We could apply it, for example, to the determination of form and forces for the deck-stiffened arch bridge in Chapter Eight, or the stone masonry footbridge in this chapter, whose solutions we achieved graphically.

The choice between a graphical solution and a numerical one for any given problem is a matter of judgment. For a cable from which to hang dinosaur models in a museum, or a stone footbridge of limited span, an error of an inch of dimension or 10 pounds of force is of no practical consequence. If you are good at graphical solutions, you can save time by skipping the numerical solutions in designing such structures. For a roof or bridge with a long span and heavy loads, a sensible strategy might be to utilize graphical solutions for early design studies, taking advantage of their quick, self-checking, transparent character, and then do a careful numerical analysis to determine final dimensions and quantities. Such prominent structural designers as Gustave Eiffel and Robert Maillart did relatively few numerical calculations. They routinely based the final designs of even their largest and most important structures on carefully drawn graphical analyses that were done at two or three times the scale of those in this book.

A NUMERICAL METHOD FOR SYMMETRICAL PARABOLIC ARCHES AND CABLES

A parabola is funicular for a load uniformly distributed over its horizontal projection. Because so many buildings and bridges are designed for loads that are assumed to be uniformly distributed, many arches and cables take a parabolic form. The mathematics of a parabola reduce to several simple equations, making numerical analyses of these structures easy and rapid.

Figure 9.14(a) shows the forces that act on a symmetrical parabolic cable of span L and sag s: these are wL, a uniformly distributed load; H, the constant horizontal component of the force at any point in the cable and its reactions; and $wL/2$, the vertical component of each reaction. In (b), in order to find an expression for the horizontal component, we draw a free-body diagram of the left half of this system. We take moments about point a and solve for H:

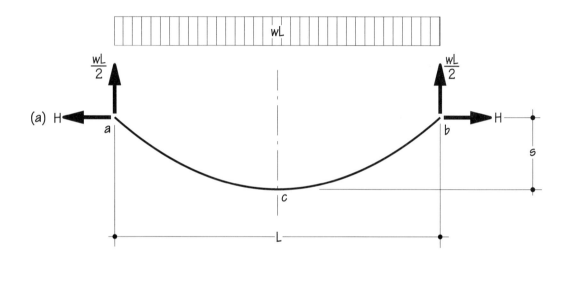

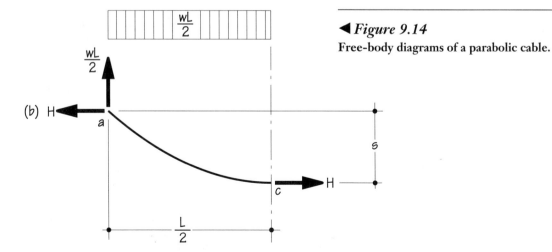

◀ *Figure 9.14*

Free-body diagrams of a parabolic cable.

$$\sum M_a = 0 = \left(\frac{wL}{2}\right)\left(\frac{L}{4}\right) - sH$$

$$H = \frac{wL^2}{8s} \qquad [9\text{-}1]$$

We would like to find an equation that describes the shape of the cable in terms of y_x, the vertical distance from the support at any horizontal distance, x (Fig. 9.15). We draw a free-body diagram of the portion of the cable that lies within distance x of the support, and take moments about a:

$$\sum M_a = 0 = wx\left(\frac{x}{2}\right) + xV_x - y_x H$$

For V_x, the vertical component of the cable force at distance x, we substitute an expression found by summing all the forces that act in the vertical direction on this free body:

$$V_x = \frac{wL}{2} - wx$$

For H, we substitute from eq. [9-1]. Solving for y_x, we arrive at a useful expression for the coordinates of any point on a parabola:

$$y_x = \frac{8s}{wL^2}\left(\frac{wx^2}{2} + x\left(\frac{wL}{2} - wx\right)\right)$$

$$y_x = \frac{4sx}{L^2}(L - x) \qquad [9\text{-}2]$$

A slightly different form of eq. [9-2] is highly efficient in the repetitive calculations needed to define a number of points on a parabola, as we will demonstrate in the next chapter:

$$y_x = 4s\left(\frac{x}{L} - \frac{x^2}{L^2}\right) \qquad [9\text{-}2a]$$

Next we seek an expression for $T_{\max}$, the maximum tension in the cable. We found in Chapter Eight that $T_{\max}$ occurs at the supports.

Figure 9.16 is a free-body diagram of a, the left-hand support of the cable. Because $\Delta y / \Delta x$, the slope of the cable at this point, is identical to the slope of its line of action, it may be defined as the vertical component of the reaction divided by the horizontal component:

$$\frac{\Delta y}{\Delta x} = \frac{wL}{2H}$$

Again substituting for H from eq. [9-1] and simplifying, we come to a useful expression for the slope of a parabola at its support:

$$\frac{\Delta y}{\Delta x} = \frac{wL}{2} = \frac{4s}{L} \qquad [9\text{-}3]$$

To find the maximum force in the cable, we add the vectors of the vertical and horizontal components of the reaction:

$$T_{\max} = \sqrt{\left(\frac{wL}{2}\right)^2 + H^2}$$

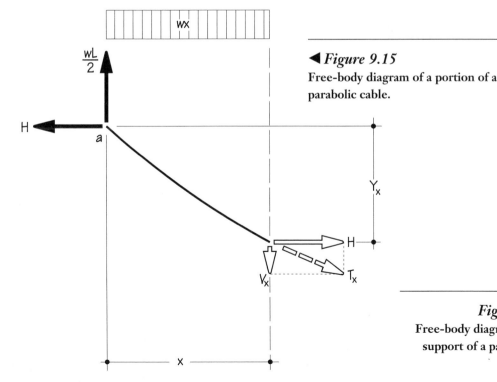

◀ *Figure 9.15*

Free-body diagram of a portion of a parabolic cable.

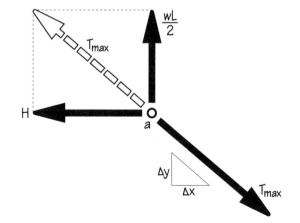

Figure 9.16 ▶

Free-body diagram of the left support of a parabolic cable.

To put this in the most convenient form, we substitute for w an expression taken from eq. [9-1]:

$$w = \frac{8sH}{L^2}$$

Simplifying, we come to the expression

$$T_{max} = H\sqrt{16\left(\frac{s^2}{L^2}\right) + 1}$$

We define the *sag ratio*, n, as the ratio of sag to span:

$$n = \frac{s}{L} \qquad [9\text{-}4]$$

We substitute n for s/L to create a simple expression for the maximum tension or compression in a parabolic cable or arch:

$$C_{max} = T_{max} = H\sqrt{16n^2 + 1} \qquad [9\text{-}5]$$

For handy reference, all these expressions for the properties of a symmetrical parabolic cable or arch are summarized in Figure 9.17. An analogous set of expressions for an asymmetrical parabolic structure will be presented in Chapter Eleven.

GEOMETRIC PROPERTIES OF A PARABOLA

A parabola has several geometric properties that will be helpful to us as we design parabolic structures such as those we will undertake in the next two chapters. Figure 9.18 demonstrates the most frequently useful of these properties, which is embodied in eq. [9-3]: **Tangents to a parabola at its supports intersect at a point that lies on a vertical line through the center of the span at a vertical distance from the closing string**

SUMMARY OF NUMERICAL EXPRESSIONS FOR DESIGNING SYMMETRICAL PARABOLIC ARCHES AND CABLES

H, the horizontal component of force at any point in a symmetrical parabolic arch or cable, is found using the following expression, in which w is the load per unit of span length, L is the horizontal span, and s is the maximum sag or rise:

$$H = \frac{wL^2}{8s} \qquad [9\text{-}1]$$

Y_x, the sag or rise at any point on the axis of the arch or cable, may be found with the following expression, in which x is the horizontal distance from the left support:

$$Y_x = \frac{4sx}{L^2}(L - x) \qquad [9\text{-}2]$$

The following form of this equation is more efficient in repetitive calculations:

$$Y_x = 4s\left(\frac{x}{L} - \frac{x^2}{L^2}\right) \qquad [9\text{-}2a]$$

The slope of a symmetrical parabola at its left support is:

$$\frac{\Delta y}{\Delta x} = \frac{wL}{2} = \frac{4s}{L} \qquad [9\text{-}3]$$

The sag ratio, n, is defined as follows:

$$n = \frac{s}{L} \qquad [9\text{-}4]$$

The maximum tension or compression in a symmetrical parabolic arch or cable, which occurs at the support, is found by using the expression:

$$C_{max} = T_{max} = H\sqrt{16n^2 + 1} \qquad [9\text{-}5]$$

▲ *Figure 9.17*

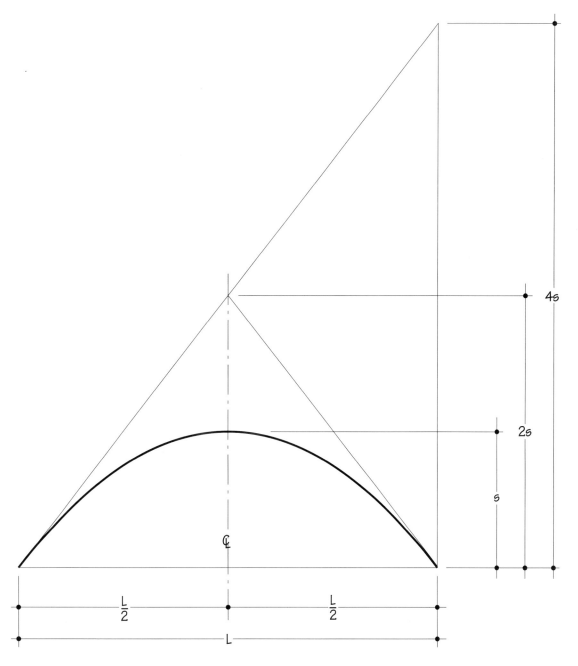

◀ *Figure 9.18*
Geometry of lines tangent to a parabola at its supports.

that is twice the sag or rise. Figure 9.19 shows that this property also applies to a parabola with an inclined closing string. This is a handy relationship because it saves us the work of constructing trial force and funicular polygons when we are finding the form of a uniformly loaded structure—the tangents at the supports are parallel to the first and last rays of the final force polygon, which allows us to find the final pole directly, as we will do several times in the remainder of this book.

Figure 9.20 illustrates a corollary of this property: **Any two tangents to a parabola intersect at a point that lies on a vertical line through the center of the horizontal distance between the points of tangency.** We will use this relationship in Chapter Twelve when we make a precise determination of the eccentricity of the pressure line through a steel arch roof structure.

Sometimes you may want to construct a parabola without going to the trouble of drawing a force polygon and a funicular polygon. In Figure 9.21, we see one way of doing this. The closing string and vertical centerline of the parabola are drawn. Tangents to the ends of the parabola are constructed through a point on the centerline that is $2s$ from the closing string. The two tangents are divided into any convenient number of equal segments, and lines are drawn between the corresponding divisions as shown. All these lines are tangent to the parabola. In an alternative construction (Fig. 9.22), an enclosing box is

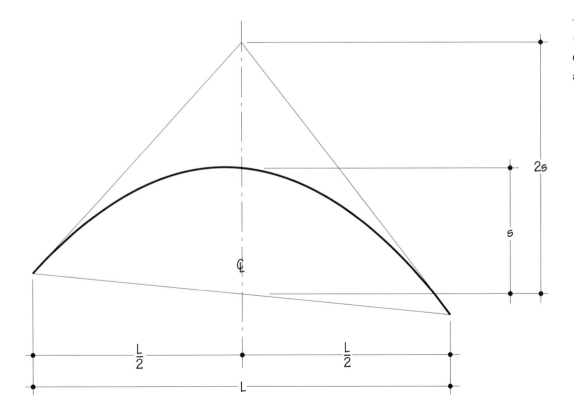

◀ *Figure 9.19*
Geometry of lines tangent to a parabola at its supports.

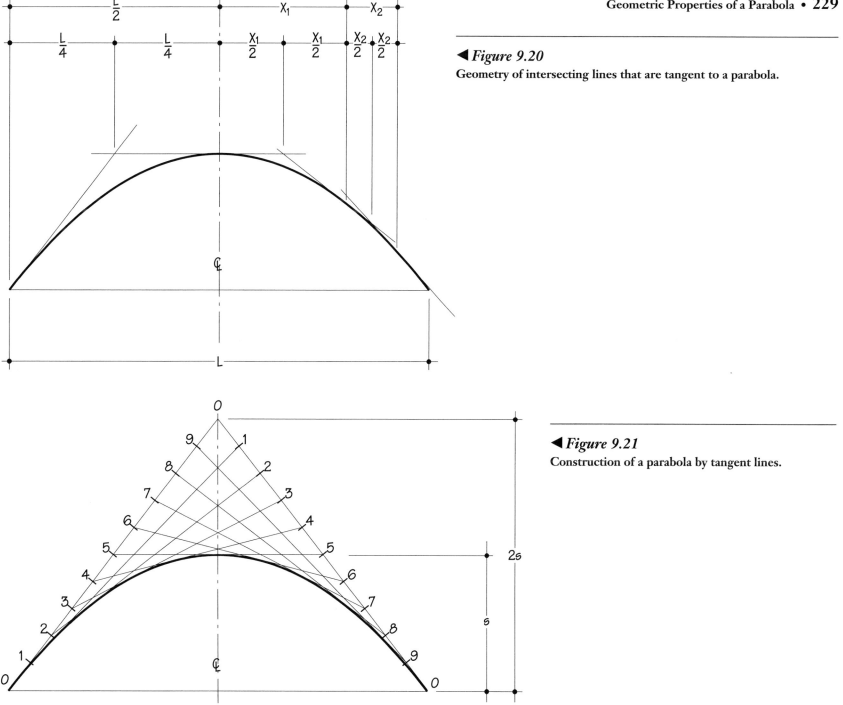

◀ *Figure 9.20*
Geometry of intersecting lines that are tangent to a parabola.

◀ *Figure 9.21*
Construction of a parabola by tangent lines.

inscribed around the end points and apex. On the perimeter of this box, the rise and half-span are divided into equal numbers of equal segments. Rays are drawn from the apex to the divisions on the sides of the box. The intersections of rays with vertical lines through the corresponding divisions of the half-span are points on the parabola.

These two constructions give identical results. Neither of them gives us the forces in the parabolic structure. However, the maximum force is easily determined either by applying eqs. [9-1], [9-4], and [9-5], or by constructing a force polygon consisting of three lines only, a vertical load line whose length is wL, and two rays parallel to the end tangents to the parabola.

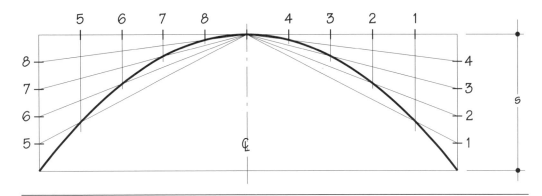

▲ *Figure 9.22*
Construction of a parabola by intersecting lines.

Key Terms and Concepts

partial closing string
pressure line
graphic statics
dynamics

bending moment
sag ratio
statics

Exercises

1. Figure 9.23(a) is a design sketch of a roof for a tennis stadium. Because of the shape of the plan of the building, the vertical loading on the steel truss arch that supports the center of the roof varies as shown in the loading diagram, (b). The arch must pass through points 1, 2, and 3 on the space diagram, (c). Find the curve of its pressure line.

2. A cable that is loaded uniformly on its horizontal projection must pass through points 1, 2, and 3 in Figure 9.24, with points 1 and 3 at the same level. Find the curve of the cable.

3. Without drawing a trial funicular polygon, construct the curve of a uniformly loaded arch whose rise is one-quarter of its span.

4. Working graphically, find the magnitude, direction, and location of the line of action of the resultant of each of the two groups of forces in Figure 9.25.

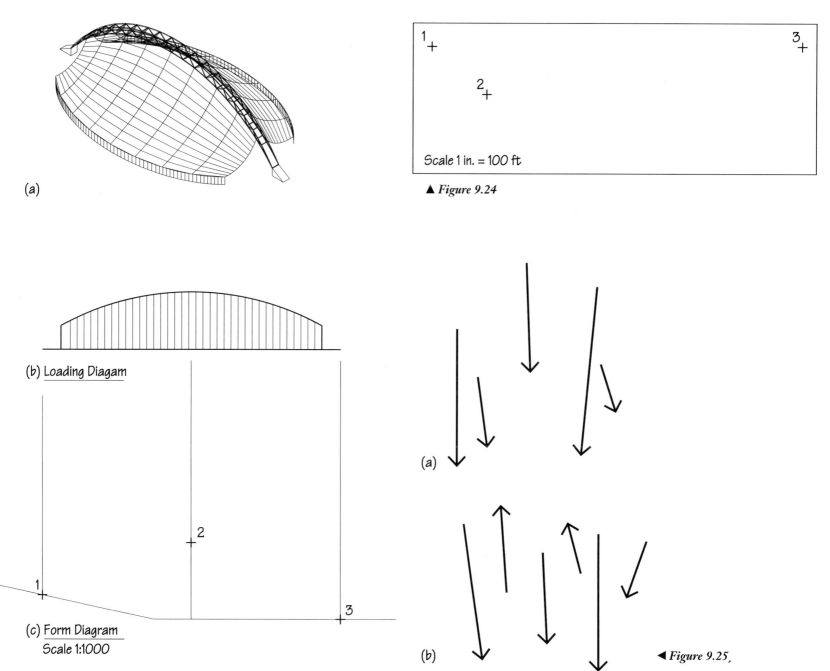

(a)

(b) Loading Diagam

(c) Form Diagram
Scale 1:1000

▲ *Figure 9.23* **A roof for a tennis stadium.**

Scale 1 in. = 100 ft

▲ *Figure 9.24*

2

1

3

(a)

(b)

◀ *Figure 9.25*

5. Find the two reactions on the truss in Figure 9.26, using both a graphical and a numerical solution. How accurate are the answers that you obtained graphically?

6. Find form and forces numerically for the deck-stiffened arch bridge in Chapter Eight.

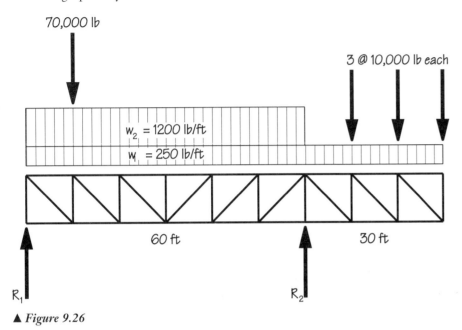

▲ *Figure 9.26*

Figures 9.27 and 9.28 ▶
The Royal Horticultural Hall in London, designed by architects Howard Robertson and J. Murray Easton and engineer Oscar Faber, was constructed in 1928. It is brilliantly daylit by four levels of clerestory windows. Its concrete arches, which span 72 ft (22 m) and are 58 ft (18 m) high, are funicular above the level of the roofs of the side aisles. To enable the arches to become vertical as they approach the floor, the flat concrete slabs of the roofs of the side aisles act as beams lying on their sides to apply a strong, inward, horizontal push to the legs of each arch. Each aisle roof is about 26 ft (8 m) deep in the horizontal direction and spans the length of the building, 150 ft (46 m). The aisle roofs are tied together by steel rods inside the horizontal band of the end wall that lies just above the clock at one end and just below the balcony at the other end, leaving no horizontal thrust to be imparted to the foundations. (Photos: Professor Dr. Chris H. Luebkeman.)

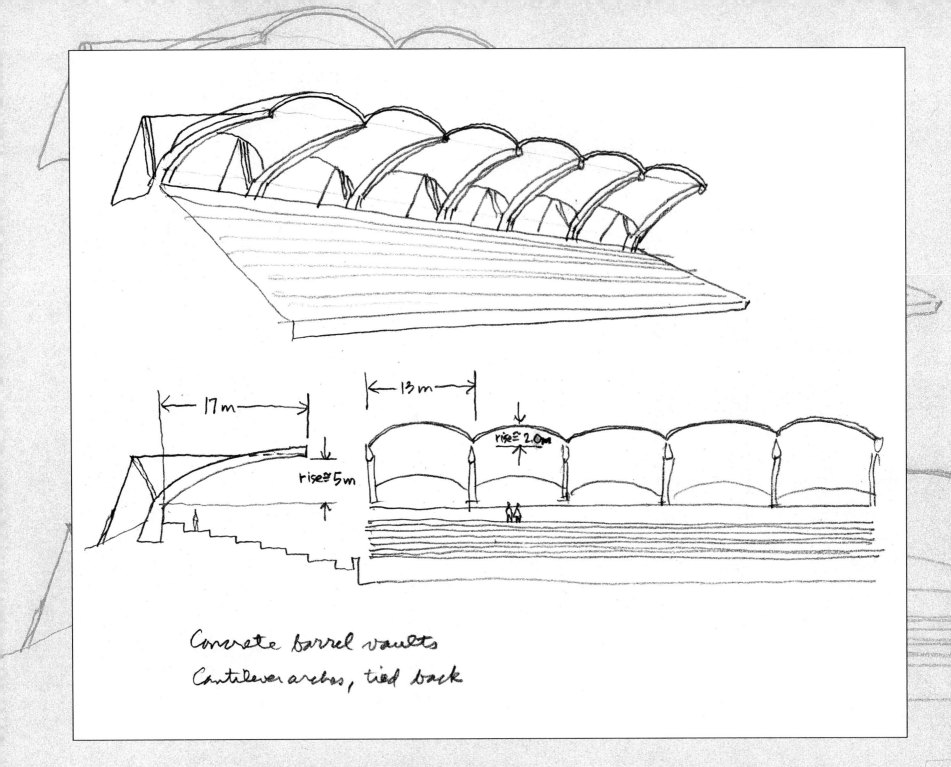

17 m

13 m

rise ≈ 5 m

rise ≈ 2.0 m

Concrete barrel vaults
Cantilever arches, tied back

Concrete barrel vaults

Chapter TEN

SHAPING A CANTILEVERED ARCH ROOF

The sketch at the top of the page shows a stadium roof design with annotations: *17m*, *13m*, *rise ≈ 5...*, *rise ≈ 2.0m*

◄ **An early design drawing of a stadium roof.**

The facing page shows sketches of an idea for a roof to shelter the grandstand of a stadium. The seating is constructed directly on a sloping bank of earth. The bedrock, a soft limestone, lies only a meter or two beneath the surface. The roof structure consists of a series of cylindrical concrete *barrel vaults* that are supported by cantilevered concrete half-arches. The thrust at the upper end of each half-arch is balanced by the pull of a horizontal stay. The other end of each stay is fastened to the top of an inclined concrete strut from which a second, steeply inclined stay is anchored to a foundation in the ground. Another foundation transmits the compressive force from the half-arch and strut to the ground.

INITIAL ASSUMPTIONS

We will build with concrete whose ultimate strength is approximately 25 MPa. For the arches and struts we will use an allowable stress of 40% of this value, which is 10 MPa. This is an average value for the composite action of concrete and reinforcing steel that is suitable for preliminary design. Even assuming that we will use the minimum practical thickness for the vaults, their stresses will be a small fraction of 10 MPa, providing in effect a huge factor of safety against the greater risks and uncertainties associated with their thinness.

In finding form and forces for this structure, we will design the barrel vaults first, then

Concrete barrel vaults

the arches, the stay cables and struts, and, finally, the foundations. This top-to-bottom order is the same one we used in Chapter Two to design the columns of a building. It allows us to follow the path of the loads as they accumulate from the topmost element through the various members and pass into the earth.

DESIGNING THE BARREL VAULT

The minimum practical thickness for the barrel vaults is determined by the diameters of the steel reinforcing bars that they contain, plus the thickness of concrete *cover* within which the bars must be embedded to protect them from corrosion and fire. Reinforcing bars of the smallest standard size, 10M, will be sufficient. A 10M bar is 11.3 mm in diameter. We will install bars in both the circumferential and longitudinal directions in the vault, creating an orthogonal grid of steel that will control cracking, which might otherwise occur in any direction from such forces as concrete shrinkage, temperature expansion and contraction, and unforeseen localized loadings such as might occur if workers pile a stack of heavy roofing materials on a small area of the vault. Where the bars cross one another, their total thickness is 22.6 mm. The Standard Building Code Requirements of the American Concrete Institute specify that for concrete *shells* (thin vaults) with bars of this diameter, a minimum cover thickness of 13 mm is required on each side of the reinforcing. A sketch of the reinforcing bars and minimum cover (Fig. 10.1) shows that the least possible thickness for the vaults is about 50 mm. But experience has shown that a shell this

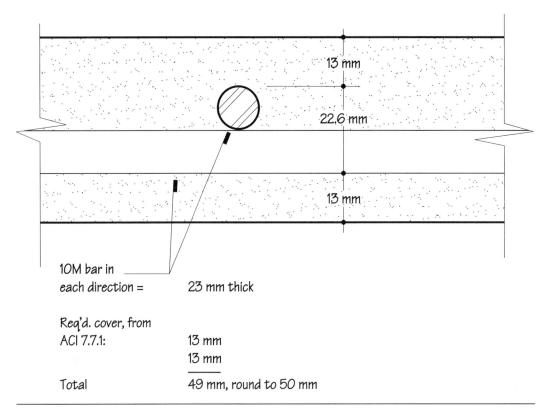

▲ *Figure 10.1*
Finding the minimum thickness of concrete in the vaults.

thin is very difficult to make; even a slight inaccuracy in the bending of the bars or the curvature of the formwork would result in a structure that does not meet minimum cover requirements and whose shape differs from the assumed geometry. The geometry of a thin shell must be correct in order for the shell to work in pure compression. Experience suggests that a minimum practical thickness for shells is 65 mm. We will adopt a thickness of 80 mm to provide an additional cushion against construction imperfections. This will make the builder's task sufficiently less exact-

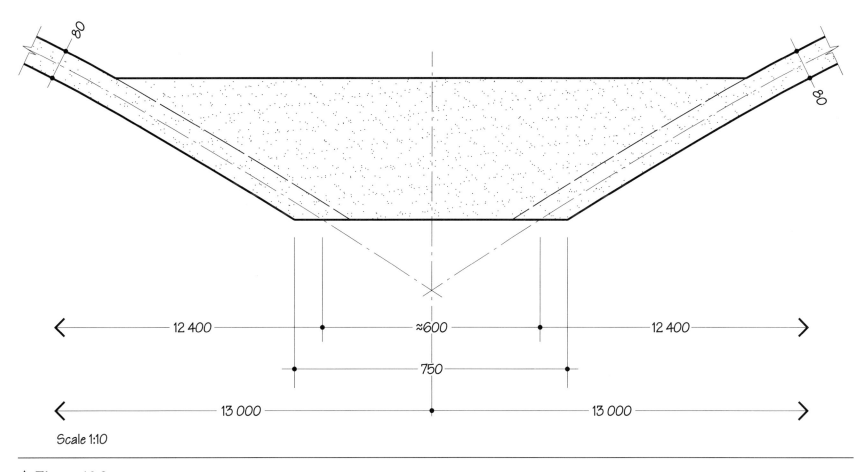

▲ *Figure 10.2*
Preliminary detail of the vault intersection.

ing that it will probably result in a lower contract price despite its use of more concrete than a shell of minimum thickness.

Our original sketches indicate that the vaults span 13 m, measured from centerline to centerline of the cantilevered arches, and rise 2 m. To simplify the form of the roof, we will not form the half-arches as discrete ribs below the edges of the vaults. Instead, we will thicken each intersection of vaults to create an integral rib. In sketching this detail, we decide to eliminate the sharp edge on the underside of the intersection, making a flat surface that is 750 mm wide (Fig. 10.2). This will make the formwork somewhat easier to construct and will avoid the problem of trying to cast a flawless sharp edge in concrete. This decision effectively reduces the span of the vaults to 12.4 m. We will keep a rise of 2.0 m.

The vaults are actually *double-curved*, because the shape of the supporting arches gives them a slight secondary curvature in a direction perpendicular to their primary curvature. The secondary curvature imparts additional strength and stiffness to the vaults and makes their exact analysis somewhat more involved. For purposes of preliminary design, however, we can make the conservative assumption that each vault acts in only one direction as a series of 1-m-wide, 80-mm-thick arches. We estimate the loads on the horizontal projection of a square meter of vault surface. The live load per unit area is taken from the local building code, and the dead load, the self-weight of the arch, is based on the density of concrete:

Dead load = (0.08 m)(2400 kg/m³) = 192 kg/m²

Live load from building code = 120 kg/m²

Total load = 312 kg/m²

The force exerted by this load = (312 kg/m²)(9.8 m/s²) = 3.06 kN/m².

FINDING FORM AND FORCES FOR THE VAULT BY GRAPHICAL MEANS

The loads are assumed to be distributed uniformly, but, to facilitate a graphical analysis, we treat them as if they are divided into 10 discrete loads. Each load is applied to the center of a 1.24-m segment of the span. This places the first and last loads 0.62 m from the ends of the span, with the other loads occurring at 1.24-m intervals between. The magnitude of each load is:

$$P = (3.06 \text{ kN/m}^2)(1.24 \text{ m})(1 \text{ m}) = 3.8 \text{ kN}$$

Figure 10.3 illustrates the graphical design of these vaults. Because we know that the funicular polygon is a parabola, we avoid constructing a trial funicular polygon by drawing funicular segments *oa* and *om* first, each along a line that

starts from a support and passes through a point on the centerline of the polygon that lies twice as far from the closing string as the desired rise, as we learned to do in Chapter 9. Rays *oa* and *om* on the force polygon are drawn parallel to these segments to find the final pole directly.

The funicular polygon may be scaled to determine the dimensions of the vault, measuring vertically from the closing string to the center of each line segment to establish points on the vault axis. The force polygon is scaled to learn that the maximum compressive force in the 1-m-wide arch is 35 kN and the horizontal thrust is 29.3 kN.

FINDING THE FORM OF THE VAULT BY NUMERICAL MEANS

The rise of the vault that we are designing is 2 m, and the span is 12.4 m. We divide the span arbitrarily into 10 equal parts of 1.24-m width and

---

Figure 10.3 ▶

Graphical determination of form and forces for the vaults.

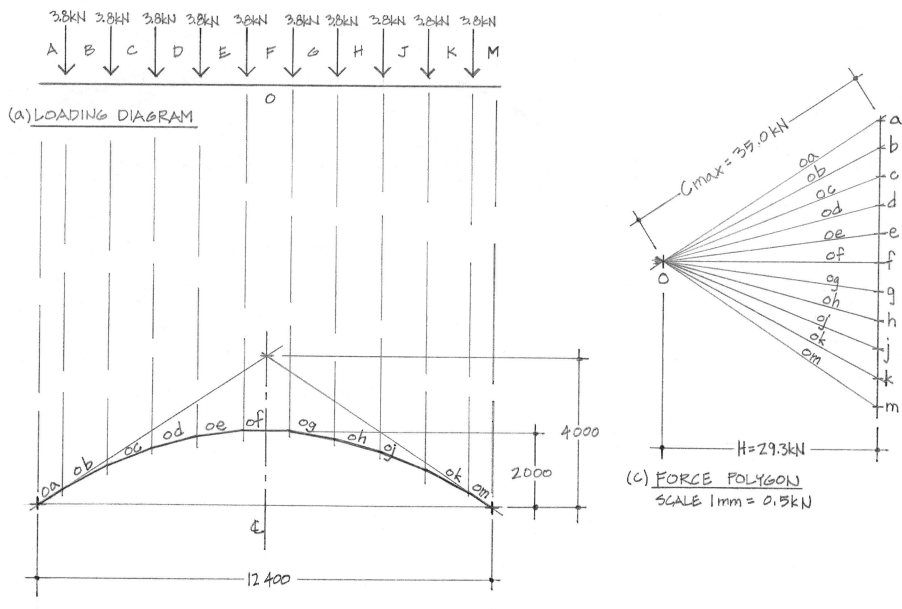

3.8kN 3.8kN 3.8kN 3.8kN 3.8kN 3.8kN 3.8kN 3.8kN 3.8kN 3.8kN

A   B   C   D   E   F   G   H   J   K   M

O

(a) LOADING DIAGRAM

4000

2000

12 400

(b) FUNICULAR POLYGON
SCALE 1:100

Cmax = 35.0kN

oa
ob
oc
od
oe
of
og
oh
oj
ok
om

a
b
c
d
e
f
g
h
j
k
m

H = 29.3kN

(c) FORCE POLYGON
SCALE 1mm = 0.5kN

calculate the height of the arch at each interval, using eq. [9-2a]. We enter these values on a drawing of the arch (Fig. 10.4):

$$y_x = 4s\left(\frac{x}{L} - \frac{x^2}{L^2}\right)$$

$$y_{0.1L} = (8 \text{ m})(0.1 - 0.1^2) = 0.72 \text{ m}$$

$$y_{0.2L} = (8 \text{ m})(0.2 - 0.2^2) = 1.28 \text{ m}$$

$$y_{0.3L} = (8 \text{ m})(0.3 - 0.3^2) = 1.68 \text{ m}$$

$$y_{0.4L} = (8 \text{ m})(0.4 - 0.4^2) = 1.92 \text{ m}$$

$$y_{0.5L} = (8 \text{ m})(0.5 - 0.5^2) = 2.00 \text{ m}$$

The height of the center point calculates as 2.00 m, providing a partial check of the accuracy of this set of solutions. From these dimensions, we can plot the form of the centerline of the vault on drawings and furnish dimensions on the construction drawings to guide the fabrication of the formwork.

FINDING THE MAXIMUM FORCE IN THE VAULT BY NUMERICAL MEANS

We examine a strip of vault 1 m wide that spans 12.4 m with a rise of 2 m. We determined earlier that the total load on this strip, W, is 38 kN. First we use eq. [9-1] to find the horizontal thrust:

$$H = \frac{wL^2}{8s} = \frac{WL}{8s} = \frac{(38 \text{ kN})(12.4 \text{ m})}{8(2 \text{ m})} = 29.45 \text{ kN}$$

The sag ratio, n, is 2 m divided by 12.4 m, which is 0.161. With these two quantities, we calculate the maximum force in the vault, using eq. [9-5]:

$$C_{max} = H\sqrt{16n^2 + 1}$$

$$= (29.45 \text{ kN}) \times \sqrt{16(0.161)^2 + 1} = 35.05 \text{ kN}$$

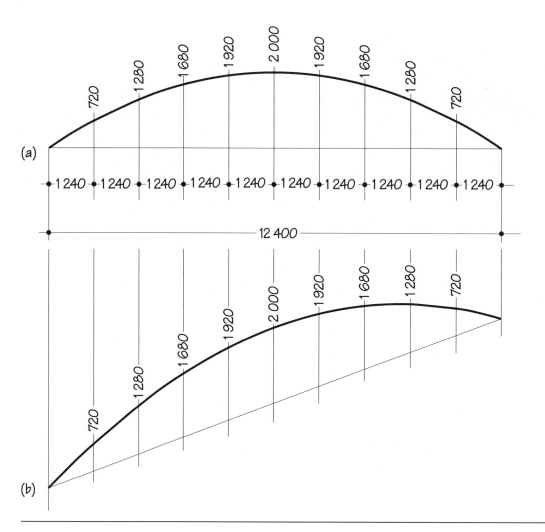

▲ *Figure 10.4*
(a) Ordinates of the vault axis. Although it does not apply to this project, notice in (b) that the same ordinates may be used to plot the form of a parabola that has an inclined closing string.

These answers correlate closely with those that we obtained graphically.

DETAILING THE VAULT

Dividing the calculated maximum force of 35.05 kN by the cross-sectional area of the 1-m-wide strip of vault, we find that the average stress in the concrete is 0.44 MPa, which is only about 5% of the allowable stress we are using for the arch and struts, a situation that is typical in thin concrete vaults. Despite this low stress, experience has shown that it is wise to stiffen the free edges of thin shells to protect them against load concentrations caused by wind pressures, drifting snow, or construction incidents. When such load concentrations occur in the interior region of the vault, they tend to be less serious than at a free edge because of the spreading of the load to adjacent material all around the place of application. In addition, any local tendency for the vault to buckle in its interior regions is suppressed by the stiffness of the surrounding surface. Along a free edge, a thin vault lacks this load-spreading, mutually supportive quality. A reinforced concrete *stiffening rib* three times as thick as the vault, which comes to 240 mm in this case, is usually adequate to stiffen a free edge. An edge rib of this dimension would make the vault look ponderously heavy. Fortunately, the rib can be recessed from the free edge by half a meter or so and still do its job adequately. This makes the rib invisible from below and preserves the elegant slenderness of the visible edge of the vault (Fig. 10.5). The sides of the rib are sloped at 30°. This permits a smoother flow of forces between the rib and the vault and facilitates the placement of wet concrete during construction. It also permits

easier installation of a waterproof membrane on the roof. If this vault were single-curved, it might also require stiffening ribs in its interior regions, but our vault, with its slight secondary curvature, will probably not need them.

We found earlier that each meter-wide strip of vault exerts a horizontal thrust of 29.45 kN when it is fully loaded. At each interior cantilevered arch, the equal thrusts of the two adjacent vaults push against each other and there is no net horizontal thrust. The arch is acted upon only by the vertical components of the thrusts of

the vaults. At each end of the roof, however, the horizontal thrust at the outside edge of the last vault is not balanced by that of an adjacent vault and must be resisted in some way. The easiest way to do this is with horizontal steel tie rods. These rods must extend from one end of the roof to the other, passing under all the vaults, in order to balance the two end thrusts against each other. These rods will be visible and will tend to detract from the graceful appearance of the roof. Furthermore, they will interfere with the erection and removal of formwork for the vaults. A solu-

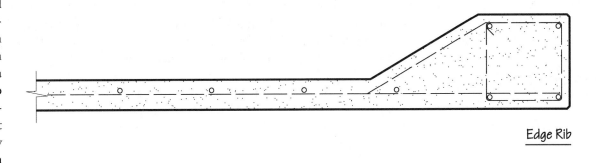

Edge Rib

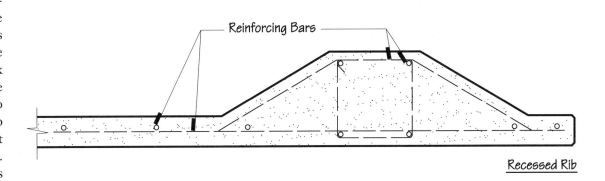

Reinforcing Bars

Recessed Rib

▲ *Figure 10.5*
Sections of stiffening ribs.

tion to these problems is suggested in Figure 10.6: we can add a cantilevered half-vault at each end of the roof, which places the line of unbalanced thrust and the resulting tie rods across the *crowns* (tops) of the vaults, where they will be much less conspicuous. This scheme is also advantageous because it permits a roof of equal total area to be constructed with one less cantilevered arch, which will save money. And the half-vaults with tie rods installed above increase the apparent lightness of the roof. We will install five tie rods across the roof. Each must resist the thrust of a strip of vault that is 3.4 m wide (1/5 of the 17 m span of the cantilevered arches). We will use mild steel bars with an allowable stress, F_{allow}, of 150 MPa. We size these bars as follows

Tensile force per bar = T

$$= \left(\frac{17 \text{ m}}{5}\right) \times (29.45 \text{ kN/m}) = 100.1 \text{ kN}$$

Required area of steel = $\frac{T}{F_{allow}} = \frac{100.1 \text{ kN}}{150 \text{ MPa}}$

$$= 0.667 \times 10^{-3} \text{ m}^2 = 667 \text{ mm}^2$$

Consulting a table of standard sizes of round steel bars, we select the smallest size that exceeds

667 mm² in area. This is a 30M bar, which is 29.9 mm in diameter and has a cross-sectional area of 700 mm².

At each end, we must anchor the tie rod to the concrete edge of the vault. The vault is only 80 mm thick, but its longitudinal edge is a free edge that must be stiffened with a 240-mm rib. We make a scaled drawing of this edge (Fig. 10.7). To avoid bending moments in the vault, the 30M tie rod must be anchored to the concrete at the center of the vault thickness. As we draw the grid of reinforcing bars in the vault, we notice that the tie rod interferes with the positions of the last several longitudinal bars near the free edge. We move these bars up slightly so that they pass over the tie rod. To maintain the required cover of concrete over these bars, we extend the taper of the rib. We also draw a small volume of concrete that extends rightward over the top of the vault to embed the 30M tie rod until the rod reaches a point where it can exit from the concrete through a nearly vertical face. This exit hole will be much easier to waterproof than a flat, sloping exit hole.

A logical way to anchor the tie rod would be to attach it to a steel end plate at the edge of the vault. The vault is so thin, however, that it would be difficult to embed a plate of sufficient

size. We can transfer the force at the end of the rod into the concrete by forming the rod into a U-bend of standard dimensions called a *hook*. The hook should lie horizontally in the center plane of the vault. To create a symmetrical pull on the rod, we weld a second hook to the first one in a mirror-image arrangement.

We must protect the exposed portions of the tie rods from corrosion. Paints must be renewed every few years, so for easier maintenance and greater reliability we will probably use a heavy coating of zinc or plastic.

FINDING FORM AND FORCES GRAPHICALLY FOR THE CANTILEVERED ARCH

The cantilevered arch, having been conceived in the original sketch as being level at its free end, may be considered to be half of a parabolic arch on a level base. To begin the graphical solution, we divide its 17-m span arbitrarily into 10 intervals of 1.7 m and estimate the load on each of its segments. We already determined that the total load of a 1-m strip of vault is 38 kN. Each arch supports half of this load, 19 kN, from the vault that bears on it from each side. This totals 38 kN per meter of arch length. We must add to this the

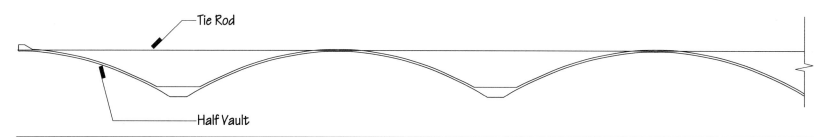

▲ *Figure 10.6*
Placing the tie rods at the crown line of the vaults.

live load that is supported directly on the 0.6-m width of the arch and an approximate self-weight of the arch itself. We scale the dimensions of the added concrete from Figure 10.2 to find that its cross-sectional area is about 0.44 m². We calculate the loads on a 1.7-m-long interval of the arch:

Vault load, D.L. + L.L.: (38 kN/m)(1.7 m)

$$= 64.6 \text{ kN}$$

Self-weight of arch:

$$(0.44\text{m}^2)(1.7 \text{ m})(2400 \text{ kg/m}^3) = 17.6 \text{ kN}$$

Live load on 0.6-m-wide, 1.7-m-long strip of arch:

$$(120 \text{ kg/m}^2)(0.6 \text{ m})(1.7 \text{ m})(2400 \text{ kg/m}^3) = 1.2 \text{ kN}$$

Total load per 1.7-m segment of arch = 83.4 kN

Say 84 kN

On our drawing (Fig. 10.8) we divide the 17-m span of the arch into 10 segments, place a vector representing a load of 84 kN in the center of each segment, and construct the load line accordingly.

We want the arch to be level at its free end. This means that the topmost segment of the funicular polygon will be level. Because the arch is parabolic, a line tangent to the arch at its support will intersect a vertical line through the crown of the arch at a height of $2s$ above the base line, which for this arch is 10 m. Thus we are able to begin the construction of the final funicular polygon by drawing its first and last seg-

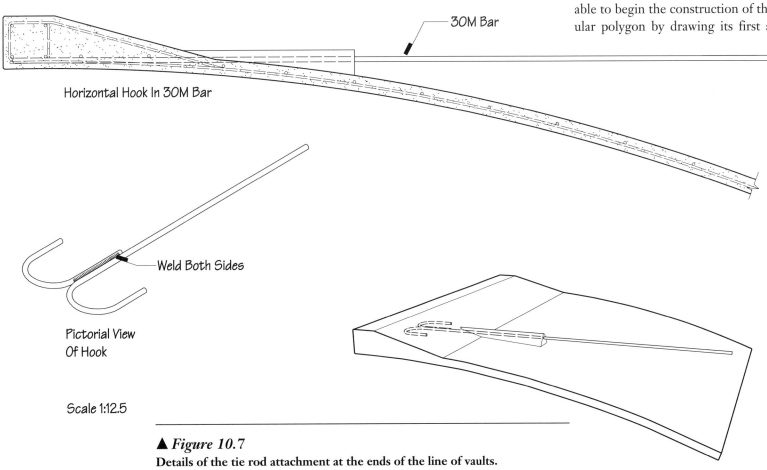

Horizontal Hook In 30M Bar

30M Bar

Weld Both Sides

Pictorial View
Of Hook

Scale 1:12.5

▲ *Figure 10.7*
Details of the tie rod attachment at the ends of the line of vaults.

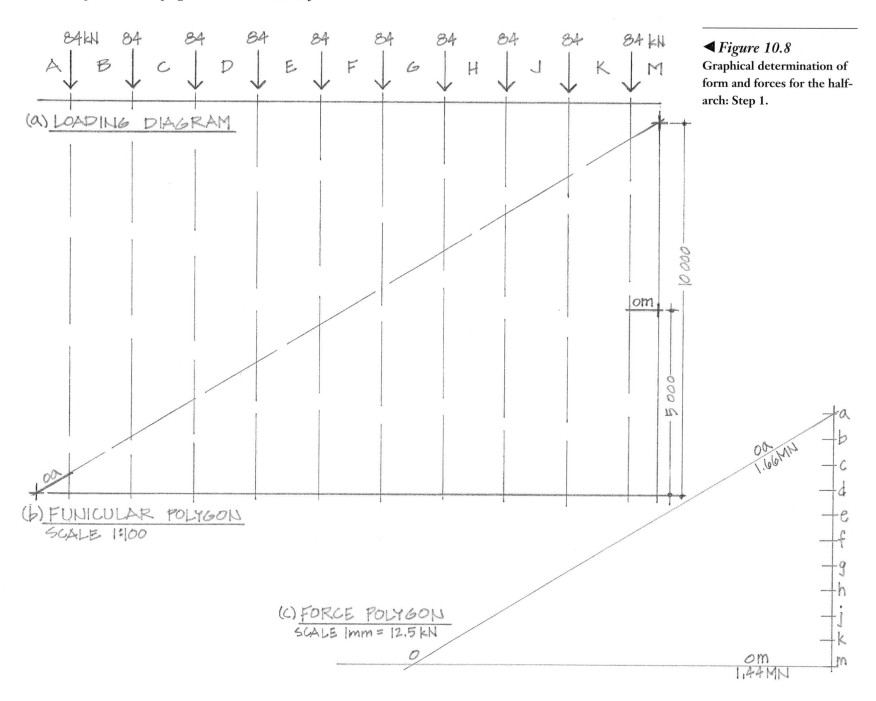

84 kN   84   84   84   84   84   84   84   84   84 kN

A   B   C   D   E   F   G   H   J   K   M

(a) LOADING DIAGRAM

10 000

0m

5 000

oa

(b) FUNICULAR POLYGON
SCALE 1:100

oa
1.66 MN

a
b
c
d
e
f
g
h
j
k
m

(c) FORCE POLYGON
SCALE 1mm = 12.5 kN

o

0m
1.44 MN

◄ *Figure 10.8*
Graphical determination of form and forces for the half-arch: Step 1.

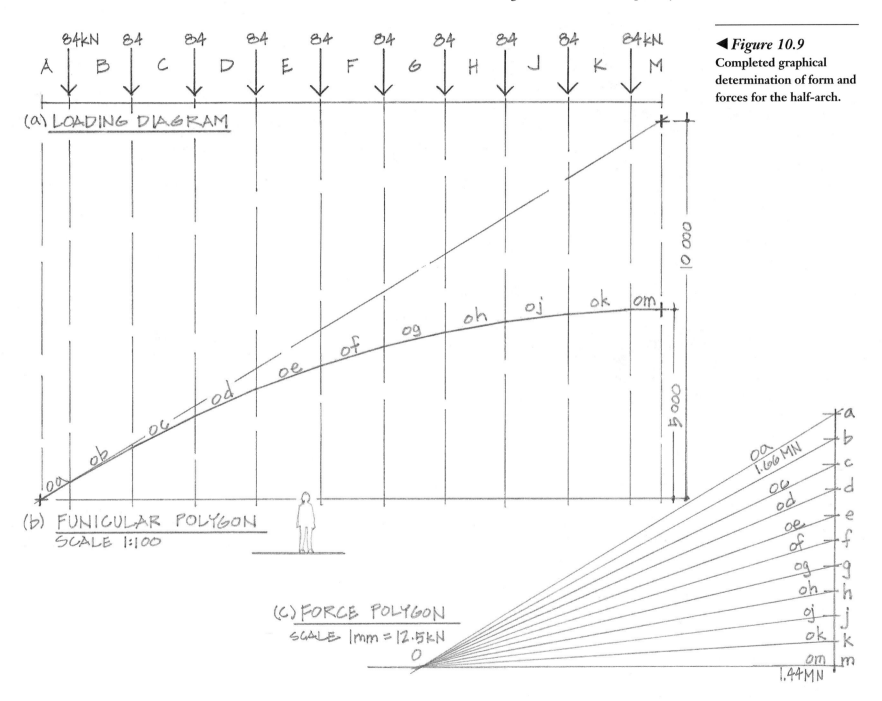

84kN 84 84 84 84 84 84 84 84 84kN

A B C D E F G H J K M

(a) LOADING DIAGRAM

(b) FUNICULAR POLYGON
SCALE 1:100

(c) FORCE POLYGON
SCALE 1mm = 12.5kN

◄ Figure 10.9
**Completed graphical
determination of form and
forces for the half-arch.**

ments, *oa* and *om*. This enables us to draw the first and last rays of the force polygon. These intersect to determine the final pole location, enabling us to construct the curve of the arch and determine the forces in it without further preparation (Fig. 10.9). The maximum force in the arch, *oa*, scales as 1.66 MN. The force at the upper end, which is also the force in the horizontal stay cable, is approximately 1.44 MN. The rise of the arch at each interval may be scaled from the centers of the line segments on the funicular polygon.

FINDING FORM AND FORCES NUMERICALLY FOR THE CANTILEVERED ARCH

A numerical solution to the cantilevered half-arch is easily achieved by assuming that we are designing a full arch that spans twice as far, 34 m, with the same rise, 5 m. The load is 49.4 kN/m. We begin by using eq. [9-1] to find the horizontal component of the force in the arch:

$$H = \frac{wL^2}{8s} = \frac{(49.4 \text{ kN/m})(34 \text{ m})^2}{8(5 \text{ m})} = 1.43 \text{ MN}$$

This is the force in the horizontal stay cable. It agrees closely with the value of 1.44 MN that we found in the graphical solution. *H* having been found, we are ready to find the maximum compressive force in the arch, using eqs. [9-4] and [9-5]:

$$n = \frac{s}{L} = \frac{5 \text{ m}}{34 \text{ m}} = 0.1471$$

$$C_{\max} = H\sqrt{16n^2 + 1}$$

$$= (1.43 \text{ MN})\sqrt{16(0.1471)^2 + 1} = 1.66 \text{ MN}$$

This value matches our earlier result from the graphical solution. We can find the coordinates of the arch with eq. [9-2a]:

$$y = 4s\left(\frac{x}{L} - \frac{x^2}{L^2}\right)$$

$$Y_{1\,m} = 4(5 \text{ m})\left(\frac{1 \text{ m}}{34 \text{ m}} - \left(\frac{1 \text{ m}}{34 \text{ m}}\right)^2\right) = 0.571 \text{ m}$$

$$Y_{2\,m} = (20 \text{ m})\left(\frac{2 \text{ m}}{34 \text{ m}} - \left(\frac{2 \text{ m}}{34 \text{ m}}\right)^2\right) = 1.107 \text{ m}$$

$$Y_{3\,m} = (20 \text{ m})\left(\frac{3 \text{ m}}{34 \text{ m}} - \left(\frac{3 \text{ m}}{34 \text{ m}}\right)^2\right) = 1.609 \text{ m}$$

$$Y_{4\,m} = (20 \text{ m})\left(\frac{4 \text{ m}}{34 \text{ m}} - \left(\frac{4 \text{ m}}{34 \text{ m}}\right)^2\right) = 2.076 \text{ m}$$

$$Y_{5\,m} = (20 \text{ m})\left(\frac{5 \text{ m}}{34 \text{ m}} - \left(\frac{5 \text{ m}}{34 \text{ m}}\right)^2\right) = 2.509 \text{ m}$$

. . . .

$$Y_{17\,m} = (20 \text{ m})\left(\frac{17 \text{ m}}{34 \text{ m}} - \left(\frac{17 \text{ m}}{34 \text{ m}}\right)^2\right) = 5.000 \text{ m}$$

These dimensions may be compared with those scaled from Figure 10.9.

The forces in the strut, backstay, and arch foundation may be found numerically by applying the expressions for static equilibrium to diagrams of the forces at each joint, as we learned to do in Chapter Three.

SIZING THE ARCH

The determination of the required cross-sectional area of concrete at the base of the arch is based on an allowable stress in the concrete of 10 MPa:

$$A_{\text{req}} = \frac{P}{F_c} = \frac{1.66 \text{ MN}}{10 \text{ MPa}} = 0.166 \text{ m}^2$$

Our early design for the arch (Fig. 10.2) provides about 0.44 m² of concrete in the arch, more than twice as much as is required. On the other hand, the depth of 0.4 m that we show in this drawing is too shallow for a free-standing arch of this span. However, in our design the arch is not free-standing, but joins the vaults on either side to form a V-shaped section that will probably prove to be sufficiently stiff against buckling.

DESIGNING THE STRUT AND STAYS

The horizontal stay carries a maximum force of 1.44 MN, which is considerable. As live loads on the roof increase and decrease, the stay will elongate and contract. To protect the rigid concrete structure from damage, we would like to minimize this movement. The amount by which a length of steel stretches under an increased load is directly proportional to the increase in the stress in the steel, regardless of the allowable strength of the steel. We could keep the diameter of the stay relatively small by making it of a high-strength steel, but for a given change in load, a smaller-diameter stay would experience a larger variation in stress, and therefore a larger change in length, than a larger-diameter stay of lower-strength steel. To control fluctuations in the length of the stay, we will make it of mild steel rods whose allowable tensile stress is 150 MPa. The required area of steel in the stay is

$$A_{\text{req}} = \frac{P}{F_{\text{allow}}} = \frac{1.44 \text{ MN}}{150 \text{ MPa}} = 0.0096 \text{ m}^2$$

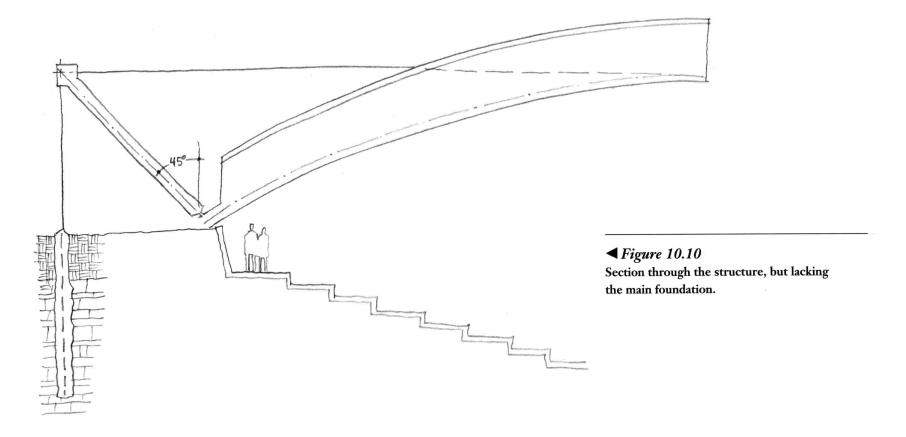

◀ *Figure 10.10*
Section through the structure, but lacking the main foundation.

The ends of the stay will be threaded to receive a nut that will transmit the force to a steel bearing plate. To account for the reduction in the working area of the round bar by the threads, we add 15% to the determined value to arrive at a required gross area of 0.0110 m² or 11 000 mm². This area can be provided by a single bar 120 mm in diameter, or two bars each 90 mm in diameter.

We sketch the strut and stays in Figure 10.10 and find their internal forces in Figure 10.11. Force *AB* is the resultant of the total gravity load on the arch, 840 kN, located at midspan. For purposes of this analysis, we substitute for the arch a strut that carries 1.66 MN of compression at the same inclination as the lower end of the arch. The force polygon (Fig. 10.11[b]) confirms that the forces that we found earlier in the arch and in the horizontal stay are in equilibrium. It also shows that if the strut is inclined at 45°, it will carry 2.03 MN of compression and the horizontal stay and a vertical backstay will both experience the same tensile force, 1.44 MN. The backstay could be anchored into a hole drilled in the limestone bedrock with *grout*, which is a fine-grained concrete with carefully controlled properties. The compressive foundation at the base of the arch will transmit 2.28 MN of force.

At a stress of 10 MPa, the strut would have to be 0.203 m² in area, which is 451 mm square. To minimize the risk of buckling and increase the appearance of strength in the strut, we decide

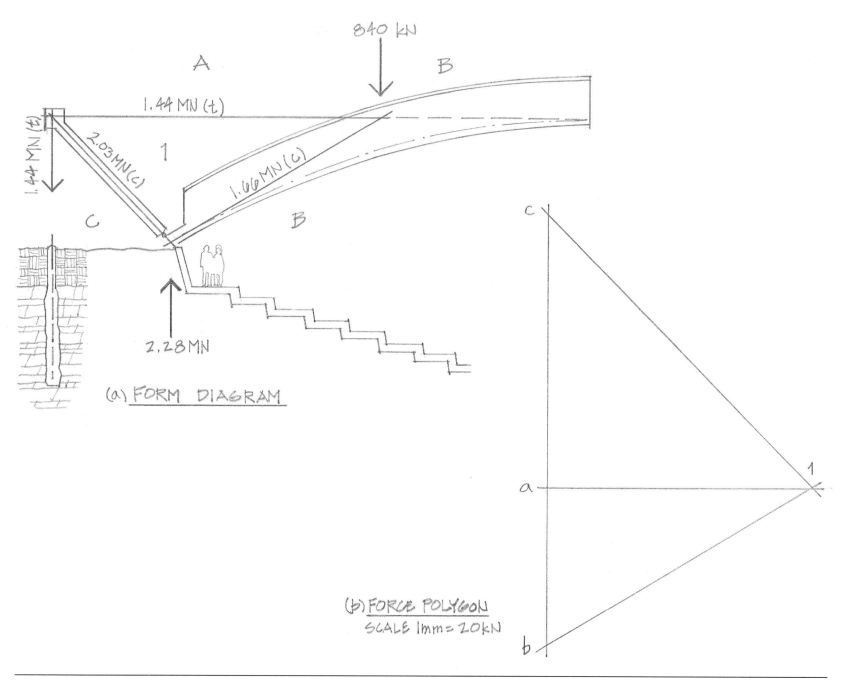

840 kN

A

B

1.44 MN (t)

1.44 MN (t)

2.03 MN (c)

1

1.66 MN (c)

C

B

2.28 MN

(a) FORM DIAGRAM

(b) FORCE POLYGON
SCALE 1mm = 20kN

c

a

1

b

▲ *Figure 10.11*
Graphical determination of forces in horizontal stay, backstay, strut, and foundations.

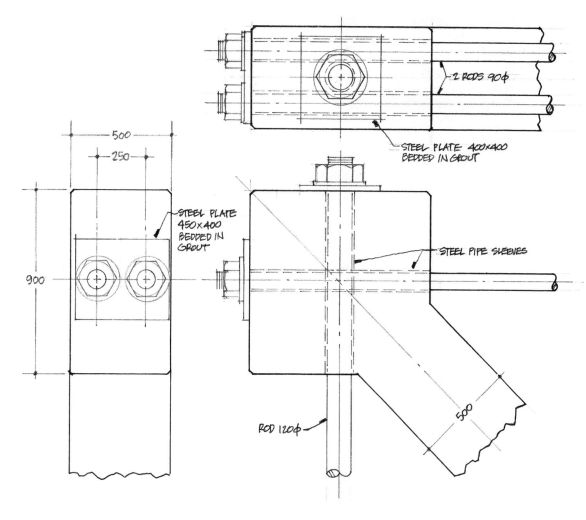

2 RODS 90φ

STEEL PLATE 400×400
BEDDED IN GROUT

STEEL PLATE
450×400
BEDDED IN
GROUT

STEEL PIPE SLEEVES

500

250

500

900

ROD 120φ

500

◀ *Figure 10.12*
Preliminary details for the head of the strut.

to adopt a section that is 500 mm square. In Figure 10.12 we lay out a preliminary design for the head of the strut that provides flat faces for each of the stay anchorages. Because the vertical backstay is exposed to vandalism, we will make it sturdy by using a single 120-mm-diameter bar (the symbol φ on the drawing is shorthand for "diameter"). To simplify the connection of the stays at the head of the strut, we will use a pair of 90-mm-diameter bars for the horizontal stay. The bars pass through greased steel pipe sleeves that are embedded in the concrete. Washers and thick steel bearing plates spread the force from each stay over a sufficient area of concrete to ensure that the actual stress in the concrete does not exceed the allowable stress of 10 MPa. The minimum size of a typical plate is calculated as follows:

$$A_{\text{req}} = \frac{P}{F_C} = \frac{1.44\,\text{MN}}{10\,\text{MPa}} = 0.144\,\text{m}^2 = 144\,000\,\text{mm}^2$$

Add area for missing concrete where bars penetrate:

$$A_{\text{gross}} = 144\,000\,\text{mm}^2 + 2\pi r^2 = 144\,000\,\text{mm}^2$$
$$+ 2\pi(50\,\text{mm})^2 = 159\,700\,\text{mm}^2$$

To ensure full contact between the bearing plate and the concrete, each plate is bedded in grout.

The twin stay bars are anchored to the upper end of the arch with a similar detail (Fig.

10.13). This connection could be left exposed, or it could be concealed within a grout-filled pocket in the end of the arch.

The horizontal stay bars will sag under their own weight. We can estimate the amount of *self-sag* by using a variant of eq. [9-1]:

$$S = \frac{wL^2}{8T} \qquad [10\text{-}1]$$

where

S is the self-sag of the stay,

w is the self-weight of a 1 m length of stay,

L is the free length of the stay, and

T is the tensile force in the stay.

We look up the self-weight of a 90-mm-diameter bar, which is 490 N/m. The free length of the stay is about 20 m, and the tension in each of the two bars is 0.72 MN. Thus, for the stay in our design:

$$S = \frac{(490 \text{ N/m})(20 \text{ m})^2}{8(0.72 \text{ MN})} = 0.034 \text{ m} = 34 \text{ mm}$$

This is less than half of the diameter of the bar. Under dead load only, the tension will be about 40% lower, so the self-sag will be about 66% higher, a total of 56 mm. This will be imperceptible.

We hinge the base of the strut to allow it to rotate back and forth slightly in the plane of the cables in response to changing loads. This avoids the high bending stresses that would occur in the strut in these situations if it were attached rigidly to the end of the arch. The hinge is created by crossing the longitudinal reinforcing bars in the strut, and by replacing most of the concrete at this point with thick rubber pads (Fig. 10.14). This creates a zone at the base of the strut that has little resistance to bending in the plane of the cables. The compression in this zone is borne completely by the reinforcing bars. The small

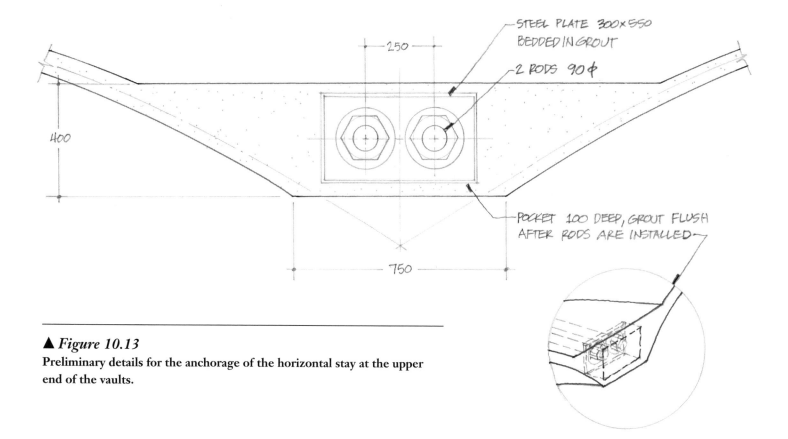

▲ *Figure 10.13*
Preliminary details for the anchorage of the horizontal stay at the upper end of the vaults.

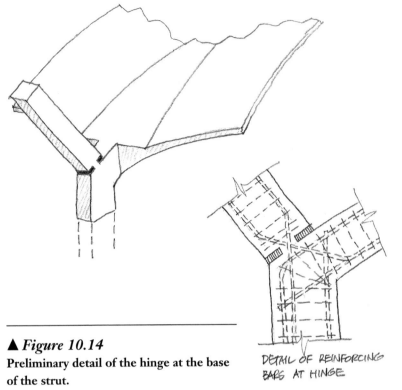

the base of the arch, we can use a rule-of-thumb value of 1.0 MPa that is given for soft limestone in the building code:

$$A_{\text{req}} = \frac{P}{F} = \frac{2.28 \text{ MN}}{1 \text{ MPa}} = 2.28 \text{ m}^2$$

$$\sqrt{2.28 \text{ m}^2} = 1.51 \text{ m}$$

The footing will be a block of concrete about 1.5 m square (Fig. 10.15).

The depth and details of the *drilled and grouted anchor* in the bedrock will be determined by the geotechnical engineer. The design of this anchor is based on the assumption that in order for the anchor to pull out of the ground, it would have to bring with it a cone of rock whose geometry and weight can be predicted from a knowl-

▲ *Figure 10.14*
Preliminary detail of the hinge at the base of the strut.

DETAIL OF REINFORCING
BARS AT HINGE

remaining volume of concrete flexes slightly as the very slight rotations of the strut take place.

The stem of the arch foundation is sized, in accordance with its force of 2.28 MN, to be 477 mm square. Again we find that this looks too slender, and it does not join well to a strut that is 500 mm square, so we adjust its size to a width of 500 mm and a depth of 700 mm.

A geotechnical engineer will design the foundations, using allowable stresses that are based on laboratory test data for actual rock samples taken from test borings on the site. To get a preliminary idea of the size of the footing under

◄ *Figure 10.15*
Completed section through the structure.

edge of the properties of the rock (Fig. 10.16). The depth of the anchor is determined by the required altitude of a cone whose weight is perhaps 20% higher than the force the anchor must resist.

What if the subsoil for this structure were a soft clay instead of rock? A drilled and grouted backstay anchor probably would not be feasible in this yielding soil. One alternative in this case would be a *deadman anchor*, which is a disk of concrete that depends on breadth rather than depth for its effectiveness (Fig. 10.17). For the 1.44-MN force from the backstay, a deadman anchor whose bottom surface is 3 m below the surface would be a disk of concrete 4 m in diameter and 0.8 m thick, comprising about 10 m³ of concrete. The weight of the truncated cone of soil on top of the disk accounts for about 88% of the weight of the anchor.

Figure 10.18 illustrates another way of coping with soft soil. An underground system of struts and ties brings both the tensile and compressive loads in the structure to a single foundation that lies on the line of action of the resultant of all the loads on the structure. There are two difficulties with this design. One is that it is costly to do so much below-grade construction. This elaborate framework would make better economic sense if were above ground and also served to support the seats of the stadium (Figs. 10.19 and 10.20). The other difficulty is that the strut in Figure 10.18 interferes with the walkway at the top of the stands. This could be avoided by modifying the design as shown in Figure 10.21. In Figure 10.22, we analyze this frame graphically to find its member forces.

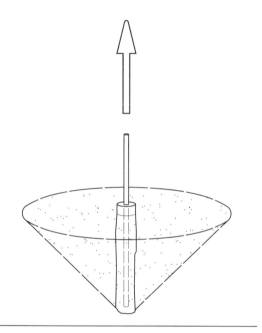

▲ *Figure 10.16*
The cone of soil that would be pulled out by a drilled and grouted anchor.

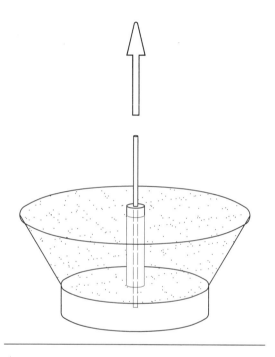

▲ *Figure 10.17*
The cone of soil that would be pulled out by a deadman anchor.

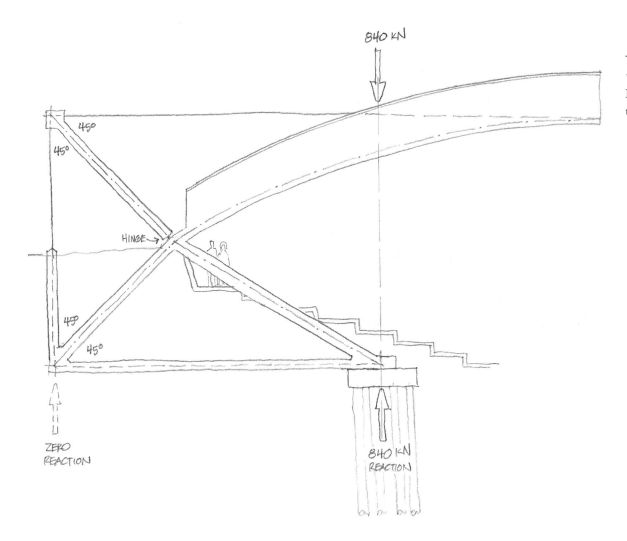

840 KN

450

45°

HINGE →

45°

45°

ZERO
REACTION

840 KN
REACTION

◀ *Figure 10.18*
**Preliminary design idea for a foundation
that exerts no uplift on the soil.**

▲ *Figure 10.19*
Roof of a stadium in Florence, Italy, designed by Pier Luigi Nervi.

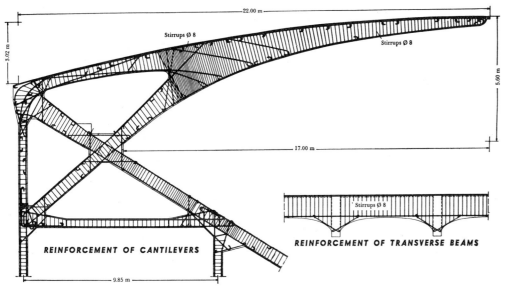

REINFORCEMENT OF CANTILEVERS

REINFORCEMENT OF TRANSVERSE BEAMS

▲ *Figure 10.20*
A section through the structure of the Florence stadium, showing the steel rein-forcing bars in the concrete. The member that slopes down toward the right serves to support the stadium seating as well as to act as an element of the roof structure. Compare this diagram with the one in Figure 10.18 and try to deduce the char-acter of the forces in each of its members. The dimensions of this structure are simi-lar to those of the structure we are designing. (Figs. 10.19 and 10.20 are taken from Pier Luigi Nervi, *Structures,* New York, F. W. Dodge Corporation, 1956.)

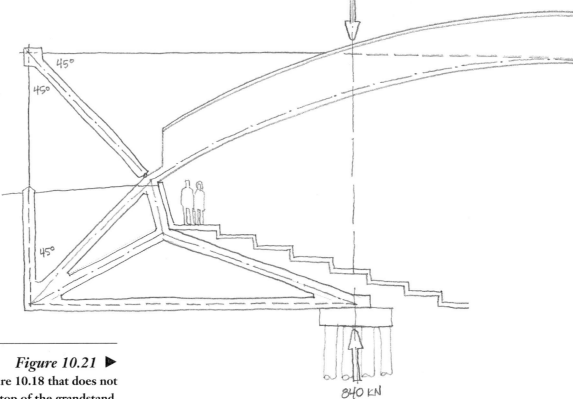

Figure 10.21 ▶
A version of the design idea in Figure 10.18 that does not obstruct the walkway at the top of the grandstand.

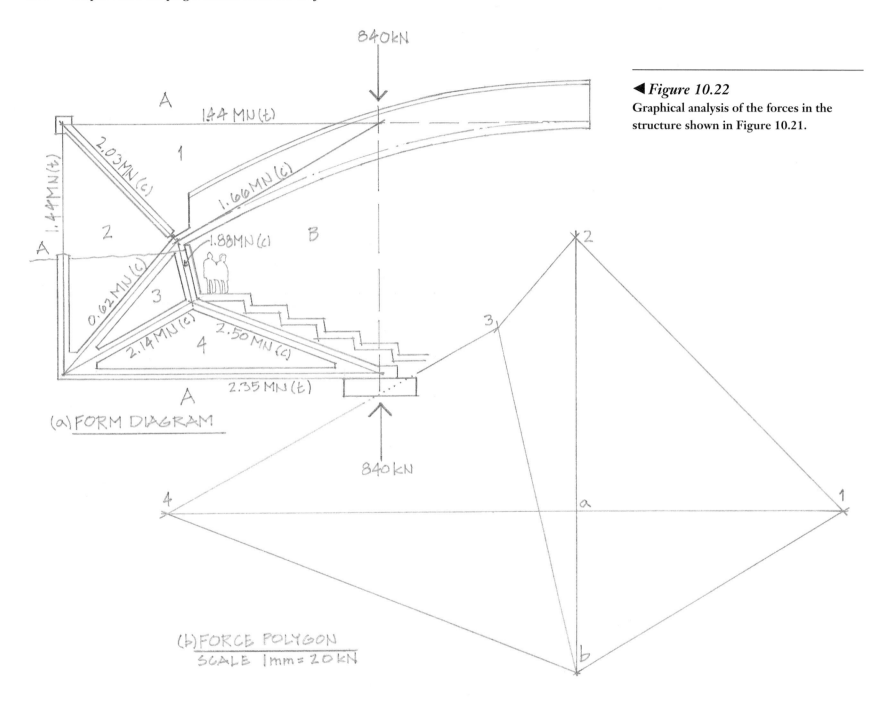

840kN

A

1.44 MN (t)

1.44MN(t)

2.03MN(c)

1

1.66 MN (c)

A

2

1.88MN(c)

B

0.62MN(c)

3

2.14MN(c)

2.50 MN (c)

4

2.35 MN (t)

A

(a) FORM DIAGRAM

840 kN

2

3

4

a

1

b

(b) FORCE POLYGON
SCALE 1mm = 20 kN

◄ *Figure 10.22*
Graphical analysis of the forces in the structure shown in Figure 10.21.

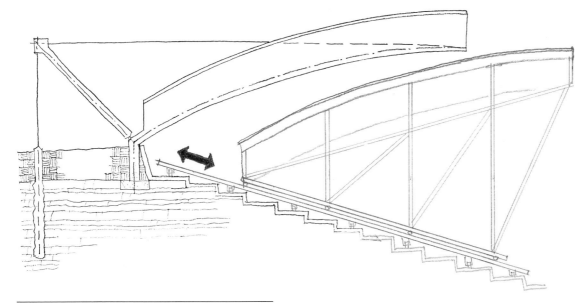

▲ *Figure 10.23*
The reusable concrete formwork rolls down an inclined track to clear the underside of the roof.

FORMING THE CONCRETE

Because it is repetitive in form, the roof could be constructed most economically with a single *bay* of formwork that can be used repeatedly. With this in mind, we evolve a design for a form that is supported on a wheeled framework (Figs. 10.23 and 10.24). To move from one bay to the next, the framework is rolled on tracks along the steps of the bleacher seats. To allow this motion to occur, the form also rolls on sloping tracks that enable it to be dropped below the bottoms of the arches, then to be pushed up again to the proper height for pouring the next bay. It is apparent, in looking at the motion of the formwork, that our decision to move the tie rods to the crown line of the vaults was a good one.

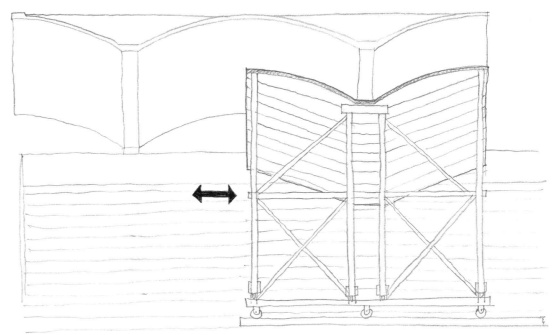

Figure 10.24 ▶
The formwork also rolls on a longitudinal track to
move from one vault to the next.

Because the roof will be constructed one vault at a time, it will be necessary to anchor each tie bar with a hook at the crown of each vault, rather than running continuous bars the full length of the roof. The curved reinforcing bars from within each vault will be left projecting out of the edge of the vault crown in each pour. These will be overlapped with the curved bars in the next pour and spliced by embedding them in the concrete. This will knit the entire line of vaults into a single, monolithic structural unit (Fig. 10.25).

FURTHER WORK

We have created a viable preliminary design for the grandstand roof (Fig. 10.26). Its shape is efficient and elegant. Its members are proportioned according to the forces that they will have to resist. We understand the basic process by which it will be constructed. This is as far as our current knowledge will take us.

Before the roof can be built, its internal network of steel reinforcing bars will have to be designed. We have shaped and sized all the concrete members in such a way that, in theory at least, they are subjected only to compressive forces and do not require tensile reinforcing. As we noted earlier, however, it is standard practice to provide a grid of bars within the vaults to resist cracking from forces caused by temperature change, concrete shrinkage, and unforeseen loading conditions. For similar reasons, longitudinal bars are installed in arches, struts, and columns. These longitudinal bars are always surrounded by smaller-diameter *ties* that resist the tendency of compressed concrete to expand and

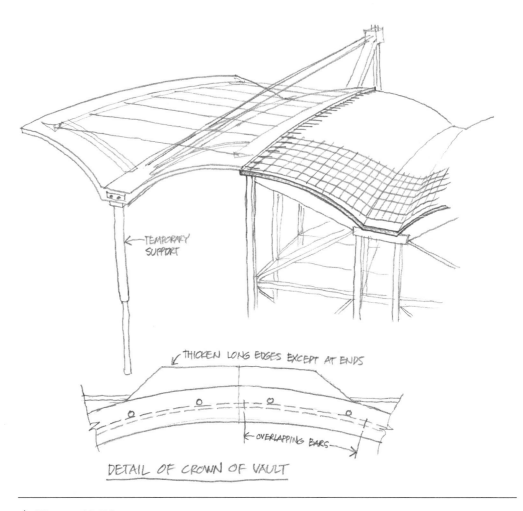

▲ *Figure 10.25*
The successive pours of concrete are joined at the crown line by overlapping reinforcing bars.

▲ *Figure 10.26*
The finished appearance of the stadium roof.

burst in directions perpendicular to the longitudinal compression (Fig. 10.27).

It will also be necessary to examine, using more advanced analytical tools, several other aspects of the design. One is the potential for the wind to lift and vibrate the roof. The dead load of the vaults and arches is more than the upward pressure that would be exerted by the strongest likely wind in most geographic regions, but winds of various velocities and directions may cause this sail-like roof to oscillate and twist in such a way that large dynamic forces would occur. Another aspect requiring investigation is the resistance of the roof to overturning, like a line of dominoes, in a direction perpendicular to the planes of the half-arches. For this to happen, the vaults would have to flex and break. The vaults are probably stiff enough to prevent such a possibility, but if this does not prove to be the case, we may have to stiffen the inclined stems of the foundations or add diagonal bracing or stiff walls between them.

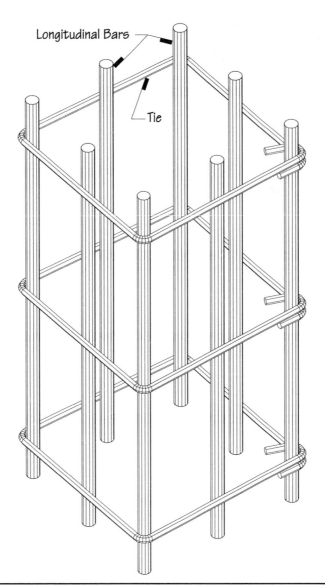

Longitudinal Bars

Tie

◀ *Figure 10.27*
Typical arrangement of longitudinal reinforcing bars and ties in the columns, struts, and half-arches. Notice how this configuration is drawn in Figure 10.20.

Key Terms and Concepts

barrel vault	shell	crown	self-sag	bay
vault	double curvature	hook	drilled and grouted anchor	ties
cover	stiffening rib	grout	deadman anchor	

Exercises

1. The forces in the members of the roof that was designed in this chapter could be reduced by moving the support of the half-arch, along with the base of the inclined strut, 3 m closer to the playing field. This would reduce the span of the half-arch to 14 m. It would place columns between the top walkway and the field, but these would not interfere with sight lines from any of the seats. Develop this design idea fully to find out how much it would reduce member forces. Design a way of sheltering the walkway that is structurally feasible and aesthetically consistent with the rest of the design.

2. The symmetrically arched vault of Pier Luigi Nervi's Exhibition Hall in Turin, Italy (Figs. 13.39-13.41) spans 85 m and rises 19.2 m from the tops of the fan-shaped supports. What is the maximum force per meter of length exerted by this roof if its total load is 375 kg per meter of horizontal projection?

Structural design is concerned with much more than science and techniques: It is also very much concerned with art, common sense, sentiment, aptitude, and enjoyment of the task of creating opportune outlines to which scientific calculations will add finishing touches, substantiating that the structure is sound and strong in accordance with the requirements.

EDUARDO TORROJA
PHILOSOPHY OF STRUCTURES

◄ *Figure 10.28* **The stadium roof at the Madrid Racecourse in Spain, 1935, designed by Eduardo Torroja. The cantilever distance is about 13 m (42 ft) and the vault thickness at the upper edge is 50 mm (2 in.). Notice the vertical backstays at the rear of the roof. Torroja avoided horizontal stay bars by warping the vault surfaces into hyperboloids that undergo tensile force along the crown lines. (Photos: Professor Dr. Chris H. Luebkeman.)**

3. Find form and forces for all the members of the grandstand roof shown in Figure 10.29. Assume that the cable is level at its outer end. The vertical planes of structure are spaced 13 m apart, and the total load on the roof is 312 kg/m².

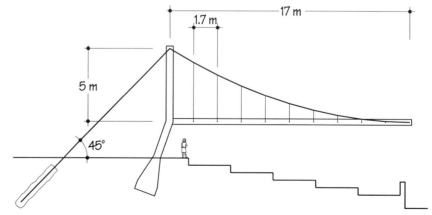

▲ *Figure 10.29* **A stadium roof.**

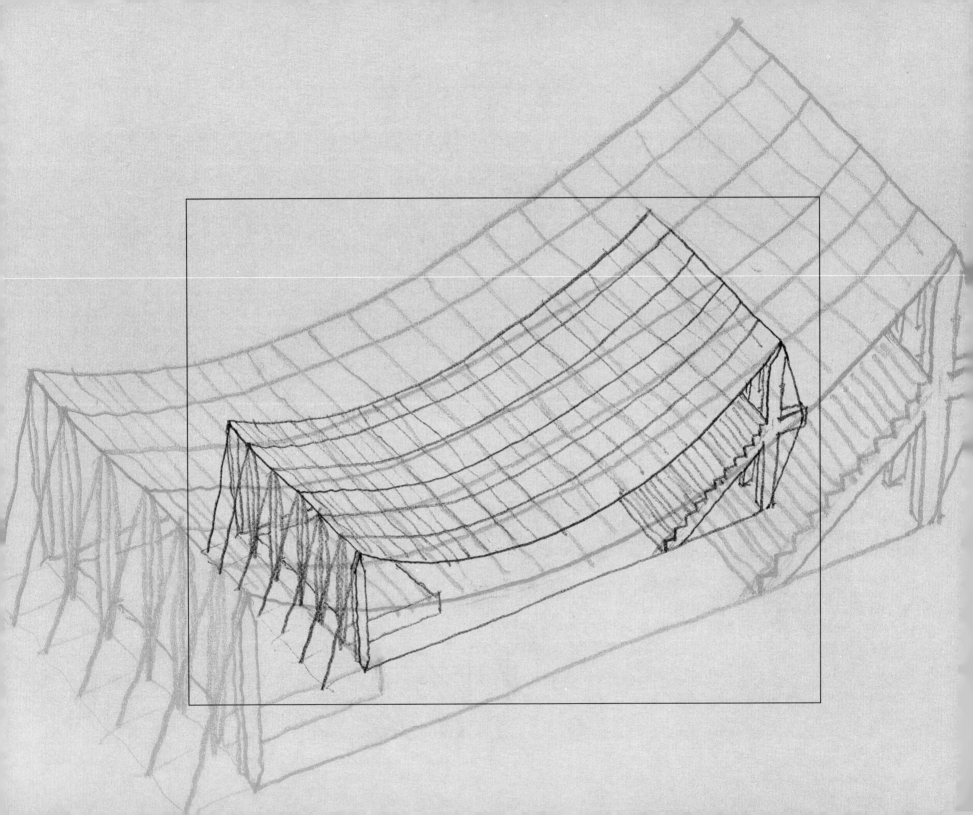

Chapter ELEVEN

SHAPING A HANGING ROOF

◀ **An early design sketch of a hanging roof for an auditorium.**

On the facing page is a sketch of an idea for an auditorium roof that is supported by parallel hanging cables. The geometry of the roof must meet the conditions diagrammed in Figure 11.1. The span of the roof, L, is 140 ft. The right-hand end of each cable is supported at point B, which is 56 ft above the floor. The horizontal line X-X, 31 ft above the floor, has been established as the minimum ceiling height. The inclined line K-B, whose slope is 1:2, assures an unobstructed view of the stage from the topmost row of seats. We need to find a cable form that will meet these conditions. In so doing, we will find the height of the left-hand cable support at point A. We also must find the forces in a typical roof cable and in each member of the supporting structures at the ends.

SETTING UP THE SOLUTION

When a cable is subjected to a load that is distributed uniformly over its horizontal projection, it takes the form of a parabola. In this building, because the roof deck follows the curve of the cable, the dead load is distributed uniformly over the length of the cable, not its horizontal projection. Therefore, under the dead load the cable will assume a shape that is nearer to a catenary than to a parabola. Given the relatively low sag ratio of this roof, however, the geometric differences between the two curves are not significant, as illustrated in Figure 11.2. Our preliminary design work will be much simpler but still sufficiently accurate if we base it on the less complex geometry of a parabola.

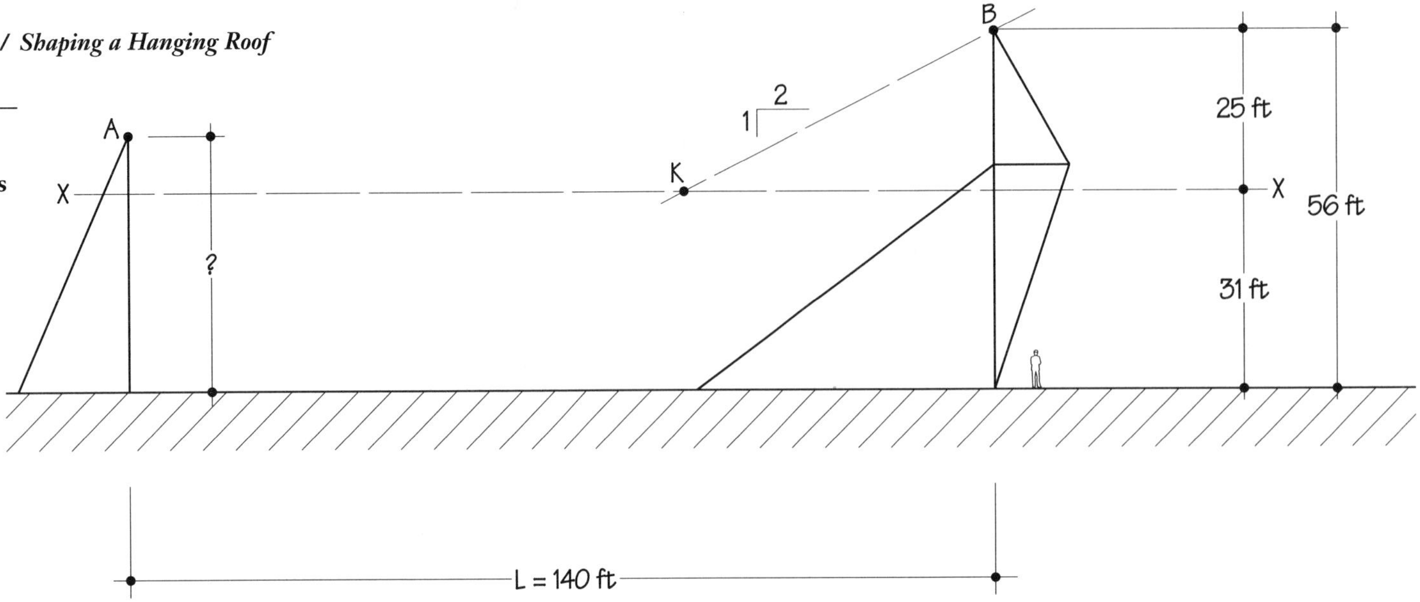

A
B
K
X
X
1
2
?
25 ft
31 ft
56 ft
L = 140 ft

Figure 11.1 ▶
Dimensional parameters of the auditorium roof.

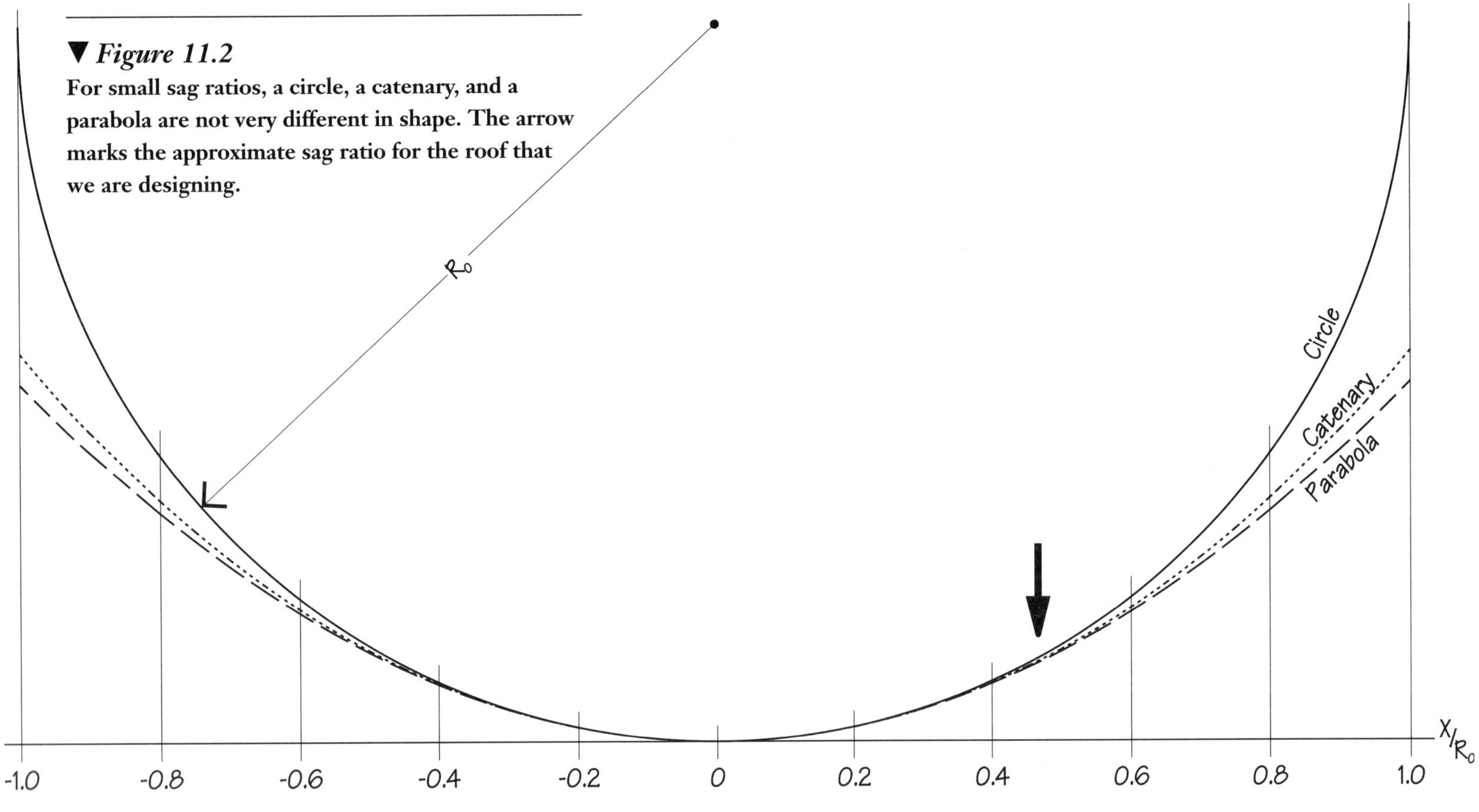

R0
Circle
Catenary
Parabola
X/R0
-1.0
-0.8
-0.6
-0.4
-0.2
0
0.2
0.4
0.6
0.8
1.0

▼ *Figure 11.2*
For small sag ratios, a circle, a catenary, and a parabola are not very different in shape. The arrow marks the approximate sag ratio for the roof that we are designing.

In Figure 11.3 we initiate our search for the form of the cable. Line *KB* is tangent to the curve of the cable at *B*. The low point of the cable, its vertex, will be tangent to line *XX* at some unknown point. Thus *KB* and *XX* are two tangents to the curve of the cable that intersect at *K*. As we learned in Chapter Nine, the intersection of two tangents to a parabola lies at the midpoint of the horizontal distance between their points of tangency. This means that the horizontal distance of 50 ft between *B* and *K* is the same as the horizontal distance from *K* to *O*, the vertex of the parabola. Therefore *O* lies at a distance of 100 ft from the right-hand support and 40 ft from the left-hand support.

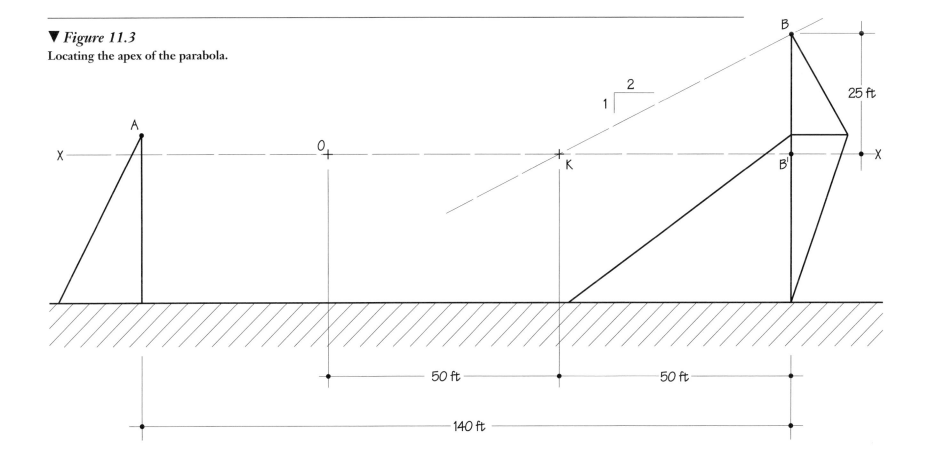

▼ *Figure 11.3*
Locating the apex of the parabola.

In Figure 11.4, we set about finding the height of the left-hand support. If we were to draw a free-body diagram of the cable, we would show three forces acting on it: the uniformly distributed load and the pulls at the two supports. The line of action of the pull at the right-hand support lies along line *BK*. The distributed load can be represented by a single resultant force that acts vertically through the middle of the span, 70 ft from each support. The line of action of this resultant force intersects *BK* at *T*. In order for the cable to be in equilibrium, the line of

▼ *Figure 11.4*

Locating the left-hand support.

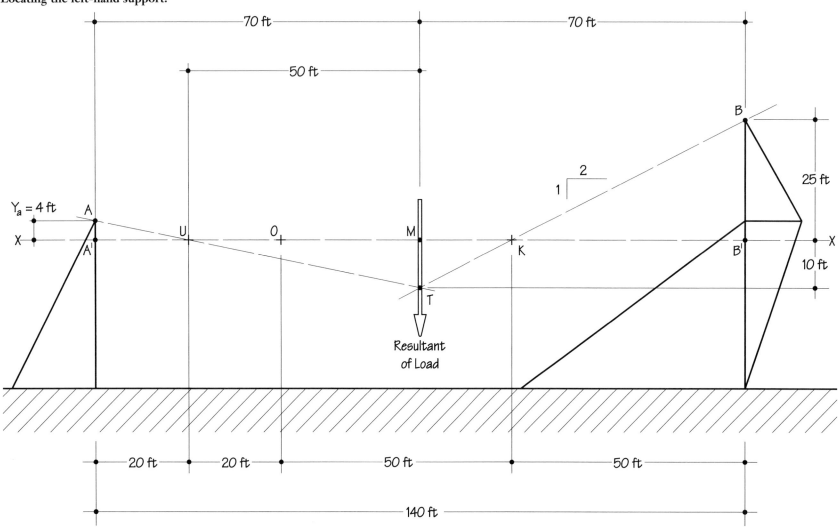

action of the third force, the pull at the left-hand support, must also pass through *T*.

This line of action, whose direction we do not know, must be tangent to the parabolic curve of the cable at the left-hand support. The intersection of this tangent with *XX*, the horizontal line that is tangent to the apex of the parabola, must lie at the midpoint of the horizontal distance between their points of tangency. We determined already that *O*, the point of tangency of the cable with *XX*, lies 40 ft from the left-hand support. Therefore *U*, the intersection of the two tangents, must be at the midpoint of this 40-ft distance, 20 ft from the left-hand support. A line through *T* and *U* is the line of action of the pull at the left-hand support, *A*.

To determine the height of *A* above *XX*, we evaluate two pairs of similar triangles. From the similarity of *BB'K* and *KMT* we determine that *MT* is 10 ft long. From the similarity of *MTU* and *UAA'*, we arrive at a dimension for *AA'* of 4 ft. Now we know the locations of three points on the cable, *A*, *M*, and *B*.

FINDING THE FORM AND FORCES GRAPHICALLY

Having found the locations of these three points, we are in a position to pursue a graphical solution without constructing a trial funicular polygon. First, we determine the applied load. The spacing of the parallel cables in the roof is given as 15 ft. The dead load is estimated at 80 psf and the live load at 40 psf for a total load of 120 psf. The relatively high dead load is based on an assumed thickness of a concrete roof deck that will help to isolate the auditorium from outside noises and to reflect sound within the enclosure.

MINIMIZING CUMULATIVE ERROR IN GRAPHICAL SOLUTIONS

Every graphical solution involves the laying out of a number of scaled intervals along a line. In Figure 11.5, we have to lay out the locations of the vectors on the loading diagram, (a), starting at a distance of 5 ft from the left support, then spaced at 13 intervals of 10 ft each, and finishing with a 5-ft dimension. Each time that we mark a measurement on a drawing, a small inaccuracy creeps in, often just a fraction of the thickness of a pencil line. If we were to lay out the vector locations on the loading diagram by measuring and marking 15 small intervals end-to-end, these tiny errors would accumulate to make it unlikely that the last interval would terminate very close to the end of the 140-ft overall dimension of the line. Similarly, in laying out the 14 equal intervals on the vertical load line of the force polygon, (c), end-to-end measurements of 0.18 in. are probably not going to result in a line that scales 2.52 in. long as it should, especially because each 0.18 in. measurement involves making an estimate of where 0.18 lies between the 0.1 and 0.2 marks on the scale. Such cumulative errors often result in funicular polygons or force polygons that do not close accurately, leading to poor results and increasing frustration.

Cumulative error can be avoided by making all measurements from one end of a line rather than end-to-end. To lay out the loading diagram in Figure 11.5(a), it is best to place the 0 mark of the scale ruler at the left end of the line and leave it there while marking off distances of 5 ft, 15 ft, 25 ft, 35 ft, and so on. On the load line in (c), the origin of the scale ruler should be left at *a* while distances of 0.18 in., 0.36 in., 0.54 in., 0.72 in., and so forth, are marked off. If the numbers are too difficult to add in your head as you go along, a pocket calculator can be used to find the cumulative dimension to each mark on the line. In this way, no mark on a line can be in error by more than whatever inaccuracy was made in its own measuring and marking, and errors cannot accumulate. With this procedure, given a sharp pencil and a steady hand, graphical constructions will close as if by magic more often than not. ∎

The heavy deck will also serve to reduce the distortions in the shape of the cable that may be brought about by nonuniform loadings such as wind pressures and drifting snow. The total load per foot of horizontal projection of the cable is equal to the load per square foot times the spacing of the cables:

$$w = (\text{load/ft}^2)(\text{cable spacing})$$

$$w = (120 \text{ lb/ft}^2)(15 \text{ ft}) = 1800 \text{ lb/ft}$$

In Figure 11.5(a), we divide the uniformly distributed load into 14 concentrated loads of 18 kips each (a kip is a kilopound, 1000 lbs). Each load is centered on a 10-ft segment of the span. On the form diagram, (b), we construct accurately the tangents to the cable at the supports, *AU* and *BK*. We draw *oa*, the ray on the force polygon (c) that represents the direction of the force in the cable at the left-hand support, parallel to *AU*. We draw ray *op* parallel to *KB*. The intersection of *oa* and *op* is the final pole, *o*. As a check of the accuracy of this pole location, we are also in a position to draw ray *oe*, which is a horizontal line that represents the direction of the cable as it passes through the apex, *O*. Ray *oe* intersects the other two rays accurately at *o*.

In Figure 11.6, we complete the graphical solution. The smooth parabolic curve of the cable is tangent to the midpoints of the straight

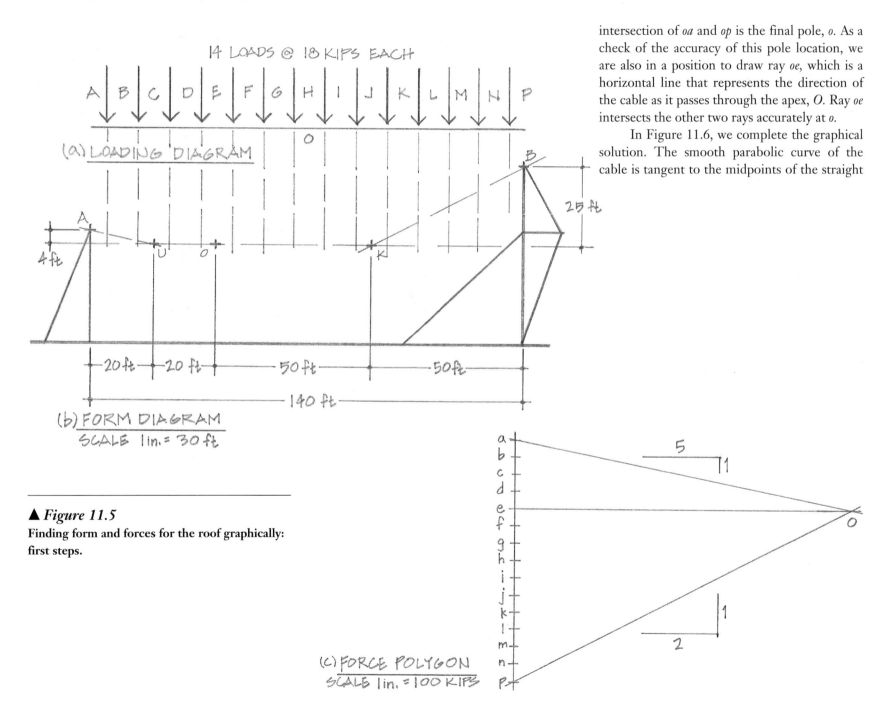

(a) LOADING DIAGRAM

14 LOADS @ 18 KIPS EACH

A B C D E F G H I J K L M N P

(b) FORM DIAGRAM
SCALE 1 in. = 30 ft

20 ft 20 ft 50 ft 50 ft

140 ft

4 ft 25 ft

(c) FORCE POLYGON
SCALE 1 in. = 100 KIPS

▲ *Figure 11.5*
Finding form and forces for the roof graphically: first steps.

14 LOADS @ 18 KIPS EACH

A B C D E F G H I J K L M N P

(a) LOADING DIAGRAM

O

B

A

25 ft

4 ft

U O K

20 ft 20 ft 50 ft 50 ft

140 ft

(b) FORM DIAGRAM
SCALE 1 in. = 30 ft

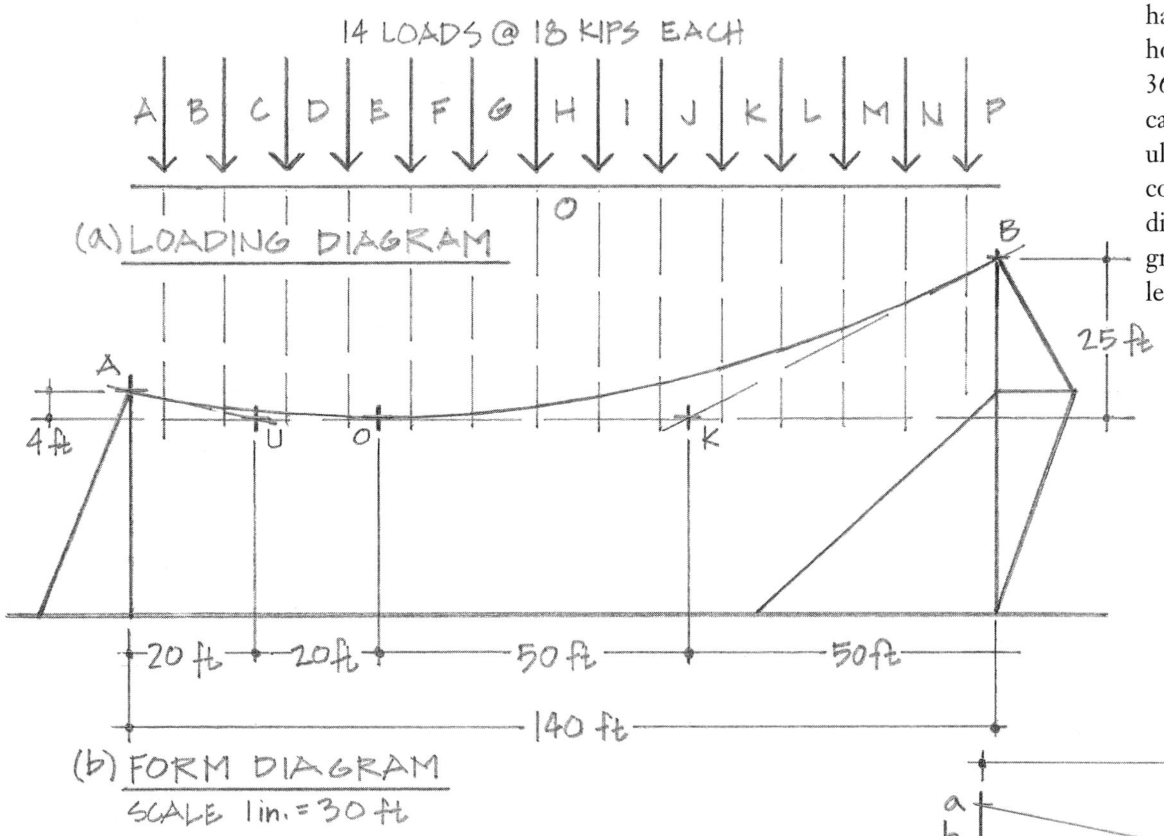

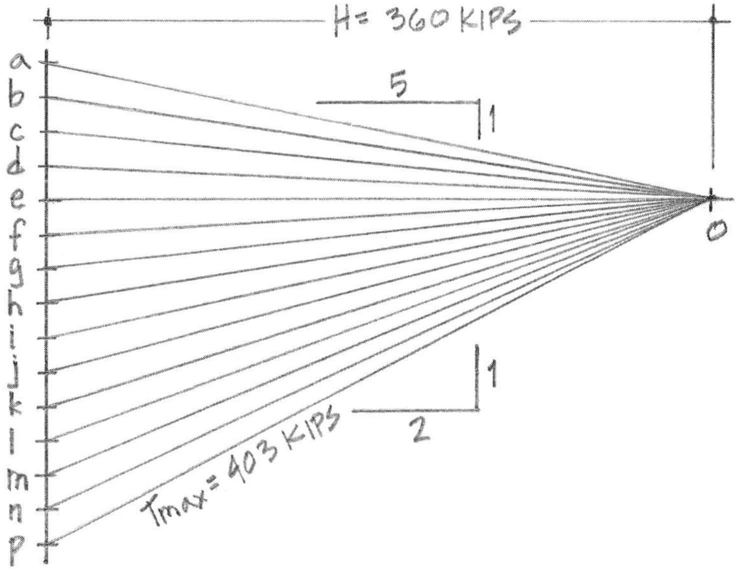

▲*Figure 11.6*
**Finding form and forces for the roof graphically:
completion.**

a b c d e f g h i j k l m n p

H = 360 KIPS

5
1

1

Tmax = 403 KIPS

2

O

line segments of the funicular polygon that we have constructed on the form diagram, (b). The horizontal component of cable force scales as 360 kips on the force polygon, and the maximum cable force as 403 kips. We could scale the funicular polygon on the form diagram to find the coordinates of points on the cable, but for these dimensions to be of useful precision, this diagram would have to be constructed at a scale at least three times as large as the one used here.

FINDING THE FORM OF THE CABLE NUMERICALLY

In the preceding chapter, we found numerical expressions for the form and forces of a symmetrical parabolic arch or cable by cutting successive sections through the free-body diagram of a uniformly loaded cable and evaluating the moments in each portion of the cable structure. It would be possible to apply these expressions to the analysis of the asymmetrical cable that we are now considering by assuming that the asymmetrical cable of 140-ft span is a portion of a symmetrical cable of longer span. For convenience, however, we will use a set of expressions for an asymmetrical parabolic structure that were derived by an analogous process. The variables are defined in Figure 11.7, and the expressions are summarized in eqs. [11-1] through [11-8], which appear in Figure 11.8. Figure 11.9 illustrates the three alternative sets of axes that may be used in defining the coordinates of points on the parabola in eqs. [11-2] through [11-4].

The numerical solution is swift and direct. We begin by substituting actual values into eq. [11-1] to find the horizontal component of the force in the cable:

$$H = w\left(\frac{L_b^2}{2b_b}\right) = (1.8 \text{ kips/ft})\left(\frac{(100 \text{ ft})^2}{2(25 \text{ ft})}\right) = 360 \text{ kips}$$

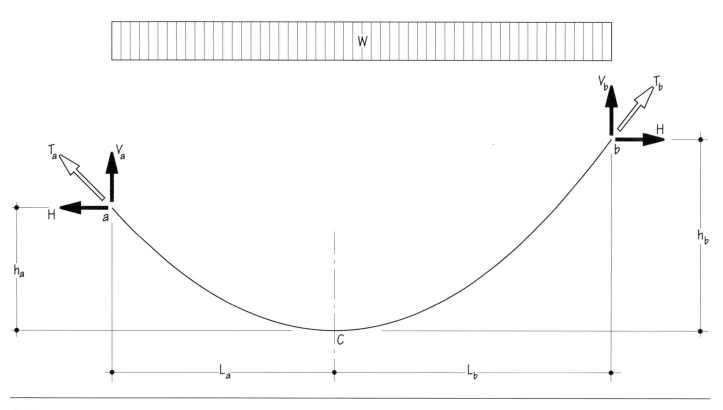

▲ *Figure 11.7*

Variables used in numerical expressions for designing asymmetrical parabolic arches and cables.

SUMMARY OF NUMERICAL EXPRESSIONS FOR DESIGNING ASYMMETRICAL PARABOLIC ARCHES AND CABLES

H, the horizontal component of force at any point in an asymmetrical parabolic arch or cable, is found using the following expression, in which w is the load per unit of span, L_a is the horizontal distance from the apex to the left support, L_b is the horizontal distance from the apex to the right support, b_a is the vertical distance from the apex to the left support, and b_b is the vertical distance from the apex to the right support (Fig. 11.7):

$$H = w\left(\frac{L_a^2}{2b_a}\right) = w\left(\frac{L_b^2}{2b_b}\right) \qquad [11\text{-}1]$$

Y_x, the sag or rise at any point on the axis of the arch or cable, may be found with respect to any of three coordinate systems, as illustrated in Fig. 11.9. With the origin at point *a*:

$$Y_x^a = \frac{b_a}{L_a^2}x(2L_a - x) \qquad [11\text{-}2]$$

With the origin at point *b*:

$$Y_x^b = \frac{b_b}{L_b^2}x(2L_b - x) \qquad [11\text{-}3]$$

With the origin at the apex, point *c*:

$$Y_x^c = \frac{b_a}{L_a^2}x^2 = \frac{b_b}{L_b^2}x^2 \qquad [11\text{-}4]$$

The slope of an asymmetrical parabola at its left support is:

$$\frac{\Delta y}{\Delta x} = \frac{2b_a}{L_a} \qquad [11\text{-}5]$$

The slope of an asymmetrical parabola at its right support is:

$$\frac{\Delta y}{\Delta x} = \frac{2b_b}{L_b} \qquad [11\text{-}6]$$

The tension or compression at the left support of an asymmetrical parabolic arch or cable is found by using the expression:

$$C_a = T_a = H\sqrt{4\left(\frac{b_a}{L_a}\right)^2 + 1} \qquad [11\text{-}7]$$

The tension or compression at the right support of an asymmetrical parabolic arch or cable is found by using the expression:

$$C_b = T_b = H\sqrt{4\left(\frac{b_b}{L_b}\right)^2 + 1} \qquad [11\text{-}8]$$

This agrees with the value that we determined graphically. The maximum tension in the cable occurs at the right-hand support. We find its magnitude by means of eq. [11-8]:

$$T_{\max} = H\sqrt{4\left(\frac{b_b}{L_b}\right)^2 + 1}$$

$$= (360\text{ kips})\sqrt{4\left(\frac{25\text{ ft}}{100\text{ ft}}\right)^2 + 1} = 402.5\text{ kips}$$

This is very close to the approximate value that we found graphically.

We can locate points on the parabola with respect to axes of reference that originate at the apex or either support; we choose axes whose origin lies at the right-hand support. Using eq. [11-3], we find the ordinate of point *A*:

$$y_x^b = \frac{b_b}{L_b^2}x(2L_b - x)$$

$$= \frac{25\text{ ft}}{(100\text{ ft})^2} \times (140\text{ ft})(200\text{ ft} - 140\text{ ft}) = 21\text{ ft}$$

This tells us that *A* is 21 ft below *B*, which places it 4 ft above *XX*, thus confirming our original determination. In similar fashion, we find the ordinates of points at 10-ft intervals for the entire span; these are diagrammed in Figure 11.10.

◀ *Figure 11.8*

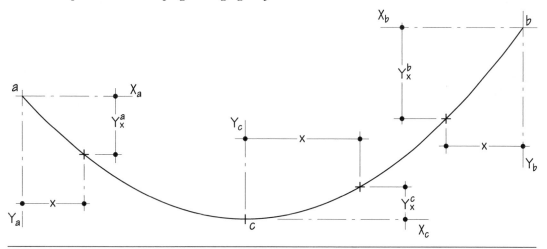

FINDING THE FORCES IN THE SUPPORTING STRUCTURES

The forces that the cable exerts on its supports are most easily dealt with in terms of their horizontal and vertical components. The horizontal component at each support, *H*, is 360 kips, or

▲ *Figure 11.9*

Three alternative sets of reference axes for calculating the locations of points on a parabola.

▼ *Figure 11.10*

Calculated vertical dimensions in feet from a reference axis through point B to points on the cable at 10-ft horizontal intervals.

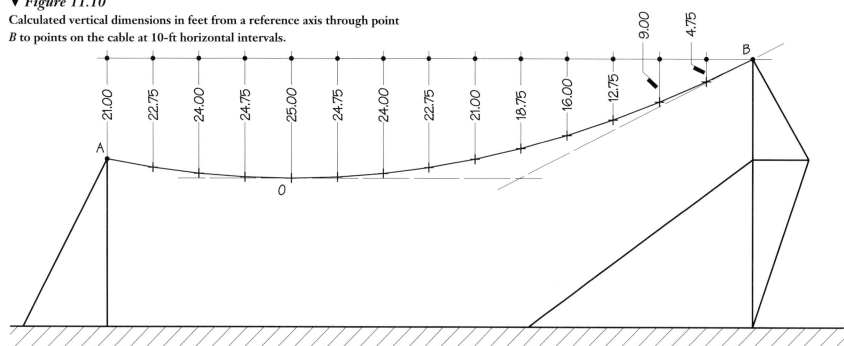

360,000 lb, as we found earlier. The vertical component of the reaction at either support of an asymmetrical parabolic cable is equal to the load distributed along the portion of the cable between the apex and that support. Thus V_B, the vertical component of the right-hand reaction, is

1.8 kips/ft times 100 ft, which is 180 kips. Similarly, V_A is 1.8 kips/ft times 40 ft, or 72 kips. We check these calculated values by comparing them to the total load on the roof, 252 kips:

$$V_A + V_B = 72 \text{ kips} + 180 \text{ kips} = 252 \text{ kips} \quad \text{O.K.}$$

Now we are in a position to find the axial forces in each member of the two supporting structures. Because both structures can be treated as trusses, we apply interval notation and solve graphically for the forces in their members. In Figure 11.11, we draw to scale a form diagram of

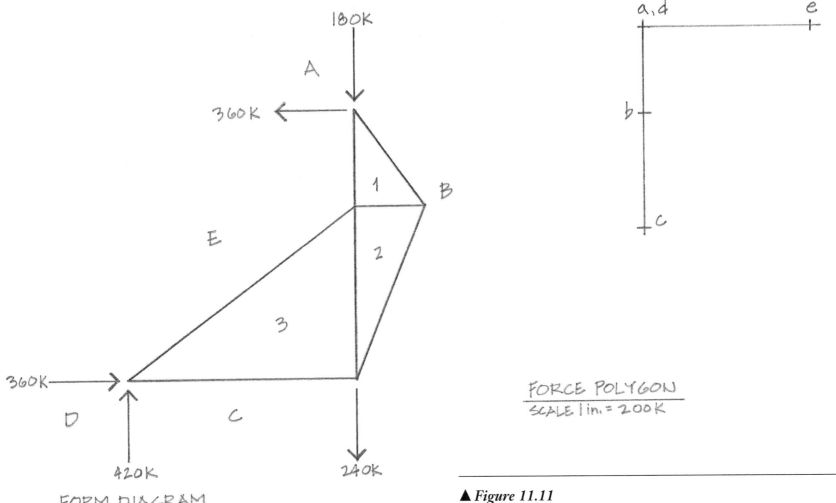

FORM DIAGRAM
SCALE 1 in. = 20 ft

FORCE POLYGON
SCALE 1 in. = 200 K

▲ *Figure 11.11*
Beginning the graphical solution for the member forces in the right-hand supporting structure.

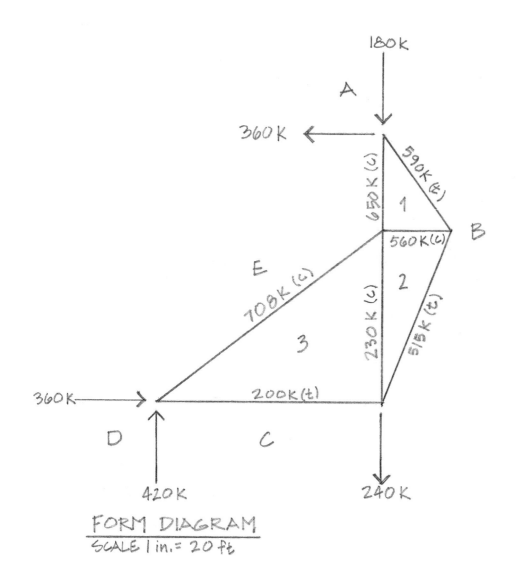

180K

A

360K ←

590K (t)

650 K (c)

1

560K (c) B

E

708K (c)

2

230 K (c)

515 K (t)

3

360K →

200K (t)

D

C

420K

240K

FORM DIAGRAM
SCALE 1 in. = 20 ft

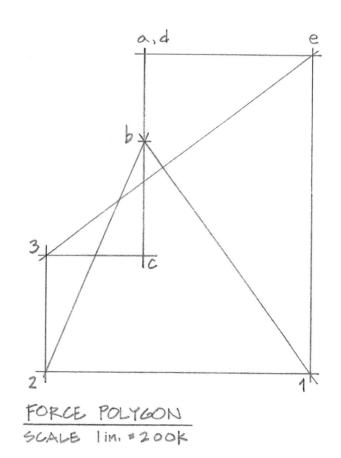

a, d   e

b

3   c

2   1

FORCE POLYGON
SCALE 1 in. = 200K

◀ *Figure 11.12*
Completing the graphical solution for the member forces in the right-hand supporting structure.

the right-hand support structure, to which we add vectors for the components of the cable force. The inclined beams that support the sloping seating in the auditorium, and the level floor slab beneath them, are considered to take part in the truss action. We assign a horizontal reaction of 360 kips from the floor slab at the lower left corner of the structure to achieve equilibrium in the horizontal direction. To find the two vertical reactions, *BC* and *CD*, we sum moments numerically. Because there are both horizontal and vertical external forces, the load line is L-shaped. The load line closes accurately, indicating that the external forces are in equilibrium. We complete the solution in Figure 11.12.

The solution for the left-hand support is much simpler (Fig. 11.13). The forces in the vertical and inclined members of the left-hand support are very large, a situation we could improve by increasing the angle between the column, *C1*, and the stay cable, *1A*.

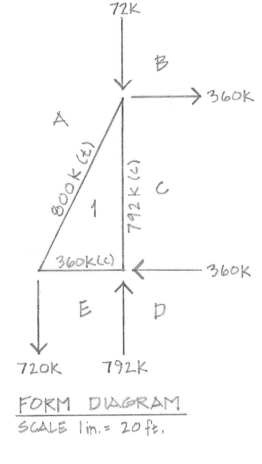

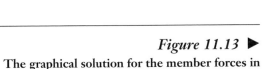

Figure 11.13 ▶
The graphical solution for the member forces in the left-hand supporting structure.

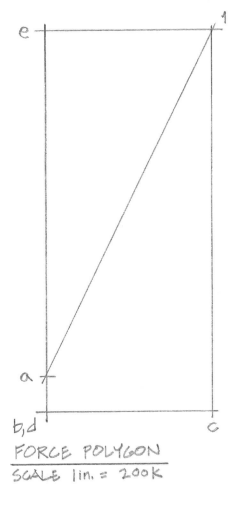

In looking at the structure as a whole in Figure 11.14, we see that a compressive force of 360 kips for each cable must be transmitted through the floor between the two support structures and onto the cable anchorage at *A″*. It may be necessary to add a stiffening rib on the underside of the floor slab in the plane of each cable to keep the slab from buckling under these loads. There is also a tensile force of 200 kips per cable in the level floor beneath the sloping seats, which will require the addition of several large reinforcing bars between points *B′* and *B″*. The effect of the action of these forces in the floor is that the structure transmits only vertical loads to its foundations. This avoids the difficulty and expense of constructing foundations to resist inclined loads.

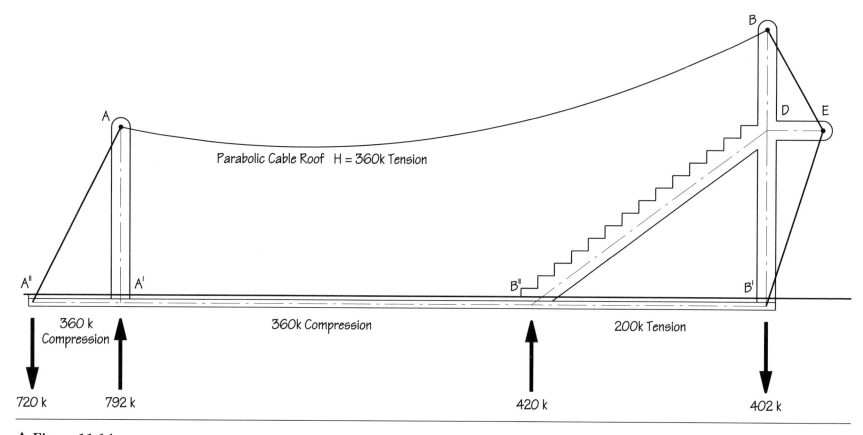

▲ *Figure 11.14*

The axial forces in the floors and foundations of the auditorium structure.

Stiffening the Cable Against Nonuniform Loads

Imagine that you are crossing a river on a primitive, loosely slung suspension bridge (Fig. 11.15). The weight of your body is large in relation to the weight of the ropes. As you move forward with each step, the shape of the bridge changes radically. In a wilderness footbridge, this change of shape is of little consequence because it can be tolerated by able-bodied hikers and will not damage the rope structure of the bridge. However, the analogous changes of shape that may take place in the hanging auditorium roof as it is subjected to varying winds and drifting snow could be disastrous, cracking the roof deck and subjecting the walls to forces they are not designed to withstand.

If the wilderness bridge includes a heavy deck of large crosswise timbers laid loosely on the suspension ropes, your weight would be small in relation to the weight of the deck, making the deck weight the dominant force in shaping the ropes. The changes of shape in the ropes that would take place as you move across the bridge would be much less than for the same

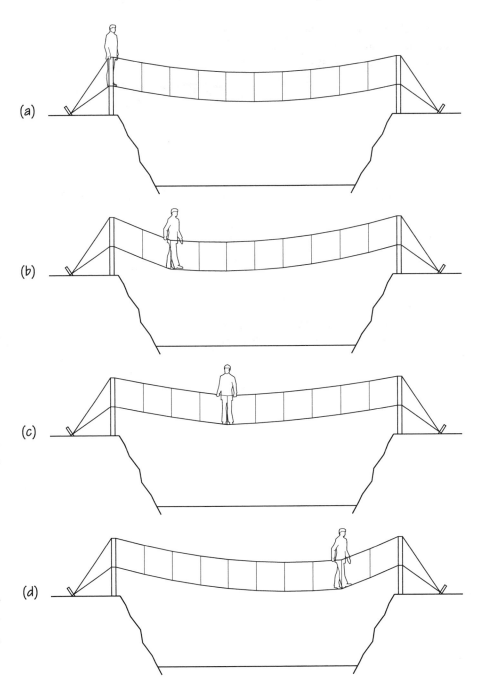

(a)

(b)

(c)

(d)

Figure 11.15 ▶
Crossing a river on a primitive rope bridge.

bridge without the heavy deck (Fig. 11.16). As mentioned at the outset of this chapter, one reason for the heavy concrete roof deck on our auditorium is to help minimize the fluctuations in the shapes of the cables under nonuniform snow and wind loads. If the deck also has a certain amount of stiffness, as this roof deck will have, its weight and stiffness can work together to further restrict distortions of the cables. However, the deck, whose depth is less than one two-hundredth of the span, is not able to contribute much to the overall stiffness of the roof. Thus, we must find a further means of stiffening the cables in this roof.

Chapter Thirteen will present a comprehensive outline of alternative ways of stiffening funicular structures against loadings for which their shapes are not funicular. For the moment, for the auditorium roof we are designing, let us consider just two alternatives, horizontal stay cables and surface action, either of which could solve the problem by itself.

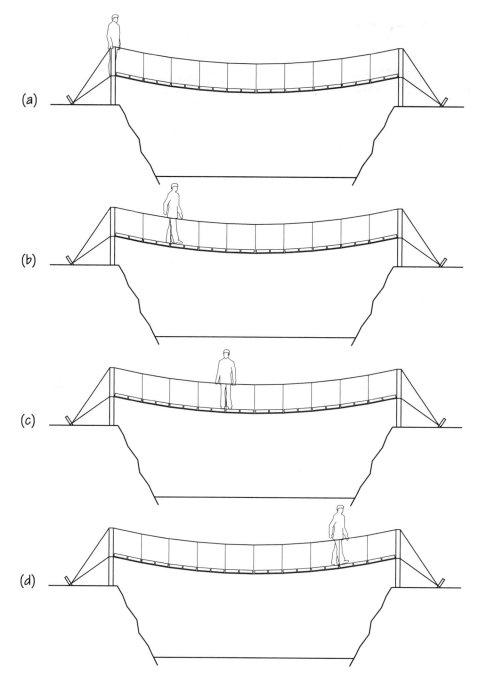

Figure 11.16 ▶
**The effect of adding a heavy deck
to the rope bridge.**

Horizontal Stay Cables

Figure 11.17(a) shows how an asymmetrical load, such as a deep drift of snow or a strong gust of wind, distorts a parabolic cable. Where the load is heavier, the cable sinks, and where the load is lighter, the cable rises. These localized, vertical displacements of some parts of the cable are invariably accompanied by lateral displacements of the cable that are especially large at midspan. If we attach horizontal stay cables to the lower portion of the main suspension cable, such lateral displacements can be minimized, which also has the effect of minimizing changes in the shape of the main cable (Fig. 11.17[b]). If we install horizontal stay cables in our auditorium, we will *pretension* them (stretch them with a permanent tensile force) to prevent them from becoming slack. We must decide whether such

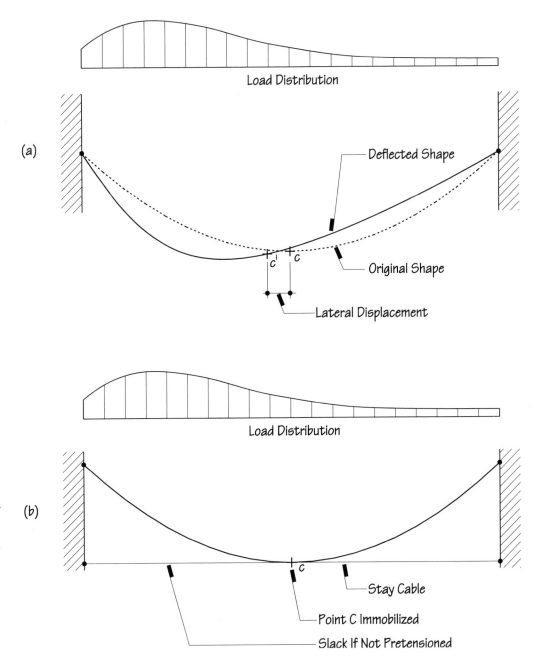

(a)

(b)

Figure 11.17 ▶
The effect of lateral stays on the roof cable.

cables would get in the way of sight lines, and whether they could become an interesting, enriching aspect of the architecture (Fig. 11.18).

SURFACE ACTION

Although the thickness of the curved concrete deck of a hanging roof is too small to be effective in preventing displacements of the cables in a direction perpendicular to its surface, the same thin slab, if it acts as a unit, is extremely rigid in the direction tangential to its surface and is able to act in that direction as a very stiff beam. Thus, if we secure the curved edges of the solid deck of the auditorium to rigidly braced side walls at midspan (Fig. 11.19[a]), the great surface rigidity of the deck will not allow lateral movements of the cables that are embedded in it (Fig. 11.19[b]).

This will restrict significantly any distortions of their shape. Though the more heavily loaded parts of the cables will be tensioned more than their less loaded parts, the shape of the cables will be unaffected because the portion of the roof slab between the loads of different magnitudes will act as a rigid surface beam that is restrained from moving by the rigid side walls. To act in this way, of course, the roof deck must be made as a single, continuous slab, not as separate panels or strips. The side walls may be braced as shown, or they may be rigid planes of concrete or masonry that act as *diaphragms*, which is much like the surface action of the roof slab.

The practical upper span limit for roofs with parallel cables is 200 to 250 ft (60 to 80 m). This limit results from the difficulty of assuring the immobility of a roof whose cables resist the

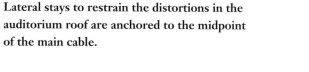

▼ *Figure 11.18*

Lateral stays to restrain the distortions in the auditorium roof are anchored to the midpoint of the main cable.

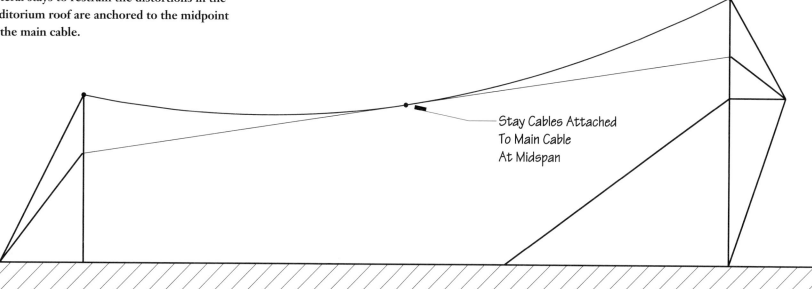

Stay Cables Attached
To Main Cable
At Midspan

actions of loads individually. In another volume, we will consider surface structures, both tensile and compressive, in which adjacent strips of the roof deck interact transversally. Surface structures experience less distortion under nonuniform loadings than the structure we have been designing, and therefore may cover larger spans.

SELECTING THE CABLE

The term *cable* is generic, referring to any flexible tension member that is made up of steel wires. The cables for very large suspension bridges are spun in place. The wires are laid parallel to the axis of the cable and bound into a single member by a tight spiral wrapping of wire. In smaller suspension structures, two other types of cables are used. A *strand* is a cable made up of

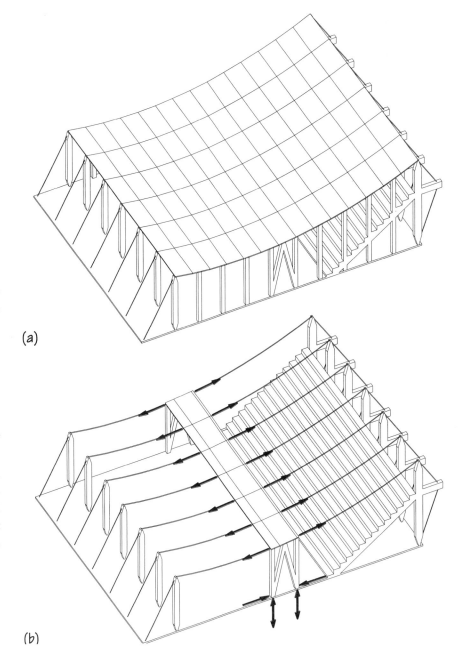

(a)

(b)

Figure 11.19 ▶
The effect on the roof cables of side wall bracing and surface action in the roof deck. The strip of roof deck between the braced wall panels acts as a horizontal beam to resist lateral displacements in the main cables.

wires formed helically in concentric layers around a center wire (Fig. 11.20[a]). A *wire rope* is composed of a number of strands laid helically around a core (Fig. 11.20[b]). A strand has a higher tensile strength than a rope of the same diameter and is therefore more suitable for the roof we are designing. A wire rope is more flexible than a strand, which is an advantage in applications such as hoisting devices and elevators.

The extremely high strength of cables in general is attributable to the method of manufacture of the wires: steel rods are *drawn* (pulled) at room temperature through a succession of dies, each of which has a circular, hardened steel orifice that is slightly smaller than that of the previous die. The drawing process reduces the rod diameter by 65 to 75%, producing a long wire whose internal crystalline structure is

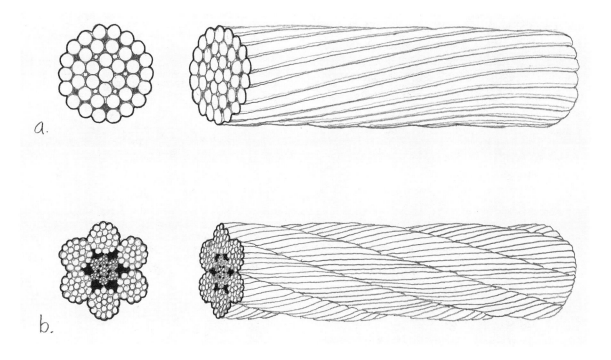

a.

b.

realigned and strengthened severalfold by the *cold working* action of the dies.

Wires for cables are coated with zinc to make them resistant to corrosion. In a highly corrosive environment, a Class C zinc coating, the heaviest, should be used for maximum protection, but the heavy coating means that fewer wires will fit into a cable of a given diameter. Thus, a cable with the lightest zinc coating, Class A, is the strongest for its size. After being coated, the wires are twisted together into cables by heavy machines that finish their work by drawing the cable through a circular die of the final cable diameter that compacts the wires tightly together.

Although these high-strength steel cables continue to be the obvious choice for most hanging and cable-stayed structures, cables of new materials have been incorporated into a few experimental bridges and buildings. Cables spun from *glass fibers* are economical and are stronger than steel, but they stretch considerably more than steel cables under load. *Carbon fiber* cables are both strong and rigid, but are relatively expensive at present. Strong, tough fibers made of *aramid*, a polymer, are widely used in tire cords and promise to have structural applications as well.

As we determined earlier, the maximum anticipated force in a roof cable of our auditorium is 402.5 kips. The safety factors that are recommended by the steel cable industry are complex; if we assume for preliminary design a factor of safety of 2.2 for the live and dead loads, we can find the required breaking strength of the cable, T_{brk}, in tons, as follows:

$$T_{brk} = \frac{(402,500 \text{ lb})(2.2)}{2000 \text{ lb/ton}} = 443 \text{ tons}$$

We select from the table in Figure 11.21 a strand with a nominal diameter of 2¾ in., with a breaking strength of 452 tons, the smallest that will suffice. This cable weighs 15.88 lb/ft, which is less than 1% of the total load that we have estimated. The weight of the cable itself is insignificant in this structure.

DETAILING THE CABLES

There are two types of end fittings used on cables, *socketed* and *swaged*. Swaging is suitable only for strands up to 1⅜ in. diameter and ropes up to 2 in. In swaging, the end of the cable is inserted into a hole in the steel fitting. The fitting is then placed in shaped die block in a hydraulic press and squeezed so tightly that the steel of the fitting flows around the steel wires and fastens to them by friction.

The first step in creating a socketed cable connection is to *broom out* the individual wires at the end of the cable (Fig. 11.22). After the broomed wires have been inserted into the tapered basket of the fitting, molten zinc is poured around them to make the connection (Fig. 11.23). Both swaged and socketed fittings develop the full strength of the cable.

Many types of cast steel end fittings are available for every size of cable. To connect cables to the foundations, we will use *closed bridge sockets* (Fig. 11.24). These incorporate a *U-bolt* that forms an adjustable connection to an anchor plate that is embedded in the concrete foundation.

◄ *Figure 11.20*
(a) Wire strand. (b) Wire rope.

Figure 11.21 ▶
(*Source:* ASTM Designation A586-92.)

Properties of Zinc-Coated Bridge Steel Structural Strand (Standards Established by the Wire Rope Technical Board)

Nominal Diameter in Inches	Class "A" Coating Throughout	Class "A" Coating Inner Wires Class "B" Coating Outer Wires	Class "A" Coating Inner Wires Class "C" Coating Outer Wires	Approx. Metallic Area in Sq. In.	Approx. Weight Per Ft. in Lbs.
½	15.0	14.5	14.2	0.150	0.52
9/16	19.0	18.4	18.0	.190	.66
5/8	24.0	23.3	22.8	.234	.82
11/16	29.0	28.1	27.5	.284	.99
3/4	34.0	33.0	32.3	.338	1.18
13/16	40.0	38.8	38.0	.396	1.39
7/8	46.0	44.6	43.7	.459	1.61
15/16	54.0	52.4	51.3	.527	1.85
1	61.0	59.2	57.9	.600	2.10
1 1/16	69.0	66.9	65.5	.677	2.37
1 1/8	78.0	75.7	74.1	.759	2.66
1 3/16	86.0	83.4	81.7	.846	2.96
1 1/4	96.0	94.1	92.2	.938	3.28
1 5/16	106.0	104.0	102.0	1.03	3.62
1 3/8	116.0	114.0	111.0	1.13	3.97
1 7/16	126.0	123.0	121.0	1.24	4.34
1 1/2	138.0	135.0	132.0	1.35	4.73
1 9/16	150.0	147.0	144.0	1.47	5.13
1 5/8	162.0	159.0	155.0	1.59	5.55
1 11/16	176.0	172.0	169.0	1.71	5.98
1 3/4	188.0	184.0	180.0	1.84	6.43
1 13/16	202.0	198.0	194.0	1.97	6.90
1 7/8	216.0	212.0	207.0	2.11	7.39
1 15/16	230.0	226.0	221.0	2.25	7.89

The top of the table header reads: **Approximate Minimum Breaking Strength in Tons of 2000 lbs.**

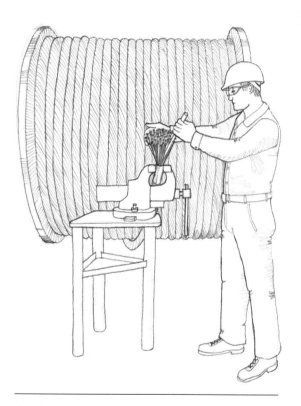

▲ *Figure 11.22*

Brooming out a cable, preparatory to making a socketed cable connection.

Nominal Diameter in Inches	Approximate Minimum Breaking Strength in Tons of 2000 lbs.			Approx. Metallic Area in Sq. In.	Approx. Weight Per Ft. in Lbs.
	Class "A" Coating Throughout	Class "A" Coating Inner Wires Class "B" Coating Outer Wires	Class "A" Coating Inner Wires Class "C" Coating Outer Wires		
2	245.0	241.0	238.0	2.40	8.40
2¹⁄₁₆	261.0	257.0	253.0	2.55	8.94
2⅛	277.0	273.0	269.0	2.71	9.49
2³⁄₁₆	293.0	289.0	284.0	2.87	10.05
2¼	310.0	305.0	301.0	3.04	10.64
2⁵⁄₁₆	327.0	322.0	317.0	3.21	11.24
2⅜	344.0	339.0	334.0	3.38	11.85
2⁷⁄₁₆	360.0	355.0	349.0	3.57	12.48
2½	376.0	370.0	365.0	3.75	13.13
2⁹⁄₁₆	392.0	386.0	380.0	3.94	13.80
2⅝	417.0	411.0	404.0	4.13	14.47
2¹¹⁄₁₆	432.0	425.0	419.0	4.33	15.16
2¾	452.0	445.0	438.0	4.54	15.88
2⅞	494.0	486.0	479.0	4.96	17.36
3	538.0	530.0	522.0	5.40	18.90
3⅛	584.0	575.0	566.0	5.86	20.51
3¼	625.0	616.0	606.0	6.34	22.18
3⅜	673.0	663.0	653.0	6.83	23.92
3½	724.0	714.0	702.0	7.35	25.73
3⅝	768.0	757.0	745.0	7.88	27.60
3¾	822.0	810.0	797.0	8.44	29.53
3⅞	878.0	865.0	852.0	9.01	31.53
4	925.0	911.0	897.0	9.60	33.60

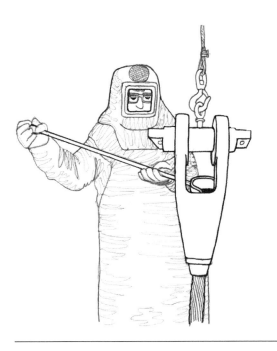

▲ *Figure 11.23*
Pouring molten zinc to complete a socketed cable connection.

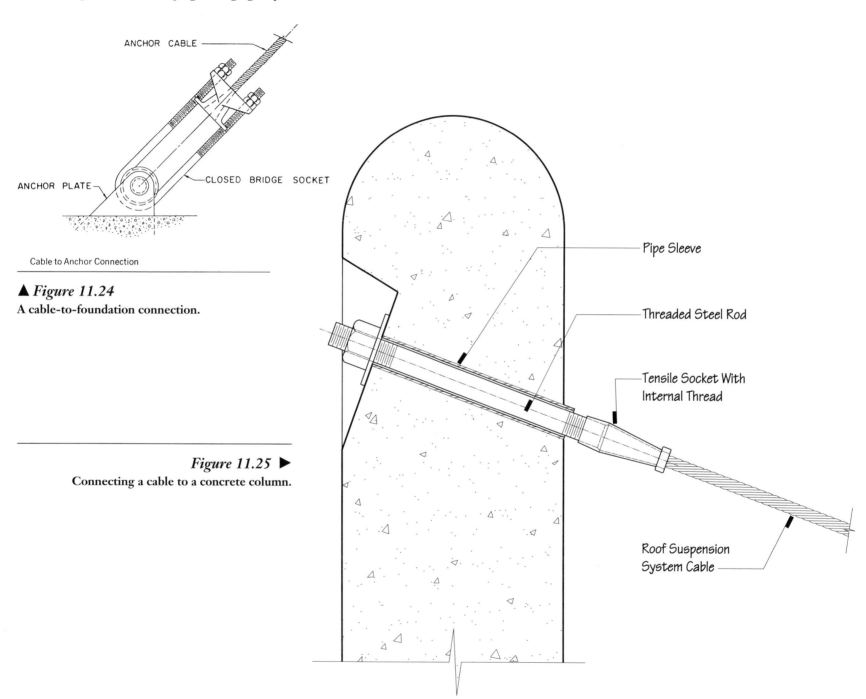

Cable to Anchor Connection

▲ *Figure 11.24*
A cable-to-foundation connection.

Figure 11.25 ▶
Connecting a cable to a concrete column.

A typical cable attachment to a concrete column is made with a *tensile socket* that contains internal screw threads that allow the socket to be screwed to a threaded steel rod (Fig. 11.25). The rod passes through a pipe sleeve that is cast into the concrete to a nut and washer that transfer the cable force to the concrete and permit some adjustment of cable length.

If we construct the end supports of structural steel instead of concrete, we will use *open strand sockets* like the one into which zinc is being poured in Figure 11.23. Study of a manufacturer's catalog (Fig. 11.26) reveals that an open strand socket for a 2¾-in. strand uses a pin of 5½ in.-diameter to transfer the load from the cable

▼ *Figure 11.26*
Typical dimensions of open strand sockets.

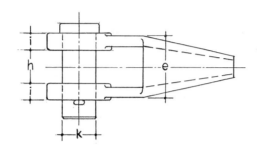
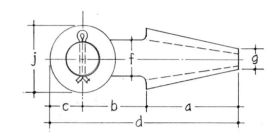

TYPICAL DIMENSIONS OF OPEN STRAND SOCKETS, IN.

Strand Size	a	b	c	d	e	f	g	h	i	j	k	Weight, lb
½	3	2.5	1.25	6.75	2.25	1.25	1.125	1.25	0.563	2.25	1.188	4
⁹⁄₁₆ & ⅝	5.5	3	1.438	9.938	2.625	1.5	1.25	1.5	0.675	2.625	1.375	8
¹¹⁄₁₆ & ¾	6	3.5	1.75	11.25	3.125	1.75	1.5	1.75	0.75	3.125	1.625	13
¹³⁄₁₆ & ⅞	6	4	2.063	12.063	3.625	2	1.75	2	0.875	3.75	2	19
¹⁵⁄₁₆ & 1⅛	6	5	2.688	13.688	4.625	2.75	2.25	2.5	1.125	4.75	2.5	35
1³⁄₁₆ & 1¼	6	6	3.125	15.125	5.25	3	2.75	3	1.188	5.375	2.75	47
1⁵⁄₁₆ & 1⅜	6.5	6.5	3.25	16.25	5.5	3.25	3	3	1.313	5.75	3	55
1⁷⁄₁₆ & 1⅝	7.5	7	3.75	18.25	6.375	3.875	3.125	3.5	1.563	6.5	3.5	85
1¹¹⁄₁₆ & 1¾	8.5	9	4	21.5	7.375	4.25	3.75	4	1.813	7	3.75	125
1¹³⁄₁₆ & 1⅞	9	10	4.5	23.5	8.25	4.375	4	4.5	2.125	7.75	4.25	165
1¹⁵⁄₁₆ & 2⅛	9.75	10.75	5	25.5	9.25	4.625	4.5	5	2.375	8.5	4.75	252
2³⁄₁₆ & 2⁷⁄₁₆	11	11	5.25	27.25	10.75	4.875	4.875	5.25	2.875	9	5	315
2½ & 2⅝	12	11.25	5.75	29	11.5	5.25	5.25	5.75	3	9.5	5.25	380
2¾ & 2⅞	13	11.75	6.125	30.875	12.25	5.75	5.75	6.25	3.125	10	5.5	434
3 & 3⅛	14	12.5	6.75	33.25	13	6.25	6.5	6.75	3.25	10.75	6	563
3¼ & 3⅝	15	13.5	7.75	36.25	14.25	7	7.25	7.5	3.5	12.5	7	783
3¾ & 4	16	15	7.75	38.75	15.25	8.5	7.75	8	3.75	14	7.25	1018

to a steel plate 6 in. thick. The socket is 30⅞ in. long and weighs 434 lb. Figure 11.27 includes two conceptual sketches of a way in which open strand sockets may be used at the tops of the supporting structures to transfer the cable loads into a steel H-column. The lines of action of the two cables and the column all meet at a single *working point*, *p*, to avoid the creation of moments at the connection. The 6-in.-thick vertical plate to which the sockets are pinned is supported against overturning and buckling by lateral stiffener plates. A heavy horizontal plate distributes the force from the vertical plates into the column. The entire assembly could be welded together from heavy steel plates, or the portion above the column could be cast as a single piece of steel.

Figure 11.28 is a preliminary sketch of an alternative design for the top of the column in which a rigid wide-flange steel member is substituted for the cable backstay. Because it avoids the expensive end fittings of the cable, this member may prove to be more economical. It would also be more resistant to the effects of vandalism and being bumped by vehicles.

With its 140-ft span, this auditorium roof is at the very lower limit of economical span length for a cable structure. The reason is that the largest proportion of cost for a cable roof is attributable to the fittings, connections, and anchorages, rather than the cables themselves. It is also virtually as easy to string a 500-ft cable as a 50-ft one. A roof with five times the span may require no more fittings and would be as easy to erect. The longer the span is, the less the cost of the fittings and erection per unit area. Of course, as we noted earlier in this chapter, if it were formed of parallel cables, the longer span would require greater attention to restraint against changes in the shapes of the cables.

DETAILING THE ROOF DECK

Figure 11.29 is an early conceptual drawing for the details of the concrete roof deck. Concrete panels 4 ft wide and 3 in. thick will be reinforced, cast, and cured in a factory. They will be made in two lengths, 16 ft and 14 ft. To stiffen the roof and to bond the panels to the concrete topping that will be poured over them after they are in place, machine-made welded wire truss assem-

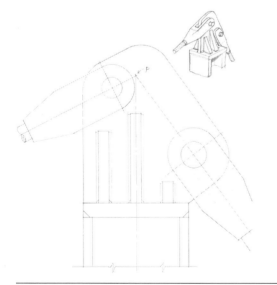

▲ *Figure 11.27*
A preliminary detail sketch for connecting a main cable and a stay cable to the top of a steel column.

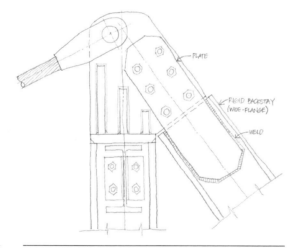

▲ *Figure 11.28*
An alternative column detail that uses a rigid backstay.

Figure 11.29 ▶
Preliminary details for the roof deck.

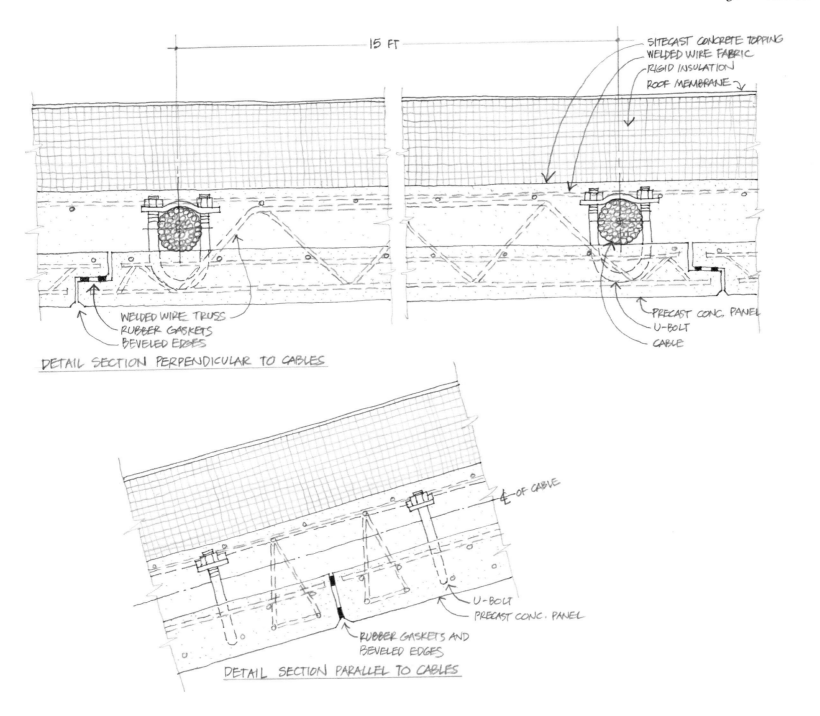

15 FT

SITECAST CONCRETE TOPPING
WELDED WIRE FABRIC
RIGID INSULATION
ROOF MEMBRANE

WELDED WIRE TRUSS
RUBBER GASKETS
BEVELED EDGES

PRECAST CONC. PANEL
U-BOLT
CABLE

DETAIL SECTION PERPENDICULAR TO CABLES

℄ OF CABLE

U-BOLT
PRECAST CONC. PANEL

RUBBER GASKETS AND
BEVELED EDGES

DETAIL SECTION PARALLEL TO CABLES

blies are embedded in the panels at intervals, with their top halves projecting above the surface. These small trusses are triangular in section for stability against buckling. Four steel U-bolts are embedded in the top of each longer panel to attach it to the two cables that support it. Each end of the longer panel projects a few inches beyond the cable and has a *dapped* edge profile that allows it to support a shorter panel that is installed in the space between the adjacent cable pair. This avoids the awkward circumstance of having the panel joint located at the centerline of the cable. Rubber gaskets cushion the bearing of one panel on another and prevent the wet concrete of the topping from leaking through. The gaskets also keep the panel edges from grinding against each other as cable loadings shift during construction. Beveled edges on the exposed lower surface give a neat, finished appearance to the panel joints. A quick calculation shows that each panel will weigh about 2500 lb, an easy lift for a small construction crane.

After the panels have been bolted to the cables, a grid of heavy-gauge reinforcing wires, called a *welded wire fabric*, will be installed across the cables and wire trusses. Then the concrete topping will be poured, embedding the cables. When the concrete has hardened, the topping, welded wire fabric, panels, and welded wire trusses unite to form a single-piece deck structure of considerable strength.

Careful consideration will have to be given to the exact sequence in which the panels will be hung and the topping poured. Thinking back to the primitive rope footbridge in Figure 11.15, we realize that we must add weight to the cables symmetrically and evenly if they are not to change shape radically during construction. One

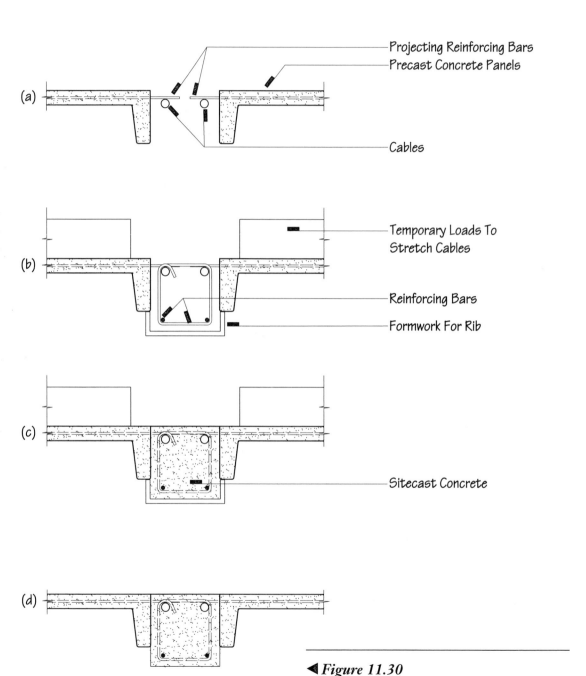

◀ Figure 11.30
How the deck was attached to the Dulles roof.

possible erection sequence would be to place alternate cross-rows of panels first, leaving empty panel-width spaces between. This would add ballast to the cables, which would restrict their motion as the rest of the panels are inserted. After all the panels have been installed, the topping could also be poured in alternating strips. Temporary or permanent horizontal stay cables could also assist in stabilizing the cables during construction.

It is instructive to study how this problem was solved in a somewhat similar building, the passenger terminal at Dulles International Airport near Washington, D.C., which was completed in 1962 (see Fig. 13.21). In this roof, precast concrete panels were placed between pairs of hanging cables to create the deck. Formwork for concrete stiffening ribs was placed around each pair of cables, supported by the panels on either side (Fig. 11.30). Before the concrete was poured, temporary loads were placed on top of the panels, stretching the cables slightly. After the concrete was poured and had hardened, the temporary loads were removed. This allowed the cables to contract slightly, compressing the concrete uniformly. This prestressing of the deck ribs enhanced the stiffness of the roof. Together with the stabilizing effect of the relatively large self-weight of the roof, it was sufficient to prevent excessive distortions of roof shape under the destabilizing effects of nonuniform snow and wind loads.

After the concrete topping of our auditorium roof has cured, a thick layer of plastic foam thermal insulation will be adhered or mechanically fastened to the roof surface, and a synthetic rubber waterproofing membrane will be installed over it to keep the building dry.

DETAILING THE TOPS OF THE SUPPORTING STRUCTURES

The tops of the supporting structures present special detailing problems, because the cables must be free to rotate slightly at the point of attachment without cracking the concrete or tearing the waterproofing membrane immediately above. Figure 11.31 shows how this movement might be accommodated at the top of each column. Two movement joints are provided in the roof deck, insulation, and membrane, one above the end of each of the cables. Steel plates welded to the top of the vertical connector plate support a small, insulated, structurally independent strip of roof. The rubber membrane on this roof overlaps the movement joints and is cemented to the membranes on the cable-supported spans, creating two flexible joints. A similar roof profile will be continued on top of a steel beam that spans between the columns.

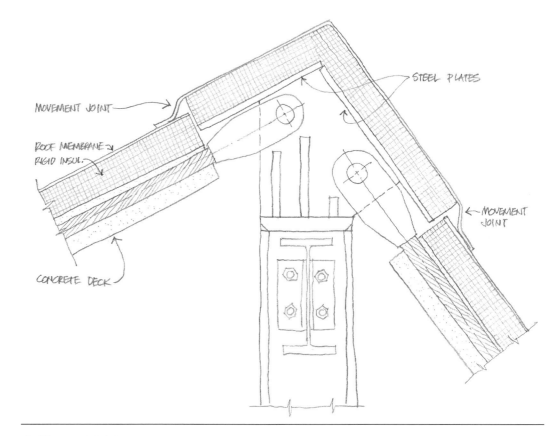

▲ *Figure 11.31*
A preliminary detail for enclosing the top of a column.

LENGTHS OF CABLES

In order to cut cables to length, we must be able to calculate in advance how long they must be. Simple numerical expressions have been developed for this purpose. We will look first at an expression for the length of a parabolic cable on supports that are at the same height. Then we will take up a slightly more involved expression that applies to structures such as ours whose supports are at different heights.

THE LENGTH OF A PARABOLIC CABLE ON LEVEL SUPPORTS

If we designate the length of the cable as l and the span as L, we can define the length of a parabolic cable in terms of the sum of the span and a difference, ΔL, between the length of the cable and its span:

$$l = L + \Delta L = L \left(1 + \frac{\Delta L}{L}\right) \qquad [11\text{-}9]$$

A close approximation of the last term of this expression is given by the equation

$$\frac{\Delta L}{L} \approx 2.6n^2 - 4n^4 \qquad [11\text{-}10]$$

where n is the sag ratio, s/L. When n does not exceed ⅛, the term $4n^4$ is not significant. Thus, for most cases:

$$l \approx L(1 + 2.6n^2) \qquad [11\text{-}11]$$

Suppose that we want to find the length of a cable whose span is 170 ft and whose sag is 17 ft:

$$n = \frac{s}{L} = \frac{17}{170} = 0.1 < 0.125 \qquad \text{O.K.}$$

$$l \approx L(1 + 2.6n^2) \approx (170 \text{ ft})(1 + 2.6(0.1)^2)$$

$$\approx 174.42 \text{ ft}$$

It follows from eq. [11-11] that if the length of a cable changes by δL, the change in the sag of the cable, Δs, is given by the following expression:

$$\Delta s \approx 0.19 \frac{\delta l}{n_{\text{initial}}} \qquad [11\text{-}12]$$

where n_{initial} is the original sag ratio. Consider a cable that has been designed to span a horizontal distance of 90 m with a sag of 7.5 m. The sag ratio, n, is 7.5/90, which is 0.0833. The correct length for this cable is 91.625 m. However, it has been cut erroneously to a length of 92 m, which is 0.375 m too long, and hung in place. What is the effect of this error on the sag of the cable?

$$\Delta s \approx 0.19 \frac{\delta l}{n_{\text{initial}}} \approx 0.19 \left(\frac{0.375 \text{ m}}{0.0833}\right) \approx 0.85 \text{ m}$$

The cable sags 0.85 m too low in the middle.

THE LENGTH OF A PARABOLIC CABLE ON SUPPORTS AT DIFFERENT LEVELS

Referring to the dimensions that are defined in Figure 11.32, the length of a cable whose supports lie at different levels can be approximated closely using the expression:

$$l \approx L + 0.65 \left(\frac{y_A^2}{L_A} + \frac{y_B^2}{L_B}\right) \qquad [11\text{-}13]$$

For the roof that we are designing:

$$l \approx 140 \text{ ft} + 0.65 \left(\frac{(4 \text{ ft})^2}{40 \text{ ft}} + \frac{(25 \text{ ft})^2}{100 \text{ ft}}\right) \approx 144.32 \text{ ft}$$

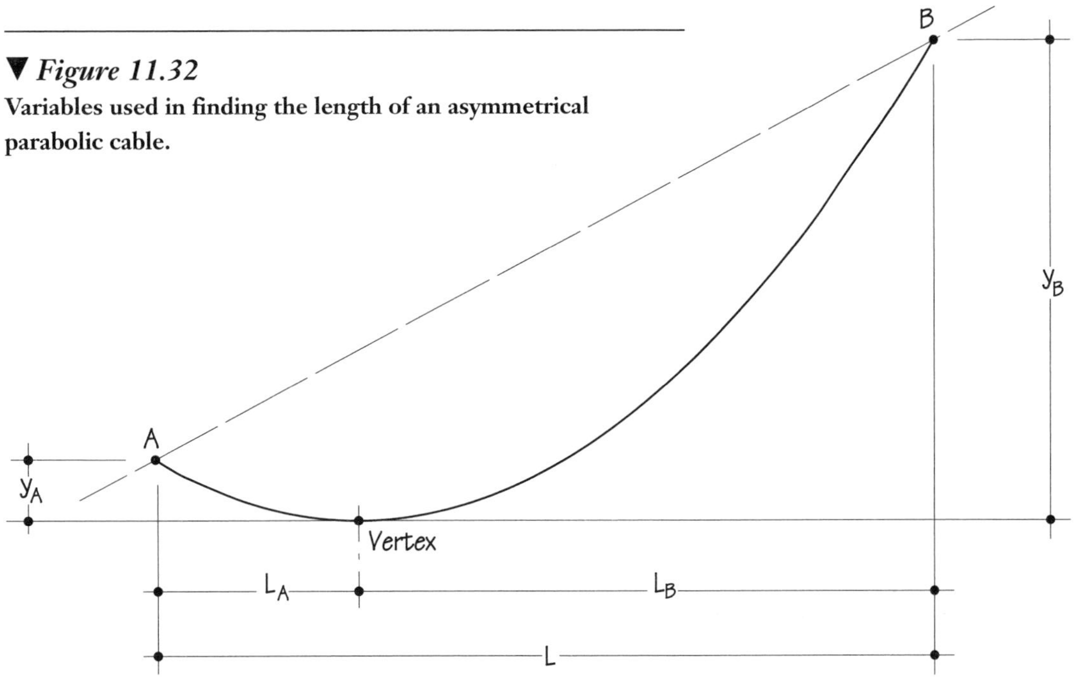

▼ *Figure 11.32*
Variables used in finding the length of an asymmetrical parabolic cable.

▲ *Figure 11.33*
The auditorium roof as designed.

ELIMINATING THE STAY CABLES

It is possible to employ surface action in the roof slab of a hanging structure in such a way as to eliminate the stay cables that bring the horizontal component of the cable action to the foundations. Figures 11.34 and 11.35 show how this is done. Solid end strips of the roof slab act as deep inclined beams that resist the total maximum force in the cables. In order to act as beams, these end strips must be made thicker than the other portions of the deck and reinforced with steel bars or strands that provide the necessary tensile resistance along the inner edges. The reactions at the ends of the two inclined beams are furnished by large compressive forces in the two edge strips of the deck. These edge strips are, of course, parabolic in profile, to match the parabolic curve of the cables. Thus, the com-

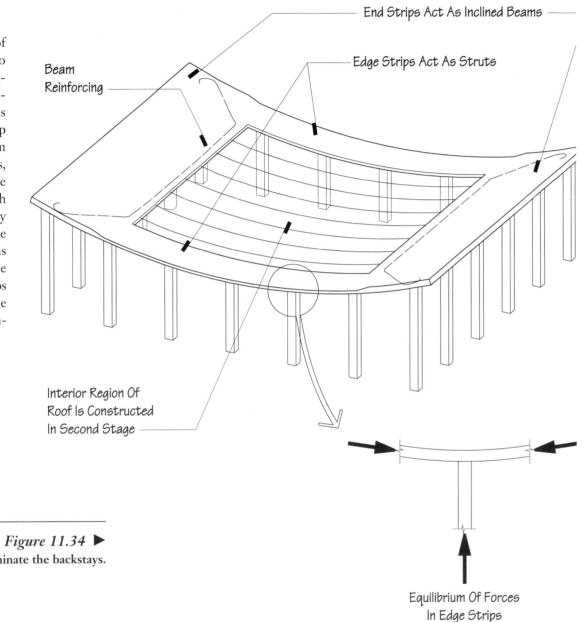

Figure 11.34 ▶

Utilizing surface action in the roof deck to eliminate the backstays.

End Strips Act As Inclined Beams

Edge Strips Act As Struts

Beam Reinforcing

Interior Region Of Roof Is Constructed In Second Stage

Equilibrium Of Forces In Edge Strips

pressive force in each curved edge tends to cause the edge strip to deflect in the downward direction, a tendency that is resisted by the upward pushes of the columns under the strip. The only nonvertical forces remaining to be considered in the walls of this structure are the lateral wind and seismic loads that must be considered routinely in any building; all the lateral pulls of the cables are absorbed within the roof deck itself.

The first stage in constructing a roof of this type is to erect the columns around the perimeter of the structure, along with the two end strips and the two side strips. Temporary shoring must be left in place to support the end strips until the rest of the structure has been erected. In the second stage, the cables and deck for the internal region of the roof deck are installed.

◀ *Figure 11.35*
Construction view of a hanging roof without backstays at the conclusion of the first stage of construction. The triangular masonry walls are expressive of the end forces from the inclined beams at the ends of the roof, but the actual work of resisting these forces is done by compressive action in the parabolic edge strips and vertical columns. (Designers: Buro Bistyp, Warsaw, Poland.)

When the distance between the side walls of this type of structure approaches or exceeds the span of the cables, the spans of the inclined beams in the end strips become excessive, and it becomes necessary to provide intermediate structures to support the beams in the horizontal direction. One way of doing this without obstructing the interior space is illustrated in Figures 11.36–11.38. A horizontal strut cuts the beam span in half. The strut is long and has a tendency to sag under its own weight, which is resisted by short, inclined struts that carry the weight of the strut down to cables on either side. The inclined struts also serve to support panes of glass for a skylight over a large lenticular opening in the roof. Further possibilities for hanging roofs that are longer than their spans are shown in Figures 11.39–11.41, in which curved edges of

Figure 11.36 ▶
Adding a horizontal strut to a roof whose width is greater than its span.

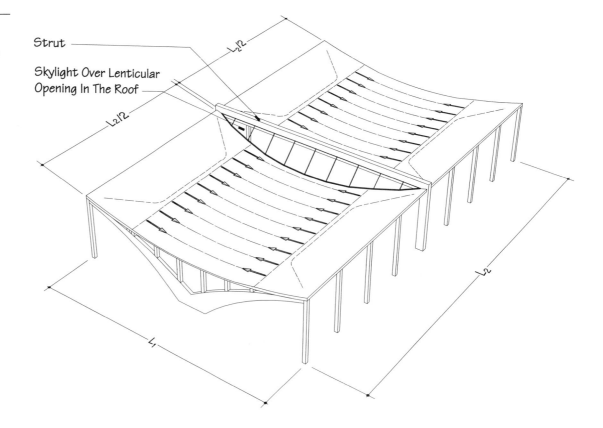

▲ *Figure 11.37*

The completion of the first stage of construction of a roof as diagrammed in Figure 11.36.

▲ *Figure 11.38*

The second stage of construction of a roof as diagrammed in Figure 11.36. (Designers: Buro Bistyp, Warsaw, Poland.)

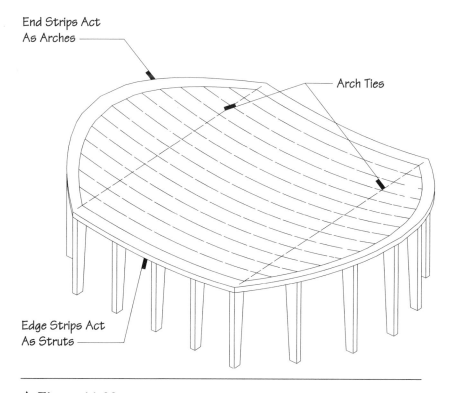

End Strips Act As Arches

Arch Ties

Edge Strips Act As Struts

▲ *Figure 11.39*

Substituting inclined arches and ties for the inclined beams to create a hanging roof without backstays.

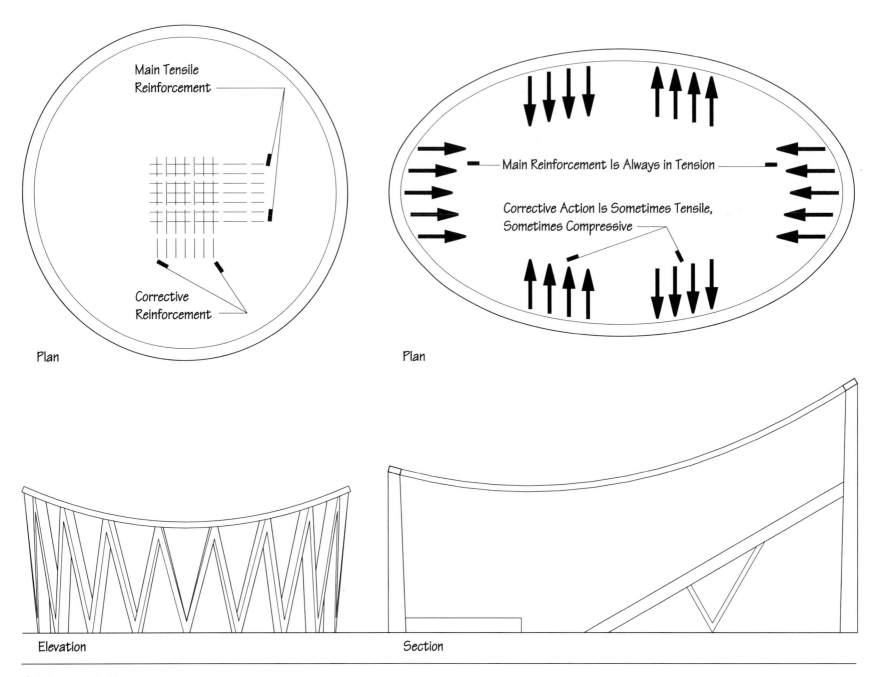

Main Tensile Reinforcement

Corrective Reinforcement

Plan

Main Reinforcement Is Always in Tension

Corrective Action Is Sometimes Tensile, Sometimes Compressive

Plan

Elevation

Section

▲ *Figure 11.40*
Circular and elliptical hanging roofs without backstays.

the roof act as inclined arches. These arches are subjected to axial forces only, much like the rims of bicycle wheels. The roof deck and its rein-forcement exert a corrective action, reacting instantaneously to any deviation of the pressure line from the axis of the arch ring by pushing or pulling the ring as needed to keep it in equilibrium. As a result of this action, the required cross-sectional area of the ring is relatively small.

◄ *Figure 11.41*
Model of a stadium roof that utilizes the principle illustrated in Figure 11.40. (Designers: Buro Bistyp, Warsaw, Poland.)

Key Terms and Concepts

surface action
diaphragm
cable
strand
wire rope

wire drawing
cold working
glass fibers
carbon fibers
aramid fibers

socketed fitting
swaged fitting
brooming out
closed bridge socket
U-bolt

tensile socket
open strand socket
working point
dapped edge
welded wire fabric

Exercises

1. Design a hanging footbridge to span 210 ft between riverbanks that differ in elevation by 7 ft. Make the supporting towers 22 ft tall. The two main cables support a deck that is 7 ft wide with a combined dead and live load of 120 psf.

2. Referring to the sketch in Figure 11.42, develop a design for a hanging roof that will drain rainwater off the lower edge.

3. Calculations show that a certain roof cable will stretch about 1.6 in. when the full design live load is applied to it. The span is 140 ft, the initial sag is 14 ft, and the supports are on the same level. How much will the stretching of the cable add to its sag?

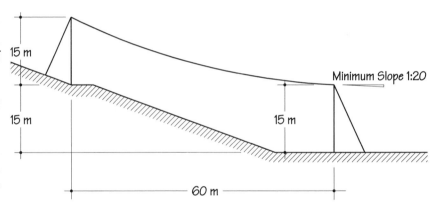

▲ *Figure 11.42*

4. A reinforced concrete parabolic arch shortens by 0.2% of its length during and after construction as a result of concrete shrinkage, creep, and compression under load. The span is 60 m, and the rise is 10 m. By how many mm does the arch shorten along its axis, and how far does the apex of the arch fall as a result of this shortening?

5. What shapes will be assumed by the freely hanging ropes shown in Figure 11.43? Assume that the weight of the rope is insignificant in each case.

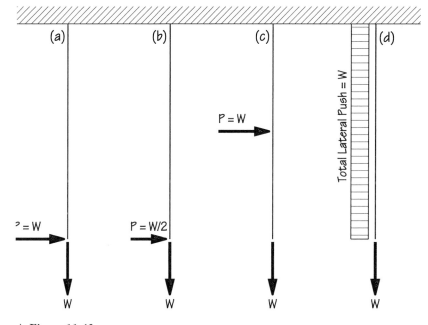

▲ *Figure 11.43*

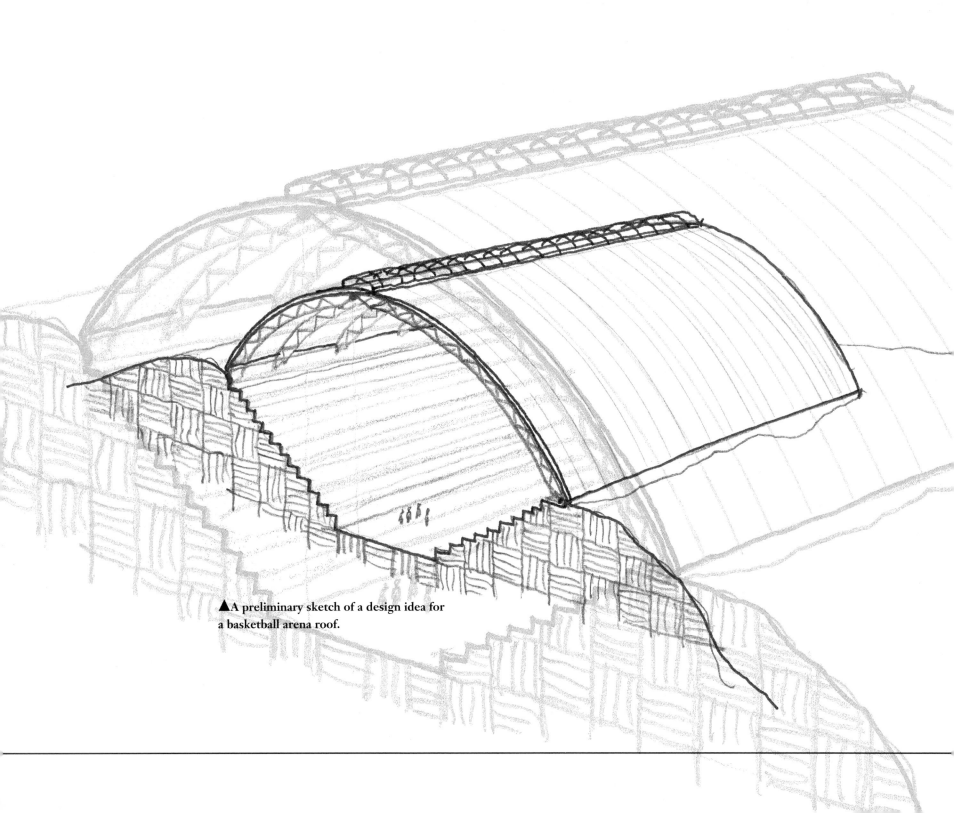

▲A preliminary sketch of a design idea for
a basketball arena roof.

CHAPTER TWELVE

SHAPING A THREE-HINGED TRUSS ARCH

The site for a proposed basketball arena is a natural bowl of rock. The roof will be supported by steel arches that span 90 m (see the facing page). Because of the asymmetry of the rock formation, the crown of the arch, which is centered over the basketball floor, will be 50 m from one support and 40 m from the other (Fig. 12.1). The rise of the arch from the right-hand support to the crown will be 25 m. The height of the left-hand support must be found. The arches will be spaced 10 m apart and will be made of steel. Each arch will have hinges at points X, Y, and Z.

ESTIMATING THE LOADS ON THE ARCH

For preliminary design, based on building code requirements and pending a detailed analysis of

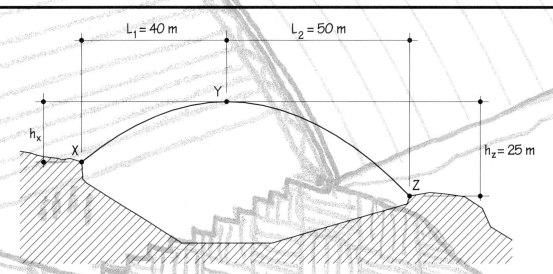

▲ *Figure 12.1*
Dimensional parameters of the arena roof.

▼ *Figure 12.2*
Finding form and forces graphically: First steps.

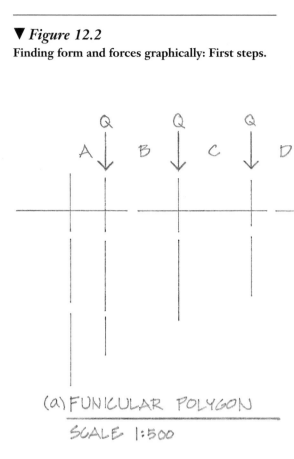

(a) FUNICULAR POLYGON

SCALE 1:500

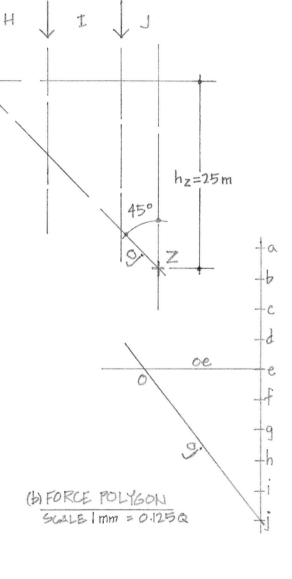

$h_z = 25\,m$

45°

Z

(b) FORCE POLYGON
SCALE 1 mm = 0.125 Q

FINDING FORM AND FORCES GRAPHICALLY

In Figure 12.2(a), we represent the uniform loading on the arch with nine concentrated forces, Q, each acting at the center of a 10-m-wide segment of the span. Each load, Q, on a 10-m segment of arch span in our graphical analysis represents the dead and live loads on a square meter of roof surface multiplied by the 10-m length of the segment and the 10-m distance between trusses:

$$Q_{DL} = (1.8\ kN/m^2)(100\ m^2) = 180\ kN$$

$$Q_{LL} = (1.2\ kN/m^2)(100\ m^2) = 120\ kN$$

$$Q_{TOT} = Q_{DL} + Q_{LL} = 300\ kN$$

We know the locations of apex Y and right-hand support Z. We know the vertical line along

wind loadings, we assume a live load on the roof of 120 kg/m². From prior projects of a similar type that have been designed and constructed by others, we estimate the mass of the trusses themselves, averaged over the entire roof surface, at about 25 kg/m². The purlins, decking, light fixtures, insulation, and roof membrane will add about 155 kg/m², for a total dead load of 180 kg/m². We convert these masses to forces:

Dead load = (180 kg/m²)(9.8 m/s²) ≈ 1.8 kN/m²

Live load = (120 kg/m²)(9.8 m/s²) ≈ 1.2 kN/m²

▼ *Figure 12.3*
Finding form and forces graphically: Completion.

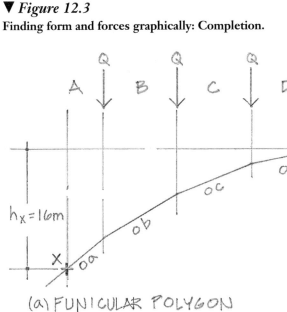

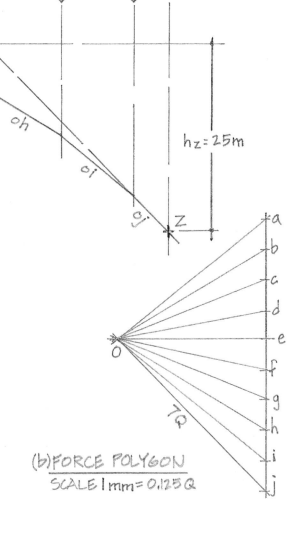

which left-hand support X is located. We apply interval notation to the loads and construct a load line. Now we must find the pole that will generate the desired curve.

The first fact that we know in advance about the funicular polygon which we are about to construct is that it will be horizontal at the apex, which is point Y. Y occurs in space E of the funicular polygon. This means that the corresponding ray oe on the force polygon will be horizontal. We draw the line of this ray horizontally through e on the load line and label it oe. We do not know yet where the pole, o, is located, but it has to be somewhere on this line.

In Chapter Nine, we found that lines drawn tangent to a parabolic arch at its supports intersect above the apex at a height above the

base line that is twice the height of the parabola. Thus, the last segment of the funicular polygon at Z, when extended upward, must intersect a vertical line through Y at a point Y' that lies 25 m above Y. The total vertical distance from Z to Y' is 50 m. The horizontal distance between these two points is also 50 m. Therefore, the last segment of the funicular polygon, which will be labeled oj, is inclined at 45°. Starting from the load line in Figure 12.2(b), we draw a line at 45° up and to the left from point j. This represents the line of the ray that is parallel to oj on the funicular polygon, so we label it oj. Where this line intersects oe is the location of the final pole, o.

We construct a full set of rays from o and, parallel to them, line segments to make up a funicular polygon that approximates the curve of the axis of the arch (Fig. 12.3). The smoothly curved parabolic line of the actual axis of the arch will be tangent to the midpoint of each of these segments. We scale the vertical location of X and find that it lies approximately 16 m below Y.

The length of the longest ray on the force polygon, *oj*, scales at 7*Q*. Earlier we estimated *Q* to be 300 kN. Thus, the maximum anticipated axial force in the arch under full live and dead loads is about 7(300 kN), or 2.1 MN.

FINDING FORM AND FORCES NUMERICALLY

Eqs. [11-1] through [11-8], which we developed in the preceding chapter, would enable us to find the form and forces for this arch rather easily. You may wish to do this for practice and to check the accuracy of the values that we obtained graphically. At this juncture, however, rather than use these equations again, we will develop instead an equivalent set of numerical expressions that are based on the curvature of a parabola. Then we will apply these new expressions to the design of the arched roof. This will prepare the way for the investigation of three-dimensional shell and membrane structures that we will undertake in a subsequent volume of this series. Numerical expressions based on the curvature of the element are extremely simple to use and are much more convenient for shell and membrane structures than the moment-based expressions that we have been using.

In deriving these new expressions, we will measure angles in radians rather than degrees. The definition of a *radian* is illustrated in Figure 12.4: it is an angle such that the length of its subtended arc *AB*, measured along the curving perimeter of the circle, is equal to the radius of the circle. It follows that there are 2π radians in a circle, from which we can calculate that a radian is approximately equal to 57.3°. The relevant advantage of the radian as a unit of measurement

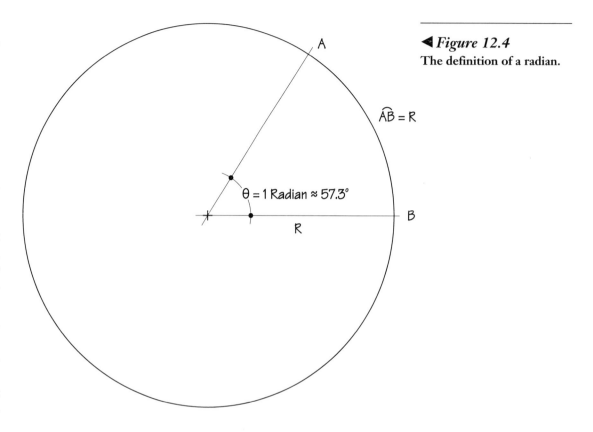

in this derivation is that an angle is measured in radians simply by dividing its arc length by its radius.

CURVATURE OF FUNICULAR LINES

Each sudden bend in the line of a longitudinally tensioned cable results from the action of a concentrated external force that is transversal to its span. Each smooth curvature of a cable consists of a gradual change of direction of its line that is caused by a transversal load distributed over a segment of the cable. Where there is no transversal load, the cable remains straight.

Figure 12.5(a) illustrates a concentrated load *Q* that produces a bend in a cable. The line of action of *Q* bisects the angle between the two segments of the cable. The equilibrium of the forces at the bend in the cable is expressed graphically by the force polygon in Figure 12.5(b). When the angle of the bend, α, is relatively small, the load *Q* approximates very closely the tension *T* in the cable times α in radians:

$$Q \approx T\alpha^{rad}$$

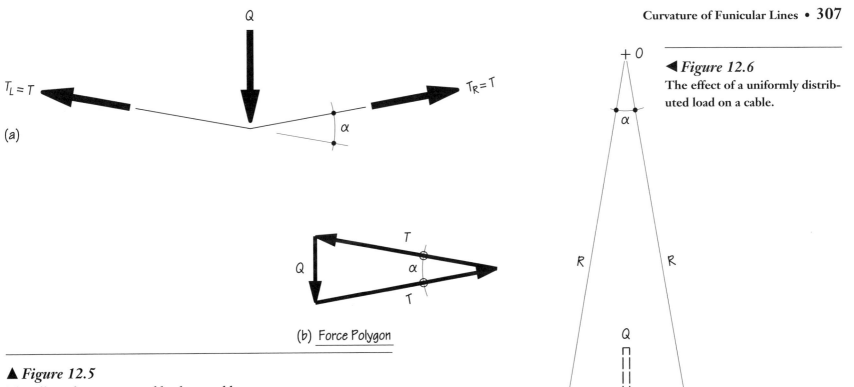

▲ Figure 12.5
The effect of a concentrated load on a cable.

(a)

(b) Force Polygon

◀ Figure 12.6
The effect of a uniformly distributed load on a cable.

Therefore,

$$T \approx \frac{Q}{\alpha^{rad}} \qquad [12\text{-}1]$$

When we replace the concentrated load Q with an equivalent loading q that is distributed uniformly over a one-unit-long segment AB of the cable, the loaded segment becomes curved, as if it were composed of many small bends, each produced by a small portion of the distributed loading (Fig. 12.6). This substitution of an equivalent distributed load for the concentrated load does not affect the value of angle α between the two adjacent straight segments of the cable.

If the distributed loading q were acting perpendicularly at each point to the line of curved cable segment AB, this segment would become an arc of a circle whose center is located at point O. The radius of the circle, R, is equal to both AO and BO. By definition, an angle in radians is equal to the length of its subtended arc divided by the radius of the arc. Therefore:

$$\alpha^{rad} = \frac{AB}{R}$$

Because we defined AB as one unit of length:

$$\alpha^{rad} = \frac{1}{R}$$

$$R = \frac{1}{\alpha^{rad}}$$

The angle α^{rad} may be thought of as representing the intensity of curvature of a cable segment that is one unit long. This can be observed in Figure 12.7, in which we see three circular segments of cable, each one unit long. A larger angle α^{rad} is accompanied by a smaller radius, a more intense curvature, and a smaller cable tension.

When the last expression is substituted into eq. [12-1], while substituting q times one unit of length for Q, we arrive at

$$T = qR \qquad [12\text{-}2]$$

This simple relationship tells us that the tension at any point in a cable is equal to the load per-pendicular to the line of the cable per unit of cable length multiplied by the radius of curvature.

This type of action, in which the load is always perpendicular to the axis of the cable, is typical of the pressure exerted by liquids, gases,

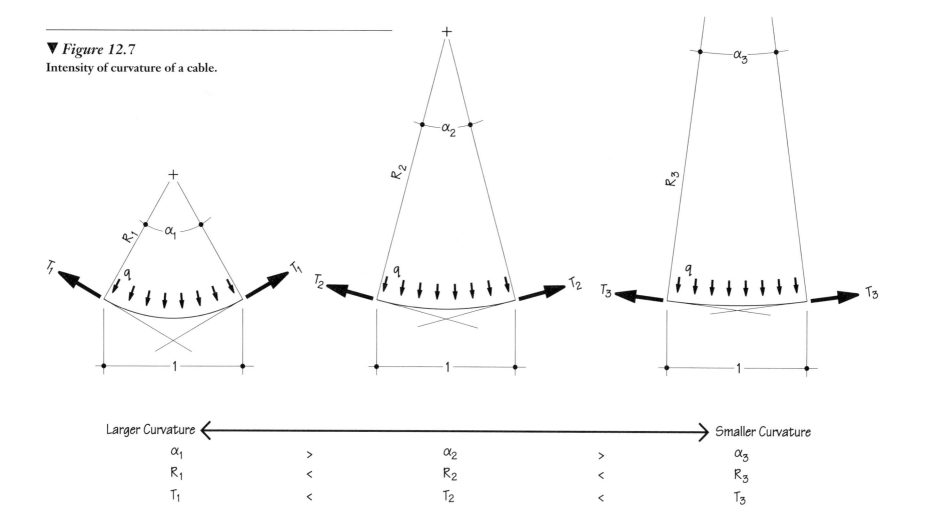

▼ **Figure 12.7**
Intensity of curvature of a cable.

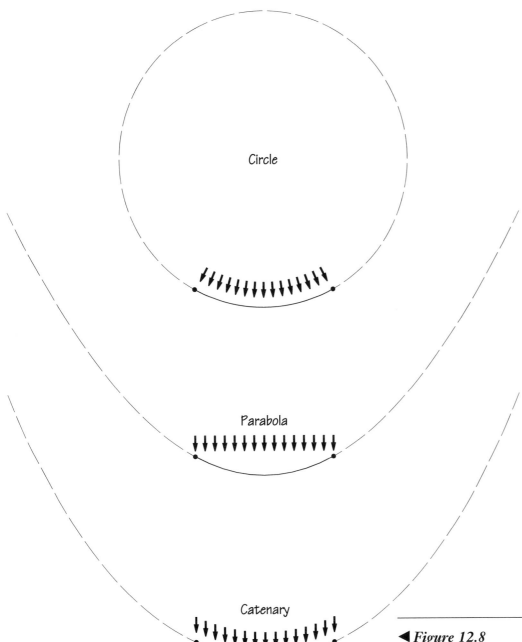

and granular materials that have negligible internal friction. For this reason it is known as *hydrostatic pressure*. When hydrostatic pressure is constant along the length of a cable, eq. [12-2] tells us that both the radius of curvature and the tension in the cable are also constant. Thus, the form that is funicular for a uniform hydrostatic pressure is a circle, which explains why pipes, pressure vessels, and large storage tanks for gases, liquids, and granular solids are usually cylindrical.

As we noted in earlier chapters, the form that is funicular for vertical loads distributed uniformly along the length of a cable is a catenary, whereas the funicular form for a uniform distribution of such loads along the horizontal projection of the span is a parabola. Because the loads on these two forms are vertical and parallel rather than perpendicular to the axis of the cable, the curvatures of parabolic and catenary funicula are variable, decreasing gradually from a maximum curvature that occurs at the apex of each. Their radii, which are the reciprocals of their curvature, reach a minimum at the apex.

In general, any line that is neither circular nor straight can be approximated by a series of small segments of circles of different radii. Thus, a shallow area at the apex of a catenary or a parabola may be difficult to distinguish by eye from a shallow arc of a circle whose radius is equal to the least radius of curvature of the catenary or parabola (Fig. 12.8). In Figure 12.9, we

◀ *Figure 12.8*
Shallow arcs of a circle, a catenary, and a parabola are difficult to distinguish from one another.

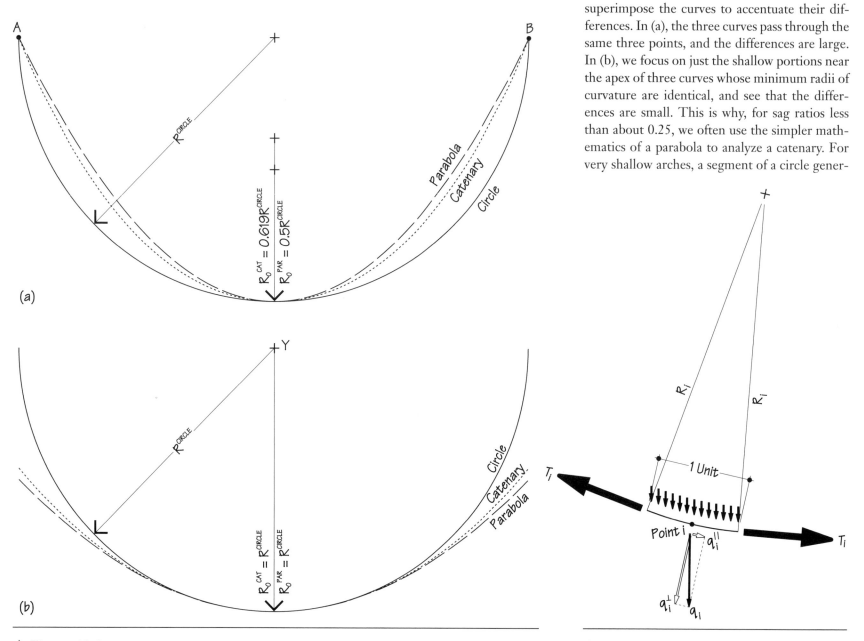

(a)

(b)

superimpose the curves to accentuate their differences. In (a), the three curves pass through the same three points, and the differences are large. In (b), we focus on just the shallow portions near the apex of three curves whose minimum radii of curvature are identical, and see that the differences are small. This is why, for sag ratios less than about 0.25, we often use the simpler mathematics of a parabola to analyze a catenary. For very shallow arches, a segment of a circle gener-

▲ *Figure 12.9*
Superimposing a circle, a catenary, and a parabola.

▲ *Figure 12.10*
The effect of a nonhydrostatic load on a cable.

ally can be substituted for either a catenary or a parabola with good results.

A simple expression similar to eq. [12-2] can easily be developed for a general loading condition, one that is not necessarily hydrostatic. Figure 12.10 illustrates such a general case. The load q_i at any arbitrarily selected point i is not

perpendicular to the axis of the cable. It can be resolved into components $q_i^\perp$, which is perpendicular to the cable at that point, and $q_i^\parallel$, which is parallel to the cable. By the same process of reasoning that we used to develop eq. [12-2], we arrive at an expression for the general loading condition:

$$T_i = q_i^\perp R_i \qquad [12\text{-}3]$$

Thus, to find the tensile force, T_i, in any point of a cable that is shaped by any arbitrary loading,

we must find for that point the perpendicular component of the distributed load and the radius of curvature of the cable. This is relatively simple to do for the vertical loads that produce a parabola. In the vicinity of the apex, the funicular line is horizontal, so the perpendicular component, $q_i^\perp$, is the same as the load itself, q. The radius of curvature at the apex, which we define as the *main radius of curvature*, R_0, is the smallest of the radii of curvature of the cable. The tensile force, T_i, at the apex is equal to the horizontal component of the force in all sections of the cable, H. Thus, for any funicular line:

$$H = qR_0 \qquad [12\text{-}4]$$

T_i, the tensile force at any point i in a vertically loaded cable, is equal to the horizontal component of force divided by the cosine of the angle of inclination at that point:

$$T_i = \frac{H}{\cos \alpha_i} \qquad [12\text{-}5]$$

To write the equation of the parabolic funicular line produced by a uniformly distributed loading, we must first determine the values of some dimensional parameters, as shown in Figure 12.11. The horizontal distance L between points A and B that lie at the same level is called the *horizontal chord*. The vertical distance s from the chord to the apex is the sag of segment ACB of the parabola. Eq. [9-1] in Chapter Nine tells us that the horizontal component of the force in

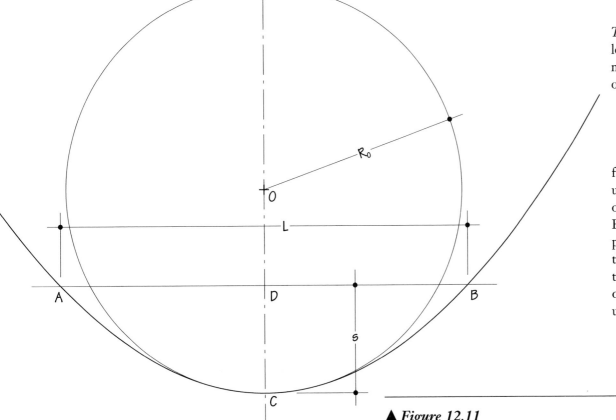

▲ *Figure 12.11*
Dimensional parameters of a parabola with a level chord.

the cable, which is the same as the tension at the apex, is given by the following expression:

$$H = T_{apex} = \frac{wL^2}{8s}$$

From eq. [12-3], we know that

$$T_{apex} = qR_0$$

Combining these expressions and recognizing that for a parabola w, the uniformly distributed load on a horizontal projection, is the same as q, we find a useful expression for the main radius of curvature of a parabola:

$$R_0 = \frac{L^2}{8s} \qquad [12\text{-}6]$$

A convenient feature of eq. [12-6] is that it will yield the same value of R_0 regardless of where the chord is located, even if the chord is inclined (Fig. 12.12).

To locate points on a parabola, we can write equations that are derived by substituting eq. [12-6] into eqs. [9-2] and [11-2]. Thus, for axes X and Y that originate at the apex of the parabola, y_x, the y-coordinate for any value x, is given by the expression:

$$y_x = \frac{x^2}{2R_0} \qquad [12\text{-}7]$$

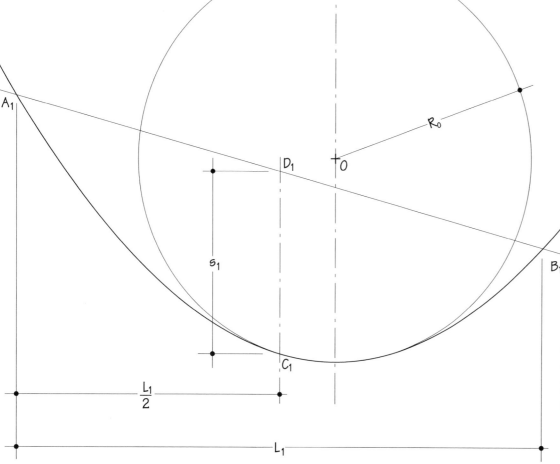

◀ *Figure 12.12*
Dimensional parameters of a parabola with a sloping chord.

Figure 12.13 ▶

SUMMARY OF CURVATURE-BASED NUMERICAL EXPRESSIONS FOR DESIGNING PARABOLIC ARCHES AND CABLES

R_0, the main (minimum) radius of curvature of a parabolic cable or arch, is equal to the square of L, the horizontal projection of the length of any chord, divided by 8 times s, the sag or rise of the parabola as measured vertically from the midpoint of the chord:

$$R_0 = \frac{L^2}{8s} \qquad [12\text{-}6]$$

With respect to axes X_0 and Y_0 that originate at any point A at the end of a horizontal chord of length L:

$$y_0 = \frac{x_0(x_0 - L)}{2R_0} \qquad [12\text{-}8]$$

For easy reference, the most directly useful of these expressions are summarized in Figure 12.13.

H, the horizontal component of force at any point in a symmetrical or asymmetrical parabolic arch or cable, is found using the following expression, in which q is the vertical load per unit of span length:

$$H = qR_0 \qquad [12\text{-}4]$$

APPLYING THE CURVATURE-BASED EXPRESSIONS TO THE STEEL ROOF ARCH

Although the foregoing derivations may have seemed arduous, the application of the resulting equations to the finding of form and forces for the steel roof arch is remarkably simple. First we will use eq. [12-6] to find the main radius of curvature of the parabolic arch. Referring back to Figure 12.1, we will base this determination on a symmetrical parabola whose span is 100 m and whose rise is 25 m:

$$R_0 = \frac{L^2}{8s} = \frac{(100 \text{ m})^2}{8(25 \text{ m})} = 50 \text{ m}$$

To find h_x, the distance below the apex of the left support, we substitute actual values into eq. [12-7], assuming as an origin for our axes the apex of the parabola, point Y:

$$y_x = -\frac{x^2}{2R_0} = -\frac{(-40 \text{ m})^2}{2(50 \text{ m})} = -16 \text{ m}$$

With respect to axes that originate at the apex of the parabola, y_x, the y-coordinate of a point on the parabola whose x-coordinate is x, is given by the expression:

$$y_x = \frac{x^2}{2R_0} \qquad [12\text{-}7]$$

With respect to axes that originate at any point A on the parabola, the coordinates of any other point on the parabola are related by the following expression, in which L is the length of a horizontal chord through A:

$$y_0 = \frac{x_0(x_0 - L)}{2R_0} \qquad [12\text{-}8]$$

T_i or C_i, the axial cable tension or arch compression at any point i, is given by the following expression, in which α_i is the slope of the parabola at i:

$$T_i = C_i = \frac{H}{\cos \alpha_i} \qquad [12\text{-}5]$$

It is often convenient to use instead of eq. [12-5] an equivalent expression that is based on sl_i, the slope of the parabola at point i:

$$T_i = C_i = H\sqrt{1 + (sl_i)^2} \qquad [12\text{-}5a]$$

This confirms the result of our earlier graphical solution.

To find the horizontal component of the thrust in the arch under a symmetrical load, we use eq. [12-4]:

$$H = qR_0 = (30 \text{ kN/m})(50 \text{ m})$$

$$= 1\,500 \text{ kN} = 1.5 \text{ MN}$$

This is also the force at the apex, point Y. The maximum compressive force will occur at the steepest inclination, which we determined during our graphical solution to be 45° at the right support. We employ eq. [12-5]:

$$C_R = \frac{H}{\cos \alpha_R} = \frac{1.5 \text{ MN}}{0.707} = 2.12 \text{ MN}$$

This differs by only about 1% from the approximate value that we determined graphically.

To lay out the axis of the arch, we could use either eq. [12-7] or eq. [12-8] to find the coordinates of as many points as we wish along its path.

FINDING THE MAXIMUM ECCENTRICITY OF THE FORCE IN THE ARCH

A force is *eccentric* when its line of action does not coincide with the axis of the member. There is no eccentricity of the forces in the arch under a uniform loading: the pressure line of the compressive forces follows the parabolic axis. However, wind and snow will often load the arch asymmetrically, causing the pressure line to deviate from the axis except at the hinges. These *eccentricities* will increase the forces in the arch. We must design the arch to support the most disadvantageous combination of the dead load on the full arch plus an *asymmetrical live load*. Experience has shown that this combination will occur when the live load is applied to only half of the arch. In the arch that we are designing, we must investigate the eccentricities created by full dead load plus live load on the right side only (from Y to Z), and also the eccentricities created by full dead load plus live load on the shorter left side only (from X to Y), to find out which are the largest. Then we can design the arch to resist the additional forces that are created by these eccentricities.

We have chosen to insert three hinges in the arch, one at each support and one at the crown. These hinges simplify our task, because any pressure line in the arch, regardless of the loading, must pass through all three of them. In Figure 12.14, we construct pressure lines through X, Y, and Z for the two asymmetrical loading conditions, and superimpose them on the funicular polygon that we constructed in Figure 12.3. (For clarity, the trial force polygons and trial funicular polygons have been removed from this drawing.) The pressure line for full dead load plus live load left rises above the pressure line for full live load plus dead load in the left half of the arch, and falls below it in the right half. The pressure line for full dead load plus live load right does the opposite. When the three pressure lines are superimposed, the result is a composite funicular polygon that consists of two slender crescents, each with a pressure line for a uniform loading that passes through its center. Each crescent is thickest at the quarter point of the span, which means that the maximum eccentricities occur at this location.

These crescents show us how to shape arches ideally for any combination of loads. If we construct the steel arch trusses so that the top chords follow the top lines of the crescents and the bottom chords follow the bottom lines, no part of the truss will experience tension under any predicted loading pattern. Under the most asymmetrical loading pattern, one chord in each half of the arch would carry all the compression and the other chord would carry no force at all. If we make the trusses deeper than the crescents at every point, the two chords will always share the compressive load in varying proportions, though their shares will be equal only under a uniform loading. If the arches were to be solid rectangular members of masonry instead of steel trusses, the crescents would have to fall within the middle third of the height of the section at every point in the span to avoid tensile stress under the most adverse loading condition. Steel, reinforced concrete, and laminated wood have considerable resistance to bending, so we would not have to make the arches as deep in these materials as we would in unreinforced masonry.

To find the magnitude of the maximum eccentricity in the arch under an asymmetrical loading, we need only to measure the vertical distance at the quarter-span point between the pressure line for that loading and the axis of the arch. The axis of the arch is the same as the pressure line for a uniform loading. In attempting to measure eccentricities at the quarter spans on

Figure 12.14 ▶
Graphical construction of pressure lines in the arch for symmetrical and asymmetrical loading conditions.

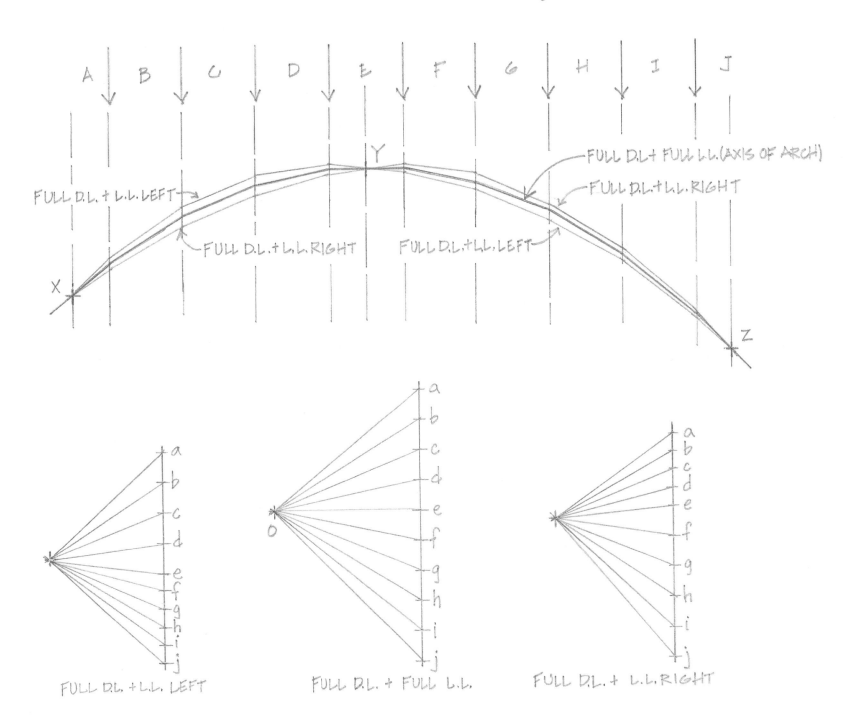

FULL D.L. + L.L. LEFT

FULL D.L. + FULL L.L.

FULL D.L. + L.L. RIGHT

How Many Hinges?

There are two basic reasons to include hinges in an arch. One is to make the arch less susceptible to stresses caused by changes of temperature and small movements in its supports. The other is to simplify site connections between its manufactured components. A side benefit of hinges is that they simplify calculations by reducing the degree of statical indeterminacy. An arch is statically indeterminate when its reactions cannot be calculated by using only the conditions of static equilibrium. Additional mathematical expressions based on the elastic behavior of the arch must be employed to find the reactions on a statically indeterminate arch. The degree of indeterminacy is equal to the number of such additional expressions that are required for a solution.

Arches are commonly built in three different configurations: **fixed-end** arches, **two-hinged** arches, and **three-hinged** arches (Fig. A). (Though a one-hinged arch is possible, the form is rarely built.)

The three-hinged arch has a number of advantages over the other two. Chief among these is that it rotates freely at the hinges to adjust to changing external conditions without any significant change in its internal stresses. If its foundations settle a bit, or the material of the arch expands on a hot, sunny day, its stresses are unaffected. A three-hinged arch is also statically determinate under any set of loadings and external conditions, meaning that it is easy to analyze either graphically or numerically. On the other hand, it is the least rigid of the three

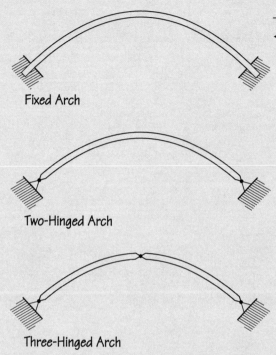

Fixed Arch

Two-Hinged Arch

Three-Hinged Arch

◀ *Figure A*

arch configurations, because it cannot develop bending resistance at its hinges. Thus, it uses somewhat more material than a two-hinged or fixed-end arch to do the same job. It is, however, the easiest and least troublesome of the three to erect.

A fixed-end arch has three degrees of statical indeterminacy, which means that it requires three additional equations beyond those of static equilibrium for its solution. Any adjustment of the arch to shifting loads, temperature

changes, or foundation settlement is accompanied by some degree of bending in the material of the arch. Bending can become severe and destructive if external conditions cause significant distortions of its shape. It is the most rigid of the three configurations, because all of its material can work to resist bending.

A two-hinged arch can adjust well to small changes in the vertical locations of its foundations, but if the distance between the foundations grows longer or shorter, significant bending stresses may result. Changes in temperature or loading also cause bending stresses, although these are less severe than in a fixed-end arch because of the free rotation of the ends. A two-hinged arch has one degree of statical indeterminacy and is intermediate in its rigidity between the other two configurations.

Fixed-end arches, except for their common use over very short spans in masonry walls, should be used for longer spans only in situations where their foundations are very stable. Two-hinged arches are often used for their simplicity and economy in stable soils. Three-hinged arches are a safe choice under almost any set of conditions. A four-hinged arch would be not a structure, but a mechanism, which is another way of saying that it would collapse under even the smallest irregularity in its loading. ■

Figure 12.15, however, we find that the distances are very small, scaling somewhere in the range of 1.0 to 1.5 m. They are difficult to determine more precisely than this because of small drawing inaccuracies and the thicknesses of pencil lines. These factors subject our measurements to potentially large errors. We must find another, more accurate, way of quantifying the eccentricities.

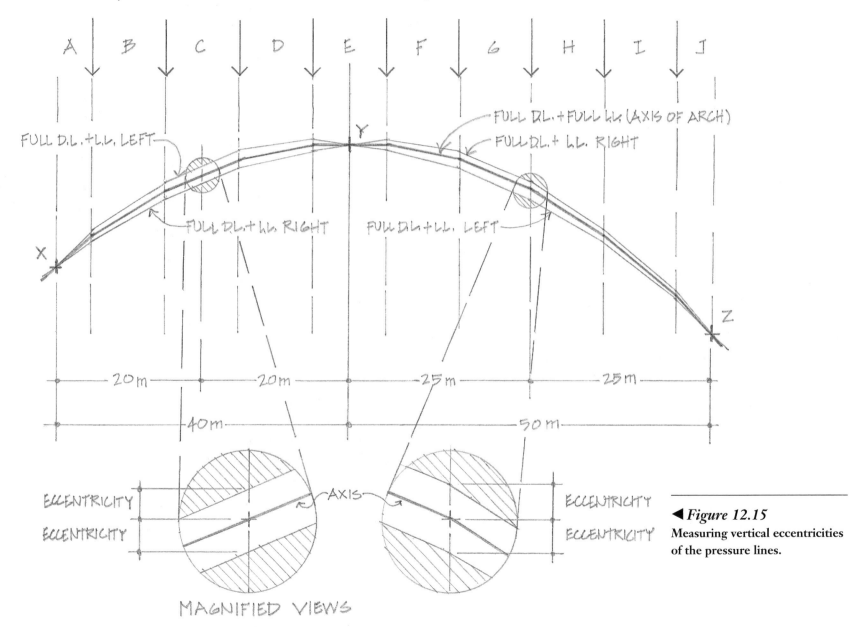

▶ *Figure 12.15*
Measuring vertical eccentricities of the pressure lines.

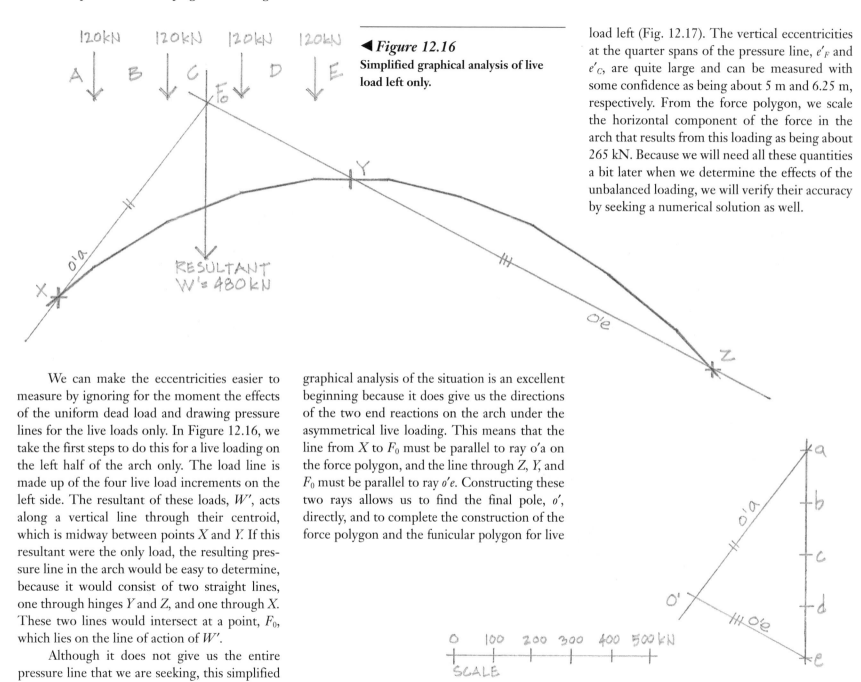

◀ *Figure 12.16*
Simplified graphical analysis of live load left only.

load left (Fig. 12.17). The vertical eccentricities at the quarter spans of the pressure line, e'_F and e'_C, are quite large and can be measured with some confidence as being about 5 m and 6.25 m, respectively. From the force polygon, we scale the horizontal component of the force in the arch that results from this loading as being about 265 kN. Because we will need all these quantities a bit later when we determine the effects of the unbalanced loading, we will verify their accuracy by seeking a numerical solution as well.

We can make the eccentricities easier to measure by ignoring for the moment the effects of the uniform dead load and drawing pressure lines for the live loads only. In Figure 12.16, we take the first steps to do this for a live loading on the left half of the arch only. The load line is made up of the four live load increments on the left side. The resultant of these loads, W', acts along a vertical line through their centroid, which is midway between points X and Y. If this resultant were the only load, the resulting pressure line in the arch would be easy to determine, because it would consist of two straight lines, one through hinges Y and Z, and one through X. These two lines would intersect at a point, F_0, which lies on the line of action of W'.

Although it does not give us the entire pressure line that we are seeking, this simplified

graphical analysis of the situation is an excellent beginning because it does give us the directions of the two end reactions on the arch under the asymmetrical live loading. This means that the line from X to F_0 must be parallel to ray o'a on the force polygon, and the line through Z, Y, and F_0 must be parallel to ray o'e. Constructing these two rays allows us to find the final pole, o', directly, and to complete the construction of the force polygon and the funicular polygon for live

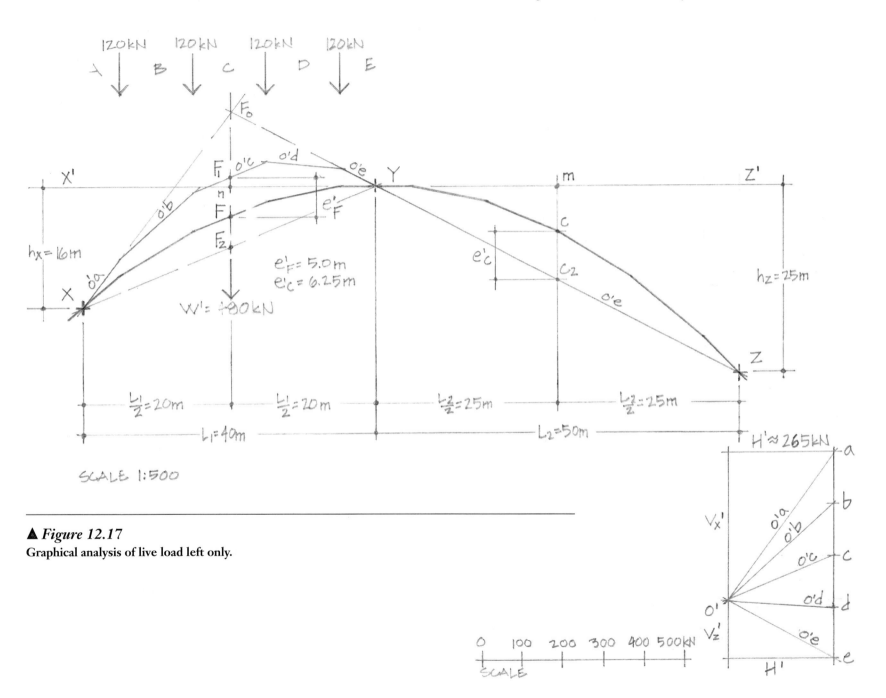

▲ *Figure 12.17*
Graphical analysis of live load left only.

SOLVING NUMERICALLY FOR ECCENTRICITIES AND HORIZONTAL THRUST

To find an exact value for H', the horizontal thrust attributable to the live load on the left half of the arch, we will sum moments about X. We make a simplified sketch of the situation (Fig. 12.18). There will be two unknowns in the expression for moments about X, H' and V_Z, which are the two components of the reaction at Z. The line of action of this reaction is YZ, which descends 25 m over a horizontal distance of 50 m, which is a slope of 1:2. This means that V_Z is exactly half of H', allowing us to sum moments with only one unknown and solve directly for H'. To simplify the operation further, we substitute for the four individual loads their resultant, W', which is a single force of 480 kN acting through K:

$$\sum M_X = (480 \text{ kN})(20 \text{ m}) + H'(25 \text{ m} - 16 \text{ m})$$

$$-\frac{H'}{2}(90 \text{ m}) = 0$$

$$H' = 266.7 \text{ kN·m}$$

This exact value is very close to the approximate value of 265 kN·m that we determined graphically.

◀ *Figure 12.18*
Sketch of forces involved in finding the horizontal thrust attributable to live load left only.

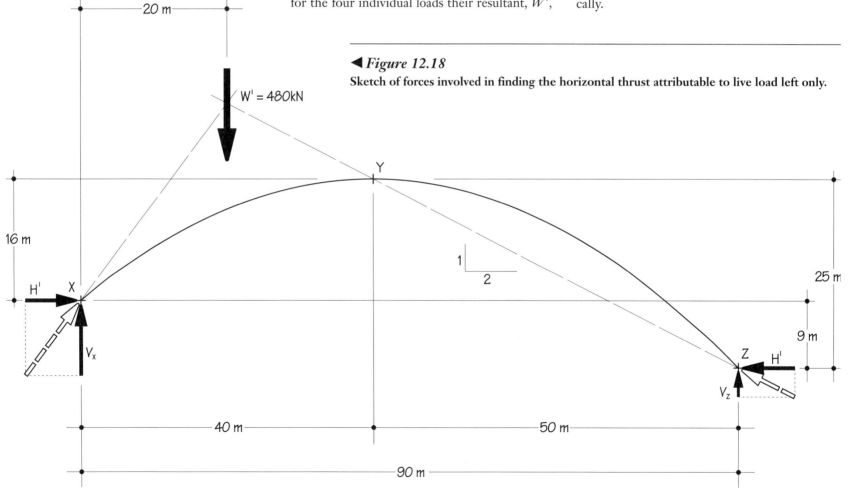

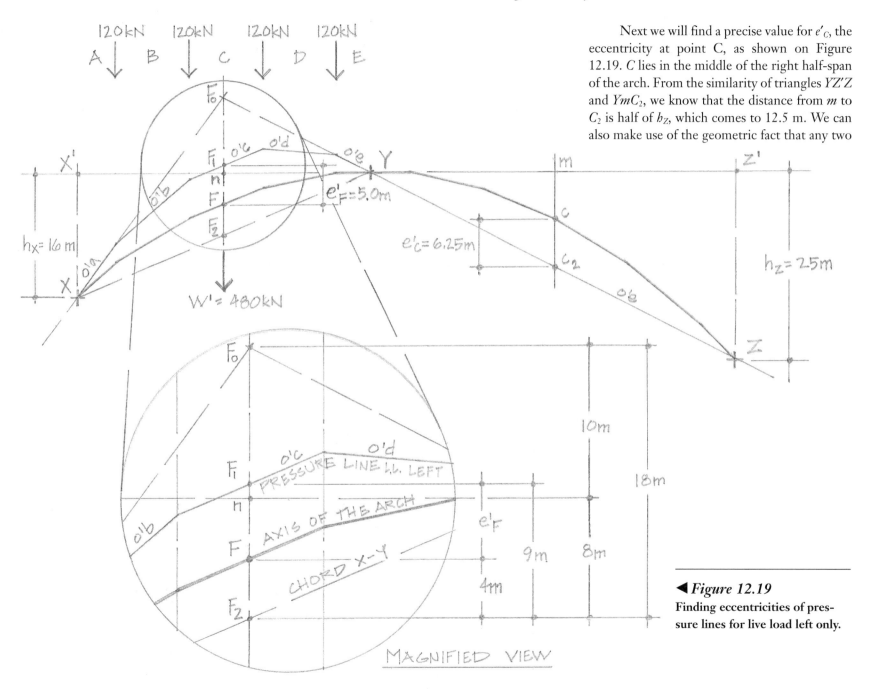

Next we will find a precise value for e'_C, the eccentricity at point C, as shown on Figure 12.19. *C* lies in the middle of the right half-span of the arch. From the similarity of triangles $YZ'Z$ and YmC_2, we know that the distance from *m* to C_2 is half of h_Z, which comes to 12.5 m. We can also make use of the geometric fact that any two

◀ *Figure 12.19*
Finding eccentricities of pressure lines for live load left only.

tangents to a parabola will intersect on a vertical line that lies halfway between the two points of tangency; the altitude of the parabola as measured along that vertical line is half the distance from the chord to the intersections of the tangents. This means that tangents to the parabola at Y and Z must intersect at m, and that e'_C is exactly half of mC_2. This comes out to 6.25 m, the same as the value that we measured earlier.

Finding e'_F is a bit more involved. Through the similarity of triangles $XX'Y$ and F_2nY, we determine that the distance from n to F_2 is half of $X'X$, which comes out to be 8 m. Triangle F_0nY is similar to triangle $ZZ'Y$, from which we can find the distance from F_0 to n:

$$\frac{F_0n}{25 \text{ m}} = \frac{20 \text{ m}}{50 \text{ M}}$$

$$F_0n = 10 \text{ m}$$

Adding the results of these two determinations, we find that the distance from F_0 to F_2 is 18 m.

The two broken lines that intersect at F_0 in Figure 12.19 are tangents to the parabolic portion of the funicular polygon for the half live load. This means that the distance from F_1 to F_2 is half of 18 m, which is 9 m. The tangents to this half of the axis of the arch intersect at n; thus the distance from F to F_2 is 4 m, which is half the distance from n to F_2. Putting all these dimensions on a magnified sketch so that we can keep track of them (Fig. 12.19), we are able to determine at last that e'_F is 9 m minus 4 m, or exactly 5 m. This is the same as the distance that we scaled from the graphical solution. The only difference in the values obtained from the graphical and numerical solutions is that there is a discrepancy of less than 1% in the horizontal thrust figure.

BENDING MOMENTS FOR LIVE LOAD LEFT

Earlier we calculated that the horizontal thrust caused by the live load on the left half of the arch is 266.7 kN·m. We have just finished determining that the pressure line for the live load on the left half of the arch reaches maximum vertical eccentricities from the arch axis of 5.0 m in the left half of the arch, and 6.25 m in the right half. Wherever the arch axis and the pressure line do not coincide, a moment is created in the arch that is equal to the horizontal thrust multiplied by the vertical eccentricity between the arch axis and the pressure line. Such a moment is called a *bending moment*, because it causes the arch to bend. The maximum bending moments in an asymmetrically loaded arch occur at points of maximum eccentricity. Thus, for a live load on the left half of this arch, the maximum bending moments are:

$$M'_C = H'e'_c = (266.7 \text{ kN})(6.25 \text{ m}) = 1667 \text{ kN·m}$$

$$M'_F = H'e'_F = (266.7 \text{ kN})(5.0 \text{ m}) = 1333 \text{ kN·m}$$

SOLVING NUMERICALLY FOR BENDING MOMENTS FOR LIVE LOAD RIGHT

Figure 12.20 shows the determination of the pressure line and eccentricities for a live load right condition. The solution procedure is similar to the one we have just concluded for live load left. The horizontal thrust calculates to be 333.3 kN, and the eccentricities are 5.0 and 4.0 meters, resulting in the following values for bending moments:

$$M''_C = 1667 \text{ kN·m}$$

$$M''_F = 1333 \text{ kN·m}$$

Earlier we found identical bending moment values for these same two points under live load left only. Thus, we discover an interesting symmetry in the behavior of the arch despite its asymmetrical geometry.

COMBINING THE EFFECTS OF LIVE AND DEAD LOADS

The horizontal thrusts, eccentricities, and bending moments we have determined to this point are the effects of unbalanced live loadings only, which we examined separately from the effects of the uniform dead load for convenience of analysis. Now we must combine the effects of the asymmetrical and symmetrical loadings on the arch to determine the range of forces and stresses that we can anticipate in the actual structure.

Dead Loads and Live Loads Distributed over the Entire Span. When the arch is fully and uniformly loaded, its internal forces will consist entirely of axial compression throughout its length. We can find the magnitude of the maximum axial force, which occurs at Z, the point of maximum slope, by using the appropriate expressions from Figure 12.13.

$$w = \frac{300 \text{ kN}}{10 \text{ m}} = 30 \text{ kN/m}$$

$$H = qR_0 = (30 \text{ kN/m})(50 \text{ m}) = 1\,500 \text{ kN}$$

$$C_{\max} = \frac{H}{\cos \alpha_{\max}} = \frac{1\,500 \text{ kN}}{\cos 45°} = 2\,120 \text{ kN}$$

All the forces in the arch are axial under this symmetrical loading pattern, so there are no

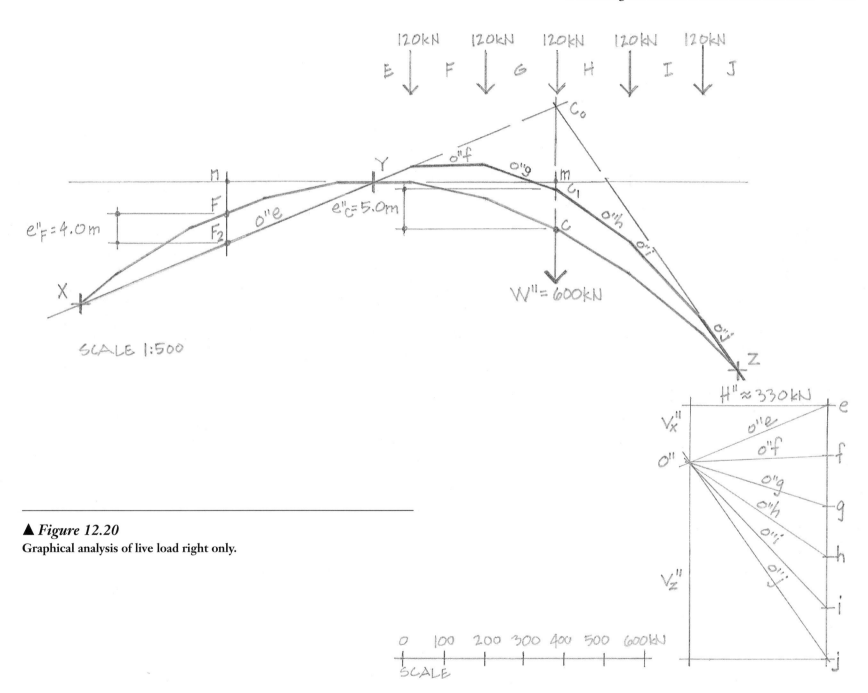

▲ Figure 12.20
Graphical analysis of live load right only.

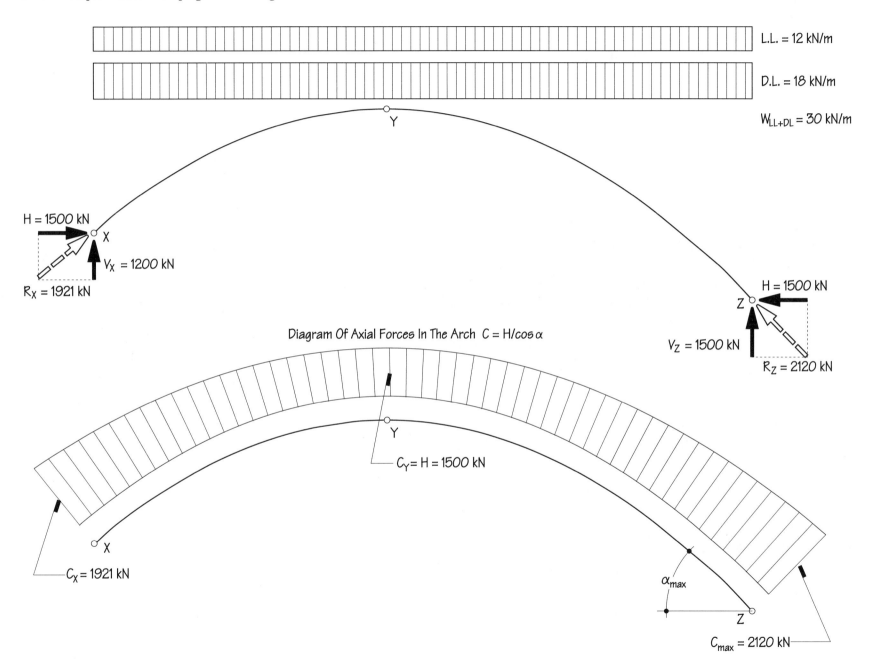

L.L. = 12 kN/m

D.L. = 18 kN/m

W_{LL+DL} = 30 kN/m

H = 1500 kN

V_X = 1200 kN

R_X = 1921 kN

H = 1500 kN

V_Z = 1500 kN

R_Z = 2120 kN

Diagram Of Axial Forces In The Arch C = H/cos α

C_Y = H = 1500 kN

C_X = 1921 kN

$α_{max}$

C_{max} = 2120 kN

◀ *Figure 12.21*

Distribution of axial forces for a uniform loading on the arch.

bending moments. Figure 12.21 diagrams the distribution of axial forces in the arch under a uniform loading. The minimum force, at the apex, is equal to the horizontal thrust.

The axial force at any point in the arch may be found by using eq. [12-4]. The angle of inclination, α_i, is often difficult to determine directly. In such a case, it is more convenient to use an exact equivalent of this expression that is based on the slope of the parabola, sl, rather than the angle:

$$C_i = H\sqrt{1 + (sl_i)^2} \qquad [12\text{-}5a]$$

At X, the left support, for example, a tangent to the parabola intersects the horizontal line through the apex at a horizontal distance from X of 20 m. The vertical distance between these points is 16 m. Thus the slope at X is $^{16}/_{20}$, or 0.8. Substituting into eq. [12-5a]:

$$C_X = H\sqrt{1 + (sl_X)^2} = (1500 \text{ kN})\sqrt{1 + (0.8)^2}$$

$$= 1\,921 \text{ kN}$$

Full Dead Load Plus Live Load Left. To find the horizontal thrust under this loading, we must add the thrust attributable to the dead load over the full span to the thrust that is generated by the live load on the left half of the span. The dead load thrust can be found as a proportional share of the thrust for the fully loaded arch:

$$H_{DL} = \frac{180 \text{ kN}_{DL}}{300 \text{ kN}_{DL+LL}} (1\,500 \text{ kN}) = 900 \text{ kN}$$

$$H_{tot} = H_{DL} + H' = 900 \text{ kN} + 266.7 \text{ kN}$$

$$= 1167 \text{ kN}$$

We have already calculated the maximum total bending moment for this loading, M'_{F-tot}, which

is entirely attributable to the live load on the left half of the span. The bending moment at any point in an eccentrically loaded arch is equal to the horizontal force in the arch times the vertical eccentricity at that point. Restating this relationship in another form and applying it to our problem, the eccentricity of the pressure line for this loading at points F and C is equal to the total bending moment divided by the thrust:

$$e = \frac{M}{H}$$

$$e_{F'-tot} = \frac{1\,333 \text{ kN·m}}{1\,167 \text{ kN}} = 1.14 \text{ m}$$

$$e_{C'-tot} = \frac{1\,667 \text{ kN·m}}{1\,167 \text{ kN}} = 1.43 \text{ m}$$

These are the small eccentricities that we found so difficult to measure accurately in Figure 12.15. They are much smaller than the eccentricities that we found in Figures 12.19 and 12.20, which ignored the effects of the uniform dead load. This is because, when calculating eccentricities for the total loading, we divide the same bending moment that was produced by the half-span live load only, by a total horizontal thrust that is now more than four times larger than it was in the earlier determination.

Next we need to find the axial compressive forces in the arch at points F and C, where the bending moments have maximum values. Eq. [12-5a] enables us to do this. To determine the slope angle of the arch at each of these points, we can utilize an interesting property of a parabola: **The slope at any point on a parabola is directly proportional to the horizontal distance of that point from the apex.** This means that because the slope at point Z is 1.0, the slope

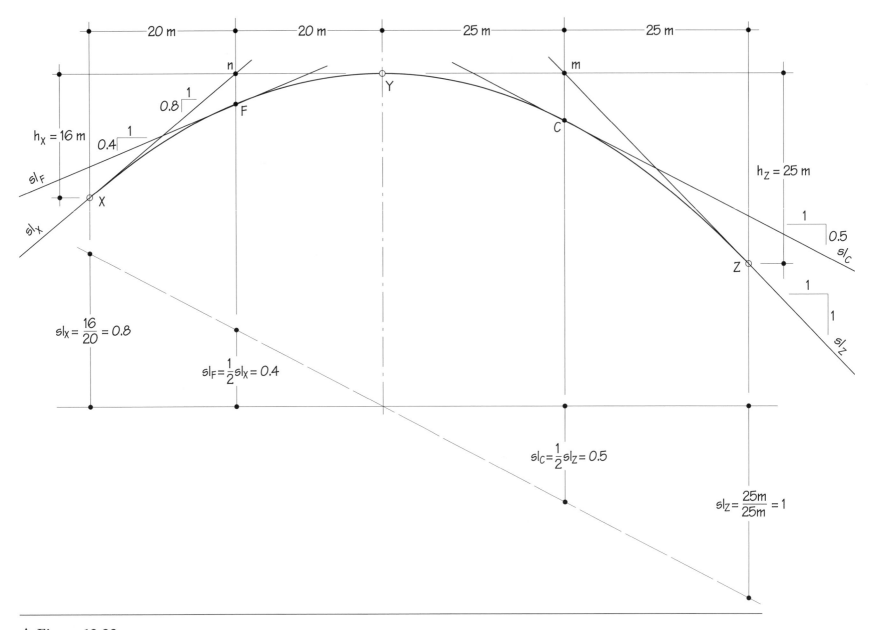

▲ *Figure 12.22*
Slopes of the parabolic axis of the arch.

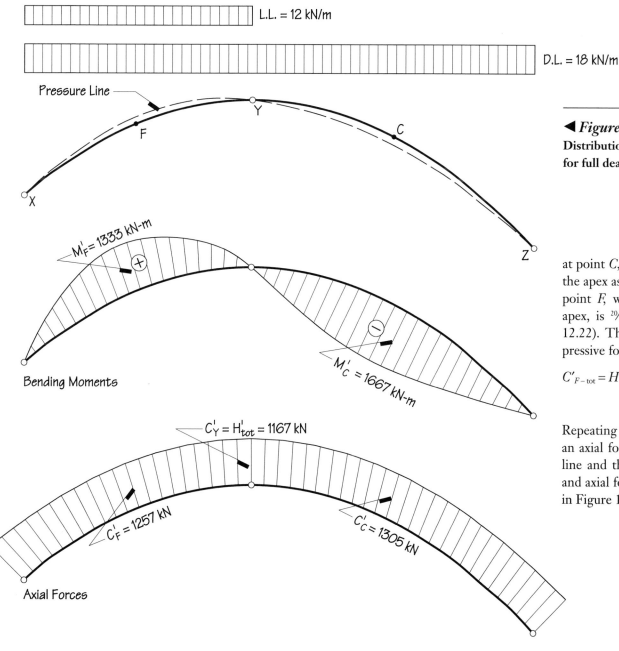

L.L. = 12 kN/m

D.L. = 18 kN/m

Pressure Line

$M'_F = 1333$ kN-m

$\oplus$

$M'_C = 1667$ kN-m

Bending Moments

$C'_Y = H'_{tot} = 1167$ kN

$C'_F = 1257$ kN

$C'_C = 1305$ kN

Axial Forces

◀ *Figure 12.23*
Distribution of axial forces and bending moments for full dead load plus live load left.

at point C, which is half as far horizontally from the apex as point Z, is 0.5. Similarly, the slope at point F, which is 20 m horizontally from the apex, is $^{20}/_{50}$ times the slope at Z, or 0.4 (Fig. 12.22). Thus we can determine the axial compressive force at F:

$$C'_{F-tot} = H'_{tot} \sqrt{1 + (sl_C)^2} = (1\,167 \text{ kN}) \sqrt{1 + (0.4)^2}$$

$$= 1\,257 \text{ kN}$$

Repeating the computation for point C, we find an axial force of about 1 305 kN. The pressure line and the distributions of bending moments and axial forces for this loading are diagrammed in Figure 12.23.

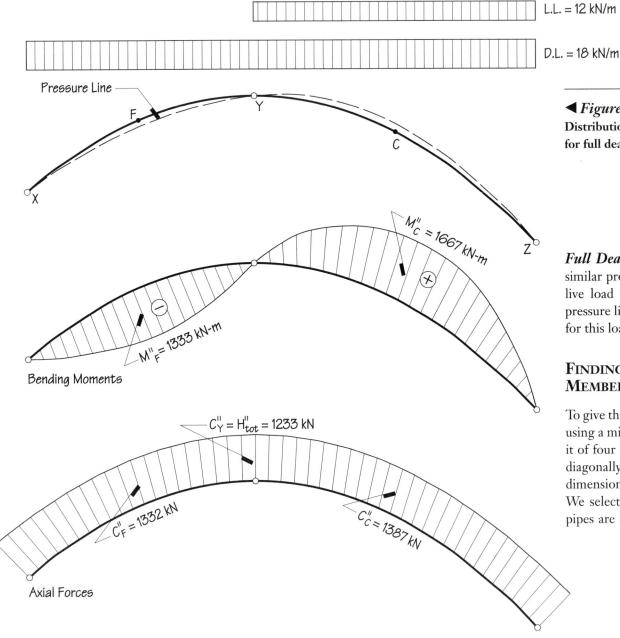

L.L. = 12 kN/m

D.L. = 18 kN/m

Pressure Line

F

Y

C

X

Z

M''_C = 1667 kN-m

(+)

(−)

M''_F = 1333 kN-m

Bending Moments

$C''_Y = H''_{tot}$ = 1233 kN

C''_F = 1332 kN

C''_C = 1387 kN

Axial Forces

◄ *Figure 12.24*
Distribution of axial forces and bending moments for full dead load plus live load right.

Full Dead Load Plus Live Load Right. A similar procedure for a full-span dead load, plus live load on the right half only, produces the pressure line, bending moments, and axial forces for this loading, as diagrammed in Figure 12.24.

FINDING THE FORCES IN THE MEMBERS OF THE ARCH

To give the arch vertical and lateral rigidity while using a minimum of material, we decide to make it of four longitudinal members that are trussed diagonally to one another in a three-dimensional, boxlike configuration (Fig. 12.25). We select steel pipes for the members because pipes are ideally shaped to resist axial compres-

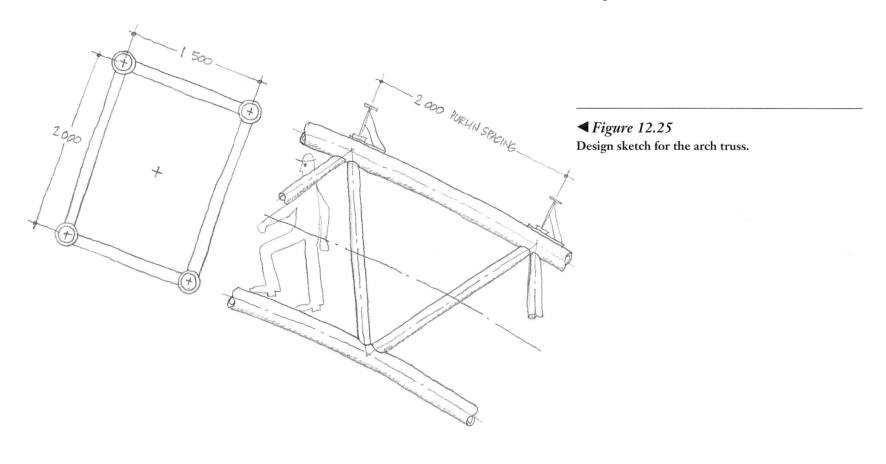

sion, and because the resulting trusses will look sleek and muscular. Pipes are also easy to paint, and they expose a minimum of surface area to corrosion. Experience-based rules of thumb for proportioning steel three-hinged arches suggest an arch depth in the range of one-fortieth to one-eightieth of the span. These relationships suggest a depth of 1.13 to 2.25 m. We would also like to have the interior of the truss readily acces-

sible for inspection and maintenance. We settle on a trial depth of 2 m and a width of 1.5 m, both measurements being taken between centers of pipes.

The most critical loading situation in the arch occurs at point C, where the action of a full dead load plus dead load right results in an axial force of 1 387 kN. This axial force is distributed equally to all four pipes, about 350 kN to each.

The bending moment at this point, 1 667 kN·m, must be matched by an internal *resisting moment* in the arch. The moment arm for the resisting moment is the truss depth of 2.0 m that we have adopted. The bending moment of 1 667 kN·m divided by the 2.0 m depth gives a force of about 833 kN in each chord. Each chord consists of two pipes, so each pipe carries a force of 833/2, or roughly 415 kN as a result of the eccentricity of the loading. This force is tensile in one pair of pipes and compressive in the other. Figure 12.26 shows how all these forces add up. The total compressive force in the upper chords is the sum of two compressive forces, 350 kN and 415 kN, which is 765 kN. The tensile force in the lower chords is the sum of 415 kN of tension and 350 kN of compression, which adds up to 65 kN of tension. With a shift of the half live load from one side of the arch to the other, the tension would shift to the upper chord, and the compression to the lower.

SIZING THE PIPE MEMBERS

Each pipe in the truss must be capable of resisting safely a maximum force of 765 kN of compression. The pipe will be restrained against buckling by the densely distributed diagonal

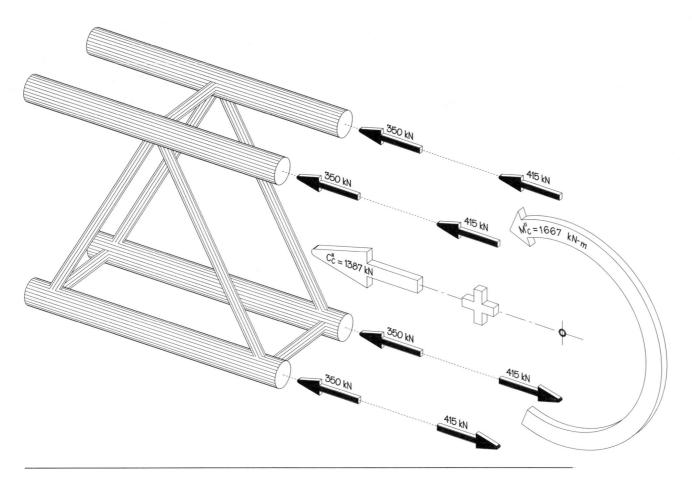

▲ *Figure 12.26*
The maximum axial force in each chord member of the truss is the sum of one-quarter of the maximum axial force in the arch plus another axial force that is attributable to the resisting moment.

members between the chords, which allows us to use the full allowable compressive stress for mild steel of 160 MPa. We calculate the required cross-sectional area:

$$A_{\text{req}} = \frac{P}{f_C} = \frac{765 \text{ kN}}{160 \text{ MPa}} = 4\,780 \text{ mm}^2$$

From the *Manual of Steel Construction* of the American Institute of Steel Construction, we choose the lightest pipe that exceeds this figure, a standard-weight pipe of 200 mm nominal diameter, which has a cross-sectional area of 5 420 mm².

The weight of this pipe is 425 N/m. To estimate the weight of the arch truss, we multiply this by 4 for the four chord members, and add 15% for the difference between the horizontal span and the length of the arch along its parabolic axis. Then we add 25% more to account for the diagonal members, hinges, and mounting brackets. This comes to about 2 400 N/m of truss span, or 240 N/m² of roof area. At the beginning of the design process, we estimated a mass for the trusses of 25 kg/m². We multiply this by 9.8 m/s² to convert it to a weight of 245 N/m²; our early estimate was very close to this

later one. The weight of the trusses is about 13% of the estimated total dead load of 1 800 N/m².

DETAILING THE ROOF

We have at least two primary options for the overall profiles of the trusses. Figure 12.27 shows the more expressive of these, crescent shapes that are based on the composite pressure lines for the half live loadings shown in Figure 12.14. Trusses of this shape would use the minimum practical amount of steel, but their inconstant geometry would make their detailed design

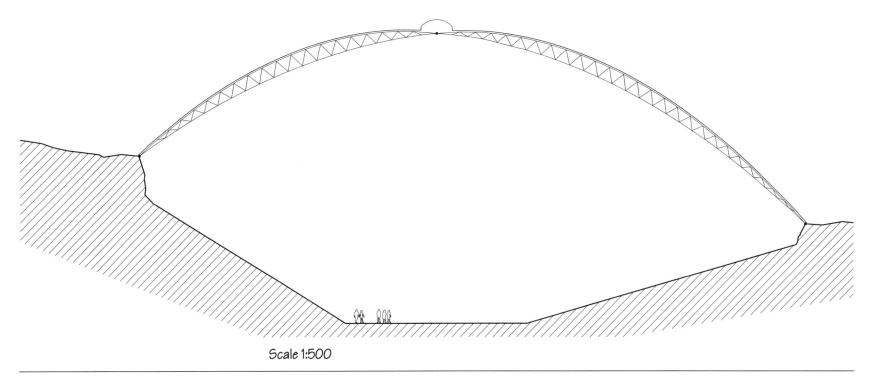

Scale 1:500

▲ *Figure 12.27*
The crescent truss option.

and assembly complex and potentially costly. The constant-depth trusses sketched in Figure 12.28 would use slightly more steel and would not appear so sleek and slender as the crescent-shaped ones, but they are likely to cost less because of the relative simplicity of their design and fabrication. We might also consider using constant-depth trusses whose axes are arcs of circles rather than parabolas. Because of their constant curvature, these would be the easiest of all to make. But they would experience slightly higher maximum bending moments than para-bolic arches because of the greater disparity between the circular arc and the pressure lines, requiring still more steel, and if they were adopted, another expressive nuance of the design would be lost.

The 10-m distance from arch to arch is too long for the corrugated steel sheet roof decking that we would like to use, which can span only about 2 m. To support this roof decking, steel *purlins* (roof beams that span across the slope) must be installed over the arches at 2-m intervals. We extend the spanning capability of these beams and simplify the joinery by making them continuous over the trusses and splicing them at points of minimum bending moment (Fig. 12.29). We have not yet learned how to assign sizes to beams; using rule-of-thumb values, we estimate that 300-mm-deep steel beam will suffice. For maximum economy and simplicity, all the purlin connections will be bolted. Because the purlins sit at varying angles to match the slopes of the arches rather than upright, they will have to be braced at the seats to prevent them from twisting.

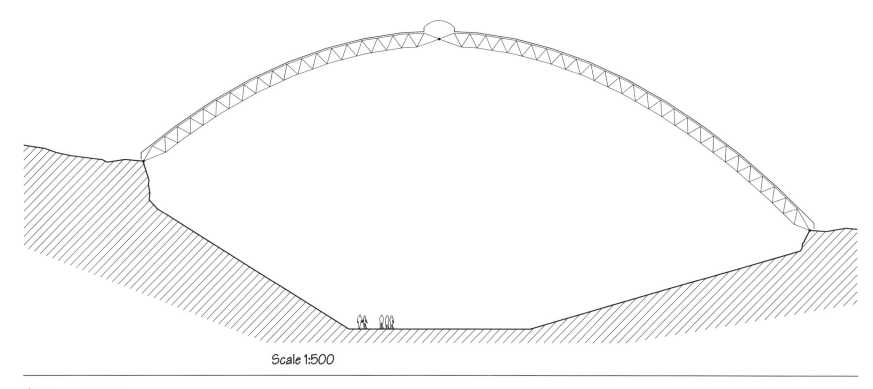

Scale 1:500

▲ *Figure 12.28*
The parallel-chord truss option.

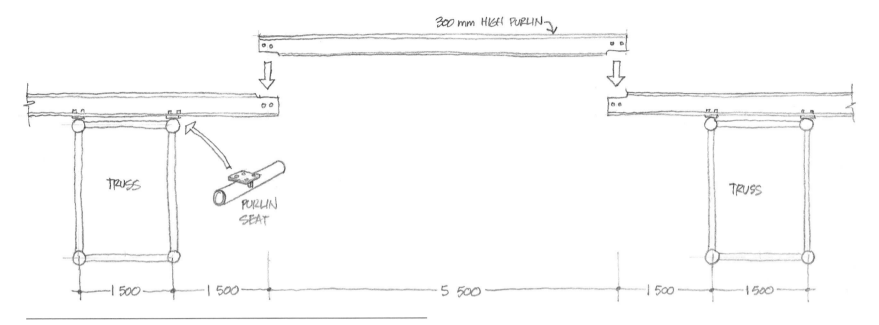

▲ Figure 12.29
First sketches of purlin details.

The decking itself is illustrated in Figure 12.30. It is formed by ridged rollers from thin steel sheet stock and is available in lengths up to 12.6 m. Long sheets of decking will allow us to minimize the number of separate pieces that must be handled, and to make each piece of decking continuous over as many as six purlin spaces for maximum structural efficiency. We will have to consult with the decking manufacturer to ascertain whether this decking is sufficiently flexible to conform to the curvature of the roof without buckling. The decking will be fastened to the purlins from above, either with welds or with *self-drilling, self-tapping screws*, which drill their own holes in the decking and purlin flange and create screw threads in the holes as they are driven with pneumatic wrenches.

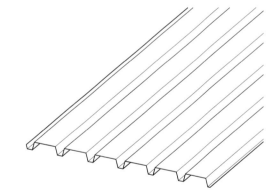

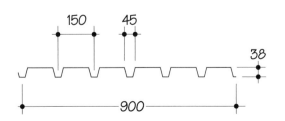

◄ Figure 12.30
Corrugated steel roof decking.

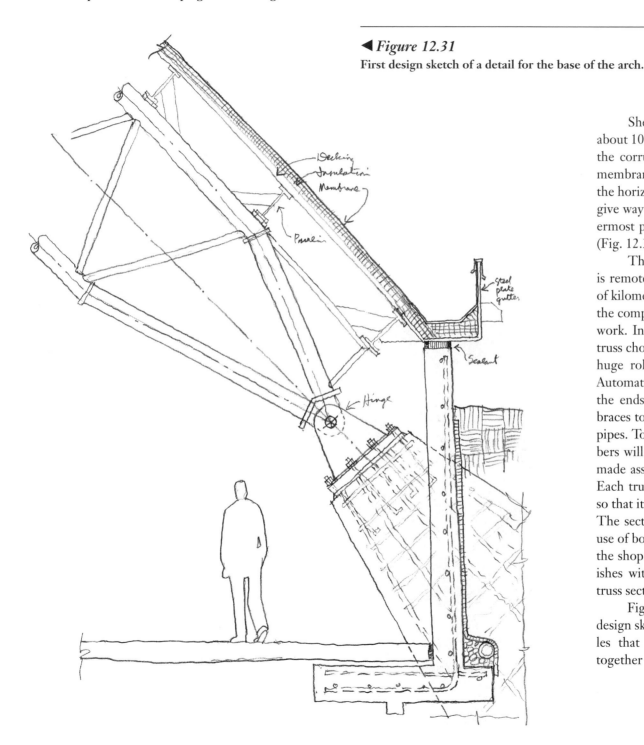

◀ *Figure 12.31*
First design sketch of a detail for the base of the arch.

Sheets of rigid thermal insulation board about 100 mm thick will be screwed to the top of the corrugated decking, and a waterproof roof membrane will be fastened to the insulation. At the horizontal edges of the roof, the decking will give way to bent steel plates, welded to the lowermost purlins, that will form rainwater gutters (Fig. 12.31).

The trusses will be *fabricated* in a shop that is remote from the site, perhaps even hundreds of kilometers away, depending on the location of the company that is the successful bidder for the work. In the *fabricator's* shop, the pipes for the truss chords will be bent to the required radii by huge rollers in a hydraulic bending machine. Automated flame cutting machinery will shape the ends of the smaller pipes for the diagonal braces to conform to the curvature of the larger pipes. To assure accurate assembly, all the members will be held rigidly in position in specially made assembly jigs while the joints are welded. Each truss will be fabricated in several sections so that it can be transported on highway trailers. The sections will be joined at the site with the use of bolted shipping joints that are prepared at the shop (Fig. 12.32). The fabrication work finishes with cleaning and prime painting of the truss sections.

Figures 12.31 and 12.33 show preliminary design sketches for the hinges. The huge knuckles that hold the hinge pins will be welded together from heavy steel plates or cast directly

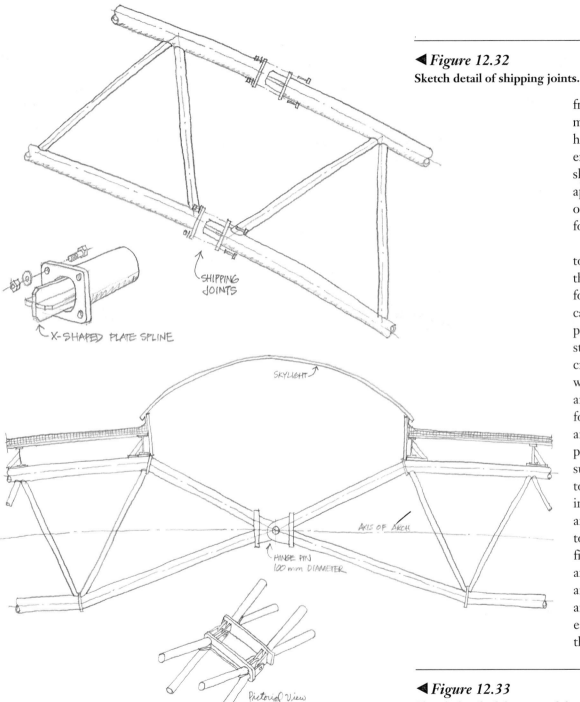

◀ *Figure 12.32*
Sketch detail of shipping joints.

from molten steel. The pins will be about 100 mm in diameter. They will be greased and driven home with sledgehammers as each truss is erected. A sealant joint at the outer walls and a slightly flexible skylight construction at the apexes allow for the very small rotations that will occur in the hinges as temperatures change, foundations settle, and live loads shift.

On the construction site, another contractor, the *erector*, takes on the work of putting up the trusses, purlins, and decking. The procedure for erection of the arches must be worked out carefully during the design process so as to avoid problems that might otherwise occur at this stage. The sections will be assembled on curving cradles at ground level. Cranes must be selected whose capacities match the weights of the half-arches, about 100 kN for the left half and 125 kN for the right half. The cranes will lift the half-arches off the cradles and onto their foundation pins. A temporary tower of steel scaffolding will support the top end of each half-arch until the top pin is inserted, after which ironworkers will install enough purlins and decking to restrain the arch against buckling. Then jacks will lower the tower, placing the arch in compression for the first time. The tower will be moved over 10 m and jacked up again to receive the next pair of arch members. It may be possible to erect the arches without the tower if two cranes can lift each pair of half-arches simultaneously and hold them in position while the top pin is inserted.

◀ *Figure 12.33*
Sketch detail of the apex of the arch.

▲ *Figure 12.34*
The basketball arena as designed.

▲*Figures 12.35*
The three-hinged steel truss arches of the Waterloo Terminal for Channel Tunnel trains are highly asymmetrical so as
to accommodate unusual site conditions in a crowded area of London. Cables are used for most tensile members. Architect:
Nicholas Grimshaw and Partners. Engineer: Anthony Hunt Associates. (Photo: Jo Reid and John Peck.)

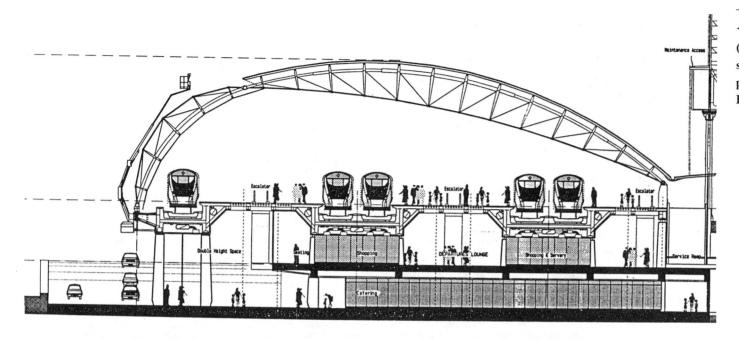

◀ *Figures 12.36*
(Diagram from Chris Wilkinson, *Supersheds*, reproduced by permission of the publisher, Butterworth-Heinemann.)

◀ *Figure 12.37*
Welded steel pipe trusses for a Royal Air Force hangar at Gaydon, England. Engineers: Ove Arup and Partners. (Photo courtesy of John Laing, PLC.)

◄ *Figure 12.38*
In this design for the Wettstein Bridge at Basel, Switzerland, architect/engineer Santiago Calatrava proposed a truss arch made of welded steel pipes. The joints at the supports are made of cast steel. (Courtesy of Santiago Calatrava, Calatrava Valls SA.)

Key Terms and Concepts

radian
hydrostatic pressure
main radius of curvature
chord
eccentricity
asymmetrical live loading
three-hinged arch

two-hinged arch
fixed-end arch
live load left
bending moment
live load right
resisting moment
purlin

self-drilling, self-tapping screws
fabrication
fabricator
erection
erector

Exercises

1. Determine both graphically and numerically the vertical position of the right support of an asymmetrical parabolic arch whose span is 288 ft, whose rise to the pin at the apex is 75 feet, and whose apex is 180 feet horizontally from the left support (Fig. 12.40).

▲ *Figure 12.39* **The Antrenas Bridge in France, constructed in 1996, uses steel pipe struts to bring the deck loads to a polygonal arch made of a large-diameter pipe. (Photo courtesy of Michel Virlogeux, Designer. Photographer: Jacques Berthellemy.)**

2. Using a scale not smaller than 1:250 and a beam compass, or working in a CAD program, investigate the following alternative shapes to the 90-m parabola developed in this chapter, each passing through the same hinge locations as the parabolic arch:

  a. The shape is a segment of a single circle.
  b. The shape is made up of two segments of circles, both of which are tangent to a horizontal line at hinge Y.
  c. The shape is made up of two segments of circles. One passes through points X, F, and Y. The other passes through Y, C, and Z.

Comment in writing on the relative suitability of each as an alternative to the parabolic shape. Given the relative ease of fabrication of a circular arch, which of these might you adopt?

3. Work out a design for dividing the parabolic trusses that we designed in this chapter into smaller sections for shipping, using a truck trailer that allows a maximum load width of 4.3 m, a maximum load length of 16 m, and a maximum load height of 4.1 m.

4. Discuss the relative merits of the two alternative placements of the apex hinge that are shown in Figure 12.41. What effect would each of these locations have on the forces in the trusses?

5. How deep must we make the arch that we designed in this chapter to eliminate any tension that might occur in its main members under the anticipated loading conditions? In general terms, how will this affect the amount of steel in the arch and the transportability of its sections?

6. Prepare a complete preliminary design for a symmetrical three-hinged steel truss arch roof for an airplane hangar whose span is 120 m and whose rise is 24 m.

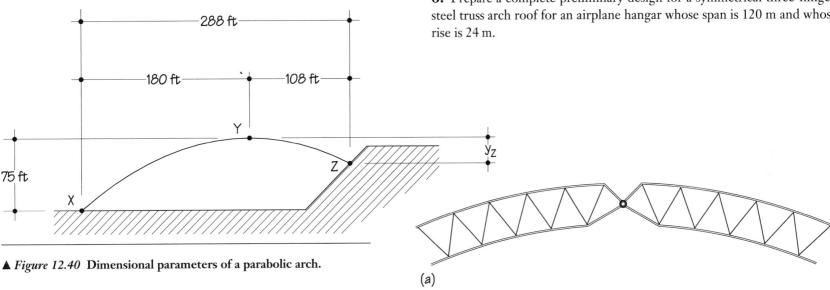

▲ *Figure 12.40* **Dimensional parameters of a parabolic arch.**

Figure 12.41 **Alternative locations for the apex hinge.** ▶

(a)

(b)

Chapter THIRTEEN

Restraining Funicular Structures

◄ The floors of the Federal Reserve Bank in Minneapolis are carried across a 270 ft (82 m) span by parabolic cables. The floor beams above the cables are supported by columns, and those below, by hangers. The cables are restrained from changing shape under nonuniform loadings by stiffening trusses at the top of the building, which also act as struts to resist the inward components of force at the ends of the cables. Architects: Gunnar Birkerts and Associates. Structural engineers: Skilling, Helle, Christiansen, Robertson. (Photo: Balthazar Korab Ltd. Photography.)

M o s t   p e o p l e   h a v e   a n   i n t u i t i v e ability to recognize the proper relationship between the form of a hanging cable and the loads that are applied to it. It takes only a glance at the cable forms in Figure 13.1 to conclude that they are more or less correct. But even a child is likely to perceive immediately that the cable forms in Figure 13.2 are absurd, because they contradict our common sense and our instinctive knowledge of funicular forms. From earliest times, unschooled builders in many regions of the world have erected funicular compression structures of stone, brick, and mud, giving vivid testimony to the human instinct for recognizing and putting to practical use the directions along which internal forces flow in solid bodies. Funicularly shaped structures, whether cables, tents, arches, domes, or vaults, transmit forces with a

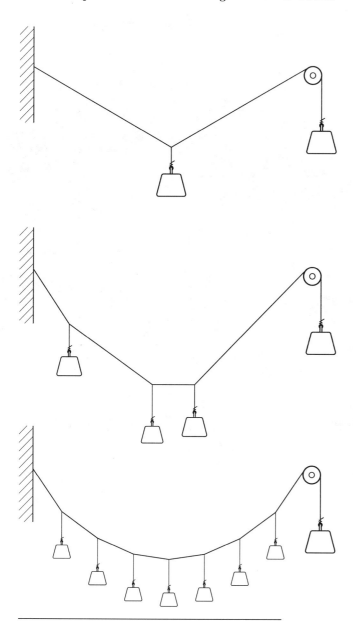

▲ *Figure 13.1*
Shapes taken naturally by loaded cables.

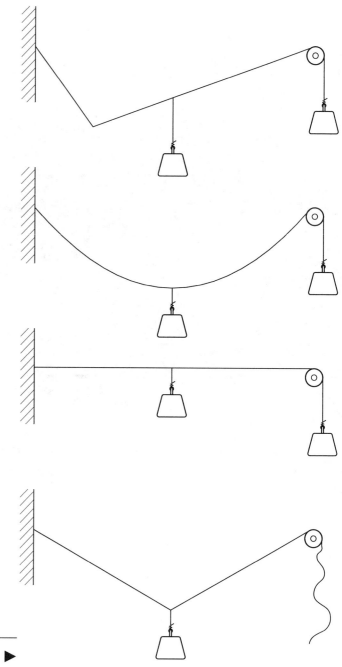

Figure 13.2 ▶
Shapes that cables cannot take.

forthright simplicity that leads not merely to a high degree of technical efficiency, but also to a satisfying perception that they are elegant and harmonious.

Today's structural materials are several times stronger in compression and hundreds of times stronger in tension than those used by yesterday's unschooled builders. We are able to build structures of relatively low self-weight that span distances and support loads many times larger than those of any previous era. For structures with the longest spans, we invariably choose funicularly shaped cables spun from high-strength steel wires. The prodigious load-carrying capacity of a hanging cable results not only from the high strength of the material, but also from the ability of the flexible cable to develop a strictly axial response to any pattern of loading by assuming a shape that is funicular for that pattern. In this way, all the material in a cable works equally to resist the axial effect of the external load. This self-adjusting action also presents us with a problem, however. In nearly all of the suspended structures we design, we cannot permit the cable to change its shape as its loading patterns change, because such changes of shape would make the structure unfit for human use. Consider a heavy railway locomotive moving across a hanging bridge (Fig. 13.3). The main suspension cables, if unrestrained, will change shape constantly to assume a maximum curvature at the point where they bear the load of the locomotive. In so doing, they will cause undulations in the deck that will make it impossible for the locomotive to proceed and that may well lead to the total disintegration of the bridge.

The true art of designing a funicular arch or cable structure lies not so much in finding the basic form, which is simple enough to do, but in contriving a suitable means to restrain the funicular members against changes of shape that are caused by loadings for which the members are not funicular. Wind creates pressure on the windward side of a curved or sloping roof and exerts a suction on the leeward side, then changes direction, creating constantly shifting

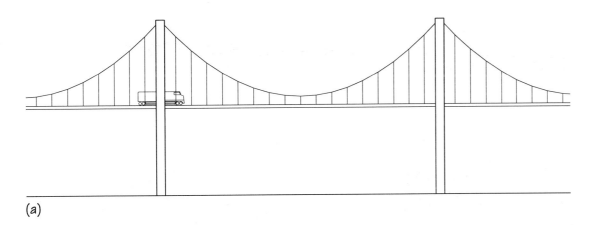

(a)

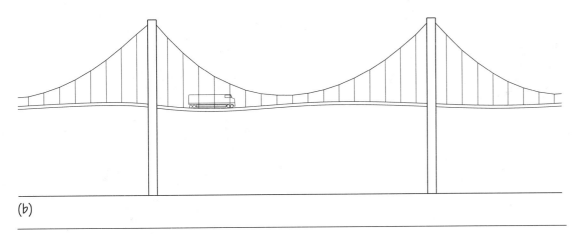

(b)

▲ *Figure 13.3*
Deformation of an unrestrained hanging bridge by a heavy locomotive.

Figure 13.4 ▶
Restraining hanging structures using cables.

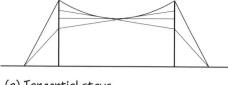

(a) Tangential stays

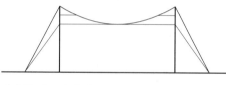

(b) Vertical stays

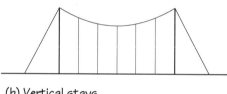

(c) Horizontal stays

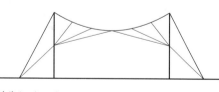

(d) Inclined stays

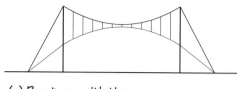

(e) Prestress with ties

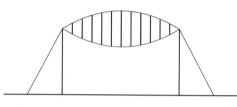

(f) Prestress with struts

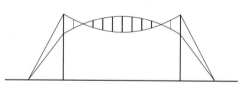

(g) Prestress with ties and struts

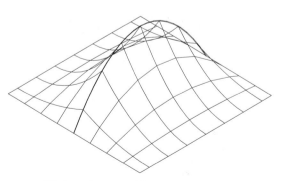

(h) Anticlastic cable net

loading patterns, none of which matches the loads for which the supporting arch or cable was shaped. Wind can scour snow off one portion of a roof, leaving it without any live load, and deposit snow in heavy drifts on other portions. Floor loading patterns change with every change of furnishings in a room and with the daily migrations of the occupants of a building. Bridge decks are sometimes empty of vehicles, sometimes full, and most often loaded with vehicles in random locations. Irregular loadings may also be created by vibrations induced by wind or earthquakes. No arch or cable can be given a shape that is funicular for all such conditions. Instead, we must base the shape on the predominant loading pattern, which is most often the dead load, and provide structural restraint to assist the funicular element in supporting other patterns of loads.

This problem and several of its solutions have been alluded to in previous chapters. Our purpose here is to conceptualize and summarize the full range of potential solutions to the restraint problem and to illustrate how they have been employed in a variety of actual structures. Figure 13.4 shows a number of ways of restraining a hanging cable by using auxiliary cables.

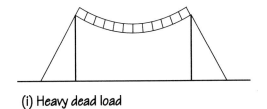

(i) Heavy dead load

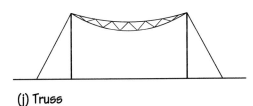

(j) Truss

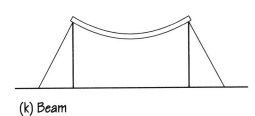

(k) Beam

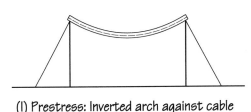

(l) Prestress: Inverted arch against cable

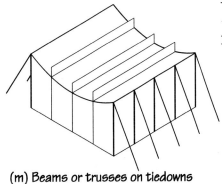

(m) Beams or trusses on tiedowns

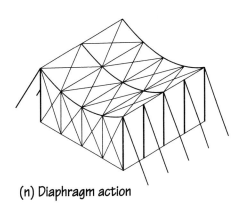

(n) Diaphragm action

◀ *Figure 13.5*
Restraining hanging structures using means other than cables.

The purpose of the auxiliary cables in each example is to restrain the primary cable from changing its shape when its loading pattern changes. The options in Figure 13.5 address the same problem, but include elements other than cables. Figure 13.6 relates to the problem of restraining a planar arch, and Figure 13.7 shows still other alternatives that present themselves when the arched structure assumes a third dimension to become a vault, dome, or shell.

Many structures combine a flat floor or roof deck with a funicular supporting element, either an arch or a cable. Figure 13.8 shows that this combination opens further possibilities for restraint, some based on stiffening the funicular member, some on stiffening the deck, and some on adding diagonal braces in the spaces between the deck and the supporting member.

These five figures present a wide range of potential solutions to the restraint problem. They may be used to review options when confronting a particular design. Rather than discuss in the abstract each option in the diagrams, however, it will be more productive and enjoyable to view how the designers of a number of actual structures have employed these solutions.

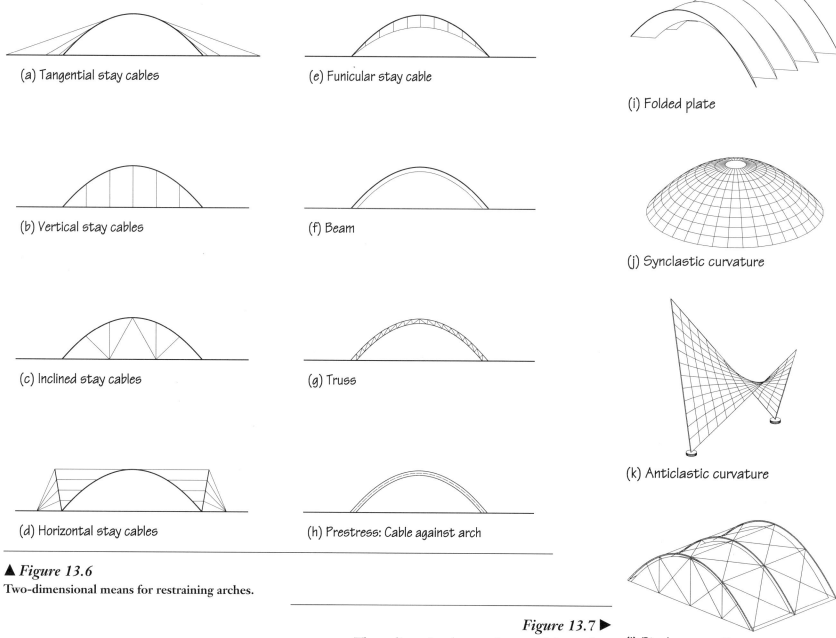

(a) Tangential stay cables

(b) Vertical stay cables

(c) Inclined stay cables

(d) Horizontal stay cables

(e) Funicular stay cable

(f) Beam

(g) Truss

(h) Prestress: Cable against arch

(i) Folded plate

(j) Synclastic curvature

(k) Anticlastic curvature

(l) Diaphragm action

▲ *Figure 13.6*
Two-dimensional means for restraining arches.

Figure 13.7 ▶
Three-dimensional means for restraining arches.

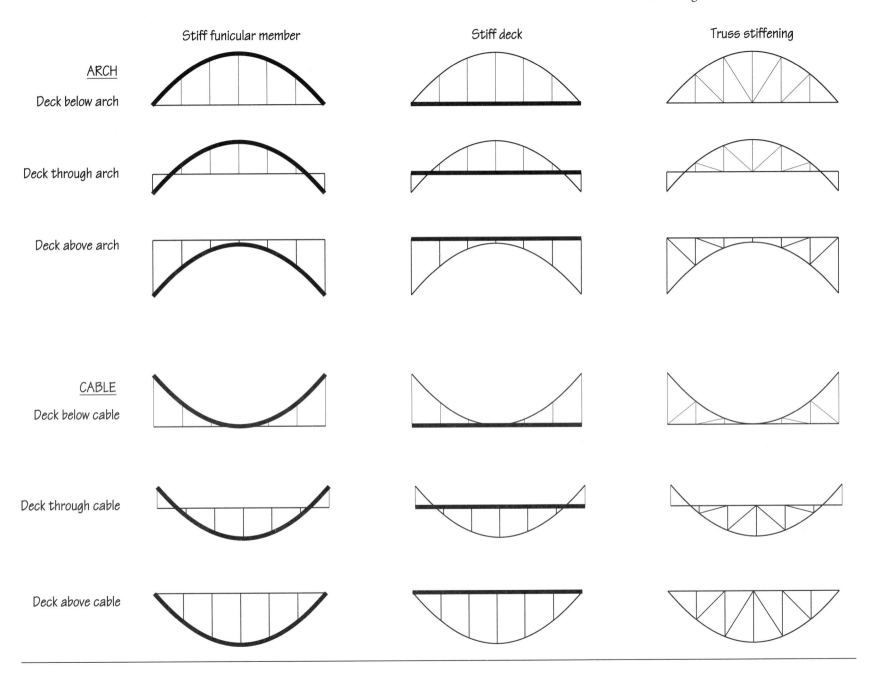

▲ *Figure 13.8*
Means for restraining funicular members in structures that include a flat deck.

RESTRAINT BY STAYS AND STRUTS

Figure 13.9(a) shows the shape of a cable that supports a uniformly distributed load. In (b), we see the effect of applying a live load to only the left half of the cable. The right half becomes straight, while the left half takes on a greater curvature than before. Point *C*, which was formerly in the middle of the span, has moved to the left. If the live load shifts to the right half of the cable only, (c), the entire shape reverses, and *C* moves to the right. A logical response to this situation is to install horizontal stay cables that prevent horizontal displacements of point *C* at midspan (Fig. 13.9[d]). If different loadings occur on the two halves of the main cable, the stay cable on the less loaded side of the span intervenes with a pulling force that corresponds to the difference in loads.

Although this simple restraint system will reduce greatly the changes in the shape of the main cable under nonuniform loads, it cannot prevent changes resulting from loads that are localized in an area that does not correspond to a half-span. By adding tangential stays at suitable intervals across the whole span, as diagrammed in Figure 13.10, we can make the main cable as rigid as we wish against any pattern of loads, no matter how random. When the loading pattern is compatible with the shape of the main cable, the stays are inactive, but they react instantly to any change in loading conditions.

In a similar manner, stay cables in several other patterns can also serve to restrain a suspension cable (Fig. 13.4[b–d]) or an arch (Fig. 13.6[a–e]). In accordance with the principle of inversion, compression struts can replace the stay cables in any of these patterns. As an exam-

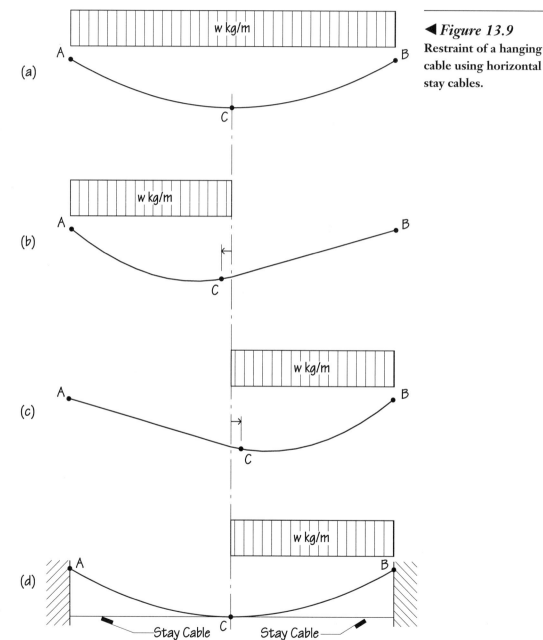

◀ *Figure 13.9*
Restraint of a hanging cable using horizontal stay cables.

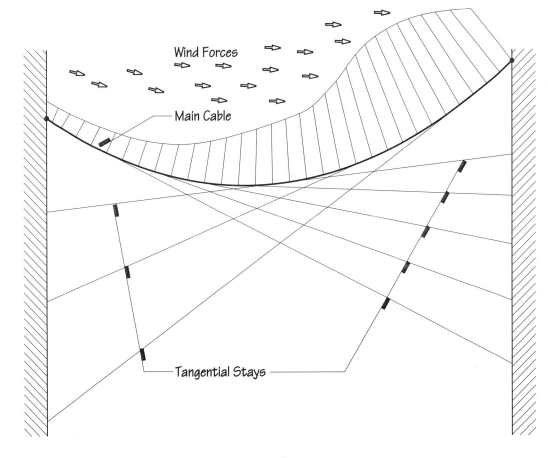

Wind Forces

Main Cable

Tangential Stays

◀ *Figure 13.10*
Restraint of a hanging cable using tangential stay cables.

ple, consider a concrete bridge on the Italian Autostrada del Sole that is supported by funicular arches (Fig. 13.11). Although parabolic in its larger outline, each arch is actually a polygon whose vertices coincide with the points at which the vertical columns bring the deck loads to the arch. Horizontal concrete struts between these vertices restrain the arches from changing shape as heavy vehicles move across the spans. It is instructive to compare the forms of these arches above the top line of horizontal struts with the arch form of the Salginatobel Bridge (see Fig. 13.28).

The four parallel steel arches of the Broadgate Office Building in London are each restrained by two inclined steel stays (Fig.

◀ *Figure 13.11*
Bridge on the Autostrada del Sole between Bologna and Firenze, Italy, 1960. Engineers: Arrigo Carè and Giorgio Gianelli. (Photo from the collection of Fritz Leonhardt, reproduced by permission.)

13.12). Analysis by the structural engineers of the building showed that these two stays alone, when considered together with the stiffness of the arch itself, were sufficient to prevent excessive arch deflections under any anticipated shift in loading.

RESTRAINT BY PRESTRESSING CABLES

The circular roof of the Utica Municipal Auditorium, diagrammed in Figure 13.13, is a so-called *bicycle wheel* structure. The gravity loads are supported by a lower set of radial cables that span between a central tension ring and a compression ring at the top of the perimeter wall. (A compression ring is a full-circle horizontal arch. Its circular shape is funicular for the radial loading exerted by the cables.) To restrain these cables against movement caused by wind uplift, vibrations, and asymmetrical snow loads, an upper set of radial cables apply downward forces through vertical tubular steel struts to prestress the lower cables. The sags of the two sets of cables are dif-

▲ *Figure 13.12*
Broadgate Office Building, London. Architects and engineers: Skidmore, Owings & Merrill. (Photo: Niall Clutton, Arcaid.)

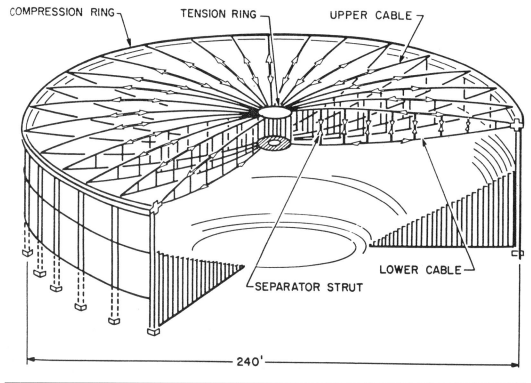

▲ *Figure 13.13*
Cutaway diagram of the Utica Municipal Auditorium roof structure. The span is 240 ft (73 m). The compression ring is made of reinforced concrete, and the tension rings of steel. The cables were prestressed by jacking apart the tension rings. The roof was prefabricated and erected in two and a half weeks, using only one tower of scaffolding. (Courtesy of Thornton-Tomasetti Engineers/The LZA Group, Inc.)

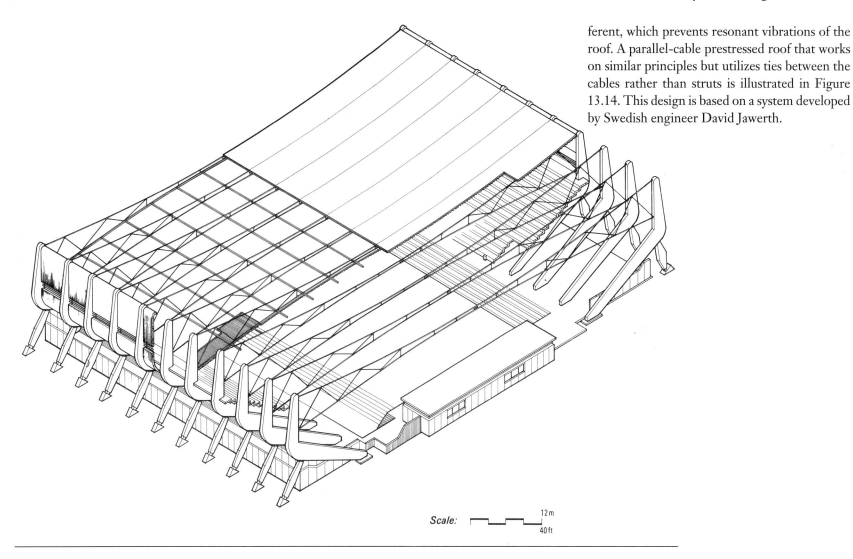

ferent, which prevents resonant vibrations of the roof. A parallel-cable prestressed roof that works on similar principles but utilizes ties between the cables rather than struts is illustrated in Figure 13.14. This design is based on a system developed by Swedish engineer David Jawerth.

Scale: 12 m / 40 ft

▲ *Figure 13.14*
In this unbuilt design for a sports center in Sokoto, Nigeria, engineer V. Mosco proposes a roof in which each suspension cable is stabilized by a cable of opposing curvature that pulls downward from beneath it. The curvatures of the two cables are slightly different so as to prevent resonant vibrations. The boomerang-shaped elements support both the cables and the seating for 4000 spectators, each serving to balance the other. The span is 73 m (240 ft). (From Andrew Orton, *The Way We Build Now,* **reproduced by permission of the publisher, Chapman and Hall.)**

◀ *Figure 13.15*
The hanging roof of the Ingalls Hockey Rink,
Yale University, built 1956–1959 by
Eero Saarinen, architect, with structural
engineers Severud-Elstad-Krueger.
(Photo: Edward Allen.)

Figure 13.16 ▶
Section drawings of the Ingalls Rink. The
arch spans 230 ft (70 m). The maximum
width of the building is 180 ft (55 m).
(Reproduced by permission of the publisher
from *Eero Saarinen On His Work*, copyright
© 1962 by Yale University.)

▼ *Figure 13.17*
Sports Arena for 8000 spectators, Maracaibo,
Venezuela, 1967. Designed by the Ministry of
Public Works.

Anticlastic curvature of a three-dimensional cable net is another way of restraining cables with prestressing forces. In the arena roof of Figures 13.15 and 13.16, a longitudinal parabolic arch of reinforced concrete supports transverse loadbearing cables that span to curving perimeter walls. Longitudinal cables pull downward on the loadbearing cables to restrain them. This principle is more easily seen in another arena roof, Figure 13.17, in which the opposing curvatures of the two sets of cables are more pronounced. The cables and fabric membranes of

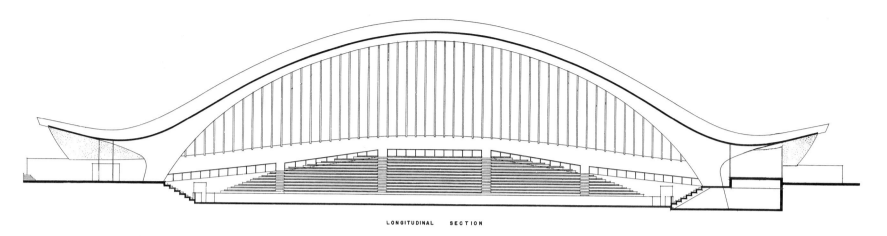

LONGITUDINAL   SECTION

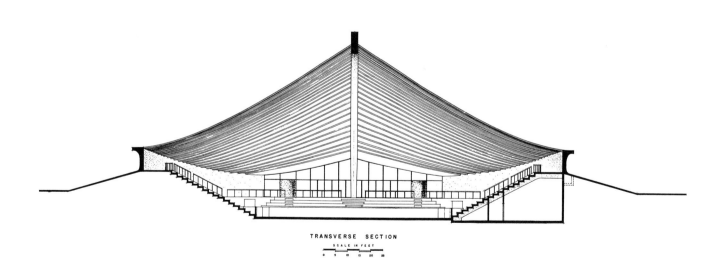

TRANSVERSE   SECTION

SCALE IN FEET

0   5   10   15   20   25

▲ *Figures 13.18 and 13.19*
Pier 6 Concert Pavilion, Baltimore, 1992. FTL architects. Buro Happold and M.G. McLaren, engineers.
(Photos: © 89 Durston Saylor.)

the tent roof photographed in Figures 13.18 and 13.19 are tensioned into anticlastic surfaces that are as poetic as they are rigid.

RESTRAINT OF A CABLE BY AN INVERTED ARCH

The principle of invertibility tells us that it is theoretically possible to replace a hanging cable

in any structural system with its inverted shape in the form of an arch. In the *stress ribbon* footbridge in Figure 13.20, the lower cable in the system shown in Figure 13.14 is replaced by what is, in effect, an upside-down concrete arch that follows the same curvature as the suspension cables. The cables prestress the arch, and the arch prestresses the cables, creating a rigid structure. To avoid excessive inclinations of the

bridge deck, the sag is minimal and the cable forces are extremely high, requiring strong end anchorages.

A much higher sag ratio was used in the stress ribbon roof of the Dulles Airport terminal building (Fig. 13.21), leading to more modest cable forces. As in the stress ribbon bridge, the inverted arch of the concrete roof deck serves to restrain the cables. The massive, outward-

▲ *Figure 13.20*
Stress ribbon footbridge, Prague-Troja, Czech Republic, 1984. The main span is 96 m (315 ft), with a sag of only 1.86 m (6.1 ft). Dopravni Stavby, engineers. (Photo: Jiri Strasky, Ph.D., P.E.)

▲ *Figure 13.21*
Dulles Airport, Chantilly, Virginia, under construction in 1962. The span is 160 ft (49 m). Architect: Eero Saarinen. Engineers: Ammann and Whitney. (Photo: Balthazar Korab Ltd. Photography.)

leaning concrete columns make a gesture of balancing the inward pull of the roof, creating a visually powerful architectural expression that reflects the forces in the structure.

RESTRAINT BY STIFFENING THE FUNICULAR MEMBER

Arches for long spans are invariably made of laminated wood, steel, or reinforced concrete, all of which are materials that are inherently resistant to bending. This stiffness is frequently employed to resist changes of shape in the arch. The laminated wood roof arches in Figure 13.22 are designed to withstand both axial compression and the maximum expected bending moment resulting from asymmetrical snow and wind loads. The reinforced concrete barrel vault in Figure 13.23 does not have to be very thick to resist axial loads, but deep concrete ribs have been added to stiffen the roof against nonuniform loadings. The steel arches in Figures 13.24 and 13.25 are trussed to restrain them from changing shape under moving loads.

In Figure 13.26, we study once again the shapes taken by a cable under a uniformly distributed load, (a), and loads distributed on either half of the cable only, (b) and (c). If auxiliary cables were added to create the form shown in (d), the curving cables would be able to maintain their shapes under any of the loading conditions shown. In an actual structure, the presence of an unvarying dead load would suggest replacement of the straight cable segments with ones that are curved funicularly for the dead load only, thus arriving at the basic form of the suspension

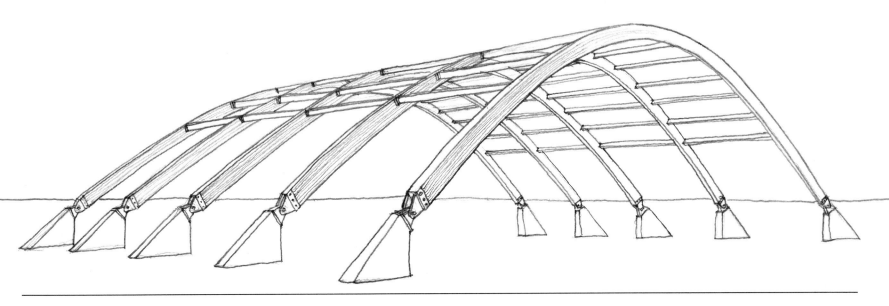

▲ *Figure 13.22*
Laminated wood arches. (Drawing by Edward Allen.)

▼ *Figure 13.23*
U.S. Navy hangar, San Diego, California. Engineers: Roberts and Schaffer Co. (Photo courtesy of Stedman & Dyson, structural engineers.)

▼ *Figure 13.24*
The arch of the Bayonne Bridge, completed in 1931, is restrained from changing shape by its steel trussing, which allows the suspended deck to be very thin. The span is 1675 ft (520 m). The bridge connects Bayonne, New Jersey, with Staten Island, New York. Engineers: Ammann and Dana. (Photo: Port Authority of New York and New Jersey.)

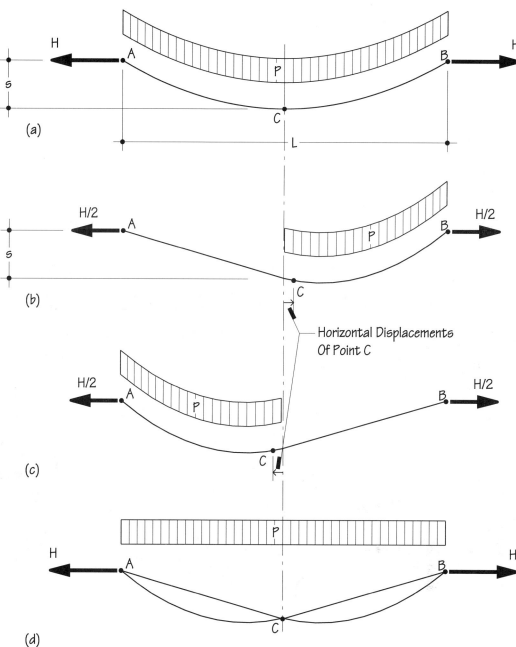

(a)

(b)

Horizontal Displacements Of Point C

(c)

(d)

▲ *Figure 13.25*
The New River Gorge Bridge, built in Fayette County, West Virginia, in 1977, spans the longest distance of any arch in the world, 1700 ft (520 m). The deep, stiff, trussed construction of the arch allows the deck trusses to be shallow. (Photo courtesy of Michael Baker Corporation.)

Figure 13.26 ▶
Restraint of a cable using a double cable configuration.

members in the bridge shown in Figure 13.27. In this structure, the designer has also stiffened the funicular members by making them into steel trusses. Hinges at the supports and the apex allow for the system to move slightly in response to temperature changes and foundation settlement.

If Figure 13.27 is viewed upside down, its form resembles that of the famous Salginatobel Bridge, Figure 13.28, whose graceful shape originated from a similar line of reasoning. Robert Maillart designed this bridge using the graphical methods that are presented in this book (Fig. 13.29). Figure 13.30 shows that the crescent-shaped concrete stiffening walls that converge at the three hinges of this bridge are integral to an arch structure that takes the shape of an inverted double T (sections *a-a* and *b-b*). This configuration is often referred to as a *box arch*. The pressure line of a uniform loading on the bridge, shown clearly in Figure 13.29, runs within the hollow space of the open-topped box, at about a third the height of the crescent at every point in the stiffening wall. If the live load is concentrated on the opposite half of the bridge only, the pressure line drops slightly, and if the live load is all concentrated on the same half, it rises slightly, but it always remains well within the confines of the crescents. Because the bridge is shaped so intelligently, its stresses remain very low regardless of the loading condition, and the steel reinforcing bars, none of which is larger in diameter than a human thumb, have little function except to resist temperature and shrinkage stresses.

As was the case with most of his bridges, Maillart had to submit his design for the Salginatobel Bridge to a competitive process in which it was judged against designs by other engineers. To be selected for construction, his bridge had to

▲ *Figure 13.27*
Tower Bridge, London, 1886–1894, John Wolfe Barry, engineer. The hanging span is 270 ft (82 m). (Photo copyright Will & Deni McIntyre, Photo Researchers, Inc.)

▲ *Figure 13.28*
Salginatobel Bridge, Schiers, Switzerland, Robert Maillart, engineer, 1930. The span is 90 m (295 ft). (Photo: ETH-Bibliothek, Zürich.)

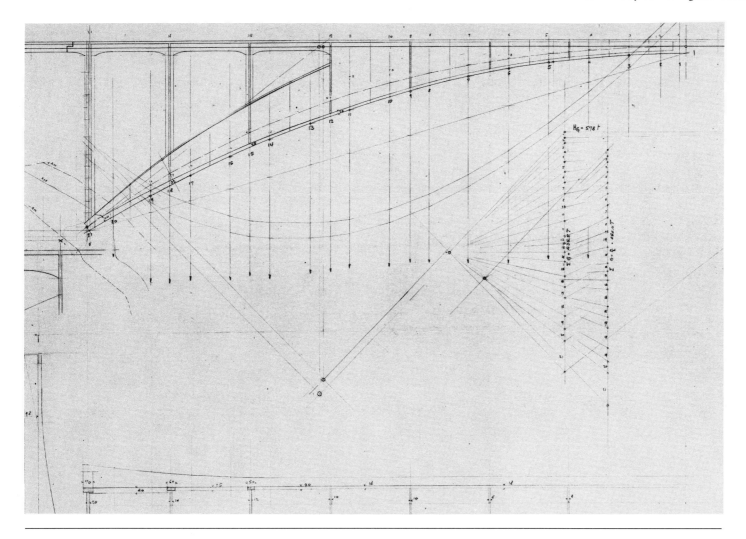

▲ *Figure 13.29*
One of Maillart's design development drawings for the Salginatobel Bridge, from the Maillart Archives, ETH, Zürich.

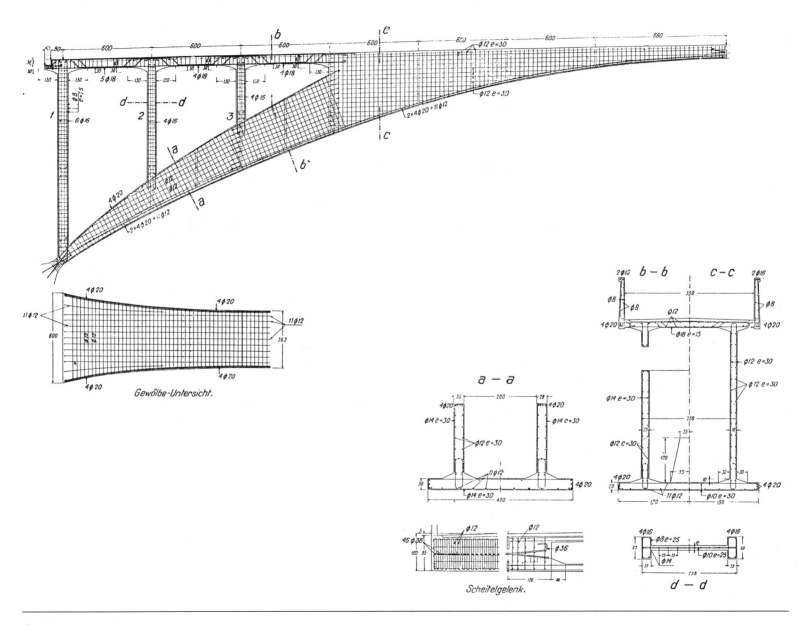

▲ *Figure 13.30*
Details of the Salginatobel Bridge. (From Max Bill, *Robert Maillart*, Zürich, Verlag für Architektur, 1949.)

be more economical than the alternatives. Much of its economy comes from its efficient shape. Also important in the low cost of the bridge was the economy of its construction process. The ingenious wooden scaffolding (Fig. 13.31) was designed to support only the weight of the wet concrete for the bottom slab of the arch and to restrain this arch slab from changing shape during the remainder of the construction process. In this way, the arch slab itself was able to provide the required temporary support for the rest of the formwork and concrete in the bridge, allowing the scaffolding to be much lighter and less costly than usual.

RESTRAINT BY STIFFENING THE DECK

The most common way of restraining the cables in a suspension bridge is to deepen the deck into a *rigidity beam*, which in most cases is actually a truss (Fig. 13.32). The rigidity of the beam enters into action only when the bridge is loaded

▼ *Figure 13.31*
Scaffolding to support the concrete formwork for the Salginatobel Bridge. (Photo: ETH-Bibliothek, Zürich.)

▼ *Figure 13.32*
A trussed rigidity beam restrains the San Francisco-Oakland Bay Bridge, completed in 1936 by engineers C. H. Purcell and Glenn B. Woodruff. (Photo: Don Knight, courtesy of National Archive.)

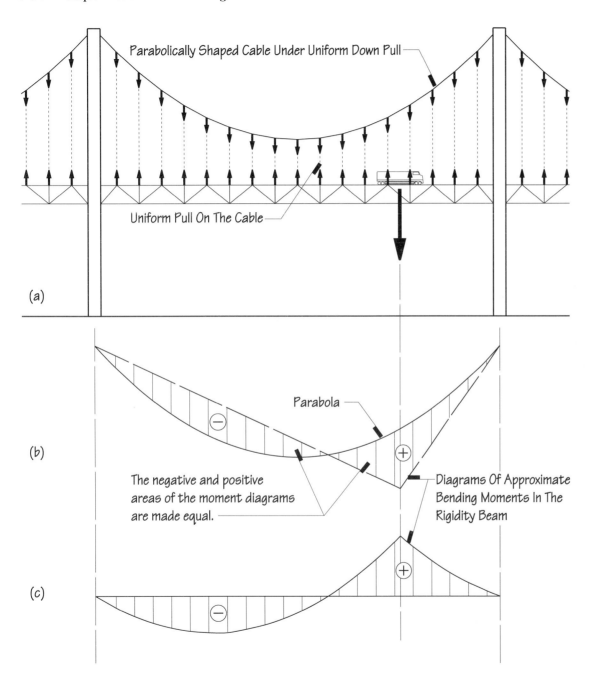

(a)

(b)

(c)

Parabolically Shaped Cable Under Uniform Down Pull

Uniform Pull On The Cable

Parabola

The negative and positive areas of the moment diagrams are made equal.

Diagrams Of Approximate Bending Moments In The Rigidity Beam

◀ *Figure 13.33*
Determining the bending moments in a rigidity beam.

in a manner that is incompatible with the shape of its cable; otherwise, a cable subjected to loads compatible with its shape deforms much less than the beam and therefore absorbs all such loads. The only role of the rigidity beam is to absorb excessive loads in certain regions of the bridge and carry them to less loaded regions. This relocation of loads makes the vertical pulling action on the cables compatible with their parabolic shape.

Figure 13.33 illustrates the nature of the stabilizing effect of a rigidity beam on the shape of a cable of a bridge that is subjected to a single large load, such as a locomotive, without taking into account any dead load. The beam transforms the single load into a distributed set of equal vertical pulls that are compatible with the shape of the cable (a). All the differences between the actual loading and the loading that corresponds to the shape of the cable are absorbed by the beam. An approximate diagram of the intensity of the bending moments in the beam may be constructed by superimposing a shape that is funicular for the single load on the shape of the cable in such a way that the negative and positive areas between the shapes are equal (b, c). In reality, the uniformly distributed dead load of the deck is sufficiently large that it contributes a great deal to the stabilization of the shape of the cable and considerably reduces the role of the rigidity beam.

◀ *Figure 13.34*
Burgo Paper Mill, Pier Luigi Nervi, engineer. (Photo: Professor Dr. Chris H. Luebkeman.)

The application of rigidity trusses to a hanging building is illustrated in the photograph at the beginning of this chapter and in Figures 13.34 and 13.35. The factory building in the latter illustrations was designed by Pier Luigi Nervi to house a very long machine for making paper. It was anticipated that the factory would be expanded over time with the addition of more such machines side by side, and it was important not to obstruct the space between the machines with columns. The concrete heads of the columns are shaped in such a way that each cable is anchored to a flat surface that lies perpendicular to its axis.

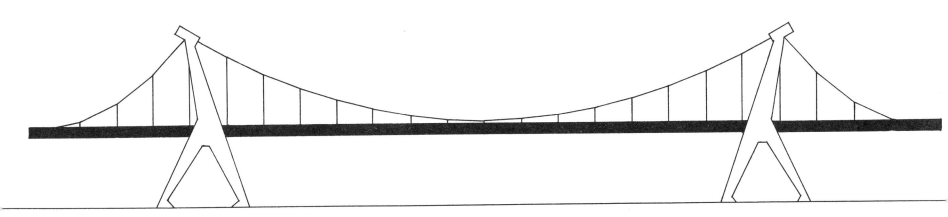

▲ *Figure 13.35*
Diagram of Burgo Paper Mill, Pier Luigi Nervi, engineer. The solid black area indicates the trussed rigidity beam. (Drawing by Edward Allen.)

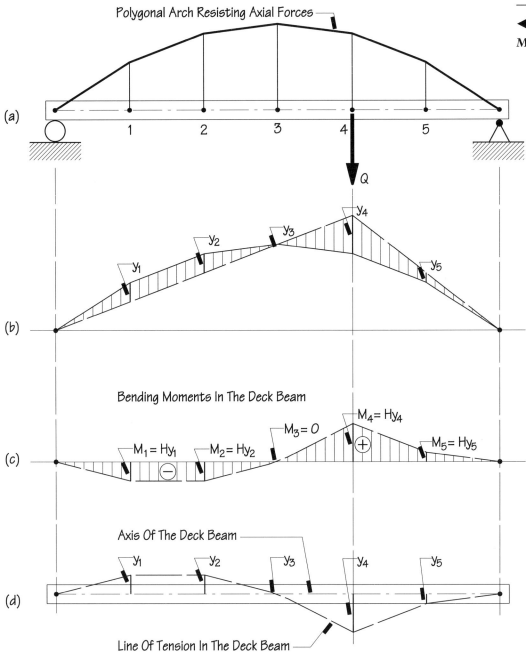

(a) Polygonal Arch Resisting Axial Forces

1 2 3 4 5

Q

(b) y_1 y_2 y_3 y_4 y_5

(c) Bending Moments In The Deck Beam

$M_1 = Hy_1$ $M_2 = Hy_2$ $M_3 = 0$ $M_4 = Hy_4$ $M_5 = Hy_5$

(d) Axis Of The Deck Beam

y_1 y_2 y_3 y_4 y_5

Line Of Tension In The Deck Beam

◀ *Figure 13.36*
Moments in a deck-stiffened arch.

The principle of the rigidity beam is applied to arched structures in the form of the *deck-stiffened arch* (Fig. 13.36). Robert Maillart built many of his shorter-span bridges as deck-stiffened arches; one of these is pictured in Figure 8.18 and in Figure 13.37. Notice that the arch itself is a thin slab, designed for axial forces only, that follows a funicular profile. The deck is a deep reinforced concrete rigidity beam.

RESTRAINT BY TRUSSING THE FUNICULAR MEMBER AND THE DECK

The bridges in Figure 13.38 are supported by very slender steel arches. The arches are restrained against changing shape by the addition of diagonal members between the arches and the shallow deck to create a very rigid structure. With pinned connections at both ends, these bridges function as restrained arches, and their form is completely logical. If one end were put on rollers, however, the arch action would disappear and the bridge would function as a truss in bending. In this case, the most efficient form for the bridge would be a parabolic truss whose depth varies from zero at the supports to a maximum at midspan, just the opposite of the actual curvature of these bridges.

RESTRAINT BY DIAPHRAGM ACTION

Restraint of a cable roof by diaphragm action is illustrated in Figure 11.19 and is described in detail in the accompanying text.

▲ *Figure 13.37*
Schwandbach Bridge, Switzerland, 1933, Robert Maillart, engineer. The arch slab is only 200 mm (8 in.) thick and spans 37.4 m (123 ft). (Photo: ETH-Bibliothek, Zürich.)

Figure 13.38 ▶
Navajo Bridges, Grand Canyon, Arizona. The bridge in the background spans 616 ft (188 m). It was built in 1929 by engineer R. A. Hanson. The new span of 726 ft (221 m) (foreground) was completed in 1995 by Cannon and Associates, Consulting Engineers. Because the depth of the canyon at this point is 457 ft (142 m), temporary scaffolding to support the bridges during construction was not a practical possibility. The trussed configuration made it possible to construct each bridge by cantilevering from the supports at both ends. (Photo: Richard Strange Photography.)

RESTRAINT BY FOLDED PLATE STIFFENING

Pier Luigi Nervi stiffened the thin concrete vaults of his Turin Exhibition Building by folding them into corrugations (Figs. 13.39–13.41). The folds increase the effective depth of the vaults many times over and avoid the need for stiffening ribs. The detail section in Figure 13.41 shows the ingenuity of the construction. The roof was prefabricated as a set of short elements, each 2.5 m wide, made of what Nervi called *ferro-cemento*, a very thin, almost fibrous construction that consists of multiple closely-spaced layers of fine wire mesh impregnated with portland cement plaster. Lateral diaphragms of the same material prevent the thin sections from buckling. After these prefabricated elements were placed on temporary scaffolding, longitudinal reinforcing bars were installed over the ridges and valleys, and concrete was poured in these two regions to knit the elements into a single, strong roof shell.

The rice storage silo by Eladio Dieste (Figs. 13.42 and 13.43) is a thin parabolic vault made of hollow clay tiles. Reinforcing bars in the mortar joints between the tiles strengthen the

It is very difficult to explain the reason for our immediate approval of forms which come to us from a physical world with which we, seemingly, have no direct tie whatsoever. Why do these forms satisfy and move us in the same manner as natural things such as flowers, plants, and landscapes?

PIER LUIGI NERVI

◀ *Figure 13.39*
Turin Exhibition Hall, 1949, Pier Luigi Nervi, engineer. (© Joe Viesti, Photographer, courtesy of Viesti Associates, Inc.)

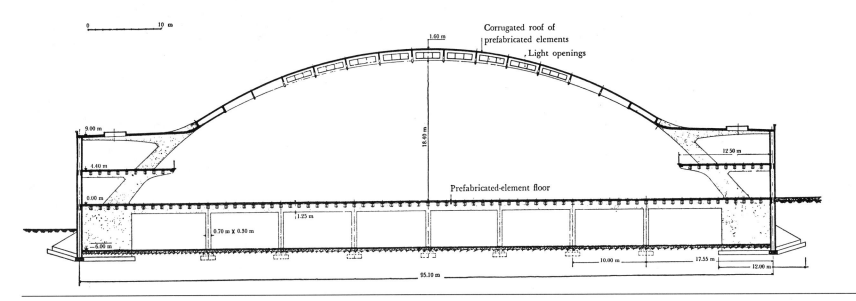

▲ *Figure 13.40*

Cross section, Turin Exhibition Hall, 1949, Pier Luigi Nervi, engineer. (Source: Pier Luigi Nervi, *Structures*, New York, F. W. Dodge Corp., 1956.)

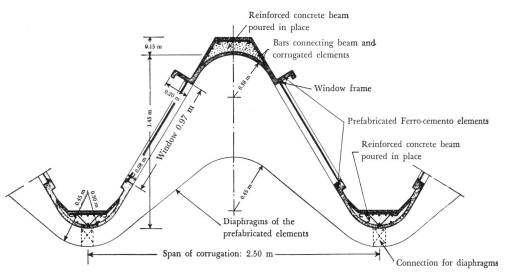

◄ *Figure 13.41*

Detail of vault, Turin Exhibition Hall, 1949, Pier Luigi Nervi, engineer. (Source: Pier Luigi Nervi, *Structures*, New York, F. W. Dodge Corp., 1956.)

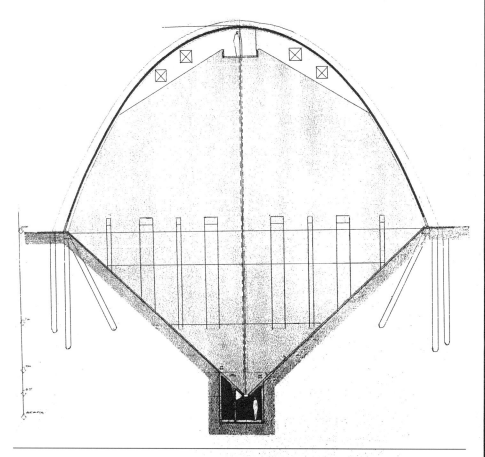

▲ *Figure 13.42*
Cross section, rice silo, Vergara, Uruguay, Eladio Dieste, engineer.
(Courtesy of Dieste & Montañez SA.)

Figure 13.43 ▶
Rice silo, Vergara, Uruguay, Eladio Dieste, engineer.
(Courtesy of Dieste & Montañez SA.)

In many cases structures have the ability to move us and attract us because they are mysteriously expressive . . . we perceive these structures not only with our eyes but with our spirit, and they display a more exact adaptation to the laws that control matter in equilibrium. . . . Giving form to a work . . . is like leaping into a void, and we want that jump to be more of a flight than a fall, . . . but we must remember that there is no art without science, and that it will take much rational effort to acquire the ability to take that jump.

ELADIO DIESTE, *LA ESTRUCTURA CERAMICA*
(BOGOTÁ: ESCALA, 1987), P. 152.

vault considerably, but its sinusoidal corrugations make it highly resistant to changing shape when subjected to the shifting pressures of external winds and internal piles of rice.

The Super Sam market in Warsaw, Poland, employs a more complex type of folded plate stiffening in which tensioned and compressed elements are balanced against one another. Figure 13.44 illustrates the evolution of the structural concept. Two retail spaces, divided from each other by a central structure for storage and food preparation, could be roofed with separate hanging roofs (a). To eliminate the diagonal backstays from the central area, the roof cables could be made continuous (b). The outside backstays could also be eliminated by adding compressive struts to equilibrate the pull of the cables (c). To arrive at the final design, the struts were curved to become arches that support half the roof load directly (d). Figure 13.45 diagrams the alternation of cables and arches that pro-

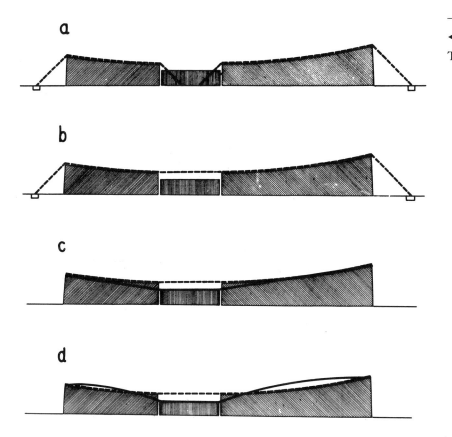

◀ *Figure 13.44*
The concept of the Super Sam roof.

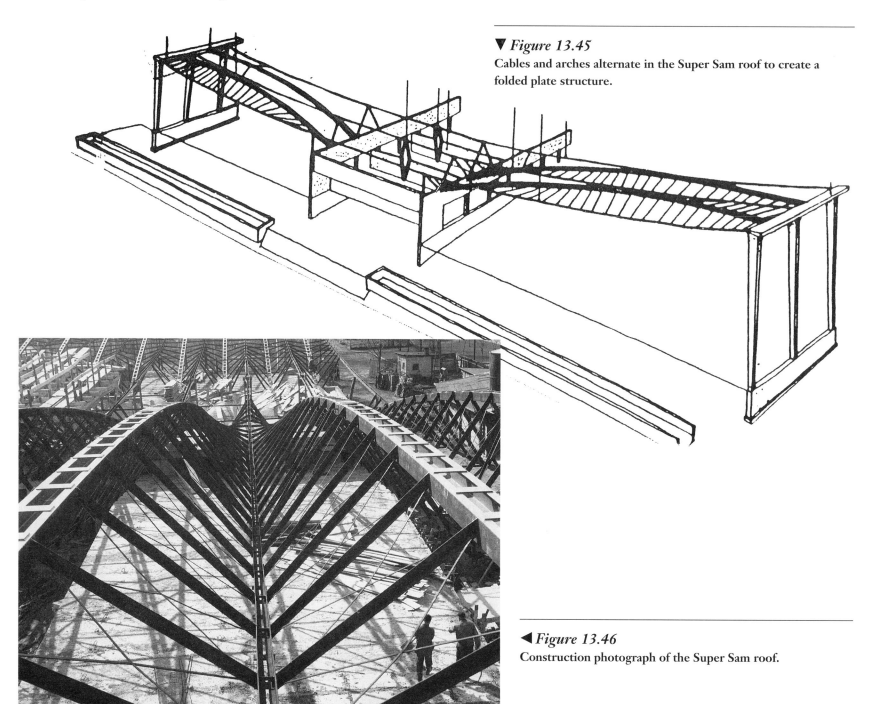

▼ *Figure 13.45*
Cables and arches alternate in the Super Sam roof to create a folded plate structure.

◄ *Figure 13.46*
Construction photograph of the Super Sam roof.

duces the folded plate. Figure 13.46 shows the construction. Each arch consists of a pair of steel channels; another pair of steel channels provides a path for each cable. Short lengths of steel angle connect the arches and cables to frame the surfaces of the folded plate. The steel framework was prefabricated in large sections that were erected on temporary supports with the aid of a crane. Then the cables were threaded through the framework and tensioned with hydraulic jacks.

The roof was covered with sheet metal on the outside and wood on the inside (Figs. 13.47 and 13.48). Triangular steel frames on the roof of the central structure prevent lateral movement of the cable under asymmetrical loadings.

Restraint by Synclastic and Anticlastic Curvature

Funicular structures that are fully three-dimensional are highly resistant to changes of shape if they are given a basic curvature that is either synclastic or anticlastic. These membrane and shell structures are discussed in another volume in this series.

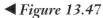**Figure 13.47**
Interior view of Super Sam.

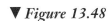**Figure 13.48**
Super Sam. Architects and engineers: Buro Bistyp, Warsaw, Poland.

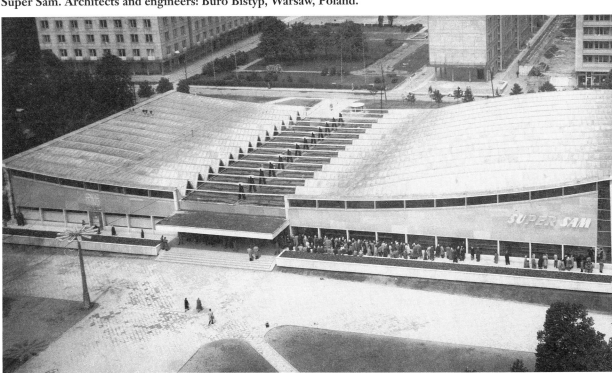

Key Terms and Concepts

restraint of a funicular element
restraint with stay cables or struts
restraint by prestressing
bicycle wheel structure
anticlastic curvature

inverted arch
stress ribbon
box arch
rigidity beam
deck-stiffened arch

restraint by trussing
restraint by diaphragm action
restraint by folded plate stiffening

Exercises

1. Sketch five other ways of restraining the concrete arch slab of the Salginatobel Bridge against the effects of asymmetrical loadings (Figs. 13.28–13.30). Write a paragraph discussing the advantages and disadvantages of each. What procedure would you use to erect each of your designs?

2. For the Broadgate Office Building (Fig. 13.12), develop an alternative scheme for restraining the steel arch. Base your design on either the parabolic geometry of the arch or the rectilinear geometry of the frame behind it. Write a brief essay presenting the rationale for your design.

3. Find the force under full live load in a cable in the stress ribbon bridge shown in Figure 13.20. Use the dimensions given in the figure legend.

Assume that there are six cables. The live load is 4.0 kN/m^2. The dimensions of the deck section are 3.8 m by 0.3 m.

4. Working graphically, determine whether the inclination of the columns of the paper mill shown in Figures 13.34 and 13.35 is such that the columns are subjected only to axial forces under a uniform roof loading.

5. Sketch four different ways of restraining a cylindrical concrete shell roof that is 6 in. thick, rises 40 ft, and spans 175 ft.

Chapter FOURTEEN

Shaping Efficient Trusses

◀ Vertical constant-force trusses with funicular outer chords stiffen a glass wall against wind loads at the Kansai International Airport in Osaka, Japan. Each vertical joint between sheets of glass is supported by mirror-image trusses inside and out. The roof trusses, triangular in section and made of steel pipes with welded joints, do not follow funicular lines. Architects and engineers: Renzo Piano Building Workshop and Ove Arup & Partners. (Photo: John Edward Linden/Arcaid)

In Chapters Five and Six, we learned to analyze trusses by using either numerical or graphical calculations to find the forces in their members. Any planar truss configuration that is made up entirely of triangles is theoretically stable, but some configurations work more efficiently than others. In this chapter, we will learn to shape a truss in such a way that it has specified structural properties. We might wish, for example, to shape a truss so that the forces throughout the length of the top or bottom chord are constant, allowing the use of a single size of member from one support to the other. This *constant-force truss* design has several potential benefits. It can simplify design and fabrication of the truss joints. It generally results in a truss that uses less material than most other truss

forms that could carry the same pattern of loads. And it usually produces a truss that is graceful in appearance, because its form responds directly to the loads that it supports. Truss forms may be optimized by either the numerical or graphical method. We will explore the numerical method first.

A Numerical Method for Finding an Optimal Form for a Truss

Drawing (a) in Figure 14.1 shows a loading pattern for a top-loaded truss. We would like to find a form for this truss such that the force in the top chord will be a constant 26,000 lb throughout its length, thus allowing a single piece of material of uniform size to serve for this member. The top

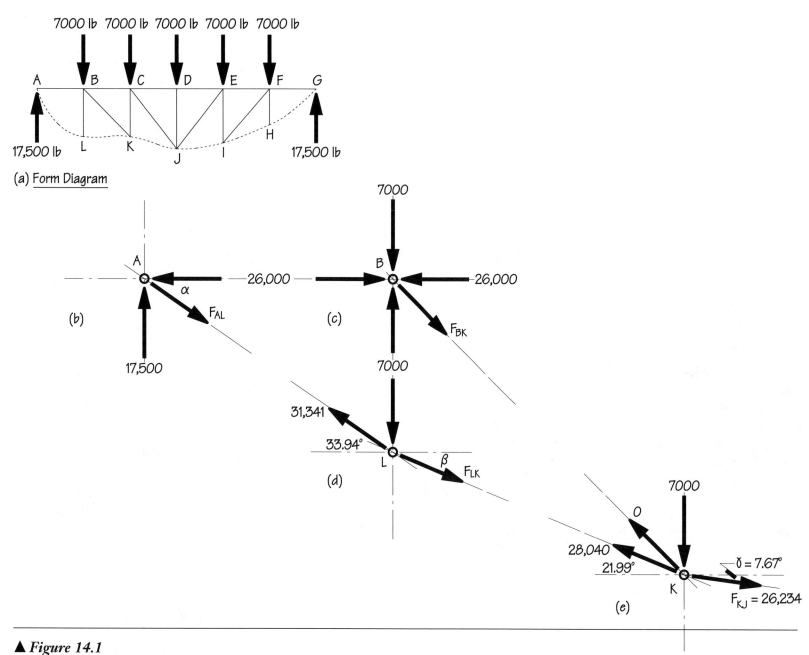

(a) Form Diagram

▲ *Figure 14.1*

Shaping a constant-force truss numerically.

chord is to be level; the form of the bottom chord is unknown, as indicated by the amorphous dotted line on the space diagram.

We begin our work at A, the left end joint of the truss, which we diagram as a free body in Figure 14.2(b). Two of the three forces that converge on this joint are known. The force F_{AL} in the bottom chord and the angle α between the top and bottom chords are unknowns. Two simultaneous equations may be written by summing the forces first in the vertical direction, then in the horizontal:

$$F_{AL} \sin \alpha = 17{,}500 \text{ lb}$$

$$F_{AL} \cos \alpha = 26{,}000 \text{ lb}$$

Dividing one equation by the other, we take advantage of the fact that the sine of any angle divided by its cosine equals its tangent:

$$\frac{\sin \alpha}{\cos \alpha} = \frac{17{,}500 \text{ lb}}{26{,}000 \text{ lb}} = \tan \alpha$$

$$\alpha = 33.94° \ (33°56')$$

$$F_{AL} = \frac{17{,}500 \text{ lb}}{\sin 33.94°} = 31{,}341 \text{ lb}$$

Moving next to joint B (Fig. 14.1[c]), three of the five forces are known: the 7000-lb load and forces of 26,000 lb from the right and the left. The diagonal BK must be a zero-force member, otherwise its horizontal component would upset the equilibrium between the identical forces in the top chord. Thus, by inspection we can assign a force of 7000 lb compression to member BL, to balance the only other vertical force on this joint. In similar fashion we deduce that these same relationships must hold true for all the joints in the top chord.

In Figure 14.1(d), we diagram the forces on the next joint, L, of the bottom chord. F_{LK}, which is the force in member LK, and the angle β are unknowns. We again write two equations by summing forces in the vertical and horizontal directions, respectively:

$$7000 \text{ lb} + F_{LK} \sin \beta - 31{,}341 \sin 33.94° = 0$$

$$F_{LK} \cos \beta - 31{,}341 \cos 33.94° = 0$$

Solving these equations, we find that angle β is 21.99° (21°59') and force F_{LK} is 28,040 lb. In Fig-

ure 14.1(e) we diagram the next joint, K, which we solve in similar fashion. By symmetry, we now know all the forces and angles in the truss.

Figure 14.2(a) is a summary diagram, accurately constructed, of the form and forces for the entire truss. Ideally, because the diagonals contain no forces, the truss could be built in the form shown in (b), assuming that the external loading on the truss never varies. The bottom chord follows the funicular line of a hanging cable that carries five equal loads at uniform intervals. The vertical struts serve only to carry

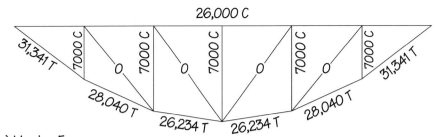

26,000 C

31,341 T   7000 C   7000 C   7000 C   7000 C   7000 C

0   0   0   0

28,040 T   26,234 T   26,234 T   28,040 T   31,341 T

(a) Member Forces

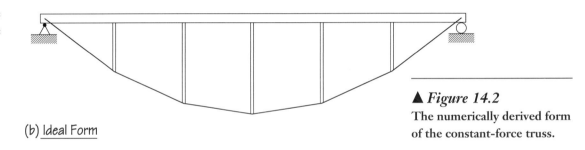

(b) Ideal Form

▲ *Figure 14.2*
The numerically derived form of the constant-force truss.

◀ *Figure 14.3*

The Shiosai Bridge in Japan, with a clear width of 3.0 m (10 ft), is used by pedestrians and cyclists. It is made of concrete with high-strength steel post-tensioning tendons. The longest span is 61 m (200 ft). The diagonals have been omitted. (Owner: Shizuoka Prefecture. Contractor: Sumitomo Construction Co., Ltd.)

◀ *Figure 14.4*

The Alamodome in San Antonio, Texas, shown here under construction in 1993, is a huge arena that seats 65,000 people indoors for football games. The main roof truss in the center of this photograph spans 378 ft (115 m). Its funicular bottom chord is made of steel cables. Its top chord is a steel wide-flange shape 3 ft (0.9 m) deep. It supports parallel chord steel trusses over the seating area and, along with its identical twin, off the photo to the right, 10-ft-deep (3 m) trusses over the playing field, which were installed after this photograph was taken. (Structure designed by Marmon Mok. Photo courtesy of Vulcraft Division of Nucor Corporation, manufacturer of the parallel-chord trusses.)

the superimposed loads to the bottom chord. The top chord acts only to resist the horizontal pull of the bottom chord at each support. If properly sized, the top chord and the verticals are stressed to capacity throughout their length. If the bottom chord is made of a steel rod or cable of constant diameter that is sized for its maximum force, it is stressed to 84% of its capacity for a third of its length, 89% for another third, and 100% for the rest. Thus, we see that there is little structural material in this truss that is not fully utilized. It is a highly efficient form.

Most trusses, of course, are subjected to loading patterns that vary over time: moving loads in bridges and floors, and changing combi-nations of wind and gravity loads in roofs. Diag-onals generally must be added to the ideal form to respond to these conditions. In some cases, however, rigid truss joints or external stiffening devices can be used to deal with changing loads so as to avoid diagonals entirely.

We know from our understanding of hang-ing cables that, because the bottom chord of the truss that we have designed in Figure 14.1 is funicular for a set of vertical loads, the horizon-tal component of the tensile forces in the mem-bers of the bottom chord is constant. It is equal to the compressive force in the top chord, 26,000 lb. This allows us to check the accuracy of our calculations by multiplying each member force by the cosine of its slope angle to see whether it equals 26,000 lb:

$$F_{AL} \cos 33.94° = 31{,}341 \cos 33.94° = 26{,}001 \text{ lb}$$

$$F_{LK} \cos 21.99° = 28{,}040 \cos 21.99° = 26{,}000 \text{ lb}$$

$$F_{KJ} \cos 7.67° = 26{,}234 \cos 7.67° = 25{,}999 \text{ lb}$$

Constant-force trusses of this shape have been used in such structures as the Shiosai Bridge in Japan (Fig. 14.3) and the Alamodome roof in San Antonio, Texas (Figs. 14.4 and 14.5). A number of recent buildings employ trusses of this shape as window mullions for large expanses of glass, where their chief role is to resist hori-zontal wind pressures on the glass (see the

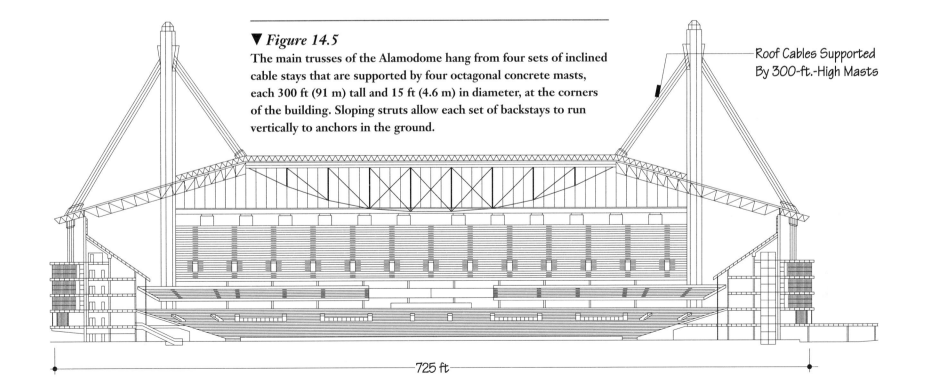

▼ *Figure 14.5*
The main trusses of the Alamodome hang from four sets of inclined cable stays that are supported by four octagonal concrete masts, each 300 ft (91 m) tall and 15 ft (4.6 m) in diameter, at the corners of the building. Sloping struts allow each set of backstays to run vertically to anchors in the ground.

Roof Cables Supported By 300-ft.-High Masts

725 ft

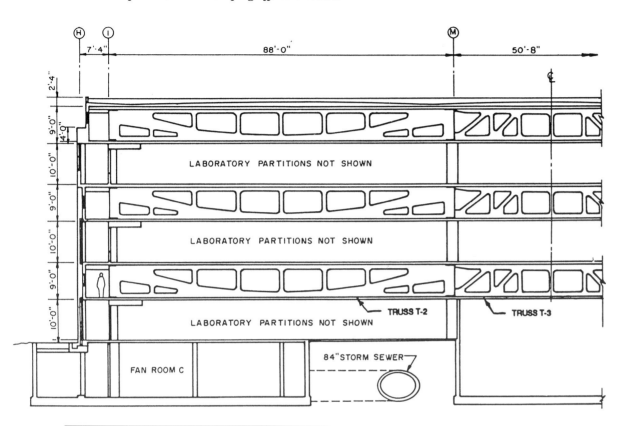

▲ *Figure 14.6*

Laboratory floors of the Ciba-Geigy Life Science Building in Summit, New Jersey, built in 1992, rest on precast concrete constant-force trusses. The funicular bottom chord of each truss consists of steel posttensioning tendons encased in concrete. Below this chord hangs a horizontal semistructural member of concrete that supports a level ceiling below. The trusses, each 9 ft (2.74 m) deep and 88 ft (26.8 m) long, provide column-free laboratory space as well as a generous zone for piping, wiring, and ductwork. (Courtesy of Weidlinger Associates, New York.)

Figure 14.7 ►

Each truss for the Ciba-Geigy Life Science Building was cast on its side. The smooth, bundled strands in this photograph are plastic-sheathed steel posttensioning cables that follow the funicular line of the bottom chord. The rest of the internal elements are steel reinforcing bars. (Courtesy of Weidlinger Associates, New York.)

photograph at the beginning of this chapter). In most cases, diagonals were added to the ideal form to resist nonuniform loadings. Figures 14.6–14.8 illustrate a precast concrete floor truss design that does not utilize diagonals, but relies instead on the stiffness of its steel-reinforced concrete members and joints to resist incidental moments caused by asymmetrical loads. A level bottom chord that has no significant role in the overall strength and stiffness of the truss has been added to this truss to support a flat ceiling.

A GRAPHICAL METHOD FOR FINDING OPTIMUM FORM FOR A TRUSS

Figure 14.9 demonstrates how the constant-force truss that we derived in Figures 14.1 and 14.2 may be shaped graphically rather than numerically. Interval notation facilitates the graphical solution. The load line is constructed in the usual manner. A line is drawn parallel to the load line at a distance of 26,000 lb to the left of it. The force polygon is then constructed in

steps (a) through (d) in such a way that all the lines that represent the forces in the segments of the top chord end at this vertical line. These intersections determine the inclinations of the various segments of the bottom chord, which are added one by one to the form diagram to the left, generating the shape of the truss. At each step, the construction of the lines on the force polygon precedes and guides the construction of the form of the truss. All the diagonals are zero-force members. The forces in the other members are found by scaling the lengths of the corresponding line segments in the force polygon.

The form and forces found by this graphical method are identical to those found by the numerical method. The main differences between the two methods are that the graphical method involves no numerical calculations and that it typically takes about one-third as much time as the numerical method to achieve the same result. The accuracy of the graphical method depends on the scale at which the drawings are constructed and the precision with which they are drafted. At almost any scale, the results are likely to be far more accurate than the degree of precision with which the external loadings can be predicted.

An expedient working method for finding a constant force shape for a truss is to arrive at the desired form by graphical experimentation, then determine exact construction dimensions and angles by numerical analysis. Given the transparency and rapidity of the graphical method for finding truss forms, only graphical derivations are presented in the rest of this chapter.

▼ *Figure 14.8*

Each truss weighs 43 tons (39 tonnes). The short reinforcing bars that project from the edges of the truss will be overlapped with similar bars from the floor, ceiling, and column elements before concrete is poured, uniting all these members into a strong, single-piece construction. Architects: Mitchell/Giurgola. Engineers: Weidlinger Associates. (Courtesy of Weidlinger Associates, New York.)

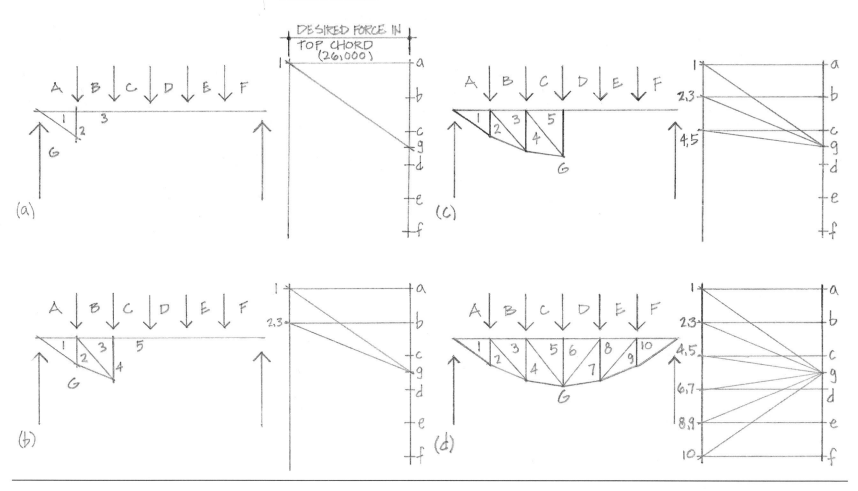

▲ *Figure 14.9*

Finding the form of a constant-force truss graphically. At each step, the lines that represent force on the force polygon are constructed first, then the lines that represent the members on the form diagram.

FINDING A TRUSS FORM THAT HAS CONSTANT FORCE IN THE CURVING CHORD

Examination of the completed force polygon in Figure 14.9 suggests that one might easily find a form for a truss in which the force is constant throughout the curving bottom chord rather than the straight top chord, a condition that would allow the efficient use of a rod or cable for the bottom chord. This derivation is shown in Figure 14.10. The lines on the force polygon (c) are constructed first for each pair of members, then the corresponding lines on the form diagram (a). To begin, working to the same scale as the force polygon, a compass is set to a radius equal to the desired force in the bottom chord, and an arc is swung about point *g* on the load

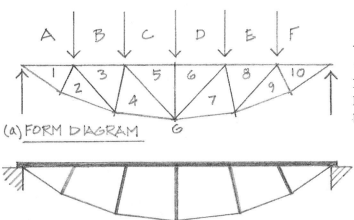

(a) FORM DIAGRAM

(b) IDEAL FORM

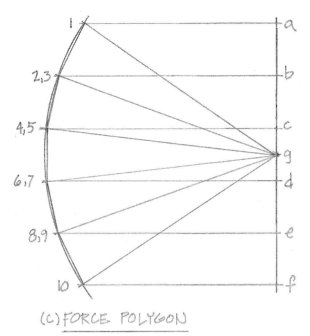

(c) FORCE POLYGON

◄ *Figure 14.10*
Finding the form of a truss that has constant force in its curved bottom chord.

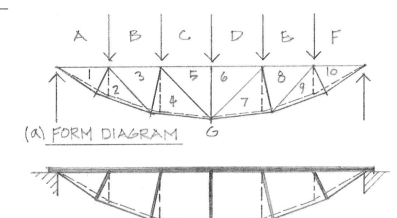

(a) FORM DIAGRAM

(b) IDEAL FORM

Figure 14.11 ►
Comparison of form and forces in two constant-force trusses.

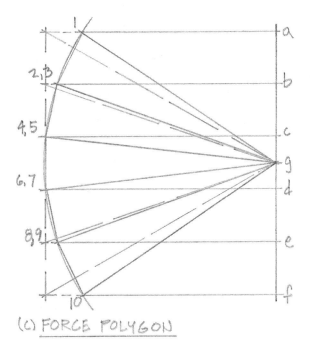

(c) FORCE POLYGON

line. The intersections of this arc with the horizontal lines that represent the forces in the top chord segments are the locations of the numbered points in the force polygon. Except at the centerline of the truss, all the internal members are inclined. Half of them carry zero force under the ideal loading condition and may be eliminated to arrive at the ideal form (b).

Figure 14.11 demonstrates the lower member forces in this truss in comparison to a truss of the same depth with constant force throughout its top chord. This highly efficient form apparently was first discovered by the American engineer George Pegram; he used it in

1894 for the slender, graceful steel roof trusses of the train sheds in the St. Louis Union Station (Fig. 14.12). Their span, 141 ft, was the longest of any roof truss in the world at that time. Engi-neer Michel Virlogeux employed the same shaping principle in a recently constructed bridge in France (Figs. 14.13, 14.14).

A similar graphical construction can be used to shape a truss that contains true vertical members while still retaining a constant force throughout the length of the bottom chord (Fig. 14.15). In this form, the diagonals carry small

▲ *Figure 14.12*
Steel roof trusses of the train sheds at the St. Louis Union Station, designed by George Pegram in 1892–1894. (Photo: Edward Allen.)

▲ *Figure 14.13*
Engineer Michel Virlogeux achieved constant tension in the four steel strands that form the bottom chord of this bridge truss by inclining the V-shaped struts at appropriate angles. The deck acts in compression as the top chord of the truss.

forces even under a uniform loading and cannot be eliminated. As in all the examples in this chapter, the construction of the force polygon precedes that of the form diagram at each step.

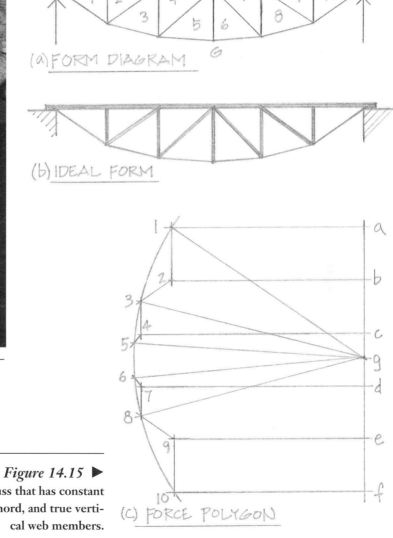

▲ *Figure 14.14*

A detail of the intersection of the strut and the tension strands in the bridge shown in Figure 14.13. The photographs of this bridge, which was constructed in 1996, were taken by its designer, Michel Virlogeux.

Figure 14.15 ▶

Finding the form of a truss that has constant force in its curved bottom chord, and true vertical web members.

A BOTTOM-LOADED CONSTANT FORCE TRUSS

If equal loads are applied along the bottom chord of a truss that has a level, constant-force top chord, an interesting form emerges (Fig. 14.16). All internal members carry zero force, and the ideal form of the resulting truss (b) is that of a funicular suspension cable with a compression strut to resist its horizontal pull. The force polygon is a mirror image of the diagram one would use to find the form and forces for a hanging cable.

If the depth of the truss in Figure 14.16 is decreased progressively in relation to its span, and if the sizes of the tensile and compressive members are proportioned to the forces they experience, we arrive at the form of a longitudinally compressed beam that incorporates a funicularly curved tendon (Fig. 14.17). This is similar to the form of a posttensioned concrete beam that is designed for a uniformly distributed load, and offers a simple way in which the behavior of such a beam may be analyzed and understood.

Figure 14.18 shows the inversion of the form of the truss in Figure 14.16, an elegantly simple truss whose ideal form (b) is that of a tied funicular arch. The force polygons for the two examples are identical, although in interval notation their letters correspond to letters that are differently located on their respective space diagrams. With the addition of diagonals, this is the

Figure 14.17 ▶

As the truss in Figure 14.16 is made progressively shallower, its member forces rise. The concrete top chord, which is in compression and must resist buckling, grows very thick. The bottom chord may be made of very high-strength steel cables so as to remain slender. The limiting case is a form similar to that of a posttensioned concrete beam.

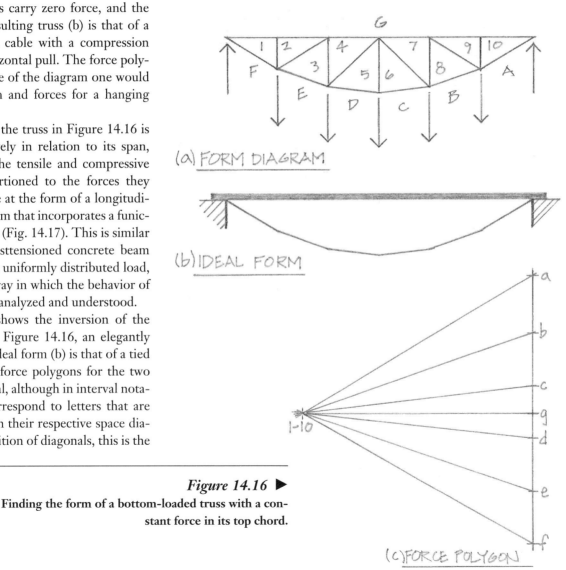

(a) FORM DIAGRAM

(b) IDEAL FORM

(c) FORCE POLYGON

Figure 14.16 ▶
Finding the form of a bottom-loaded truss with a constant force in its top chord.

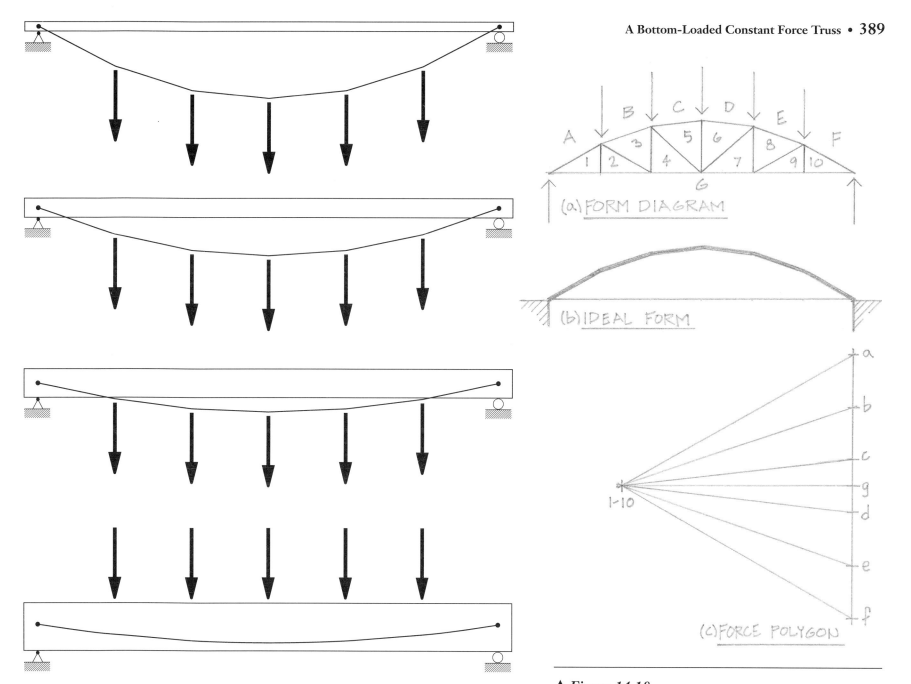

(a) FORM DIAGRAM

(b) IDEAL FORM

(c) FORCE POLYGON

▲ *Figure 14.18*

Finding the form of a bowstring truss, which is a top-loaded truss with a constant force in its bottom chord.

▲ *Figure 14.19*
Steel bowstring trusses support the roof of an elementary school.
(Photo courtesy of Vulcraft Division of Nucor Corporation.)

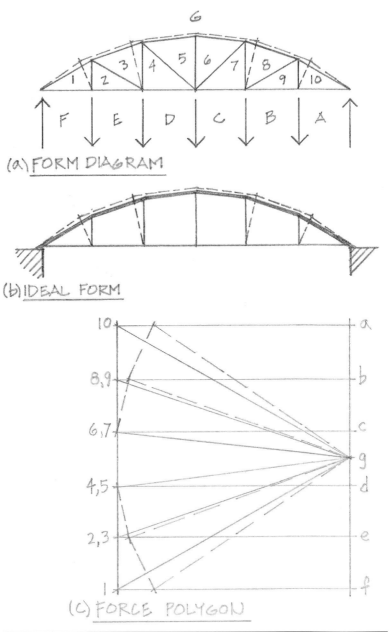

(a) FORM DIAGRAM

(b) IDEAL FORM

(c) FORCE POLYGON

▲ *Figure 14.20*
Finding the form of a tied arch, a bottom-loaded truss with constant
force in its bottom chord. The broken lines demonstrate that the
Pegram form of this truss, with its inclined interior members, experiences even lower forces than the traditional tied arch form.

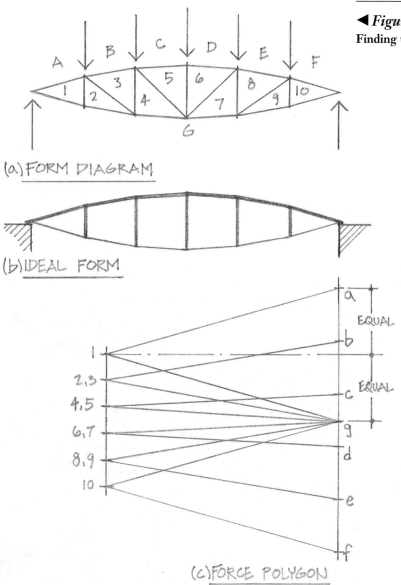

◀ *Figure 14.21*
Finding the form of a lenticular truss.

(a) FORM DIAGRAM

(b) IDEAL FORM

(c) FORCE POLYGON

highly economical *bowstring truss* of wood or steel that is widely used in roof structures of industrial and commercial buildings (Fig. 14.19). For ease of fabrication, a segment of a circle is often used for the top chord instead of the ideal shape, which is a parabola. This results in a negligible loss of efficiency, which is reflected in the small forces that occur in the web members of the truss under a uniform loading.

A further exploration of this line of investigation is shown in Figure 14.20. The truss is bottom-loaded, but is constructed to have a straight bottom chord with constant force throughout. The resulting form is that of an arch with slender tensile verticals that transmit the applied loads to the arch and a horizontal tie that resists the thrust of the arch. This form is widely used in *tied arch* bridges (Fig. 1.12). The broken lines indicate the further economy of designing a tied arch so that the force is constant throughout the arch rather than the tie.

A LENTICULAR TRUSS

A *lenticular truss*, also called a *Pauli truss* after its inventor, the German engineer Friedrich August von Pauli, has the unique property that within each panel, the forces in the top and bottom chords have the same absolute value, but are opposite in character. The shape is generated from the force polygon (c) in Figure 14.21. In each panel of the truss, the inclinations of the top and bottom chord segments are made equal, as shown. Lenticular trusses were widely used in the nineteenth century for road and railway

◀ *Figure 14.22*

The Saltash Bridge, designed by Isambard Kingdom Brunel in 1859, is an early example of the use of lenticular trusses. Each truss spans 455 ft (139 m) and has a midspan depth of 62 ft (19 m). The top chord is a tube, elliptical in cross section, made of wrought iron plates riveted together. Each bottom chord is a chain made of long wrought iron links. The bridge is located near Plymouth, England. (Photo courtesy of The Institution of Civil Engineers, London.)

▲ *Figure 14.23*

This late-nineteenth-century lenticular bridge still carries traffic in western Massachusetts. (Photo: Edward Allen.)

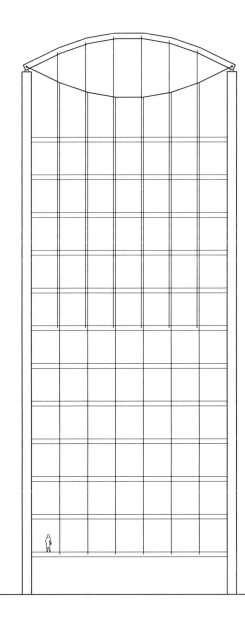

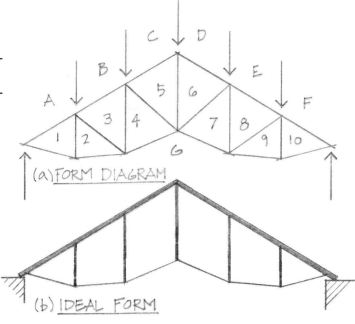

◄ *Figure 14.24*
Lenticular trusses supported by elevator and stair cores can furnish economical support for a tall building. Half the building's floors are hung from the top chord, and half from the bottom chord, thus balancing the forces in the truss.

(a) FORM DIAGRAM

***Figure 14.25* ►**
Finding the form of a constant-force gable truss.

(b) IDEAL FORM

A CONSTANT-FORCE GABLE TRUSS

Gable trusses may be optimized in the same general manner as flat trusses. Figure 14.25 shows the shaping of a gable truss in which the force is constant throughout the top chords. The inclination of the top chords is given by the desired pitch of the roof that is supported by the truss. A vertical line is constructed to the left of the load line at a distance that yields the desired force in the top chords; this distance is measured along lines *a1*, *b3*, *c5*, *d6*, *e8*, and *f10*, whose inclinations are the same as those of the top chords. The form of the bottom chord is determined by the

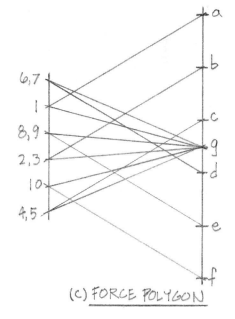

(c) FORCE POLYGON

bridges (Figs. 14.22 and 14.23). More recently, they have been proposed as an efficient means of supporting hangers that carry multiple floors from the top of a high-rise building (Fig. 14.24).

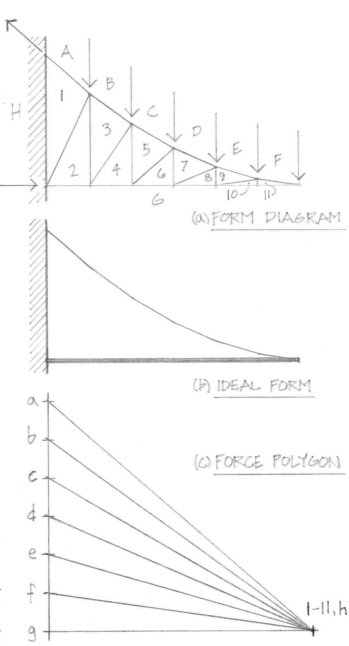

▲ *Figure 14.26*

Concrete constant-force gable trusses in the Magazzini Generali warehouse at Chiasso, Switzerland. Robert Maillart designed this structure in 1924. Longitudinal struts prevent out-of-plane movement of the trusses. The detailing of the cantilevered roof overhang and columns is particularly expressive. (Photo: ETH-Bibliothek, Zürich.)

lines that radiate from *g* on the force polygon (c). Concrete roof trusses of this form, without diagonals, were used by Robert Maillart in a warehouse at Chiasso, Switzerland (Fig. 14.26).

CANTILEVER TRUSSES OF OPTIMAL FORM

Figure 14.27 illustrates the shaping of a cantilever truss that carries five identical top loads while maintaining a constant force in its level bottom chord. As with the other trusses in this chapter, the form of the truss is derived from the form of the force polygon. The verticals and diagonals in this truss carry no forces under the ideal loading condition. The ideal form of the

Figure 14.27 ▶

Finding the form of a top-loaded, constant-force cantilever truss.

truss is that of a funicular cable held away from the wall by a strut that has constant axial compression throughout.

The truss in Figure 14.28 is the cantilevered equivalent of a lenticular truss. Its orientation on the page is that of a tower that is subjected to lateral wind forces. Its form is generated by a force polygon that has been constructed in such a way that the top and bottom chord forces are identical in magnitude in each panel. The resulting form suggests the shape of the Eiffel Tower, a structure that was designed using graphical methods (Fig. 14.29). This form of tower is very efficient in resisting wind forces with nearly constant internal forces throughout its height.

▲ *Figure 14.29*

The Eiffel Tower, designed by Gustave Eiffel and Maurice Koechlin for the 1889 Universal Exposition in Paris, was by far the tallest structure in the world at the time of its construction at a height of 300 m (1000 ft). With such an efficient shape, its structure is astonishingly light: If its members were melted down into a solid block as large as its base, the block would be only 64 mm (2.5 in.) high. (Photo © Bill Bachman, Photo Researchers, Inc.)

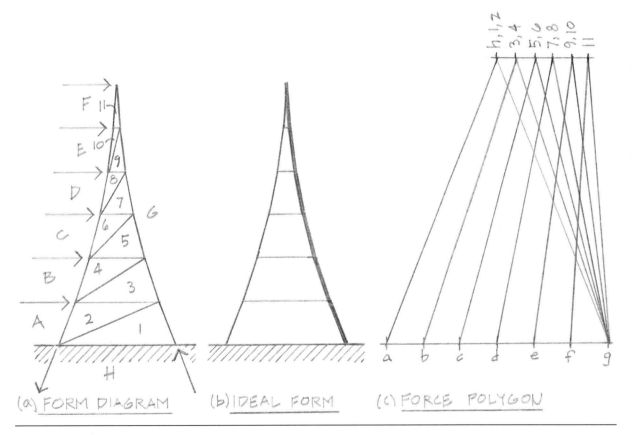

▲ *Figure 14.28*

This tower is the cantilevered equivalent of a lenticular truss. The top and bottom chord segments in each panel experience forces of identical magnitude.

OPTIMAL TRUSS FORMS: THE GENERAL SOLUTION

Most of the examples given to this point have been level, symmetrical trusses with symmetrical gravity loadings. The method that has been used, however, is general and may be applied to inclined and irregular loading and support conditions. Figure 14.30 shows an inclined truss with varying loads, one of which is nonvertical, applied at irregular intervals. The force polygon has been manipulated to produce a truss form that has constant force throughout its top chord. Because of the nonvertical load, the hinged end reaction is inclined, and the resulting load line is a quadrilateral. All the lines that represent the forces in the segments of the top chord on the force polygon have been constructed to the same length, which produces an inclined web member in the ideal truss.

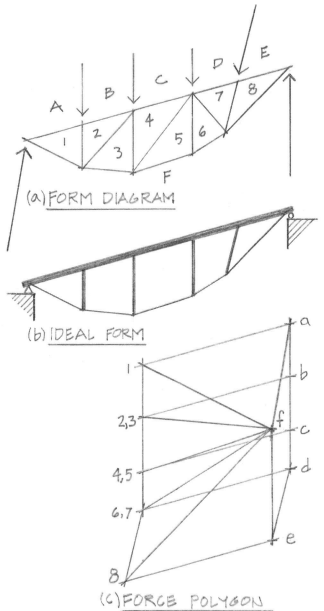

(a) FORM DIAGRAM

(b) IDEAL FORM

(c) FORCE POLYGON

◀ *Figure 14.30*

Finding the form of a constant-force truss with a sloping chord and an irregular set of loads.

Suboptimal Truss Forms: The Camelback Truss

In many situations, an external constraint is placed on the form of a truss. Such is the case with a bridge truss whose portals at each end must be tall enough to clear the vehicles on the roadway or track that passes between the parallel trusses of the bridge. Figure 14.31 demonstrates the shaping of a *camelback* truss, a form frequently seen in road and railway bridges. The heights of members *1-2* and *9-10* are fixed by vehicle clearance requirements, thus determining the inclinations of top chord segments *G-1* and *G-10*, and the inclinations of *g-1* and *g-10* in the force polygon. For the rest of the truss, the construction of the force polygon precedes the construction of the form diagram at each step. The four center segments of the top chord are configured so that they carry equal forces. This allows them to be the same size, which simplifies fabrication and increases overall structural efficiency. An alternative construction, shown in broken lines, provides for constant force throughout the bottom chord.

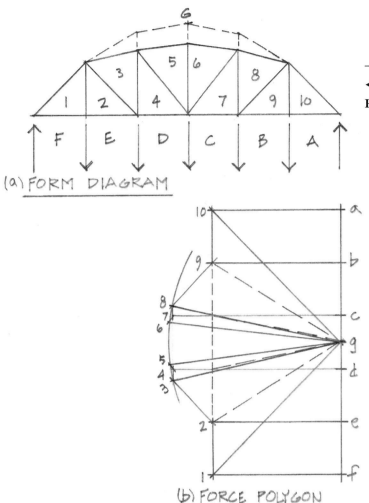

◀ *Figure 14.31*
Finding the form of a camelback truss.

VISUALIZING FORM IMPROVEMENTS IN TRUSSES OF NONOPTIMAL SHAPE

An important advantage of the graphical method of truss analysis over numerical or computer analysis during early stages of design is that the force polygon furnishes ample, easily discernable clues as to how the form of an arbitrarily shaped truss might be improved. Consider the *scissors truss* (a) in Figure 14.32, which supports a gable roof while maintaining a lofty, soaring interior space. A glance at its accompanying force polygon reveals that the maximum member forces in this truss are roughly twice as high as the total external load. If this is to be a welded steel truss, these high forces might be of comparatively little consequence; but if the truss is to be made of wood, it is likely that some of the connections will need so many bolts or timber connectors that they will be impossible to make. In examining the force polygon further, we find that the member forces are so large because the lines in the force polygon that represent the forces in the ends of the top and bottom chords (*a-1* and *g-1*, for example) meet at so sharp an angle. If these two lines met at a less acute angle, their lengths would be considerably shorter.

Acting on this clue, we might flatten the bottom chord to increase the angle between the chords, producing a triangular truss (b). Even without measuring, we can see by comparing this force polygon with that of the scissors truss that this strategy has practically halved the maximum chord forces. This is good, but the lofty, soaring quality of the enclosed space has been lost. How can we get it back, without returning to a truss form that has excessive member forces?

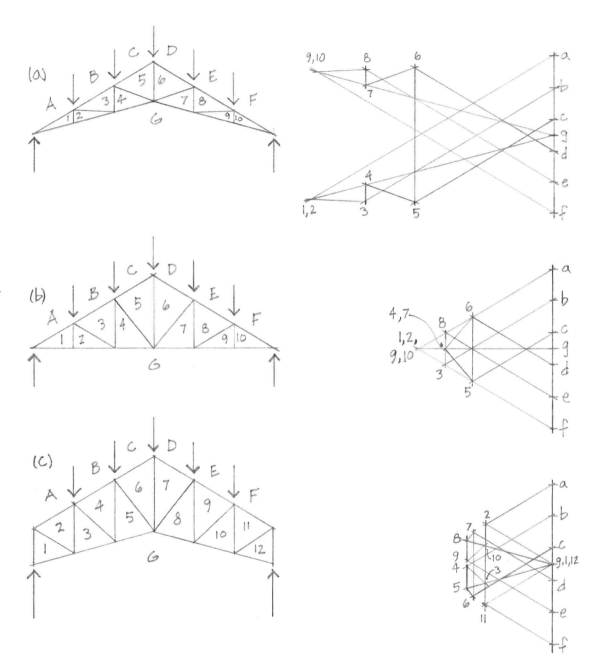

◀ *Figure 14.32*

Suboptimization of the form of a roof truss, in which the relative compactness of the member force diagram is a measure of the efficiency of the truss.

Realizing that the maximum chord forces occur at the ends of the truss, we could increase still further the angle between the top and bottom chords at the very ends, but pull the bottom chord back up in the middle panels so as to give a more pleasing shape to the enclosed space (c). Comparing the three force polygons, we perceive instantly, even without measuring, that the forces in this truss are by far the lowest of any of our three designs. Perhaps this third design contains too much interior volume to be economical or desirable—no matter, we can try other alternatives that retain the basic form of the third truss but reduce its overall height somewhat, because we are now in a position to guess that their member forces will probably not exceed those of the triangular truss option.

This type of experimentation lies at the heart of the structural design process. It is facilitated by the rapidity of the graphical method of analysis and by the ease with which generalizations may be made about the overall performance of each truss simply by noting the relative compactness of the force polygon. Numerical analyses tend to take longer, and the bare numbers that they yield are of little help in figuring out how to improve the form of the truss.

▲ *Figure 14.33*

Constant-force bowstring trusses of steel are designed to support the heavy column loads of a 15-story laboratory building that was subsequently constructed above them on Roosevelt Drive in Manhattan in 1990. The polygonal chord of each truss is shaped so that it is funicular for the particular loads and spacings of the line of columns that it carries, resulting in considerable variation of form from one truss to the next.

[Structural design] is not a science. Science studies particular events to find general laws. [Structural] design makes use of these laws to solve particular problems. In this it is more closely related to art or craft; as in art, its problems are under-defined, there are many solutions, good, bad, or indifferent. The art is, by synthesis of ends and means, to arrive at a good solution. This is a creative activity, involving imagination, intuition and deliberate choice.

• Ove-Arup, *Ove Arup & Partners, 1946–1986* (London: Academy Editions, 1986), p. 9.

▲ *Figure 14.34*

The truss members are heavy wide-flange shapes, welded at the joints. Despite their considerable weight, these optimally shaped trusses, by replacing the inefficient plate girders that had previously been designed for this project, saved $1 million worth of steel. (Photos by Bernstein Associates. Trusses designed by Ysrael Seinuk for Cantor/Seinuk Partnership.)

Key Terms and Concepts

constant-force truss

bowstring truss

tied arch

lenticular truss

Pauli truss

camelback truss

scissors truss

Exercises

1. A six-panel, parallel-chord truss supports a gravity load of 6 kN at each joint along the top chord. The span is 12 m. Find a depth for this truss such that the maximum chord force is 36 kN.

2. A seven-panel truss supports a gravity load of 1000 lb at each joint of the bottom chord. An additional vertical load of 4000 lb is applied to the joint that lies just inside the right-hand support. Shape this truss in such a way that its level, straight top chord has a uniform force of 7000 lb throughout its length.

3. The straight bottom chord of an eight-panel truss lies at an angle of 15° to the horizontal. Each joint along the top chord is subjected to a gravity load of 1500 lb. Shape this truss so that the force is constant at 12,000 lb throughout the top chord.

4. A truss has a main span of six panels and an overhang at one end of two panels. All eight panels have the same horizontal dimension. Each joint along the top of the truss is subjected to a gravity load of 8 kN. A level chord extends from one end joint of the truss to the other. Shape this truss in such a way that the level chord experiences a force of 32 kN throughout its length under the given loading.

5. A cantilever truss of five equal panels has a straight top chord that slopes down from the wall at an angle of 15° to the horizontal. Three bottom loads of 10 kips each are applied to the outermost joints. Shape this truss so that its top chord has a tensile force of 40 kips throughout its length under this loading.

6. A ten-panel bowstring truss supports nine gravity top loads of 6 kN each on its interior nodes. Find a shape for this truss so that it will have a constant force of 42 kN in its bottom chord. Construct and analyze a second bowstring truss of the same maximum depth whose top chord is a segment of a circle. Compare the member forces in the two trusses. Are they significantly different?

UNIT CONVERSIONS

Length and Area

1 in. = 25.4 mm	1 mm = 0.0394 in.
1 ft = 304.8 mm	1 m = 39.37 in.
1 ft = 0.3048 m	1 m = 3.2808 ft
$1 \text{ in.}^2 = 645.2 \text{ mm}^2$	$1 \text{ mm}^2 = 0.00155 \text{ in.}^2$
$1 \text{ ft}^2 = 0.0929 \text{ m}^2$	$1 \text{ m}^2 = 10.76 \text{ ft}^2$

Volume and Density

$1 \text{ ft}^3 = 0.0283 \text{ m}^3$	$1 \text{ m}^3 = 35.31 \text{ ft}^3$
$1 \text{ yd}^3 = 27 \text{ ft}^3 = 0.7646 \text{ m}^3$	$1 \text{ m}^3 = 1.308 \text{ yd}^3$
$1 \text{ lb/ft}^3 = 16.018 \text{ kg/m}^3$	$1 \text{ kg/m}^3 = 0.0624 \text{ lb/ft}^3$

Mass

1 lb mass = 0.454 kg	1 kg = 2.205 lb mass
1 kip mass = 454 kg	1 tonne = 1 000 kg = 2.205 kips
1 ton = 2000 lb = 907 kg = 0.907 tonne	1 tonne = 1.102 tons

Force and Moment

1 lb force = 4.448 N	1 N = 0.2248 lb force
1 kip force = 4 448 N	1 MN = 224.8 kips force
1 lb-ft = 1.356 N·m	1 N·m = 0.7375 lb-ft
1 lb-in. = 0.1130 N·m	1 N·m = 8.8496 lb-in.

Stress and Pressure

1 psi = 6.89 kPa	1 kPa = 0.145 psi
1 psi = 0.00689 MPa	1 MPa = 145.14 psi
$1 \text{ lb/ft}^2 = 4.884 \text{ kg/m}^2$	$1 \text{ kg/m}^2 = 0.205 \text{ lb/ft}^2$

STANDARD SIZES OF STEEL REINFORCING BARS

Inch-Pound Reinforcing Bars

Size Designation	Nominal Weight, lb/ft	Nominal Dimensions	
		Diameter, in.	Cross-Sectional Area, in.^{2}
#3	0.376	0.375	0.11
#4	0.668	0.500	0.20
#5	1.043	0.625	0.31
#6	1.502	0.750	0.44
#7	2.044	0.875	0.60
#8	2.670	1.000	0.79
#9	3.400	1.128	1.00
#10	4.303	1.270	1.27
#11	5.313	1.410	1.56
#14	7.65	1.693	2.25
#18	13.6	2.257	4.00

SI (Metric) Reinforcing Bars

Size Designation	Nominal Mass, kg/m	Nominal Dimensions	
		Diameter, mm	Cross-Sectional Area, mm^2
10M	0.785	11.3	100
15M	1.570	16.0	200
20M	2.355	19.5	300
25M	3.925	25.2	500
30M	5.495	29.9	700
35M	7.850	35.7	1000
45M	11.775	43.7	1500
55M	19.625	56.4	2500

SELECTED REFERENCES

Addis, Bill. *The Art of the Structural Engineer.* London, Artemis, 1994.

A beautifully illustrated essay on recent works of structural design.

Allen, Edward, and Joseph Iano. *The Architect's Studio Companion: Rules of Thumb for Preliminary Design* (2nd ed.). New York, John Wiley & Sons, 1995.

A succinct guide to selecting, laying out, and assigning preliminary member sizes to structural systems for framed buildings in wood, steel, and concrete.

Ambrose, James. *Design of Building Trusses.* New York, John Wiley & Sons, 1994.

A comprehensive look at the design of roof trusses, including an extended treatment of graphical analysis by Harry Parker.

Bill, Max. *Robert Maillart.* Zurich, 1949.

The classic book on Maillart's structures.

Billington, David P. *Robert Maillart and the Art of Reinforced Concrete.* Cambridge, MIT Press, 1990.

A handsomely illustrated treatise on Maillart's design innovations.

Billington, David P. *Robert Maillart's Bridges: The Art of Engineering.* Princeton, Princeton University Press, 1979.

The definitive guide to the subject, including a location map.

Billington, David P. *The Tower and the Bridge: The New Art of Structural Engineering.* Princeton, Princeton University Press, 1983.

An exciting introduction to the design of large structures.

Cowan, Henry J. *Architectural Structures.* New York, Pitman, 1980.

An excellent introduction to the mathematics of structure.

Engel, Heinrich. *Structure Systems.* New York, Van Nostrand Reinhold, 1981.

Illustrated with lovely drawings and photographs of models, a revealing study of the potential of building structure, especially at longer spans.

Faber, Colin. *Candela, The Shell Builder.* New York, Reinhold, 1963.

The definitive work on the master designer of concrete shell structures.

Frampton, Kenneth, Anthony C. Webster, and Anthony Tischauser. *Calatrava Bridges.* Zurich, Artemis, 1993.

Photographs and insightful essays on the work of a leading structural designer.

Francis, A. J. *Introducing Structures.* Oxford, Pergamon Press, 1980.

An intuitive guide to structural function.

Gordon, J. E. *Structures, or Why Things Don't Fall Down.* New York, Plenum Press, 1978.

A revealing look at how structures work.

Harris, James B., and Kevin Pui-K Li. *Masted Structures in Architecture.* Oxford, Butterworth, 1996.

A well-illustrated review of suspended and cable-stayed roofs.

Imbesi, Giuseppe, Maurizio Morandi, and Francesco Moschini. *Riccardo Morandi.* Rome, Gangemi Editore, 1995.

Illustrated with numerous drawings and photographs, the complete works of a noted engineer, with text in both Italian and English.

Kellogg, Richard E. *Demonstrating Structural Behavior with Simple Models.* Fayetteville, 1994.

How to construct ingenious models of plastic foam to illustrate every type of structural behavior. This book may be ordered from the author by telephone (501-521-6587) or by fax (501-575-7429).

Leonhardt, Fritz. *Bridges: Aesthetics and Design.* Cambridge, MIT Press, 1984.

Written by a leading structural engineer, a stunning picture gallery of bridges with insightful commentary and advice on design.

Lin, T. Y., and Sidney D. Stotesbury. *Structural Concepts and Systems for Architects and Engineers.* New York, Van Nostrand Reinhold, 1988.

A comprehensive, semimathematical guide to preliminary design of building structures.

Mainstone, Rowland. *Developments in Structural Form.* Cambridge, MIT Press, 1975.

A readable, richly illustrated, historically based introduction to structures.

Moore, Fuller. *Structural Systems.* New York, McGraw-Hill, 1998.

A clear, understandable, nonmathematical presentation of the broad realm of structural devices, illustrated with images of famous buildings.

Nervi, Pier Luigi. *Aesthetics and Technology in Building.* Cambridge, Harvard University Press, 1966.

A treatise on structural design by a leading twentieth-century engineer.

Nervi, Pier Luigi. *Structures.* New York, F. W. Dodge, 1956.

Insightful writings of a great structural designer, illustrated with drawings and photographs of his own buildings.

Otto, Frei. *Tensile Structures.* Cambridge, MIT Press, 1973.

An imaginative, all-inclusive study of the potential of lightweight structures by an innovative structural designer.

Otto, Frei, and Bodo Rash. *Finding Form.* Munich, Deutscher Werkbund Bayern, 1995.

A provocative, beautifully illustrated compendium of structural innovation.

Polano, Sergio. *Santiago Calatrava: Complete Works.* Milan, Gingko, 1996.

The buildings and bridges of a ground-breaking architect/engineer.

Rosenthal, H. Werner. *Structure.* London, The MacMillan Press, 1978.

A superb text on the shaping of structures.

Salvadori, Mario. *Why Buildings Stand Up.* New York, McGraw-Hill, 1982.

An intuitive introduction to structures by a leading engineer and educator.

Salvadori, Mario, and Robert Heller. *Structure in Architecture.* Englewood Cliffs, NJ, Prentice-Hall, 1963.

An understandable introduction to structure, aimed at students of architecture.

Schodek, Daniel. *Structures.* Englewood Cliffs, NJ, Prentice-Hall, 1980.

An excellent text on configuring and sizing building structures.

Straub, Hans. *A History of Civil Engineering.* Cambridge, MIT Press, 1964.

A revealing, readable introduction to the development of our understanding of structural function.

Thompson, D'Arcy. *On Growth and Form.* Cambridge, Cambridge University Press, 1977.

The classic treatise on the relationship between forms in nature and the functions that they serve.

Torroja, Eduardo. *Philosophy of Structures.* Berkeley, University of California Press, 1958.

The major theoretical writings of a great engineer.

Torroja, Eduardo. *The Structures of Eduardo Torroja.* New York, F. W. Dodge, 1958.

An illustrated exposition of Torroja's work.

Wilkinson, Chris. *Supersheds* (2nd ed.). Oxford, Butterworth, 1996.

A picturebook of exciting longspan roofs.

Wolfe, William S. *Graphical Analysis.* New York, McGraw-Hill, 1921.

A complete introduction to graphic statics with numerous examples.

Index